ROMANCE in the GARDEN

John H. Tobe

ROMANCE IN

Artist: Yolanda Lamoure

THE GARDEN

GEORGE J. McLEOD, LIMITED.
PUBLISHERS AND PUBLISHERS REPRESENTATIVES

73 BATHURST STREET, TORONTO 2-B, ONTARIO

Printed and Bound in Canada
by
THE HUNTER ROSE CO. LIMITED

CONTENTS

v

'Tis the Simple Things . . .

Zounds! The things one sees on the farm and in the country!

I was watching the squirrels the other day. You see, already a few of the hickory and other nuts are beginning to fall and the squirrels are busy caching them away so that they will have some to eat during the winter. They sit back on their haunches with their bushy tails sticking up like a rudder and peel the husk off like a banana skin. Then their saw-like teeth rip through the shell and they pick out the meat clean . . . with their fingers. Down on the farm, here in the raspberry rows I watched a young skidaddler taking raspberries right off the canes, pulling them until they tore away from the stem.

Have you ever watched on a cold night in the fall, before everything is hatched up for the winter, how the cats will find a warm place to sleep? I have seen them lying on the bellies of the pigs, or on the backs of the horses and cows. They like the body heat of the other animals and the big animals like them, too, because it does not allow all the heat of their body to escape . . . a sort of co-operative effort to keep each other warm on those chilly nights.

We don't have gophers around here but one day out West I watched a family of them cavorting about. As I walked closer to them the mother of the brood of about ten called to them in a shrill piercing voice. She herded them into their hole and crawled in before the last of them. But one brazen young pup remained on the outside. I walked slowly towards it. The mother gopher shrieked, scolded, and pleaded, and she looked so strange, tragic, yes, and funny with her head stuck out of the hole, yacking away, but this young fellow paid no heed.

Finally she came out of the hole, went after him and began to whollop him with her forearms, scolding him at the same time. Then the young stripling began to wail and whimper, but he did as his mama told him . . . crawled into the hole . . . and she in after him.

I remember old Maud . . . well, she wasn't so old then. She was a big Percheron and she had a lot of horse-sense. It was a heck of a hot summer day. She was in the barnyard and as usual the flies were there by the million. It was before the days of DDT and other potent insecticides . . . flies weren't so easy to get rid of as they are now.

1

Well, she got tired of swishing the flies off her back with her tail and twitching them off her flank with her skin, and swinging her neck around. So she headed for the barn. In her manger a batch of kittens were huddled. She didn't like this and the kittens didn't seem to be afraid of her. So she lifted them with her mouth carefully, taking each separately by the scruff of the neck and carrying them out, away from her stall, then put them on the barn floor where they scampered away.

You think only a dog follows his master? Well, every time I walk into the field, one, two or all three of the cats will follow me. It just depends on whether or not they are around when I begin my trek. They are lined out after me in single file and they move exactly at the same gait I do. When I stop to look at something they stop too, and play with each other, jump about, or roll on the grass, but they are always there, the older cats and the one kitten.

Dogs do learn slow—or is it because they never know when they are licked? Whether they tangle with a skunk or porcupine they always seem to come back for more. My neighbour's big dog is a boxer. If he ever landed on a skunk his weight alone would crush him to death but he never gets that close. The skunk seems to aim straight and he catches it like an arrow—right in the eyes. This blinds the dog temporarily . . . as a matter of fact, for three or four days. You should hear him howl, bloody blue murder. Yet, if a skunk should cross his path he's at it again . . . and gets the same treatment.

Old Nig came home with his face resembling a walrus . . . quills bristling from all angles and he was crying pitifully. I got busy with the pliers and pulled out the quills. He was suffering, yet smart enough to stand still and let me pull them out, one by one. I am telling you that a porky's quill goes into the flesh easy but comes out hard because they have spines that catch the flesh on the way out.

I have had the dog come back after I thought I had removed all the quills and he would push his face into my hands, moaning. Upon examining it closer I would find there were one or two I had missed. The dog had sense enough to come back and get the job done right.

You would think after suffering like this that a dog would learn his lesson but no, the next time a porky is in the neighbourhood, back home comes the dog whimpering and moaning—the entire front of his face again bristling with porky quills!

I am very fond of ducks but I have given up raising them. Gosh, they're cute when they are small with their yellow throats and furry breasts. The way they waddle about is cute to see. I have watched them grow and as fall came I began to look forward to a dandy duck dinner. But . . . my dreams would be rudely shattered by seeing them

2

fly off with a quacking bunch of wild ducks . . . every single one of them. So, no more duck raising for me!

One day, the hired man, his wife, and I were stuccoing the help-house. We had a fair sized chunk of the plaster stuck on the wire netting that was fixed to the boards when suddenly the plaster began to move in various places. We watched, bewildered—it looked as though the place was erupting with bubbles like hot springs in Yellowstone. Suddenly a piece popped off, then another piece, and another, and as each piece lit on the ground it continued to move . . . then hop!

Then it dawned upon us they were toads or frogs. Somehow they had gotten into the plaster mix and were put on the wall along with

the plaster. We had to go over all the walls carefully patching up the holes . . . but we made sure wherever we put a patch that there wasn't a hopper in it.

Watching the antics of the birds in the Mulberry tree is something to remember. Because the tree is so heavily laden and as no one ever chases them from it, the birds regard it as a haven or sanctuary. Delicious food is there in super abundance, practically through the entire summer. There are big birds, and little birds, dowdy ones, and those that have fancy plummage, birds from near, and birds from far, silver throated, and raspy voiced.

Sometimes I wish I'd studied ornithology instead of botany. Better still had I studied both. As it is, I know a little about one and nothing about the other. But their chatter or singing, or whatever you may call it hardly ever ceases from dawn till dusk. They are pleasant companions to have about.

I have never heard of a cat raising puppies, or a dog bringing up a batch of kittens but some time ago one of my youngsters brought home a tiny squirrel whose mother had been killed. At that time our cat had just had a batch of kittens so the little squirrel was put among them and the cat raised it just like one of her own.

It was really an amusing sight to see the so-called kitten scamper along the walls and ceiling and the amazed look on the cat's face as she saw her offspring racing over her head. She actually looked as though she expected the young 'un to crash at her feet. But the squirrel didn't remain too long . . . it evidently found its own and left for parts unknown.

Probably these things won't interest those of you who are city folk but on the farm and in the country these things are an everyday part of life and living. You see, we lack the excitement and turmoil that is part and parcel of the city and we must be content with the smaller and less important things.

Northern Escape

Are you troubled, harassed, worried or bored? Then come with me!

Just a little ways from here is a brook that babbles. No, I am not being unkind to the rains, melting ice and snow, that I love as a brother. If 'tis a roar, I won't call it a whisper. There are brooks that sing, others that gurgle, some that flow, those that murmur and even ones that run. True, there are those that meander and glide. Some trip, others dance and then there are those that trickle, trip and lilt . . . and did I say those that ripple, rush, chant and prattle? Then there are those that gush and rise and spread.

I came upon a dreamy stream deep in the forest in the north country. We were short-cutting through . . . making a portage between two small lakes and the canoe had to be carried about three-quarters of a mile to the other water where we hoped to find some good fishing.

The vegetation on both sides and surrounding this little rivulet was as lush as could possibly be found anywhere in the north country and the coursing waterway was covered on all sides by tall straight trees. There were Birches, Pines, Balsam, Tamarack, Maple, Oak, Spruce and Cedar. I don't recall at the moment the other kinds but the shelter and other conditions made it an ideal place for vegetation of every type that could stand the slight shade with sunlight that filtered through the trees.

4

Then how peaceful, how serene—what a wonderful place to relax and dream! But, lo, that wasn't possible for the same conditions that made growing things so luxuriant, healthy and lush was also conducive to the breeding of mosquitoes and insect life. Unless one were well protected against the ravages of those insects, you couldn't exist there more than a few minutes. I don't know how early in the year the mosquitoes are there but I know they were there quite late—yes, late into the fall.

You know one must really love the north country to be able to even tolerate it with all those mosquitoes, flies and other biting insects.

Come, let us wander. 'Tis time to dream of enchanted woodlands, of rippling rivulets, of rills and hills, of forests filled with singing birds and playful sprites of nature.

Yes, 'twas Homer who sang of Arms and the Man. I chant of forests, rivers, winding hills and singing rills. I take you to peace—Homer led you to war and strife!

Hedging An Art

Is privacy necessary in a garden? Of course it all depends on the way you live or your viewpoint on life.

I had a young fellow doing a job for me a while ago—he was a carpenter. Came Saturday morning and he didn't turn up and I had to have that job done before the weekend and Saturday was the only day left. So I paraded down to his house and said, "Why didn't you turn up this morning to finish that job?"

"Couldn't", he said, "I've something else very important I want to do."

"Let me tell you", I replied, very much annoyed, "My business is important, too, and I want you to come and get it done."

"No, sir, not today", he insisted.

"Fine", I said, "But you won't get paid for the job if you don't."

So, reluctantly as the dragon, he came and finished the job and he sulked and sulked. I felt sorry for him but I needed the job completed and stood right with him until he did it.

It thus happened he didn't get through till about 4 o'clock Saturday afternoon and curiosity was just killing me . . . What did he want to do that was so important? I also knew he needed the money that he would earn.

"What was so all-fired important that you didn't want to work this afternoon?" I bluntly asked him.

"Well", he told me, "My neighbor lent me his fast outboard motor boat for today I wanted to take the wife and kids for a ride in it up and down the river."

"Surely", I said, "You can go for a ride in the boat now and get all the boating you can stand before it gets dark. The sun doesn't set till after 9 o'clock. Besides you can get the boat most any day if you want it."

"Baloney", he sputtered—his voice filled with emotion. "All the town people would be crowding out there lining the dock and the river front between two and three o'clock in the afternoon and here you have made me work at that time. And who wants to ride a boat when nobody will see you?"

See the predicament I am in? I don't know whether you want everybody to see your garden or whether you want it for the beauty, the comfort, the contentment and happiness that it gives you.

Now if you want to attain a greater or lesser degree of privacy it can be easily accomplished by common sense hedging. No, you don't need a fence. Fences usually become unsightly, are costly to erect and expensive to maintain. A hedge needs only a fraction of the cost of a fence to erect and there is no maintenance cost.

I'll start with *Privet*. In my opinion it is the finest all round general purpose hedge plant in the world . . . oval or round shiny leaves, dense all the way up from the ground, fast growing and requires clipping but once a year. It can be easily kept dense to a height of 4 to 5 feet although most people prefer it only 2 to 3 feet tall. The foliage is attractive, small to medium, leathery and dark green and hangs on until late, late fall. In fact the Ovalifolium variety will hold its foliage all winter if the winter is mild and down south it is evergreen. If you want it to be neat and dense, 9 inches apart is just about right for planting.

Privet   Chinese Elm   Multiflora   Barberry

Chinese Elm is an excellent fast growing hedge plant. It can be kept quite dense. The leaves are not shiny but finely toothed and

6

exactly the same as the regular Elm except much smaller. I believe it is the fastest growing hardy plant in creation and will grow from 1 to 3 feet a year. It requires clipping at least twice a year to keep it orderly. To have a dense hedge it is advisable to plant them 9 inches apart. Chinese Elm also make a nice tall screen. It will grow to a height of 6, 8 or 10 feet but of course you sacrifice density if you allow it to get this tall. I know of no disease that attacks it and it's very easy to grow. If you need a hedge in a hurry and at low cost then Chinese Elm is the answer.

Multiflora Rose is a wonderful plant for a natural hedge or screen, but remember, and I emphasize this, it is not suitable or adaptable to clipping. To get best results from it, it must be allowed to grow in its own natural way. It has a neat drooping habit. The leaves are of good color. It is thorny and will definitely keep animals, even the smaller ones, as well as children, out. It is not as fast growing as either Chinese Elm or Privet and takes about 3 years to reach maturity but then you have a screen that is just about as fine as anything one could possibly want. It will spread about 3 to 4 feet and grow from 5 to 6 feet high. It is not advisable to use it in a small yard or garden. It definitely is ideal for large estates, playgrounds, schoolyards, institutions, farms and enclosures of all types. If you've got a big lot, it would probably be entirely satisfactory, even in the city. Plant one foot apart, not closer.

Japanese Barberry is a slow growing plant, very prickly with nice attractive little green leaves that turn reddish in the fall and then nice bright red fruits, too, that hang on pretty well for the winter. It can be grown in its natural fashion which is very attractive or it can be clipped. It is more tolerant to semi-shaded locations and moisture conditions than either Privet, Chinese Elm or Multiflora Rose. It does not grow fast but it is a good plant and requires very little sun. Plant one foot apart, or closer.

Continually I am beset by folks who want to plant flowering shrubs and treat them as a hedge. To this I say, "No". No man can serve two masters. A shrub can be a hedge or a hedge row or a specimen plant but it cannot be all of them at once.

Even the well known Red Leaf Barberry doesn't make a good hedge because in order to have the shrub at its highest pitch of stateliness and beauty, it must be planted individually and allowed to grow as is its wont. Then it is graceful, colorful and lovely. As a clipped hedge it reminds me of these modern crew-cut hair-do's.

Spirea Van Houttei as a shrub is delightful and pleasant but as a hedge . . . No! It becomes too woody and after it is clipped when through blooming, you don't have much of anything.

Caragana is used throughout the west and where the climate is apt to be very severe. It does make a fairly suitable hedge but I would only plant it where nothing else is available or will grow. But as far north as Edmonton I've seen most of the hedge plants that we list here growing and doing all right. So I don't know why you should take less than the best . . . and any of the items listed here are better and more attractive.

So take my advice, friends and neighbors, and don't plant a flowering shrub and try to make a hedge out of it.

Now if you want a hedge row—that is, spacing your shrubs along the perimeters of your garden or property—fine. Just set them about 5 feet apart and let them go to it. It will give you a picture of undulating beauty for probably 5 or 6 or even 7 months of the year.

Some people desire the formal, confined, clipped lines of a hedge and others like the informal flow and that's where the hedge row is ideal.

Here are a few words about evergreen hedges . . . In the northern latitudes there are but a few evergreen plants that are suitable and used for hedging and they are as follows: Cedar (Thuja), White Spruce, Norway Spruce, Yews and Boxwood. But no matter how interesting or attractive they may sound on paper, I strongly advise caution and restraint in their use.

The Cedar is probably the least costly but in any event you are going to have a tall job on your hands to keep it attractive and healthy. Both the White and Norway Spruce actually become grotesque and ugly as they get older, if kept trimmed. You see they are not adapted to the hacking and pruning process that is involved . . . and they show their resentment.

Should you be determined on having an evergreen hedge, I'd mention my personal favorite and the finest of all hedging material—the good old English Boxwood. And let me tell you something else—it is a lot sturdier than you imagine. It's not the cold that gets it but the sun. If you have a location where you have semi-shade or partial shade, I recommend the Boxwood. It will thrive and do well—not the Korean one but the real old fashioned English one which costs much less.

In actual tests within many miles of the nursery I have found that wherever shade or semi-shade was provided Boxwood did exceptionally well. I repeat—cold isn't what bothers it. It's too much sunlight. It can't seem to stand the full blast of our northern sun.

But if the location is an open one where you get full sun and you still want an evergreen, then the Japanese Yew or Taxus cuspidata cannot be beat. It will tolerate the most difficult terrain and it is about as attractive as anything you can get but—oh—oh—oh—it is costly! You can probably buy Boxwood plants two or three years old at a reasonable figure but the Yews will cost at least twice as much.

I might add that these two hedge plants are for connoisseurs, millionaires or folks who just have to have the best—no matter what!

Botany Lesson For Now

Well, we're going to talk about how some of our shade trees got their names and we'll start with Ash . . . and run down the alphabet.

Ash—Way back when, spear shafts were made from the willowy Ash and if you know the Ash wood, you'll know it's hard, white, fine wood. Today they make axe and hammer handles from Ash—yes, and I should say baseball bats and hockey sticks, too. It comes from the Anglo-Saxon word "æsc" which meant "spear". Seems very logical, doesn't it?

Amelanchier—Also known as Juneberry, Serviceberry, Sarviceberry, Blueberry tree and Saskatoon. I could find no record of the actual derivation of the name. We do know that the fruit of the Amelanchier was used by the Indians to a great extent, as a berry and also for making their famed "pemmican" and even today is considered as good as our best Blueberry.

Alder—I can only gather that it was a corruption of the Latin word "Alnus" from the word "al" meaning "near" and the word "lan" meaning "the bank of a river". The Alder follows the paths of streams, thriving on their banks and exulting where they bend, twine and turn. It is found practically nowhere else.

Beech—It appears that back many centuries ago the tablets made from Beechwood were used for writing and the Anglo-Saxons called it "boce" or "boc" and from that same original word we get the word "book". So you see the Beechwood was our first book.

Birch—It is known by every boy in Europe or America as the Bark Tree. The name comes from the Anglo-Saxon "beorc" or "birce" meaning "bark tree". There may be some connection between Birch, church and kirk—but that's for the future. Sufficient to add that the young boughs or shoots were used and probably still are by schoolmasters to impart discipline and knowledge to the *seat of learning*.

Basswood—This is a tough one. The inner bark of the Lime Tree, Linden or Basswood was called bast. It was used in making matting

9

and cordage and the bark of the tree was also used. You see a bast is a thick mat or bassick but they also used the wood of the Lime Tree for making masts. Who knows? . . . Maybe they used it for making bass fiddles.

Balsam—I can find no definite connection between Balsam and our native tree, Abies balsami. It is a fact though that any substance or liquid that was aromatic and had some curative powers was referred to as a Balsam. Well, it is admitted that the sap of the Balsam was aromatic, resinous and abundant. Maybe the Indians used it in the treatment of cuts or bruises or as a balm in some other way. I should mention here that the Balsam actually makes one of the finest of all trees for Christmas decoration.

Cedar—That seems to come from the Arabic word "kedre" and it meant "power". Of course they were referring to the Cedar of Lebanon, for example, or the other true Cedars. Their Cedars were of mighty fine strong timber and they grew to majestic proportions. Therefore it was fitting that they would call the Cedar a name that meant "power'. Incidentally, don't confuse the true Cedars with our Cedars. Our so-called Cedars are members of the Thuya family, whereas the Cedars of the east or true Cedars are Cedrus.

Chestnut—I'm referring here to the native North American Sweet Chestnut. The wood of this tree is hard and fine with a good grain, nice color and its very durable wood was used to make chests. Logically the fruit was called Chestnut and the tree, Chestree. This fellow was originally found in the territory known as Castonea in Sicily and it is strange that the German word for "chest" is "caston". And you've also heard of "castonettes" which are two hard pieces of wood used to make sounds and music. Probably these were made from the Chestnut tree, too. Suit yourself—whichever derivation you prefer, you can have.

Dogwood—In the original spelling it was "Dagwood". But it is Dogwood in our modern dictionary. But in the older dictionaries you can find where in French, Italian, Spanish, Portuguese, Latin—yes, and even Gaelic and Irish—it meant sort of a pistol or dagger. So evidently the wood of Dogwood was made into a form of arms for defence or attack. They also made dags, goads and skewers out of the wood which were used to drive cattle forward. That is what a goad originally was. Of course skewers are used for sticking into meat. Another explanation of the word Dogwood was because the wood was once used to make a brew with which mangey dogs were bathed and cured. But I'm quite sure the "Dagwood" explanation is more logical and reasonable.

10

Elder—It was called "Eller" and "Ellarn" which in Anglo-Saxon meant "kindler". This is understandable because the light hollowed wood would make very easy kindling and help to quickly start a fire composed of harder and larger wood.

Elm—It gets its name from the Latin "ulmus" which meant "punishment" because the sinewy, tough, unbreakable wood of the Elm was made into rods or sticks with which the overseers belabored slaves and you can readily understand that an overseer wouldn't want to use a stick that broke and, believe me, you can depend upon it—an Elm stick wouldn't break no matter what you did to it. It might splinter, but break—hardly ever. The name is a very fine choice.

Hawthorn—If you know the tree and its habit and prickles, you'd quickly see why the Anglo-Saxons called it "haegthorn" which meant that it was used as a thorny hedge to prevent encroachment by animals or even humans . . . and that's just the way it's used today. throughout England and various parts of America.

Hazel—Back in the olden days the rods made from Hazel wood were used by shepherds and drovers for moving cattle about. The word "haesel" in Anglo-Saxon meant "a baton of authority". Well, the idea would be that the animals would quickly know who's boss—the man who is wielding the Hazel rod.

Hemlock—The origin of this name is absolutely obscure but we do know that from the old English it was Hymlice and Hymlic and Hemlic. What it meant or what the connection is no one seems to know. The cup of Hemlock which Socrates drank was not from the juice of the Hemlock tree but from the plant, Conium maculatum.

Hickory—This name is one of purely American origin. It appears to be a condensation of the word "Powcohicora" from Virginia and referred to the oily liquor that was made from the pressed Hickory nut kernels. The proper name of Hickory is Carya.

Honey Locust—This is properly Gleditsia triacanthos—named after a botanist called Gleditsch (makes me wanna scratch). It is continually confused with the Robina or the Black Locust. I tried to locate the connection of the "honey" and the Locust with this tree but all my research revealed nothing. It does however have sweet scented, rather inconspicuous, greenish flowers. Who knows—I may find it some time in the future.

Ironwood—Many trees known in America are called Ironwood. In fact any tree that has a tough wood and whose name the people didn't know was referred to as Ironwood. In this case they generally speak of Ostrya virginica. This is a rather slender growing tree but unusually hard. I can find no other derivation or connection to the name.

11

Larch—This comes from the Celtic word "lar" which means "fat" . . . because of the fact that this tree produces large quantities of resin and the word "larichs" was corrupted to Larch.

Locust—Here we steal from the Teutonic. In German the Locust is called "Heuschrecke" and it is so called from the resemblance of the branches of the tree to the legs of a flying locust. The name for a Locust tree in German is "Heuschreckenbaum".

Maple—We have to go back to the original Celtic to find the word "mapwl" which referred to the knotty excrescences of the trunk. This was highly esteemed for making furniture. The Anglo-Saxon word was "mapulder" and if you know any German, you'll recognize the word "meuble" which means furniture. So it is clear that Maple was used quite extensively in the olden days for making utensils and furniture and with good reason—it is a sound, white rubbery wood.

Oak—The Anglo-Saxons called it "ac" but its meaning is obscure. I'm always inclined to believe that it was taken from the Latin where it was called Quercus which is its proper name and if you say it quickly, Quercus and Oak sound quite similar. But the word "acorn" seems to suggest that it was the corn or fruit of the "ac".

Pine—Try as I might, I couldn't get anything out of this. In Latin it's Pinus which is similar to the Greek. The Anglo-Saxon is "pinn". In Danish it's "pign". In French and Portuguese it's also "pin". In Spanish and Italian it's "pino". But how it was derived heaven alone knows! Days later . . . ah, I've found it at last—Theophrastus named it "pinos" but the Celts called it "pin" or "pyn"—referring to a mountain or rock which fairly indicates that the tree was known to grow in mountainous country and also in rocky terrain.

Poplar—The name here is practically a give-away. In Rome it was called "Arbor populi"—the tree of the people. And it could be such, too, because it is very common and grows everywhere. The name does sound like "popular" which means it was a popular tree. All this is so very simple—totally unlike most of the names with their broad derivations.

Rowan—This is taken from "runa" which in the old Norse tongue meant "charm". This is the old Rowan Tree or European Mountain Ash, as we know it. The branches or twigs of this tree were supposed to have supernatural powers and it was swung and wielded about to keep witches and evil spirits away.

Spruce—This comes from the German and this refers to the many short branchlets which are quite characteristic of all Spruce trees. Evidently our word "sprout" comes from the same origin because the "sprossen" were sprouts that seemed to appear all over the tree.

12

Sassafras—It appears that this word comes from the Spanish word "Saxafrage" because it's supposed to have similar medicinal qualities. Also, they make a beer from the young shoots and an oil is extracted from the wood which is used, or used to be used, quite extensively by perfumers. Branches are delightfully aromatic.

Sumach—There was a preparation made in the olden days from the leaves, the shoots and the plant. It was used for tanning, dying, staining and also medically as an astringent. There are records to show that the chopped up leaves made a very satisfactory substitute for tobacco. It's certainly abundant in the fall and I don't know why folks don't try it. Maybe they could save some money and some taxes, too. The name is practically the same in old French, old English, Spanish and many other European tongues.

Sycamore—This is a tree of the Scriptures and its origin is rather interesting. The Scriptural tree was Ficus sycomorus which was derived from an Asiatic or Egyptian word meaning "sukon" for "fig" and "morus" for "mulberry". It was the Mulberry-leaved Fig tree and because our Sycamore has a leaf that resembles that, we call it Sycamore.

Tamarack—It is the word used in Canada and the United States for our native Larch. It is distinctly a native Indian name and has no connection with its proper name whatsoever, which is of European origin. The tree is a native of the Alps. Search, search, search—but no more info could I find.

Willow—In German it is "wilge" or "wichel". The Anglo-Saxon is "wilig" or "welig" and it seems to have something to do with wicker and the willowy branches of the Willow could be used for wicker work and weaving.

Walnut—Evidently the Walnut grew in abundance in Wales and it found its way to England where they called it a foreign nut from the word "wealh" meaning "foreigner" or "stranger" and the word "hnut" meaning "nut". Therefore a Welshman, a Celt and a nut— a foreign nut—Walnut.

The Cow's Tale

About twenty years ago when I was just getting started in the Nursery business, I called on a customer and good friend of mine by the name of Jim Thompson.

I'd known him for many years and he was a splendid type of individual—a Scotsman of sterling character. He was a hard worker and had bought his farm with a tiny down payment and was struggling very hard to keep things going and retain possession of his farm through those lean years. In those days a dollar was a lot of money and a day's work was cheap. You could get good help for $1.00 a day —yes, and that didn't include board either.

Now Jim wasn't the most exuberant fellow in the world but when I called on him that day, he seemed to be in an unusually bad way. He didn't smile, he wasn't very happy and I didn't get the usual pleasant greeting.

"What's the trouble, old fella?" I said, as we met and shook hands.

He blurted out "I've been swindled—that's what!"

This shocked me because I knew Jim wasn't the kind of man who could be swindled very easily.

"O.K., let's hear all about it, fella", I said.

"Come out to the barn with me," he said, "I want to show you something."

So I followed him into his big bank barn and he led me into the stable and pointing to a tethered cow, he said, "Take a look at her and see what you think of her."

I walked around it and examined it below, above and from the side. You'd have thought I was an expert cattle judge examining the livestock at the Coliseum. It sure was a beautiful beast. It was the longest animal I'd ever seen.

"That sure is a beautiful beast, Friend Jim," I said.

"Looks don't mean a thing," he replied.

"Why what do you mean?" I said.

"Well, she's going to die," he said almost tearfully.

"It doesn't look as though it's going to die to me. It looks mighty healthy and as pretty as a picture, too," I replied.

"Still," he repeated, "It's going to die and there's nothing that anybody can do about it."

. . . Then he said, "I'll start at the beginning. You know John Busko—well he knew I was looking for a cow. So he came to see me. He told me he had a wonderful cow for me—just the one I needed. So I went down to his place and he showed me the animal. I fell in love with her and bought her on sight."

"How much did you give for it?" I asked.

"$150.00," he replied.

"Well, to be honest, I think you got the animal dirt-cheap," I said.

"So did I", he went on, "But after I'd had her home for a day or two I discovered that the beast wasn't eating. At first I thought it was the change that was affecting her and that in a day or two she would come around. But after almost a week had gone by and she still hadn't

14

eaten, I got worried. So I called the vet and asked him to come out. Well, when the vet got here, he took one look at the beast and jumped six feet off the ground. He was shocked to see that cow in my barn and here is the story he told me . . .

"This was a champion English cow. It was brought to Canada—in fact, it wasn't just brought—it was flown to Canada by the Minister of Agriculture, with the intention of improving the breed of Ontario cattle. Before the cow could be bred to the best of Ontario bulls, it went off its feed and wouldn't eat. One vet after another was called in to see what they could do but no matter what they tried, they just couldn't help the animal a bit. As a result it was sold to me at a very low price for slaughtering or to see if I could do anything with it before it died of starvation. Well, I experimented with everything I knew on that beast but I couldn't get it to eat a morsel and it was getting thinner and thinner every day. I knew it was only a matter of time before it would be dead. So when John Busko came around, I sold it to him for $50.00 with the strict understanding that it would be beefed. And now I see that you've bought it from him for dairying."

"I told the vet that I'd paid $150 for it and he began to froth at the mouth. So you see," Thompson said to me, "I've been swindled. That $150.00 that I paid for the cow was all the money I'd saved from my tomato crop."

Now I knew just how hard he and his family had to work to have $150.00 left over from tomatoes because he was only getting 27½c a bushel from the canners. I thought of the hours of sweat and toil . . . the plowing, harrowing, cultivating, spraying, picking and carting that went into the effort before he earned that amount of money.

Jim continued, "I was depending upon that cow to supply us with our milk, cheese, butter and cream. I've got a big mow full of good Lucerne hay for her. In fact it would be one of our mainstays for the winter. We have potatoes, turnips, squash, carrots and cabbage in the cellar as well as some of the stuff that the wife canned up. Well, that along with a good cow would sure be able to keep us very nicely until crops came again next summer. But now—no cow— no money!"

I was about to ask why he didn't borrow some from the bank but that was back in 1930 and 1931 and you could just imagine Jim prying a buck loose out of a bank in those days.

By this time we had walked back to the house and I noticed an old shotgun hanging on the wall. My mind was racing like a fire engine . . . "Listen, Jim, will you do something for me? Don't ask any questions but do as I ask and perhaps you can get your money back.

15

Could you oil up that old shotgun, make it look slick and shiny, and wander around where your neighbors will be sure to see you carrying it? Say nothing to nobody. If they ask you what you're doing, just don't say anything."

"Truly", said Jim, "I don't think the old shotgun would work, but I'll do as you say."

Now I better tell you a little bit about this man, Busko. He was quite a character—a very capable individual but always on the lookout for an easy buck and he didn't worry too much who got hurt in the process. He was quite a trader and had a little farm but most of his money was made in trading and little business deals. I knew this man very well because he had worked for my brother when he first came to this country from Russia. I also knew that behind his bluff, hearty, cheerful manner, he was a coward and I thought that this little scheme I had in my head would work.

So I took my leave of Jim and drove down the road to the first neighbor and there I stopped. We chatted for a few minutes and I asked him if he needed any nursery stock. Then I just casually told him that old Thompson was out looking for John Busko and intended to shoot him on sight . . . and added that it was something to do with a cow. Then on I went along about my business.

I must have made at least seven or eight more calls that evening and besides trying to sell nursery stock, I dropped the same sort of message about Jim looking for John Busko with a shotgun and that he intended to shoot him on sight.

The last call I made that evening was at John Busko's home. He only had a few acres and didn't depend on his farming for a living. He greeted me in his usual hearty, pleasant way and he really was a chap of good disposition.

After asking him how things were and such, I came right to the point. I said, "John, I've got some bad news to tell you. It's about Thompson and that cow you sold him. I was in to see him and he told me he was going to kill you and he's got his shotgun all ready to go to work."

When John heard this, he began to quake and his face turned as white as milk. I continued, "Listen, John, if you're smart, you'll get around to his house quick and get things fixed up." Then I got in my car and I drove down the road.

By the time I got home that evening I was quite sure that everybody in the district knew that Jim Thompson was out looking for John Busko and I also knew that a good many of the women folk called up Busko's wife and warned her.

For the next while my calls took me to the other side of St. Catharines towards Beamsville, Grimsby and Hamilton. I'd leave early in the morning and never get back till late at night so I really didn't know what was going on around home.

Well it must have been months later when I again drove into Jim Thompson's rutty old driveway. This time I met him at the barn and he certainly looked pleasant and chipper.

"How are you feeling today?" I greeted him.

"Brawley," he said, "Brawley!"

"That's sure a heck of a lot better than the last time I saw you." I said. "Tell me, how did things work out?".

"Pretty good—pretty good!" said Thompson, "The next day Busko, with his wife, and with the kids in the back for obvious protection, drove out to see me and he said he couldn't pay all the money back but he gave me $100.00. Then his wife pleaded with me not to hurt him or do anything rash and she promised that he'd pay the other $50.00 to me as soon as he could. I didn't say a word and they drove out the driveway again."

"Then", Jim went on, "An unusual thing happened with that cow. 'Twasn't more than two or three days after Busko was in and paid me the money when the boys were just driving up the horses from the back field where they'd been hauling some manure and spreading it. The big Percherons went up the ramp and stood at the end of the barn to be unharnessed before going in to get their dinner. There and then, as often happens, one of the horses had an evacuation and dropped a pile and you could see the vapor rising from the steaming manure. At that very instant Ivan, my son, was bringing the cow over to the trough to give her a drink and, as she passed the horses, she made a dash for the steaming pile of manure . . . and before she could be stopped, she had her face in it and had swallowed quite a mess of it. No matter how hard we yanked and pulled her, we couldn't get her away from it. She stood right there and gulped some of it down.

None of us had ever seen such a performance in our lives and we thought it an insane action that might kill her and we did our best to stop her. After a little excitement, we eventually got her moved back to her place. Then, the strangest thing happened. In the morning we expected to find her sick or sicker than she was before . . . but instead of that, she was eating and she's been perfect ever since. She's the best beast in the whole country—no, sir, there isn't one like her—and she gives the best milk and pails and pails of it."

Sure, I've heard of the luck of the Irish but this is the first concrete example I've had of the luck of the Scotch.

17

A Life of Ease for You

Well, folks, I have a confession to make. I am admitting my stupidity and my ignorance. Not as though you didn't know it before, but not everyone will admit it.

For a lifetime I've been searching—hunting—seeking—for any easy way to make a living. But, no—never could I come close to a bona-fide way.

But now after all these long years of struggling, when I'm worn to a frazzle, along comes the answer. I should have seen it 10 years ago—even longer.

Yes, today I know a proposition that would have made me rich long ago and what is more important—independent—with little work attached . . . giving me leisure time to do the many things I've always wanted to do.

Think of it—I needed only to work a few weeks during the entire year and live in luxury and comfort for the rest of the twelve months!

Now I know you're all "agog" and concerned and eager to hear what this fabulous thing is and of course you don't believe a word I'm telling you and say, "It can't be true!"

But, folks, it is true and if you'll just shut off your motor and relax, I'll tell you how it's done and perhaps you're not too old yet to follow this advice and reap these bounties and benefits. I hope you're not too late anyway.

I am told from the best authorities that 1,000 Sugar Maple trees will give a man an income for life annually—a fixed income—a sure income.

Upon checking various sources, the data I have before me indicates that there is an unending demand for all of the Maple Syrup and Maple Sugar that this country can supply.

So why not get yourself a piece of land that would be suitable for Maples and plant yourself a Hard Sugar Maple tract, orchard, forest or bush?

Judging from the best data I could obtain, it will take about 12 years or so before you can first tap your trees. From then on the trees will be in better shape and you'll be able to get a bigger yield with each continuous spring.

Tapping usually lasts anywhere from February 15 to April 15 which means, at the most, a maximum of 6 weeks, but it sometimes lasts as little as 2. You can judge that it does last anywhere from 2 to 6 weeks from minimum to maximum.

Actual experience, in fact, proves that tapping does not harm the

18

tree nor does it render it useless for timber or other wood products in later years.

The ideal situation would be to get yourself a tract of land where Maples can be planted. It need not be cleared . . . this would be costly. Just plant your Maples in places wherever you find soil and conditions right. Get a large enough tract so that you can plant 1,000 trees and place them quite far apart.

If you're going to plant them on cleared land, then you can probably interplant with Christmas trees. I don't think Pine would be suitable because Pine like sandy soils but Spruce and other types of Evergreens would probably take to the same soil that the Hard Maple likes.

You'd best buy Maples 3 or 4 years old because Maples, 1 or 2 years old, are awfully, awfully small. For the first few years the Maple grows very slowly but after it's 4 or 5 years old it begins to shoot along at a pretty fast pace.

While I'm on the subject, I might also tell you that there are other trees that yield Maple Syrup. One is the Black Maple which is properly known as Acer saccharum nigrum which yields about as much Maple Syrup as our Hard or Rock Maple, properly Acer saccharum.

Wait—there are still two other kinds of Maple that I know of that give Maple Syrup. One is the Red or Swamp Maple and the other is our common Silver Maple that we see growing everywhere. Both of these give Maple Syrup but only about half the sugar content of the good Hard Maple or Sugar Maple.

I do believe that you can get started in the business for a paltry few hundred bucks. You either buy a piece of bush or get a tract free from the government and plant a few trees every year. In 10 or 15 years you will reach independence. You won't need to pay any high insurance premiums and you'll assure yourself a living because you'll have good healthy work for but a few weeks a year. For certain you'll want to go out and see those trees and walk around and inspect them quite regularly so you'll have some more healthful exercise. This will insure your health and happiness.

Now take it easy, folks! Don't all rush to the Maple bush or the tall timbers at one time. Rushing is bad for the heart—Make haste slowly!

Next Year Will Be Better

Could be you city folk may use the same phrase when things aren't so good or when the plans you've made fail to materialize. But on the farm that is what we live for from year to year . . . "Next year things will be better."

Only the good earth can impart such hope to a man's soul. When crops are bountiful and the harvest is good the prices we get for our produce are usually low. On the other hand when produce is scarce, when the fields haven't produced and the trees haven't borne a very good crop, then prices are high. I guess it's like that everywhere in the world. When we could get big money for our stuff nobody has any.

Have you perhaps wondered why of all the occupations in the world farmers are so poorly paid? No, it isn't an accident because accidents, like lightning, don't keep striking time after time after time in exactly the same place. From the information that I can gather and from what I have experienced myself, about 7 out of 10 years on a farm are unprofitable or lean years.

I'm going to ask you now . . . Are farmers fools? Are they less capable than other men? Do they lack vision? Are they lazy? Are they devoid of ambition?

Perhaps as a Canadian farmer you may say to yourself, "Well, the weather and climatic conditions are against us."

But that is not the reason. In most parts of the Dominion our weather will mature big crops that are suitable for the northern latitudes without any difficulty and, further, farmers all over the world from the equator to the Arctic Circle have the same problems . . . good crops and poor crops, diseases, bad weather, storms, not enough rain or too much and such. It seems sure that farming is a world-wide fraternity and I say, "Why, oh, why is there so much trouble about arranging a fair rate of payment for the man who tills the soil?"

In spite of the questions I've asked above, the man who tills the soil must have hope and vision in his soul, in his heart and his mind. No, a farmer cannot be a lazybones. The fact that he is able to stay on the farm at all is a tribute to his capable management, his intelligence and ability to work. Further, no man plants for tomorrow unless he is ambitious.

Now, if a farmer is as capable as I have just mentioned then why doesn't he hie himself to the city and get a government job or work for some large company and be just as well off as the other fellow? Nowadays they have guaranteed wages, holiday pay, hospitalization, pension plans, unemployment insurance and any number of other benefits. They really have about everything that a human being could want. Then, I ask again, why doesn't a farmer strike out to the city and get the same things that the other fellows are getting?

Well, a heck of a lot of men have already done just that as you well know. But they belonged to the city because no man who has the farm in his soul ever leaves the farm—at least, not for good.

Yes, why doesn't the farmer go into the city and he, too, drink his fill of the nectar of prosperity? Well, I'll tell you why . . . because it is given to some men to provide for their fellow men—because some men are born "their brother's keeper".

Hold your sympathy and crocodile tears. Don't feel sorry for the farmer. Anyway some folks say that a farmer is always crying. They may be partly right and if he is, in most cases he has something to cry about because he is the man who feeds all of us and gets but a small share for himself and he has to sweat blood for it.

The farmer, who has his hay or his grain cut in the field ready to be brought inside, prays that there will be no rain. On the other hand, the fellow in the next concession who hasn't cut his crops needs a good rain to fatten the kernels and to give his fields the last extra bit of growth and he is praying for a good rain. So you see there's a conflict, an endless, continuous conflict, going on. Even the good Lord would be torn and in doubt as to which course to follow.

It must be that the good Shepherd in his wisdom made things this way . . . because what's good for one is bad for another but if we were all in the same boat at the same time and the same place, a squall could capsize the whole works and starvation for mankind would be the result.

Well, I haven't come to the heart or the truth of the matter yet and that is that a man is on the soil because he wants to retain his

21

soul, his freedom, his independence—because he is the only man in the world who is still free—in many senses—yet captivated and owned exclusively by the land upon which he works, toils and slaves. Let us say—he's a willing slave.

Farmers don't drive Cadillacs. They're lucky if they can drive the lower priced cars and have them paid for. I've never known a farmer who owned a Cadillac anyway. Perhaps he wouldn't want one if he did have a chance . . . but don't risk offering him one!

Autumn Stroll in the Woods

A Sunday in early October was the nicest fall day so far this year and I took my first stroll into the woods.

Here I was definitely in search of some Jack-in-the-Pulpit bulbs. I wanted to get a few to plant alongside the fence where they would get some shade and establish them so that I'd have them there for now and evermore.

I was quite surprised to find that the Trilliums were still in full leaf. The seed pods had disappeared. Whether they had blown away or whether they had been carried off by insects I don't know. But the plants were still in good shape here in this part of the wood that I was strolling through.

I followed the waterway, a sort of creek bed and a natural drainage ditch, although there was little or no water in it, and on both sides it was lined with plants that thrive in these dampish locations. False Solomon's Seal seemed to be everywhere and occasionally I could spot a Trillium and then I found May Apples in clumps at the base of practically every large tree that grew along the water course.

Here, too, one will find a few Dogwoods—yes, I mean the real Dogwood tree or, properly, Florida Dogwood. You don't see them around much but here in this piece of native woodland along the bank of this stream the Dogwoods were growing in abundance. At the base of each of the taller and older (not more than 10 years) Dogwood trees were many young ones clustering about . . . They looked healthy and in good shape too. There's no doubt about it. If this piece of woods is left alone in a few years it will be thick with these wonderful native flowering trees.

Then I noticed a lot of Red Elder, Honeysuckle and, of course, many of the common ordinary Dogwood shrubs. There were the Clintonias with those stark blue berries or blue beads, whichever you would call them, and there were the Baneberries with those queer, unusual black and white berries that you hear called Doll's Eyes.

22

Yes, at last I spotted my Jack-in-the-Pulpits. They're easy to find because the cluster of real red berries are a tell-tale sign no matter where they hide. I dug up a few of the plants. At the base they have a bulb that is shaped somewhat like a Gladiolus except that the top seems to rise like a pip.

Originally I'd started my treks to the woods because I wanted to gather some hickory nuts. I mean the genuine native old Shagbark Hickory—the one that has a bark that looks so ruffled and unkempt. I had a customer in California who was longing badly for an old Hickory tree so that he might have the shade and the nuts near his home. He was evidently from Ontario and one of the things that he remembered was the Hickory trees that grew around his farm home. So he wrote and asked me if I would get him a pound or so of nuts and I agreed to do so last year but for some reason or other there just didn't seem to be any nuts when I went out to gather them. So I resolved that this year I'd start early and be sure to get them for him.

Well, I did start early. Just as soon as I noticed some of the nuts falling in late September I began to gather them in my pockets and on two occasions I managed to get altogether probably half a pound. Well, this time I wanted to be sure and complete the order so I was determined to find more Hickory trees.

I searched under the Hickory trees—that is every Hickory tree I could find. There are quite a few and I picked the large ones. They were quite old and should have borne a good crop of nuts but, believe it or not, no matter how hard I searched I couldn't find a single nut this time. I even crawled over a fence in one place near the road and faced a steep embankment. I knew the nuts would roll down the bank or would stop where the ground levelled off.

Well, I followed all the logical paths that I knew but no, sir, not one nut did I find. Believe me, I searched at these various locations for more than an hour and was defeated at every instance. Most of those I did find were under the large old trees along the road quite close to town. Probably the passing motor cars and heavier traffic scare off the squirrels. But even here I had to search in the matted grass. I found some by walking slowly under the trees and when I felt a bump like a pebble under my feet I usually found a lone Hickory although sometimes it was a big Acorn. They were everywhere. If it were an Acorn 'twould be crushed under your step—If a Hickory —nary a bit of harm would it suffer. Hickory shells are as hard as flint.

The conclusion I reached was that the squirrels probably prefer these Hickory nuts to all or most other nuts. There were Acorns around by the millions and the squirrels could have them in huge quantities but there they were. But only a stray or lost Hickory nut could be found.

I didn't see much wildlife on this trip to the woods . All I saw was one lone snake. It was a beautiful looking garter and I pressed my stick at a sharp angle over the top of him and held him firm. He struggled for a moment and then lay absolutely still. I examined him very carefully and then released the pressure of the cane and he slithered quickly away.

No, ma'am, I didn't even see a Jack rabbit, a groundhog or a squirrel on this hike.

The Masses' Drink

'Tis wonderful to come suddenly upon enlightenment or explanation of something that has puzzled one for years.

BEOR, BEAR, BIOR, BIAR, PIAR, BIER, BIERE, BIRRA, BEOIR, BIORKH, PEVO, PIVO. . . .

No matter how you spell it or pronounce it or in which language, it all comes out the same and goes down the drain.

I've gone into beer parlors on many occasions in my lifetime— not to drink beer—heaven forbid—perish the thought—definitely not but merely to watch the antics of the inhabitants or the imbibing imbibers therein.

Now you can understand, too, that if you go into one of these places and make use of their ample facilities, they expect you to sit down. If you sit down you have to buy something and as this place didn't serve ginger ale, I had to accept the wares that they did have.

What astounded me was the copious quantities consumed by the semi-inebriated inhabitants of this elaborately magnificent establishment.

I found the stuff bitter to taste (recent great discovery). Therefore what made it so appetizing and desirable? That, as Hamlet said, "is the question". Assuredly not to me is it either desirable or appetizing but to others that I told you about above it most certainly is, and that has been puzzling me—yes, and worrying me—for years and years.

Now I have found the answer and because you're my pal I'm going to share this great discovery with you. The report was made by Dr. O. S. Fowler and Dr. Paul C. Carson of Denver. This queer microbe

24

was found in stale beer by a Russian in 1915. (He is still in it—not the Russian—the microbe). It was named bacillus alkaligenes because it alkalizes living tissues.

The alkali killed other microbes, especially the disease kind. The doctors made their first human experiments on themselves, finding no bad effects when the alkali microbe was put by the millions into eyes, nose or mouth.

For dental decay, they put it in toothpaste or a rinse, to be used once a day. They found acid mouths become alkaline and remain so.

Dr. Fowler said he used the microbe in more than 100 abdominal operations and obtained a definite decrease in post-operative infection. It has been used also, he said, in severe eczema and other skin disease cases with good effect.

Just a reminder (my own idea—not the doctor's) and I beg you to note very carefully . . . this was stale beer. In order to make your beer stale you'd best leave it stand at least 5 minutes before drinking . . .?

Incidentally, here are the languages from which the words in the heading were taken . . . Anglo-Saxon—beor and bear; Fries—biar; Icelandic—bior; Old High German—bior, pior; Dutch—bier; German —bier; French—biere; Italian—bierra; Irish—beoir; Gaelic—beoir; Armenian—biorkh; Polish—pivo; Ukrainian—pevo.

What is a Copse?

Do you know the term? It's rather unusual and seldom found nowadays. I know it is used in England but I've never heard it used in Canada. I've come across the word now and then in horticultural reading—especially the old periodicals and articles.

The dictionary says that it's a small woods, a thicket, a thicket of brushwood, a coppice. It's also referred to as "coppywoods".

Then as I searched further in various places I came across the following reference. It is also known as a spinney or grove with undergrowth—also spinny and spiny.

In some of the earlier English literature you come across the line "Near yonder copse where once a garden smiled". I think that was written by Goldsmith. A man by the name of Dyer said, "Copsy villages on either side" and it was Kingsley who wrote, "The downs rise steep, crowned with black fir spinnies".

For many years I have advocated and suggested to folks who had a good sized garden space to set aside one corner and plant some evergreens—that is the taller Scotch Pine, Red Pine, White Pine,

Spruce and such. As these trees grow, let them grow just as they want—tall, spindly or whatever the situation may be and let the grass and whatever it is under them grow in its natural way too. Just forget that this space exists until a few years have gone by. But perhaps it might be best though to keep the grass cut. Otherwise your neighbors will think that you're going seedy.

Then in a few years you will have a natural rustic location on your property or near your garden where you can find sanctuary for meditation now and then and I'll wager that the birds will find the place long before you do and they'll sing while you think.

This thing to my mind would be a copse. Of course you wouldn't object if the kids played "cops and robbers" in this place, would you?

In this plantation or spinney, let's call it, I wouldn't confine the planting entirely to evergreens. I'd put in a White Birch for contrast and of course beauty and maybe a Ginkgo tree. Also, there would be no objection if you wanted to stick any other kind of tree in there, too . . . maybe even a nice Linden.

As a matter of fact I'm not telling you what to grow there at all. But, remember, this little nook or cranny will give more than shade. It will lend character and substance to your entire property. In my humble opinion, too, it would be another case of tail wagging the lion—the copse may become the most delightful place round thereabouts.

One of the things to remember about planting a copse is to be sure and set it away from the house—that is, the farthest point possible . . . to sort of make it a refuge. And you know—distance lends enchantment.

Now you can mow the grass in your copse if you want to but, brother, you're going to have a full scale operation on your hands. I'd just let it grow sort of catch as catch can and if the weeds get too tall, I'd borrow my neighbor's scythe or sickle and cut down some of the tall grasses if they began to tickle my nose.

After that if you want to put some shrubs like Lilacs and others in among the trees, there is no law against it. Actually, though, you should select the types of trees, especially among the deciduous ones, that tend to grow tall and upright rather than spreading. And plant the trees fairly close to each other—anywhere from 6 to 8 feet apart.

If you want an exceptionally good item for your copse, plant a Hornbeam or, as it is properly known, Carpinus betulus. Yes, we have them. They're rare and hard to get and few nurseries on the continent have them but we do.

Another good item for your copse is the Bolleana Poplar. This is a straight tall growing fellow that has attractive bark and good foliage. Ah, yes, don't forget to scatter around your copse a good quantity of spring flowering bulbs like Snowdrops, Crocus, Daffodils, Tulips and of course Colchicums and be sure to plant some of those trees and shrubs that you can count on for fall colors. In this way you will get continuous beauty 12 months of the year . . . Oh, and don't—don't ever forget to put a Dogwood in the group. It will love that type of company.

For fall color you want Prunus cistena, Barberry, Enkianthus, Amelanchier, a Silver, a Crimson King and a Sugar Maple. The latter are a little hard to get.

Well, by now you think I've really given you a Herculian job but one thing is sure—it won't require any care or attention and it will be lovelier each succeeding year.

O.K.—O.K.—you don't have to do it! I just told you about it. Just as an afterthought it occurred to me that it would make a darn good place to set up your dog house—no, I'm not kidding—I'm dead serious . . . not for the dog, silly, but for you! If you're anything like me, you spend most of your life in the dog house so why not make it interesting?

Squirrel in the Tree Tops!

Nature's Wisdom Has Been Questioned . . . But Never Disproved.

Snow covered the fields in all directions as far as the eye could see —but the road was centre bare—while on the shoulders ice had formed from the melting snow and traffic.

I had to walk carefully for fear of a limb-shattering slip, because 'twas cold—click, click, click, click—not my heels but the cane.

You see since I last told you about my wandering I've acquired a cane which I use on my walks. I bought it at the exhibition from a hawker I knew in the old days. He only charged me 75c for what appeared to be a birchwood cane. It certainly was worth every bit of the 75c I paid for it. So I became a cane-toting gentleman.

You know what prompted the investment of money in this elegant cane was because I'd read an article in a magazine where it said that a cane gave a man a distinguished air and his gait made him look elegant and fancy. Yes, that's me all right—suits just like a shovel would fit in the hand of Toscanini.

Well, then along came Christmas and my staff ever-mindful of my needs bought me a real high-class, fine, walnut-colored cane with a genuine silver ferrule. They also bought me a metal carrying case.

27

They had pity on their poor old boss after seeing him lug his home-work day after day, evening after evening home in a broken old card-board box that used to fall apart every now and then, strewing his papers helter skelter all over the car, on the road and around the office.

So now I am the possessor of a handsome metal carrying case for my papers and 2 elegant canes. Boy, you should see me strut! I look fancier than the young man in the thing that goes, "In spring a young man's fancy . . ."

As I reached Onslow's this day a squirrel was skipping about but when it heard the click of the cane, that is the metal against the pave-ment on the road, it became frightened and quickly scaled the nearest tree and then up and up to the next tree.

I was moving at a good clip and so kept pace with the squirrel. It skipped deftly from tree to tree by means of the closest entwining branches. I followed—Maple to Birch and then a Basswood, Pine, another Maple, then another Pine, then an Ash and then another Maple.

The plight of the squirrel intrigued me. I knew he was frightened by the sound of the click which he thought actually was a gun being fired and he was running for his life.

Abruptly we came to a Maple tree that was completely unlike the other Maples due to the fact that its branches grew almost perpendicu-lar, rather than in the usual spreading fashion of Maples. I thought to myself, "Here, sonny boy, you've made the error of your day. This could cost you your life" . . . if I were a trigger-happy gun-toter.

Then my eyes followed him as he went speedily up one branch to another—up higher, higher and higher until he got to practically the uppermost branch in that erect-growing Maple tree. I thought of this little fellow again, "You've made a valiant effort to escape from what appeared to be imminent serious danger—but now you are in a real jam."

Nature's ingenuity—seek . . . you'll find it everywhere—take note of evergreens growing alongside deciduous or other trees. You'll find that there are few, if any limbs close to the neighboring tree. Or, if there are, they are dead or dying. But, on the other side where they can grow freely, they are long, strong and sinewy.

Or else you will see where the evergreen has shot up above the com-peting trees, surrendering the right to its nether limbs and growth, giving its all to attaining height—and at the top the growth is lush, dense and furry.

Such was this Spruce . . . then, as the squirrel got to the top, he hesitated but only momentarily. Suddenly, he leapt into the air. You see I had not noticed that one of the topmost branches of the Maple came almost close to a huge Spruce tree which was quite a distance away but yet some of its uppermost hanging branches way up high leaned over within a few feet of the Maple.

At last he was in the safety of the Spruce which had thickly grown, compact branches of green along every inch of its stems and tips. I saw him for only one more second and then he was gone. I walked underneath the Spruce and as carefully as I peered and spied in walking round and round, I could not locate him. The evergreen foliage of the Spruce was so dense that it was impossible to see him and he had found sanctuary. He was lost in the swirl of lush green branches and bows—safe from hunters or other intruders or even nosey friends like myself.

Now I reflected—in his trek the squirrel had passed other evergreen trees which were Pines but their branches were sparse and would not afford him the protection that he needed.

I thought he didn't know where he was going—but I was wrong. He knew from the start where he could find protection and he headed straight for it.

Yes, I still believe if given a chance that nature protects her own.

World's Most Amazing Plant

Linnaeus called this horticultural phenomenon "the most wonderful of plants".

The Venus Fly Trap (properly Dionaea muscipula) can be found only in one spot of the entire globe—in a small section of North and South Carolina.

Up until a few years ago you, I or anyone else could go down to their native, low lying habitat and gather up as many of these plants and their seeds as we would like and cart them off. But this practice evidently reached great proportions and it began to appear as though these depredators could or would cause the plant to become extinct.

Wisely the government of the State of North Carolina enacted legislation to protect the Dionaea muscipula and now plants or seeds cannot be lifted and removed from the state without a permit.

However permits are regularly granted to educational and scientific bodies for the removing and exporting of these most unusual plants.

This is the only plant in existence that actually catches its own food. It doesn't sit and wait for it but stretches out and opens its arms in all directions. The moment that an insect or animal touches the fine trigger hairs that lie unnoticed in the outstretched pouch it snaps shut like a fish! The interlocking sinews, like teeth or gears, mesh shut preventing the escape of the captive.

Then special juices begin to flow and the trapped insect is completely digested. It is stated that this plant is actually the closest link between plant and animal.

This voluntary movement when it catches its prey is something that is commonly associated only with animal life. Actually the Venus Fly Trap has no true leaves but has a cluster of narrow life-like arms and at the end of these arms are perched the fringed hinged traps whose strange action gives the plant its distinction. If a young spring frog enters or crosses the trap it quickly snaps shut and he becomes loosely but snugly held a prisoner.

Biologists who have checked the digestive process of the Venus Fly Trap say it is somewhat similar to that of an animal. The plant has the ability to distinguish between a digestible and indigestible object. If the trap closes on an edible object it remains closed for about 9 days. This is the time required to digest its prey. Then it re-opens. Now if an indigestible object such a piece of wood, a leaf, a piece of straw or any similar indigestible matter is placed in the trap it will close but will re-open in a few hours. How the plant can tell the difference between them has so far remained a mystery. The softness or hardness of the object apparently make no difference. Charles Darwin mentioned that it was one of the most extraordinary plants he had ever observed. The best theory so far advanced to explain the action of the plant comes from a scientist who investigated closely and he says that the plants are usually found in soils very deficient in nitrogen. As insects are a good source of the necessary nitrogen the Venus Fly Trap attempts to make up this deficiency by catching insects. How it developed the efficient method of snaring its prey has never been discovered.

The Venus Fly Trap is a small plant seldom growing more than 5 or 6 inches in height. Nor does it spread any more than this. The traps reach a mature size of 1½" in diameter. The plant is a perennial growing from a small bulb. It has a fairly attractive white flower which seems to stand straight out from the centre like a mast. The seed is jet black, hard and tiny.

A plant does not reach full maturity until it is 3 or 4 years old. The individual traps live for about 6 weeks after opening. Then they turn black and die off to be replaced by new traps. There may be two traps to a plant or a dozen. It varies.

The plant can be kept growing indoors if proper conditions are given but it will go dormant and then can be brought back into growth.

Here's how to keep your plant healthy:

1. Do not overwater but keep slightly damp.
2. Give full sunlight.
3. Protect from winds or draughts. This is important.
4. Never use fertilizer.
5. Allow natural dormancy to take place.

Let's Live Longer

Of course this is probably old stuff to those of you who are gardeners but I just can't help but remark about the things I see and hear.

I read horticultural publications from Australia, Great Britain, United States, Canada and, yes, even the foreign language ones from Germany, France and Belgium. Some of these publications have obituary columns and other places where they mention an old nurseryman, gardener, farmer, seedsman, planter, agricultural worker and such has died. The ages?—74, 77, 79, 82, 86, 89, 90. These figures are from the last batch I came across. I'm not exaggerating. That's true. These fellas seem to be blessed with long life in abundance.

Then I pick up my daily papers and I read of this business tycoon dropping dead at 55, this one at 40—shucks, it seems that hardly any of them reach 60 and it's next to a miracle for some of them to get to be 70. So is it not just and proper and logical that I reach the conclusion that gardening, working with nature and with God is a blessed occupation and does give a man long life?

Yet that's what your garden can do for you —Give you healthy long life!

Probably you will wonder how I derive my logic for some of these statements. Well, stop, think and follow me a moment. When a man is concerned with planting something and making it grow —it doesn't matter whether it's a seed, a cutting or a tree from a nursery — the fact that he

31

takes the time to plant it himself and work in the soil marks him as a man of understanding and reflection. He must of necessity practise patience and, of course, he must understand what he's doing. Well, this begins to work upon his mind, upon his body and his soul and the stresses and strains of his life, of his work seem to melt away. He soon becomes more philosophical and understanding of the work he does and of the people he works with. This lessens the tension. It is the tensions that are the true killers. One will learn to be relaxed and not to worry because worry doesn't help anything. Thus, you see why a gardener lives longer than any other class of people.

I know that working on the land with nature teaches a man to live. It just can't be otherwise. One seems to acquire a special blend of philosophy. It seems inevitable even though you're not striving to learn. The knowledge seems to overtake you instinctively. You learn that nature's ways are best, steady and relentless—easy but sure and positive. It is the only way, the true way, yes, nature's way to good health, good life, contentment and happiness.

Gardeners must be active and alert and this promotes good health and good habits. The miracle of life is re-enacted every day before their very eyes. They are not prone to living excesses. They do not drink too much, seldom over-eat or gorge themselves. There's not too much laughter but a smile and a chuckle here and there. They work every day. They take no long recesses nor drawn out holidays. A little every day is better than a lot in one day and nothing the next.

'Tis true, too. They are better dispositioned than most folks because they face life philosophically, broadly, with understanding and compassion for themselves, their fellow men and their animals on the farm. They have learned to truly love, appreciate and enjoy the simple things in life. You know and I know that there are multitudes of simple things in life that are neither costly nor hard to procure. They are there for everyone to share. There's no man in our country who loves his home more than the man of the land.

Don't envy him . . . follow him!

By George — A Hick

All of us have heard the expression "Let George do it". Strange to relate this has a distinctly horticultural flavor.

Way back in the time of the ancient Greeks the word "ge" meant the earth and "ergon" meant to work. Combine them and it meant "one who works the land" and definitely indicated a farmer.

Perhaps some of you have studied Latin and will remember the famous Georgics. I think Virgil was the author. It deals entirely or exclusively with field husbandry and if you ever read them you'd see just how much those ancient Greeks did know about field husbandry and cultivating the land in general.

Today we usually refer to a farmer as a "hick". Evidently in those days they called them "George". Maybe it would be nicer and perhaps more elevating if we called our farmers Georges even in the present day and, come to think of it, a long line of our kings were called Georges. I wonder would they be flattered to think that we're calling them farmers.

The Georgics . . . evidently published or written nearly 2,000 years ago . . . is even today considered a very fine high rated comprehensive text book on agriculture.

The term "Georgic" meant anything belonging to or pertaining to the farm and rural life.

Gardening — The Leveller

When I was a young chappy in knee pants . . . sure enough we wore knee pants in my day . . . we looked like baseball players . . . nowadays the only people who wear knee pants are the fellows in court . . . no, no, not police court—the court of St. James, or St. Jeans. (St. Jeans would be more suitable wouldn't it?) . . . Anyway, back in them thar days there was a poem in my old reader about "Death—The Leveller". Oh, I don't know who wrote it—Browning or Blacking or somebody.

Anyway, the gist of the poem was that when all is said and done and we're laid on our bier (That's the way some of my sousy friends would like to die) all are equal—the rich, the poor, the mighty and the meek, the fat and thin, the short and the tall, the blondes and the brunettes and the redheads and the hellcats.

Well, I'm sure that gardening is just as good a leveller as the old fellow with the sickle or the scythe. When you're out working in the garden, the big tycoon who earns $50,000 a year, the practised surgeon who earns $25,000 a year, the busy executive or politician who earns $25,000, $30,000 or $40,000 a year . . . well, when you get them in the garden with a trowel, a rake or a spade, then you've got them down to size . . . because there the man or woman doesn't exist who can earn more than $1.00 an hour.

Yet you see, basically we all get down to earth some time. So here's something that you can share and enjoy in common with the Prime Minister, the millionaire, the artist, the author or the orator. When they get into a garden they're not a dang bit better than you are. In fact you might even be better than they.

Bobbin' Robin

Spring sent me a messenger. I heard a robin this morning chanting gleefully away outside my window.

I was almost startled because this is the first week in March and it is still quite wintry and cold outside.

He was singing away gaily and I could translate every word of his song . . . "Come on—get up—get out", he said, "Things are astirring —spring's acoming. There's no time to waste. There's much to do. Folks will soon be wanting their trees and seeds and things, and you'd better get them ready."

"Well, there are all those things to be done that you were going to do last fall—remember? . . . That lower field of Evergreens on the knoll that must be moved over to make room for that new planting . . . The last of those fruit trees that you couldn't get out when it froze . . . And you started to plough up that field you had in tomatoes and only got half way through."

I'm sure hoping this year we'll be able to get on the land early— real early. Old Cock Robin, you red-breasted troubadour, you sure do sing cheerfully but I've known you to be wrong about those early springs before. Still, I'm glad to see you . . . even though you do make a mistake now and then.

After all is said and done, if you can come out through the snow, the slush, the rain and the chilly winds of March and April with but a nest in the tree for protection, who are we to complain—with warm clothing and heated homes. So sing up loud and clear! Yours is a voice that is not stilled by do's, don'ts, but's, can'ts, conventions, rules and regulations. Yours is a soul that laughter cheers—mine is a heart that is full of tears! Sing, robin, sing—with all your heart! You know no borders. The world is yours and you do it no umbrage. You are indeed heaven blessed!

Nature's Prize

What thought do those of us who call ourselves gardeners ever give to sub-soiling or the conditions that exist for a plant below the soil's level?

There are two plants that are known and esteemed as nature's great sub-soilers. They do their work very effectively. This team of sub-soilers do a better job of looking after the regions below the soil's surface for the benefit of nature and mankind than any mechanical or other means devised by man. One of them is the Clover.

The other, and more important, member of the team is the Alfalfa. I was about to say "esteemed Alfalfa" but then I realized that it was not esteemed except by the few who know and understand the plant.

The root of the Alfalfa penetrates the soil, reaching every nook and cranny and it works 7 days a week, 24 hours a day. It never rests but continues its life's work of improving conditions below the soil level. The tiny roots work their way by penetration through the hardest soils, the poorest soils, the richest soils—to great depths . . . yes, 5, 10, 15, 20, 30 feet and more, and longitudinally they have been known to travel hundreds of feet. Yes, I'm talking about the roots of one plant. Moreover, making a place for water and air to get in—which is what the soil needs.

There is a record in the United States Department of Agriculture that states that Alfalfa roots were found penetrating through crevises in the roof of a tunnel 129 feet below the surface of an Alfalfa field.

It is understandable and reasonable that this great penetrating root system, reaching such a long distance and so many depths, will encounter elements that are unknown probably a few inches from the surface of the soil where most plants get their nourishment.

Therefore, continuing on this vein, an Alfalfa root and the Alfalfa plant will contain more vitamins and more elements than any plant in existence.

That makes good sense, doesn't it? Hence, if we are intelligent enough to utilize the plant, the seed or the roots, we in turn must benefit by our bodies having a source of elements that they so badly need for regeneration and balance.

It also has the natural ways and means of extracting nitrogen from the air and using it in its roots and eventually, if and when the roots die and decompose, the nitrogen is left in the soil and the soil is enriched.

The big puzzle to me is why man has not found reasonable ways and means of utilizing this marvelous food? Yes, he thought enough of his animals to prepare it for them and to sow millions of acres of it throughout the world for their use but he hasn't been smart enough to use it for himself. No one has taken the trouble to actually find ways and means of using it in our daily food. I'm sure that each and every one of us would be healthier if we did include Alfalfa in one form or another in our regular fare.

It is believed that Alfalfa is the oldest plant known to man. It is the most valuable forage plant ever discovered.

Here let me quote a learned Professor, addressing the National Hay Association at St. Louis in 1904. His name was Spillman. He was an agrostologist of the United States Department of Agriculture.

"In this area it will give from 2 to 3 crops a year. In Texas and farther south, it will give 4 to 5 large crops a year. In California they cut Alfalfa 11 times a year."

"Nitrogen is one of the important elements that the soil lacks in most all localities and Alfalfa has the means of bringing this nitrogen from the air into the soil. It is recorded that the roots of the Alfalfa will leave in the soil 8 to 10 times as much nitrogen as there was before. Alfalfa users never have to buy nitrogen and that is one of the most important elements used in fertilizers.

"No other agricultural plant leaves the soil in such splendid condition as Alfalfa does. It turns the air, the moisture, the sunshine and the earth into foodstuffs and green and purple grass into nectar and sweet perfume. It immediately forms a partnership of all the microorganisms and works in close harmony with them".

If this hasn't sold you on the values of Alfalfa, nothing will. And each and every fact and statement is true. Alfalfa can transform plain, ordinary, useless farmland into banks of undulating meadows, full hearted soils rich in plant food.

Alfalfa was carried by the Persians into Greece with the invasion of Xerxes in 490 B.C. It was carried into Rome in 146 B.C. and later used by the Romans during their conquest of Greece. Even Pliny mentions and praises it as a forage plant and it has been in cultivation in Italy since then.

The name Alfalfa is Arabic and actually means "good fodder".

It appears that it was introduced into Spain by the Moors from Northern Africa at the time of their conquest of Spain about 711 A.D. From Spain it crossed into France and then to Belgium and England. It was highly spoken of by an English writer of the 15th Century.

In England it is more often known by the name of Lucerne than it is Alfalfa. The Alfalfa term is used in Canada and the United States. The names seem to be interchangeable.

It is known by more names than any plant of my acquaintance. It would take probably half a column to list all of the names by which it is known and the word Clover plays an important part in it because half of these names have the word Clover attached to them. For example it is called French Clover, Mexican Clover, Lucerne Clover, Alfalfa Clover, Chilean Clover, Brazilian Clover, Syrian Clover, Blue Snail Clover, Branching Clover, Stem Clover, Monthly Clover,

Horned Clover, Perennial Clover, Blue Perennial Clover, Burgundy, Welsh Clover, Sicillian Clover and the plant isn't Clover at all. One of its common names, though, is Purple Medick.

Alfalfa has a long, long life. It has been proven in fields in Mexico that it has been continuously productive without replanting for over 200 years. There are many cases in France where it has definitely been known to have flourished for more than a century. In the United States it ordinarily lives from about 10 to 20 years although there is a field known in New York State where it has been successfully mown for over 60 years. It is called Everlasting and I believe it has every right to that name.

In height it usually grows from about 3 to 5 feet although there have been records that show that it has grown more than 10 feet.

The plant has a tender tap root with many branches tending downwards yet with considerable lateral growth. But as this tap root goes downwards it keeps sending out laterals—new ones all the time. The tap root goes deeper and deeper, sending out its laterals at every level. The top laterals die off and in their place decay occurs and leaves space for air and water to penetrate which is truly fertilizing the soil. It is considered by far the most efficient deep reaching sub-soiler and renovator known to the horticultural world.

Beauties in Flowering Shrubs

You know it's pretty hard for a father to play favorites with his children. It's not smart and it's often dangerous because your children will wind up with a complex.

Well, I'm sort of in the same predicament when I have to choose between various forms of beauty in the garden. It is understandable that a garden is really never complete unless it has variety—annuals, perennials, flowering bulbs, flowering shrubs, trees, evergreens, roses and so on.

However, dollar for dollar, hour for hour, season for season, I doubt if there is any group in the plant kingdom that gives so much beauty, comfort and protection in a permanent way as do the flowering shrubs.

I'm not going to pay tribute to all of them although they all do have varying merit. I'm going to mention those that are perhaps dear to my heart or have proven themselves hardy, dependable, attractive and flowerful.

1. *Forsythia*—You just can't garden without it. For ten long

years I refused to have one in my garden, mostly because I thought it was redundant. As I'd walk or drive around the country on some mighty cold April days I began to admire that hardy, beautiful, golden-flowered plant that stood up so bravely in spite of the howling winds, the biting frost, and ice and snow. I have quite a few of them in my garden now and I doubt if anything else gives me so much joy.

2. *Chaenomeles* (Japanese Flowering Quince)—This is a slow growing fellow but follows right close on the heels of the Forsythia for early blooms. It is a true Quince and bears "canable" fruit. Although it can be had in flowers of various colors, the one we commonly know has scarlet blooms that cover the bush from top to bottom. It is prickly, having fairly sharp thorns that will keep children and dogs away from it. I've seen some of them that were older than the "hills of home" and still doing well.

3. *Spirea Van Houttei*—For many years it has been known as the world's most planted shrub. I'm not particularly fond of it but if left alone it makes a display of small white blooms that look like the foam of Niagara Falls. It is used for hedges, accent, specimen and practically every other planting need known.

4. *Kolkwitzia* (Beauty Bush)—Ah, if ever there was a perfect shrub, this is it. I think it was Robert Fortune who discovered it somewhere in his travels in the north of China. I've read his first volume and no mention of the Kolkwitzia was made. But never mind its pedigree. It's the most glorious shrub in Christendom, Mohammedandom or any other dom—inion.

Beautiful, delicate pink flowers in such profusion as to rival the stars in the heavens. The shrub itself has the most elegant, gracious habit. It grows slowly but for such beauty . . . you can wait.

5. *Philadelphus coronarius* (Sweet Mockorange)—This tall growing shrub gets more compliments and comments than any item that I have at home. It's an old timer. Those in my garden are over 25 years old and are still in virile neat condition. The Greeks used it to decorate the brows of their victorious warriors or was it athletes? Apart from their fragrance, the flower is beautiful and always reminds me of the flower of the Dogwood.

6. *Deutzia scabra*—This tall growing shrub has attractive double flowers . . . white with pinkish tinge. Very much like the Mockorange in habit and growth but the flowers are more double. Doesn't have a common name to my knowledge.

7. *Weigela* (Cradle Shrub)—This is another beauty that came from China and its flowers resemble the Kolkwitzia except that they

are larger and you can get them in pink and red. They're not nearly as graceful but much more colorful. It's a good shrub and grows to about 4 feet. I call it the Cradle Shrub because it was named after a German botantist called Weigel which means "cradle" in German.

8. *Berberis thunbergi atropurpurea* (Red Leaf Barberry)—Put one of these in a nice sunny place and for sheer glorious color of foliage and form it will rival any shrub in the garden. Makes a nice hedge, too, but it must have a lot of sunlight. I like it best untrimmed. A splendid item.

9. *Buddleia* (Butterfly Bush)—Also called Summer Lilac. It will die back to the ground in the cold winter but makes tremendous growth and blooms abundantly all summer long. Has a delectable fragrance and the butterflies flock to it by the "trillions". Rightfully called Butterfly Bush. It got its name from an English clergyman called Buddle.

10. *Althea* (Rose of Sharon)—For mid-summer and fall bloom this shrub is hard to match. Flowers are identical with the large Hollyhocks. The bush grows large and dense and is one of the largest of all shrubs. It grows up to 6 feet tall and 3 to 4 feet wide. Full and densely foliated. It has 1001 uses. You can have them in various colors, singles and doubles. Linnaeus thought it was a native of Syria but China seems more logical. It starts to bloom in late July and often continues till fall. Botanically—Hibiscus syriacus.

11. *Hydrangea Paniculata Grandiflora*—Not many shrubs can surpass the Hydrangea when it comes to size, beauty and utility. It starts to bloom in July and the huge trusses still hang there all winter long. The blooms don't fall but cling tenaciously. You've seen them . . . large conical-shaped panicles. They change color, too, right through, starting off with white, then pink, mauve and intermediate shades of purple and red. They grow 3 to 4 feet high but if trimmed into a tree, which is easily done, it becomes even more beautiful.

12. *Blue Hydrangea*—Twenty years ago we listed this shrub and were laughed at by all the nurserymen throughout Canada. They said it wouldn't grow and bloom in our latitude but today practically all of the leading nurseries list it. So evidently it is growing and doing all right. I'm trying hard to think of a more attractive shrub—bold, clean, beautiful and impressive—that blooms during the latter part of the summer but I can't bring one to mind.

Where conditions are suited this shrub will reach a height of probably 4 feet and the floating blue flowers are incomparable. The trick is that you've got to keep the frost-tender terminal buds from freezing in the northern latitudes. This can be accomplished by cutting

39

it back early in the spring and getting the new late growth to flower or by protecting it in the fall and winter against the real cold weather.

If your soil isn't acid, the blue flowers will be pink or violet. If you want to be sure that it will be blue, make sure there is a lot of acid peat in the soil. Proper name—Hydrangea macrophylla (hortensis).

13. *Kerria japonica*—I usually run hot and cold about this shrub. Sometimes I think it's lovely and other times I more or less ignore it. It is distinguished among all shrubs of my acquaintance because of the fact that the wood is bright green, winter and summer—it's more noticeable when the leaves are off in the winter because the bark is stark-naked at that time.

It has a peculiar habit of growth—shooting up all over the place like bamboo. There are two forms generally known—one is the single flower which is like a Cosmos of lovely gold color and there is a double one just like small pompon Chrysanthemums. It is the double one that is most popular. It blooms chiefly in the spring but you can count on blooms intermittently, more or less, throughout the summer.

It doesn't have a common name that is generally used but I have heard it called Japanese Rose. I don't get the connection except that the leaves of the plant do resemble those of a Rose. It's hardy practically anywhere.

14. *Anthony Waterer Spirea*—There are so few really good low growing shrubs that Spirea Anthony Waterer is planted wherever a low growing shrub is desired. However, this isn't its only cause for greatness. It is hardy. It starts to bloom in July and continues right on sometimes until frost. The flowers are a pleasing bright crimson and it seems to thrive under adverse conditions and will tolerate most types of soils.

15. *Tamarix*—This fellow doesn't seem to have a common name either—at least, I couldn't find any. But they are also called Tamarisk.

This is a most unique shrub with light, feathery foliage and most unusual, graceful, feathery plumes of rosy pink—mostly in dense racemes which are grouped in a large terminal panicle. It blooms during August and September. It is excellent in a group planting where you want something to stand out.

Pentandra—Grows 10-13 feet and blooms August-September.

Hispida—Of dwarfer habit and grows only 3-4 feet. Flowers August-September.

16. *Snowberry and Coralberry* (Symphoricarpos)—There is nothing particularly attractive about these shrubs but they have their uses. Believe me, when you have a difficult situation that requires handling

40

like smoke, shade, dampness or open wind-swept places or to stand the worst of city conditions, then you can fill in with Symphoricarpos. Beautiful girls may be a dime a dozen but those that can cook, wash, sew and knit may not be so plentiful and bring premiums on the marriage market. So it is with Symphoricarpos.

The Orbiculatus or Coralberry has reddish-purple fruit that birds love and it bears them plentifully. It is commonly called Indian Currant.

The other one is the Snowberry or commonly called Waxberry. Everybody has seen them. It has those whitish marbles that sit all over the bush in mid-summer and fall.

17. *Alpine Currant* (Ribes alpinum)—This makes a good hedge for shady locations. It is ideal for city conditions. It comes into leaf very early and the leaves hang on until very late. I've often recommended it for locations where practically nothing else would grow and yet one didn't want anything to grow eventually too tall. It can be easily kept controlled. It's good for that troublesome spot.

18. *Smoke Tree* (Cotinus coggygria)—This is a close relation of our native Sumach. Everybody seems to love this unusual shrub because of its clouds of feathery, purplish-green flowers that appear in mid-summer. Of course the foliage has a bright, glowing fall color as well. So this makes the shrub even more desirable for practically every garden.

19. *Andromeda* (Pieris japonica)—Here is just about the finest shrub that you can find anywhere. In habit it is slow growing and that probably is an asset rather than a liability. In the early spring, before most plants have even stirred, the plant is covered with beautiful white, scented flowers that resemble Lily-of-the-Valley almost to perfection. The flowers seem to last and last and then the foliage seems to take on a reddish or bronzy color. Then as the flowers begin to fade and fall the plant starts in with its new growth which is really quite becoming. In the fall the new tiny buds of the flowers that are to appear next spring are covering the plant. Undoubtedly a delightful subject. It is evergreen with oblong leaves about 1½ to 3 inches long. They are shiny and deep green.

20. *Viburnum carlesi*—There may be sweeter smelling flowers but they have never come within range of my nose. The very fragrant white flowers appear early in the spring, in globular heads, actually before the leaves fully appear. One of the features of this shrub, too, is the extremely handsome foliage which vies with the beautifully scented blooms. For years it has ranked as one of the top shrubs because of its fragrance. It is also called the Korean Spice Viburnum.

41

As I told you at the start, I'm not trying to describe all of the shrubs but I've just given you my impression of the ones generally seen.

Simple Addition

So you had a garden. Yes, now 'tis fall. In the spring you worked your land and prepared it for the plants and seeds to come and then later you planted, you sowed, cultivated, insecticided and whatever else was necessary. Then in late summer you enjoyed the bounties of your crop.

Now 'tis fall. What did you get out of your garden? . . . Vegetables, berries, fruits? Believe it or not, these were the material gains but that perhaps was the least that you garnered from your garden.

Will you not spend a moment to think of the other things that your garden gave you? Did you not get exercise and accumulate health, strength and well-being? Did not your soul revel with joy and pleasure for being in the great outdoors having the benefits of the sun to shine upon you? Did you not enjoy the planning and plotting? Did not the anticipation send charges surging through your body and mind? Surely your eyes feasted on the garden and things around you. Did your ears not absorb the songs of the birds? Yes, all these things —because you had a garden!

Did you not reap relaxation, comfort and unbounded interest as the days unfolded about you? Did you not find solace under the shade of the spreading willow tree? Did you not find your mind filled with nobler thoughts and plans? The relaxation that you found as you lay under the tree and the winds wafted health and scented breezes past your nose. . . . Yes, it is from our garden and from nature that we learn how to appreciate, to understand and to love all mankind. You cannot help but enrich your soul and your heart from the beauties of nature that surround you.

Kind thoughts and generous deeds go hand in hand with working with the earth. Each day brings its interests, its hopes and visions and we strive to fulfil them—knowing full well that tomorrow will bring new problems, new questions and new answers. But this is life and that is how it is to be lived if one wants to enjoy the wonders which our Heavenly Father has bestowed upon us.

About Pollination

Let's talk about pollination. This subject, one of vital importance to orchardists and home gardeners, is not usually appreciated or discussed as broadly as it should be.

You may not realize it but you just can't grow fruit successfully on a commercial basis, or get the best of results from a garden or home planting, unless you have at least a fundamental knowledge of pollination.

To begin with, all fruits are placed in one of these three categories ... (1) self-fruitful, (2) partially self-fruitful, (3) self-unfruitful. In this third group you could say self-sterile—the terms are synonymous.

It is of vital importance to note that no variety of pear can, by any stretch of the imagination, pollinate a variety of apple, plum, or peach. Cross-pollination must and does only take place between and among the same species. Different varieties of apple are required to pollinate an apple. Different varieties of pear are required to pollinate pears, and so on.

Peaches generally are considered self-fruitful and that means that one peach tree can and does set fruit without the aid of any other peach tree. The only peach tree variety that is generally known in America as being self-unfruitful is the old J. H. Hale but this variety is only grown in certain sections of the country and even then in somewhat smaller quantities. They used to be very popular because the fruit attains an enormous size but it seems to have fallen into disfavor and is seldom, if ever, found any more.

Here's another thing. When we say a peach tree is self-fruitful, it means that the blossoms on a peach tree are capable of fertilizing themselves and bearing proper crops of fruit.

Very few varieties of Plums are considered self-fruitful and it is best to remember here also that, generally speaking, there are two types of plums—the European and the Japanese. Being somewhat different to each other, they do not generally pollinate each other. That is, a European will seldom effectively pollinate a Japanese and vice versa. But there are exceptions. For example, Reine Claude which is a European type will pollinate Shiro and maybe others. Red June, a Japanese kind, will also pollinate Shiro.

Pay strict attention now for the success or failure of your crop may lie right here. If one variety of apple, for example, blossoms very early and the other variety does not open its flowers till very late, it is easy to see why you could not expect any great success in cross-pollination—if any. In such cases it must be realized that proper fertilization of the flower is not being provided even though you have more than one variety.

Turning to cherries, none of the sweet varieties, or the black cherries as we know them, are self-fruitful. You must have two different varieties of sweet cherries if you're going to set a crop of fruit. I

43

know of no sweet cherry that is self-fruitful. However, the Montmorency is entirely self-fruitful and requires no outside pollination. It is good to remember at this point that the Montmorency Cherry which we know as the pie cherry or sour cherry does not pollinate the sweet varieties.

There are what is known as semi-sweet or half-sweet cherries. They actually are a hybrid between the sweet and the sour. These are self-sterile and require pollination the same as the sweet cherries do.

Apricots are considered partially self-fruitful. Therefore it is advisable wherever possible to have another variety of apricot or two different varieties if you want to get a good set of fruit. But it has been established that apricots will bear a crop even without another apricot close by.

I should mention here that one variety of apricot known as the Riland definitely does not pollinate itself satisfactorily and is considered self-unfruitful.

Nectarines, like peach, are entirely self-fruitful and only one variety is required. No pollination from outside sources is neecssary.

Quince are considered to be sufficiently self-fruitful.

Filberts or hazelnuts are definitely considered self-sterile. They will not bear if planted alone. Therefore you must get another variety if you want to get nuts.

There are some varieties of apple that will pollinate themselves, but, to all intents and purposes, it should be accepted that apples require cross-pollination. If you want to get dependable crops be sure to plant different varieties of apples in proximity to one another.

In this instance pears are very similar to apples. While there may be some varieties that will pollinate themselves I have never heard of them. Generally speaking, you'd be safer if you accepted the fact that pears, too, are self-sterile and require pollination from other varieties.

Looking the pollination business over on a rather broad scale, it is wise to understand a few basic matters. One is that you may plant two varieties of cherry, or any other fruit for that matter, and still get poor cross-pollination or small crops. This is due to the fact that these two varieties are not fully compatible. You'll find this occurs in apples, pears and cherries—yes, and in plums, too. You must find two varieties of the same fruit that will effectively pollinate and by a little study and examination you will definitely find that one variety does the job much better than another.

Let us turn to cherries for a moment. Napoleon, which is called a white cherry but actually is the old Royal Anne or Oxheart, is one of the finest of all cherries in flavor, size and quality. Napoleon definitely will pollinate *almost* any variety of sweet cherry. This isn't to be taken as a blanket statement but it is definitely believed that it will pollinate almost every variety of sweet cherry. The only two varieties of cherries that the Napoleon will not pollinate effectively, to the best of my knowledge, are Bing and Lambert.

Now in pears the Bartlett and Seckel varieties don't pollinate each other effectively. As far as Kieffer and Bartlett, Barlett will definitely pollinate Kieffer but Kieffer in turn will not effectively pollinate Bartlett. It seems that Bartlett is a very poor pollen-maker and it is not considered a good pollinator for any variety of pear. Generally it seems that the Kieffer sets huge crops of fruit without the aid of any other pollination so I'd begin to suspect very strongly that Kieffer is to a great extent self-fertile although I've no proof that this is true.

Among the good varieties of apples for pollinating purposes, you can count on some of the best varieties including Cortland, Delicious, Yellow Delicious, Jonathan, Rome Beauty and Wealthy.

All commercially grown varieties of strawberries are self-fruitful but bees and others insects are necessary for the transfer of the pollen.

Currants, red and black, are generally self-fruitful but there are one or two kinds that do require cross-pollination. One of these is the Boscoop Giant. It will bear heavy crops of large black currants if another kind is close by. Red and black currants do not effectively pollinate each other.

Gooseberries, raspberries, blackberries, boysenberries and grapes are all considered self-fruitful.

Re nut trees . . . Filberts and Chestnuts definitely require cross-pollination for a proper set of nuts. So be sure to set out at least two varieties. The English Walnut is self fruitful but it, too, produces only female flowers when young and the male flowers appear only as the tree gets older. Therefore two kinds are required to get good crops —at least, when the trees are young. Nut trees which are catkin-bearers are dependent upon wind for pollination—not insects. It is believed that the Black Walnut, Butternut and Japanese Walnut are all self-fruitful.

Pollination can be effectively created or accomplished even if there are no trees of the desired varieties available. Many growers have successfully brought branches of blossoms from the desired tree from hundreds of miles away and hung them in the tree that they wanted pollinated and have got the best of results.

Occasionally you will note that fruit begins to set after blossoming but then when the fruit is partly formed it falls off the tree or decays

45

or dries up. This, in most cases, is due to improper, faulty or lack of pollination.

From what I can judge after watching the actions of the Mulberry I'm quite convinced that our Mulberry, that is the Mulberry grown here, which is the White Mulberry, is completely self-fertile and does not require pollination.

Herein lies a catch. You may have a Mulberry tree that is five or six years old that bears no fruit—yet it blossoms. You will think I have passed along incorrect information to you—but listen . . . This is one of nature's protective devices at work. Flowers of only one sex are formed. If they get outside pollen, O.K., you get fruit. If not . . . barren!

You see nature abhors inbreeding and tries to avoid it. But if after a few years no pally pollen—then both male and female flowers will appear and you will get your big crop of fruit.

But there's another variety of Mulberry—I believe it is called the Black Mulberry—and I know that this does require another tree for pollination.

It is worthy of note here, too, that some varieties of trees have blossoms that are very hardy and resistant to cold and bad weather, whereas others are tender and are easily injured. Then again some varieties of some fruits, when they blossom, blossom for a long period —the blossom remaining fertile and active for days and sometimes weeks. It is notable here that cherries are not in that category. They come out in bloom and pollination must take place within a couple of days. Otherwise it is considered a failure. You will hear among the cherry growers that, when the cherry blossoms appear and you have a spell of muggy or damp or rainy weather, the cherry crop is a failure inevitably. This is not so with practically any other variety of fruit but with cherries it is an accepted fact.

Again on this same theme, apricots are the earliest blooming of all fruits. They open up and show their beautiful colors before any other variety of fruit and they really are a treat to behold. They seem to bring spring a month or so closer. If the apricots were not really tough and hardy they would lose every flower and not a fruit would set. But because the apricot is tough and can stand these conditions, you usually get a fair crop of fruit. It's just a matter of pollination, I believe, rather than the cold weather because if they couldn't stand the cold weather, they wouldn't bloom that early. And remember, they don't get too much co-operation from bees and other insects during the damp and cold early spring. They must depend on rain and wind.

Whither Goest Thou?

Let's take the road back before it's too late. No, I don't mean the back road. But let us return to nature before the "Finished" sign is hung upon us.

The philosophers have been debating for countless years whether or not man is going backward or forward. Well, I have my own ideas but I'm not saying. Yet lately I've noticed a very promising omen. Yes, there's a light glowing because I've found there are thousands and, yes, maybe tens of thousands of people every year taking to gardening and that is a very good sign.

Now America is a new nation and it is understandable that when folks come from oppressed countries, countries where they were denied religious and other freedoms, where it was hard to make a living, where food was scarce . . . when they reach this new land flowing with milk and honey that they would get into the hustle and bustle of things and spend their days, weeks and hours just making money. So we accept that fact.

But then after a while when man has a roof over his head and a few dollars in the bank, he begins to think of more important things—how to live. So then he takes to gardening.

I have information to prove that gardening has become the fastest growing hobby in America. To me that says conclusively that man is growing wiser because no matter what hobby he pursued and got himself engrossed in, there isn't one that could give him the health, the pleasure, the feeling of well being, the sustained interest that gardening can give him.

Still there's another important factor. Each and every member of the family, male or female, young or old, can take part in this wonderful God-given hobby. Even the austere American Medical Association states, "Gardening is one of the best methods of relaxing from the fast pace of modern living".

No, I am not one of these advocates that thinks that everybody can go and live off the land like Thoreau did. Sure, it would be a wonderful dream but I know it isn't feasible. I know it could never happen. So why dwell upon it unless you just want to dream and kid yourself? I'm thinking about myself. I wasn't always a gardener. Thirty years ago I didn't know a garden from a cement floor. But when I found out, there was no power on earth that would keep me from it except death. I love the land in any form—the poor land because it I would like to make richer—and the six feet that will some day rest my bones.

You know I think that gardeners like ourselves are missing a bet. We are sharing in this wonderful God-given gift but there are many of our friends and neighbors who do not know about it. Why don't we go on a conversion tour and tell our friends and neighbors about gardening? Why can't we teach them to enjoy the world's finest hobby? Now you know you'd be doing them a favor if you converted them to gardening and probably keep them out of a pub or prevent them from being killed racing around in motor cars or flying. Whatever you save them from, you'll know you'll be preserving them for better things because from gardening and the love of the soil stem the best things in life.

So You Like Climbers

Well, that makes my task easier because I was going to talk about annual climbers anyway.

One thing about these climbing plants is that they usually germinate readily and grow like a bat out of a cave. They've pretty well got to grow that fast if they're going to complete their life cycle in one year which is the intent and purpose of every annual.

Now they have many applications. You can use them to cover a tree stump, a trellis, veranda, an arbor, a wire fence or even the old familiar outhouse. You know, strange as it may seem, they like that place best. I wonder why?

You don't have to start these vines indoors or in flats or in any other way. You just plant the seed where you want the vines to grow —and get out of the way fast. It's generally pretty safe to plant them early in May.

Don't plant the seeds too deep. About two or three times their diameter in depth is sufficient and set them about three inches apart.

Then if they all come up you can thin them out to anywhere from eight to twelve inches apart.

If you do want to start them indoors I'd suggest you put them in individual pots or bottomless plant cubes. You can get a head start this way and still not disturb them when you put them outdoors.

Balloon Vine—Commonly called Heart Seed and Love-in-a-Puff. A tropical American vine that grows about 10 feet. It has tiny flowers and very interesting 3-angled inflated hollow balls like balloons from which it gets its name. Proper name—Cardiospermum halicacabum.

Black-eyed Susan—Ah, that's the one for me. Not Susan—I mean the flower. Also called Clock Vine. It's the brightest colored, most profuse blooming vine in cultivation. It has white and gold flowers with a dark throat that will tickle you silly. Proper name—Thunbergia alata.

Canary-bird Flower—This fellow is sort of related to the Nasturtium group. Not a rank grower but will reach 10 to 15 feet. It bears curiously cut yellow flowers with curved green spurs. Actually to some, and vaguely to others, it resembles a canary bird in flight. This grows easily almost anywhere. Proper name—Tropaeolum canariensis.

Cardinal Climber—This fellow will grow up to 15 feet. It is closely related to the Morning Glory. It has beautiful crimson flowers with a white throat, about 2 inches long. Very popular. Proper name— Quamoclit sloteri.

Cathedral Bell Vine—Also known as Cup-and-Saucer Vine. This chappy belongs to the Phlox family and this is the only one of that family that climbs. This one better be started indoors. This fellow's a regular "doggone-it" and grows to 25 feet or more, climbing by leaf tendrils. The flowers are large, violet-colored, well shaped and set off by a large leafy calyx. It does look like a cup and saucer. It can even stand a little frost. Proper name—Cobaea scandens.

Glory Flower—This vine originally comes from the Andes. It is extremely handsome because of its orange-red flowers in loose racemes. It is stem-climbing, tendril bearing and the fruit is a slender pod about 1½ inches long. Its proper name in Greek means "pendulous fruit". It is properly—Eccremocarpus scaber.

Glory Star or Cypress Vine—A very fast grower that reaches up to 20 feet. The foliage is fern or thread-like and the flowers are scarlet or white. Proper name—Quamoclit pennata.

Gourds—They have a place wherever a vine is desired or wanted. I doubt if there is a living person who won't be delighted, fascinated, thrilled, perplexed and such by the varying shapes of the fruits of this plant. They want a lot of heat, moisture and rich soil and they'll grow like "Topsy". A few of the varieties are Mock Cucumber, Snake Gourd, Dishrag Gourd and the Bottle Gourd. There are those that are shaped like bananas, oranges, peaches. I'm reasonably sure that you can find a Gourd that is shaped like any fruit or utensil in the world. While some of them may be grotesque in their appearance, still others are extremely decorative, graceful and beautiful. They're wonderful for covering porches, screens or fences which they do very quickly. It's properly known as Cucurbita pepo ovifera.

Hyacinth Bean—If you want abundant foliage this is the one to grow. It has pea-shaped purple flowers and also white flowers and the seeds are edible. It should start to flower early in July and continue until cut by the frost. Proper name—Dolichos lablab. (You can talk plainer than that.)

Japanese Hop—Sorry, fellas, but this doesn't bear the real hops so you can't go into the brewing business. This has very attractive leaves and belongs to the Mulberry family. It will grow 25 feet but likes to grow at an angle. This is the baby you want for unsightly buildings. Who says that an outhouse is unsightly? I've often heard it said that it is at times the most welcome sight a man ever saw. Proper name —Humulus japonicus.

Kenilworth Ivy—Also called Coliseum Ivy, Erin's Beard and Climbing Sailor. This is a shade lover and has attractive, lilac-blue flowers with yellow throats. It is a very useful vine for hanging baskets or window boxes. It doesn't get out of bounds—seldom exceeding a length of 3 feet. You'll like it for small trellises in the living room and it does stand indoor conditions beautifully. Its proper name is Cymbalaria muralis.

Morning Glory—These are considered the quickest growing and showiest of all annual vines. They are best sown where wanted and do well in practically all locations and types of soil. For screening, their large, dark green, heart-shaped leaves are hard to beat and the flowers—trumpet-shaped in many lovely clear colors—make this group of plants one of the most popular in cultivation. Their flowers close at noon but they give of themselves so profusely that even a dull morning is made cheerful and bright by having seen them. You can grow them indoors and out. Botanically they are called Ipomoea.

Nasturtiums—You didn't know there were climbing Nasturtiums? Well, this is it. Against a trellis it will reach great height during the summer. It has a wide range of colors. Proper name—Tropaeolum majus.

Scarlet Runner Bean—It is also known as Multiflora or Flowering

Bean and Painted Lady. It has a profusion of brilliant, showy flowers and, need I tell you, the beans are good to eat, too. This is the fellow that was grown many hundreds of years ago by the Aztecs—probably one of the "grand-daddys" of the beans we know today. Properly its name is Phaseolus coccineus.

Squirting Cucumber—This is a trailing vine of the Gourd family and comes to us from the native moist forest of the middle and eastern Mediterranean. It gets its name from the fact that when the fruit is ripe the seeds violently squirt out of the pod along with a sort of liquid jelly surrounding it. I'd also like to tell you that a powerful cathartic known as Elaterium is made from the fruits of Squirting Cucumber. It's properly known as Ecballium elaterium. It has attractive yellow flowers.

Sweet Peas—Considered the most highly and intensely developed of all annual flowers. Grows to about 6 feet and does best on a trellis or other support. There is a wide range of colors—mottled, solid, striped, plain petals, wavy petals and ruffled—with sweet fragrance. Two distinct forms are available—summer flowering for outdoors and winter flowering for indoors and cutting. Academically—Lathyrus odoratus.

Wild Cucumber—This baby will climb to 20 feet. It has small white flowers which mature into 1½ inch cucumber-like fruits that are spiny and unique. Proper name—Echinocystis lobata.

An Orchid for You

The growing of Orchids is becoming more popular in America every day . . . and I have been doing my share to popularize them with Tom, Dick and Harry.

More than 10 years ago when we first started to grow Orchids we occasionally sold a plant to somebody who got the bug or heard about them and wanted to try them. Since then thousands of folks have joined the cult and now the number of Orchid growers in America, I dare say, would reach into the tens of thousands.

I'm very happy about this because I guess more than any individual in my native Canada I was responsible for encouraging, publicizing and supplying the folks who wanted to grow them.

51

When I was down in Laredo, Texas, on the Mexican border many years ago I contacted a man who hires the Mexicans to go down into the forests to get them. They don't only go into Mexico for them but down into Nicaragua and Guatemala . . . yes, and most of the other Central American Republics too. They grow down there like hair on a dog's back in the most inaccessible spots and in the crotches of tall trees. The best ones are found deep, deep in the jungle.

It was my hope to go down to Central America this summer and see the scene at close quarters but circumstances didn't permit this adventure so we'll put it on the calendar for some future date.

Anyway we just got a new lot in—1,500 of them and now we're getting another 1,000 from India . . . and replacements and new purchases keep coming in all the time. I don't know which are the most spectacular but in India they seem to have entirely different varieties.

Altogether we have a list that comprises over 100 individual genera and species of Orchids. I don't know anybody in America who has a more extensive list.

I have the biggest list of many things in America as you hear me spout. Still you have never heard me say that I have the biggest bundle of money and probably if you're as smart as I think you are, you'll quick like a fleeting buck understand why. The axiom is have less variety and more money!

Due to the fact that our list is rather extensive it is obvious that in some varieties we have but few. Often it is strictly a case of first come, first served. It never fails when someone wants Laelia autumnalis, sure as fate, 11 other people want it and we have only 10.

Unlike a factory we can't shove a slab of metal into a machine and stamp out a few more.

Growing Orchids from seeds is a fabulous and intricate occupation. You actually require a chemical laboratory . . . yes, including test tubes and culture mediums.

Then how do they grow in their native heath? Ah, that's it—we don't have that humid hot climate . . . thus, the test tubes. But we'll go into that some other time.

Strange as it may sound, Orchids are astoundingly simple to grow. Yes, I mean exactly what I say. They require less care and less attention than the commonest garden or house subject.

They are practically indestructible but there is one prime requisite . . . moisture or preferably humidity. Yet, water lying around their pulpy, thick roots will kill them surer than arsenic.

You see, the majority perch up on a tree where they get the

continuing ocean fogs and mists—yet no water threatens their roots by drowning.

Therefore (and mark this as 3A priority) give them water once, twice or more often daily but make sure it drains away like water off a swan's back. Why do I say swan instead of duck? That's easy—a swan is taller and therefore the water has a better fall, insuring surer drainage.

One more thing . . . Set the plant as high up on the medium as possible—just covering with sufficient osmunda, tightly packed about, to act as an anchor.

Now while I'm on the subject I'm going to give you some instructions on how to handle the Orchids. The experts all tell you to use Osmunda Fibre and that is generally accepted to be the best medium for growing Orchids. We have on our own volition added Sphagnum Moss, either mixed with the Osmunda or sprinkled on the surface. Why? . . . Because it retards the evaporation of moisture better than any other known medium.

You'll find the Osmunda Fibre tough stuff. You'll never believe that an ordinary fern or fibre could be so wiry but its use is that it holds exactly the quantity of moisture which Orchids require.

Now here is how you mix it for the various varieties of Orchids. Pay attention because I won't repeat it.

For Cattleyas, Dendrobiums and Laelias: 3 parts Osmunda Fibre and 1 part Sphagnum Moss.

For Cymbidiums or Cypripediums: 3 parts fibrous loam, 2 parts Osmunda Fibre and 1 part Sphagnum Moss.

For Vandaceous Orchids: 1 part Sphagnum Moss to 1 part Osmunda Fibre.

Now you're an orchidarian.

Building a Lawn

This is not a treatise nor is it a scientific research program or pursuit. Here I'm going to try to tell you in the simplest possible language and in the shortest possible time how to grow a lawn.

To begin with, it is hoped and expected that you will have enough common sense to get some decent loam or top soil if the soil in your home grounds is not satisfactory. Now you don't need anything fancy or special. You need plain ordinary decent earth and if you don't know what this is then I'm afraid I can't tell you in this instance. But if you wrote to me and explained your ignorance, I'd be happy to enlighten you.

53

Now assuming that you start off with common ordinary soil—it may be too light and it may be too heavy. If it is real sandy, then it is light and if it is good heavy clay, then it's too heavy. In either case a top dressing of peat moss from $\frac{1}{2}$ in. to 2 inches in depth would quickly correct the condition.

But let's start again. Your soil is in fair tilth and requires no special correction or improvement. You can dig up your garden plot which you are going to seed if you like, but it is not imperative or even necessary. What you should do is clean it up neatly and tidily. Then go over it with a heavy rake and rake the devil out of it until you have made a fairly rough surface. This would be best done after a rain while the earth is crumbly but not soggy.

No, I don't think you need a machine to sow your seed but get good seed, proper seed, perennial seed. If you use the best mixtures, which are perennial and life-long lasting, which I am strongly recommending, you will require only 2 to $3\frac{1}{2}$ lbs. per 1,000 square feet. If you use cheap or common mixtures, which often contain mostly annual grasses, you will require anywhere from 5 to 7 lbs. per 1,000 square feet. So it is obvious that you would have something wrong with your head if you used anything but the good mixtures. A bargain mixture is never any better than the price you paid for it and most often it is worth a lot less . . . for the simple reason that when a product costs a man little, he can tack on a good profit but when the price is fairly high, then large profits are not possible and you usually buy them at a far more reasonable margin.

I recommend broadcasting by hand—using one steady motion. Start on the east and walk straight up and down, north and south, working towards the west—using this same steady motion of broadcasting your seed. When you have reached the west side, start at the west and work back to the east. When that is completed, go to the north side and work south. Then when you've got to the south, work back to the north. This will give you as good a coverage as you ever could obtain with a machine or any other method known.

When you have finished broadcasting your seed as outlined, get your rake and rake your plot over again. This will in practically all cases bury your seeds properly and put them in prime condition for germinating.

Your lawn should be watered once or twice a day with the lightest possible spray that you can get out of your hose. If you use a heavy spray or heavy fall of water, you will only wash the seed into one pile and I strongly advise against that. Keep watering until germination takes places. It should start in 5 to 7 days and be completed in 2 to

3 weeks. But watch out—never allow your seed bed to dry out at any time at all. Otherwise you may loose your entire stand. Again, don't drown it or you may cause rot of the roots and lose your lawn, too.

Here I'm going to offer another method of sowing a lawn. This is my sure-fire way!

Some people want to be positively sure of getting a good stand and this method will insure that to the highest degree known. I dare any man or woman to show a better way of growing a lawn quickly and in the best of tilth and health. This method is exclusive to myself. I have been advocating it for 7 years now and I've never known a failure. Each and every time that this method is used, it's been an unbounded success. I am still waiting for the first complaint or for the first friend or customer to tell me that this method didn't prove completely successful.

If you're interested, here it is. Rake your lawn exactly as outlined for the previous method. Then sprinkle damp peat through a sieve over the entire area of your lawn to a depth of about ¼ of an inch. This isn't as hard to do as it sounds. You need an ordinary sieve— the kind they used to use in the olden days when they had coal furnaces—you know, an ash sifter. That would do and if you haven't got one, you can buy a piece of hardware cloth at the hardware store with ¼ in. holes and nail it onto a little box or build one from a few pieces of wood and you've got a proper medium for distributing peat moss.

After you have distributed the peat moss fairly evenly over the entire area to a depth of about ¼ of an inch or more (remember, the peat moss has to be damp), sow your seed in the same way as mentioned before. When this is done properly and carefully, again sprinkle another ¼ of an inch of peat moss over the entire area. Then leave it alone. Water with a very light spray once a day. Germination should start in 5 days and continue until practically every seed that you planted has sprouted.

You will get a stand of grass that will astound and amaze you. If the germination test of your seed shows 90% or 95%, then each and every one of these will be growing within 2 or 3 weeks. This method will work on light soils, heavy soils, poor soils and even the hard baked soils. To the best of my knowledge and belief, it's foolproof.

Warning—whichever means or method you follow, use no fertilizer either before or after sowing. You don't need it. Leave lawn clippings where they fall. Never gather or rake them up. It may look untidy for a few days after the first clipping in the spring but it is wonderful and you'll never need any fertilizer. This will maintain your lawn in good condition.

Anem — Means Wind

(So—O.K.—I'm Anemotobe).

Either you love, appreciate and understand nature or you don't. If you've reached your present age without any affection for the natural then I'm truly sorry for you—nothing I can say will improve the situation.

But on the other hand, if you do recognize the wonder and the beauty and the grandeur of nature then here is something that may be of interest to you.

In dealing with plants that depend upon bees and other insects for pollination, it is simple to understand that nature will do what it has to do to make sure that insects come for that needed visit.

Thus you will note that such insect-needing plants have attractive flowers, perfume and the size, shape, figure, color and honey nectar are all moulded and created to attract their pollinators in the best way known to nature.

Now, in dealing with the Anemophilous flowers, you will remember that none of these things are necessary because these are wind-pollinated. So nature doesn't waste these beauties and attractions upon flowers that are going to be pollinated by the wind. But here we find microscopic differences—for instance, between the shape and appearance of their pollen grains. They are lighter, smoother and often flatter, to spread out as much surface as possible and thus help the wind to do its job more effectively.

Nature has done this work of differentiating between wind and insect pollinated plants so effectively that a botanist or any good horticulturist or gardener can, by examining the flowers, with little difficulty assign to each one its proper division. For example, the anthers or pollen bags of the wind-fertilized flowers are invariably more pendulous than in the other group. For these wind-fertilized fellows the pollen is produced in greater quantities—infinitely more than normally can be utilized. And yet, remember, to create pollen it takes an awful lot of work on the part of the plant. But by producing enormous quantities of pollen, it insures pollination somehow.

I'll give you an example here—the catkins of the Poplar, the Birch and the Hazel. All of these fellows depend upon wind-pollination and they do make enormous quantities of pollen—actually so that it can be dispersed by the four winds and still perform its functions of procreation.

56

Have you ever wondered why certain plants bloom so early in the spring and why so many of them that flower so early, blossom on bare stems and branches without a leaf to be seen? I don't know whether or not it ever struck you as being strange but to me it has always affected my curiosity and upon investigation it is revealed that invariably these plants, trees, or shrubs that flower on bare branches are ones that depend upon the wind, the rains and the elements for cross-pollination.

And the reason the flowers come out so early is because they know full well that early in the spring the gales and the winds are stronger and more frequent and also the rains that catch the pollen are blown into the crevices of the flower when pollination is required.

Yes, they are anemophilous.

Now, looking at the northern latitudes . . . Any plant that flowers in April doesn't have much chance of being fertilized by insects because at that time very few insects are around and up and about. A bee, for example, couldn't fly or do its work unless the weather was good and warm—about 60 degrees, I would say.

This being the case, these plants don't have a chance of getting any pollen from insects. They depend upon the wind and therefore they don't want any interference by leaves because that would only deprive them of a chance of getting some of that life-giving pollen. Actually leaves, in this case, would be a hindrance or a liability.

No, nature doesn't function that way. The world doesn't exist by happy chance. Therefore the plants that bloom when in full leaf attract bees to do the job by means of scent and nectar. As most of these pollinating insects fly they can get about and go where color, scent and promise of ambrosia is best. Therefore each plant makes its flower as attractive as possible—some by subtle perfume—others by strong fragrance—some resort to brilliant colors—others rely on combinations of pink, white, red and yellow.

Wait . . . there's another little angle. Plants that grow close to the ground couldn't very well attract bees. So there's not much point in having sweet smelling attractive flowers when the bees and other flying insects couldn't see them. These low growing plants, when they flower, give off an unusual or often fetid odor, like carrion or decaying vegetation or animal matter. Anyway, to many or most insects it smells like food and on they come . . . the marching, the crawling, the hopping insects—all those who are not so good at aerial acrobatics—and they do the work of pollination for Stapelia, Skunk Cabbage and hosts of other similar plants.

Bless you, Mother Nature—you're stupendous!

Old Order Changeth

Have you ever felt like a fool? If you haven't, you are indeed a competent, lucky or egotistical individual. I have felt like a fool manys and oft . . . in fact too oft.

When I see the mistakes I've made, the opportunities I've missed, and the errors in judgment I've allowed to pass, it makes me sick in the pit of my stomach.

When I look back at the tombstones of my follies behind me, standing like a regiment on parade, I wonder how I ever managed to survive. How could one man do so many things wrong and still be able to live and see the light of day?

There's not much danger of my ever getting a swelled head or thinking I'm pretty good because that conglomeration or array of headstones would quickly disperse any such notions.

Yes, it's just about 27 years that I've been in the nursery business and during all that time I've been telling folks when they plant a balled and burlapped evergreen "to leave the wrap intact around the root and just plant it the way it is".

Because of the shortage of help I've had to get out in the field and do a little slugging myself the last while—something I haven't done in a few years— and I've dug up and balled and burlapped thousands of Evergreens so I've learned a thing or three.

For example, I found out that the knots that are tied in the burlap take a long time to rot. Then something else I found out shocked and startled me and I am anxious and eager to tell you about it.

About 4 or 5 years ago someone dreamed up the idea of treating these burlap squares with a chemical.  The idea was probably brilliant. This treated or dyed burlap served a two-fold purpose. One—instead of the drab brown burlap, it was colored green and it made a harmonious match . . . a green evergreen and green ball. It really did look more attractive and had more consumer appeal and was ideal, especially for the city lots and garden centres.

Of course, the second purpose was to make the burlap rot-resistant. Now while we dig most of our Evergreens to order, we're not concerned about durability; in fact, we prefer it not to be durable so it will quickly disintegrate in the soil. But to the fellow operating a garden centre or sales station in the city it often meant life and death. I know that after an evergreen sat around for a few weeks often when it was lifted to make a sale the bottom just fell out of it and that wasn't conducive to good salesmanship or customer relations. So therefore, the boy who came up with this idea of treating the burlap squares so they would not rot really produced something that these operators wanted.

O.K.—O.K.—I'm as guilty as the rest of them. I used them, too, for a short time. But now comes the pitch.

In digging evergreens this year I found that whenever the treated burlap was used not only did the burlap not disintegrate and become part of the organic content of the soil but it actually prevented a proper union of the ball with the soil. What this treated burlap did was actually create a shim . . . because around the original ball another rim of soil was formed, connected to the original with the fine hairy roots that had penetrated the holes of the burlap, and when the evergreen was lifted this rim just dangled.

There isn't any doubt about it. The chemical used in treating these burlaps was harmful to soil bacteria, prevented proper root development and union of the ball with the soil. In all probabilities this could lead to the death of a plant, in two or three years . . . if not death, definite harm or poor growth development.

You don't have to pay any attention to what I'm relating here. You don't have to believe me, but what I've told you is what I have seen and felt with my own eyes and hands—not in just a couple of cases but in handling thousands of Evergreens from below the soil level, and don't let anyone tell you that I'm full of prunes or jungle juice because I'm not—at least not in this instance.

Sure, the sales station operator is going to defend himself and tell you that this isn't the first lie that Tobe has told, but you will be the judge and jury. You're the guy who pays the piper, so the tune is of your choosing.

My best advice is to remove all bags but I'm afraid that the chemical may have already done some damage to the roots. Better buy evergreens that have not been contaminated by whatever that chemical is or contains.

Bushels of Beauty

This is the latter part of October and we have a field that is ablaze with color. Yes, glorious, magnificent or marvelous could be used to describe it.

People have been coming from almost everywhere to view the kaleidoscopic scene. Yesterday was Sunday and the folks streamed up and down the rows examining the plants and flowers.

Never have we had a better showing of fall blooms and it's due entirely to the Azaleamums and Chrysanthemums.

Some years ago we gave up growing the taller varieties of Chrysanthemums. We felt that they were too difficult because they had to be tied and staked and even then the swirling winds broke or levelled them and they were a mess. They never show their true beauty until September and October and by then the winds are vicious. So we just decided that the tall Mums had to go.

But who cares—we've got so many beautiful low growing ones that we couldn't possibly find room for the taller ones anyway.

We have over 75 distinctly different varieties and they represent practically every color one could dream of . . . yellow, white, red, purple, bronze, pink, orange . . . and each and every one with its variety of variations.

Some are the huge blooms like the florists sell you at $1.00 or $1.50 per flower. Others are of the pompon type and some are in between. Then there's the beauty that looks exactly like a daisy and is fragrant too. It's really a sparkler, an eye-catcher and a joy-giver.

We try to keep the heights of our Chrysanthemum plants below 18 inches and the Azaleamums 12 inches and under. In this way we can get a nice mound and that's where we get the comparison to a bushel basket.

Each plant has its own typical habit of growth. Some tend to grow dense and bushy. Others shoot out at various angles but each gives of its glorious color magnificently.

I don't know what you think about the period of bloom of various flowers. Everyone seems to be concerned about planting something that will give the most bloom for the longest period. Well, if you can beat Mums then you have got something. You can have Mums start to bloom for you in late July—although ours are planted late, usually about mid-June, and they don't start to bloom until August. But then August, through September and all of October, which comprises about three months, we have the grandest parade of flowers that it is possible to see and usually, if we don't get heavy frost, they last most of November, too.

This is, as I said before, written in late October and there is only one variety of Mum that has finished its blooming cycle and this is the fellow that must have started away back early in August. Every other plant in the field is there in full bloom and in its perfection.

So if everything is taken into consideration it appears that you can get between 3 and 4 months of continuous bloom from these grand plants.

Cost-wise I would say they're the lowest cost item that you could have in your garden. If you're growing Petunias or Marigolds you have to sow them every year and probably start them in the greenhouse. Then you transplant them and eventually place them in your garden. With these garden-hardy Mums you plant them once and each following year you have more and more plants to transplant.

Therefore penny-wise, work-wise and bloom-wise they are the finest flowers in creation. There's absolutely no plant to be found anywhere that gives you as much and as beautiful bloom and such sparkling color, especially when it's most desperately needed—during the dull, drab months of fall.

Do You Have Ulcers?

If you do I have a consolation for you. It is claimed that you gotta have brains to have ulcers. I've got a chap who works for me and he came and was belly-aching on one or two occasions about having trouble with his stomach and he claimed he had ulcers. So I reassured him but definitely. I told him that he couldn't have ulcers— that he was just bragging when he thought he had, "Because," I said, "you can't have ulcers for the simple reason that you gotta have brains to have ulcers." So now that he's cured I'm going to mention for those of you who do have trouble of that nature that there are ways and means that are simple and natural by means of which you can alleviate your bellyache.

About a year and a half ago in Growing Flowers I wrote and told about somebody recommending the use of olive pits as a cure for ulcers. Well, this sounded so doggone radical and unusual that I don't think very many people believed me or tried them. But on the other hand, a few people did try them and they took the trouble to write and tell me of the success they met. Those who wrote to me of course claimed that swallowing the olive pits, that is about 4 olive pits a day, definitely did clear up the trouble.

I can assure you that this is true because in my own home my wife suffers from this condition and she can find relief in two or three days by using the olive pits. And brother, let me assure you, she is just like all other good wives, my most ardent critic, disbelieves everything I say and thinks I can't do anything right but eat and sleep.

Some time ago I was talking to a friend of mine who is a doctor and he laughed uproariously when I told him about the pits, and as a matter of fact, he said that it was utterly ridiculous because the olive pits would be eliminated by the stomach. So I immediately slapped down a ten dollar bill and said, "Wanna bet?"

"Why", he said, "It's ridiculous! The stone must be ejected from the bowels."

So I still persisted and wanted to know if he wanted to bet. He ridiculed the idea but he didn't cover that $10.00. So I said, "Put up or shut up." He's been silent since.

So don't let anybody kid you and tell you different. The pits are definitely dissolved and used by your stomach organs.

Now, here is an even simpler method of fixing up your ulcer condition and this is from sound medical advice. I'll quote it to avoid getting into trouble and if you are suffering from ulcers I humbly suggest that you read this and perhaps it can be of help to you.

"In treating patients for ulcers, cabbage juice should be given before resorting to surgery, doctors are told in the Stanford Medical Bulletin.

This advice comes from Dr. G. Cheney of San Francisco, clinical professor of medicine at Stanford Medical School and originator of the Vitamin U cabbage juice therapy. His article analyzes results given by the new treatment since its introduction six years ago and compares them with results yielded by conventional ulcer therapy as reported in medical literature.

'Benign gastric ulcers as a group, including small, large and huge lesions, all tend to heal completely and relatively rapidly while receiving Vitamin U therapy,' he says. 'Only three of 65 cases failed to heal when they were adequately followed. The causes of failure in these three were dense scar tissue which replaced the normal lining of the stomach wall and severe liver damage.'

Average healing time for ulcer craters with the usual medical therapy—bed rest, strict diet, and various drugs—was six weeks. For those treated with Vitamin U, most of whom were not confined to bed, it was three weeks.

Regarding complications which may arise from stomach ulcers, the Stanford investigators reassured doctors that cabbage juice therapy does nothing to increase occurrence. 'The presence of a cancer would be no more or less important than with other forms of non-surgical treatment. No patients treated with Vitamin U are yet known to have developed cancer subsequently.'

As to a recurrence of ulcers after Vitamin U therapy, he pointed out that the treatment is based on the theory that a lack of this so-called vitamin in the diet causes the ulcers to begin with.

Relapses are to be expected if a patient does not continuously re-ceive an adequate intake of Vitamin U in the diet or as medication. In this series of patients 15 are known to have developed new ulcers, but except for two (one with liver damage, the other with a pancreas gland complication), the relapses have responded promptly to repeated treatment with Vitamin U."

If you have ulcers and haven't tried either of these remedies don't come bellyaching round here or within sound of anyone who reads this article.

Seeds and Their Needs

Let me tell you a little bit about seed germination.

You're one of our customers. You buy a 25c package of seed. You write to us a little later and tell us that your seeds didn't germinate at all or germinated very poorly and you immediately assume that we are frauds, fakes, cheats and bandits.

So let's examine the situation and see the true picture. Of course you realize that most of the plants that we grow either in the greenhouse or outdoors come from elsewhere than our own backyard. If we depended upon the food and the beauty that our native plants would produce we might have lean farin' and shallow beauty. So remember, to start with, that most of the plants that we grow have their origin in China, India, other parts of Asia, Africa, Europe and, of course, other parts of the world.

Bear in mind that a seed is a very intricate piece of mechanism and, believe me, it would need to be because the world's balance depends upon its ability to sustain itself and be ready to grow at the proper time. If the seed germinated and grew at any time and at any place the world would soon cease to exist. That is why nature has provided that intricate mechanism so that the seed will sprout and grow at a given time, at a given place or under certain specific conditions.

Some seeds require cool conditions to germinate and others warm. Then light is another important factor. Some like a little light. Some require more light. Others want semi-darkness and others, even total darkness. For instance, if all seeds germinated as soon as they were mature they would start to grow in the late summer, fall or early winter and as the seedlings grew then the winter cold would freeze and kill them and there would be no seeds to germinate and plants to grow in the spring.

Of course man is ingenious and by means of artificial light, heat, greenhouses and whatnot he can make most seeds sprout and grow at almost any time. However, never does a year pass without a lot of trouble here at the nursery. Some seed refuses to germinate according to schedule. We had an example of this with Delphinium seed last year. We procured fresh seeds of the best varieties, sowed them according to the best techniques, placed them in a cool shaded place and nothing happened. We tried it again two months later. We got about one seedling out of each flat. Then one of the girls planted a dozen flats in March—unknown to me. Practically every seed sprouted . . . Delphiniums are supposed to love the cool or late summer to germinate.

Some seeds respond to freezing, others to being kept cool for a period and many of our finest and rarest seeds are kept in the refrigerator.

The same customer who writes and complains about not getting germination doesn't always say that he allowed the seeds to dry out periodically. He'd water them in the morning and within an hour or two the starting medium was bone dry. He had the flat in a sunny window where the early morning sun poured in and raised the tem-

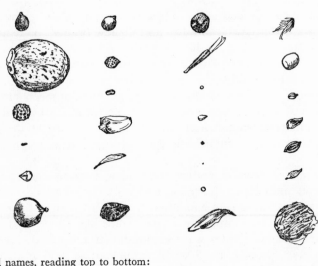

Seed names, reading top to bottom:

Dictamnus	Hop Vine	Sweet Peas	Gazania
Castor Bean	Passion Flower	Marigold	Mung Bean
Thunbergia	Hyssop	Petunia	Carrot
Nemesia	Saffron	Pansy	Gooseberry
Rose	Gerbera	Browallia	Dill
Job's Tears	Morning Glory	Begonia	Lettuce
		Irish Shamrock	Nasturtium
		Zinnia	

64

perature too far above the seeds' requirements and then the soil would dry out and there would be no moisture for the rest of the day. In the morning the procedure would be repeated.

The seed requirements for germination may vary from 42 to 80 degrees and having the earth too hot or too cold renders germination poor or not at all. Actually there is a tremendous tolerance on the part of seeds. But yet there are limits beyond which they cannot go.

When dealing with hard-coated seeds it may be necessary to crack, scar or open the outer hard coat. In most cases that's what freezing does. Some seeds are not fully mature when they drop from the plants. They have to go through a sort of maturing or curing process. Some seeds won't grow if they're covered and some seeds won't grow if you don't keep them covered.

It seems everybody wants fresh seed yet that term is a myth. Seeds sold during 1957 must have been harvested in 1956 at least. But while age does affect the germination and viability of some seeds there are, however, very few seeds that don't have a life cycle of at least two years.

Barnum Says

"Keerect"—you get 100 marks on this one—perfect! . . . "There's one born every minute".

In this wide world of ours there are always a few individuals who are not content or satisfied to accept things the way most folks do.

You might call them malcontents, the chaps with the itchy feet or the boys who walk around dreaming. But in whatever guise you find them they are apart from the rest of the mob.

These fellows are characters. They don't let anybody else do their thinking for them.

They don't accept everything that the newspapers write as gospel. They heckle politicians. They are the guys who ask questions and do a little thinking and soul searching. They are sometimes called manure disturbers—so what!

It was these lads from time immemorial who have built empires, founded new dynasties, braved the dangers of the unknown . . .yes, they sailed with Drake, Magellan and Columbus. They were the boys who were in the boat with Ulysses . . . yes, and they're the same fellows who marched with the Ghengis Khan, Alexander and Napoleon.

Don't look around, up or down! I'm talking to you! The fact that your father or mother migrated to America 5, 25 or 125 years ago tells me that you are born of the stuff that relentlessly moves onward.

You could never be slaves because you would rather die fighting. You would correct the evil or die trying . . . but never accept it.

Well, now that I've led you along this primrose path—you didn't think I was doing it for nothing, did you? There was a pattern to the method of my madness. I wanted to get you into the frame of mind where you'd think you were pretty wonderful and then you'd be a push-over for my proposition.

Do you know what the Metasequoia is . . the Sequoia, the Redbud, the Mimosa and all the other items I'm listing below here? No one that I know of has ever tried growing a Sequoia in this latitude but I know for a fact that old Layritz when he was but a boy, 60 or more years ago, planted a Sequoia, not very far from Victoria at his nursery. It was growing there a few years ago when I visited his establishment. It was then a tree that stood probably 50 feet or more in height.

So, therefore, I'm positive that the Sequoia will grow in Vancouver. I know they're growing in England. I know some of them are growing in Pennsylvania.

Now why don't you try one? Why don't you try a Redbud or a Mimosa or a Gardenia or a Camellia? Sure, they're of doubtful hardiness and they may be winter-killed but with a little protection, a little care and such you may be the first to get one to grow.

I know for a certainty that there are Redbuds growing in the Niagara district . . . yes, and also quite a few of them in other parts of southwestern Ontario. There's also Bald Cypress growing in this district . . . yes, and Pawpaw, too.

Someone, somehow, somewhere along the line had the courage to plant them and they survived. I'm surprised that some of the universities haven't tried and played with these items in their botanical enterprises.

I wish I had the time to do it but there's no use kidding myself. I've got too many unfinished jobs now without starting any more. My terrain even now is littered skull upon skull with projects that I dreamed of, hoped for and started but . . . Sure, you may lose these items but I'll bet you some of them will do all right with you.

Now just think of the personal satisfaction that you'll get out of it. Besides, it's a challenge. Too many of us right now are leading the life of blissful indolence. We get up in the morning, have our breakfast, go to work, finish our stint at the office or factory, go home and eat and have a snooze and half watch television, smoke a cigarette, have a glass of beer and go back to bed again. That's what we call living and most of us think it's wonderful.

Sharpen up, fella. Dare to be different. It's a challenge being hurled at you. Take it up. Put a bit of interest and excitement and daring into your life. I throw the torch to you.

Telltale Trees

If ever you're contemplating purchasing a farm, here is a little advice that you may do well to heed and remember.

Take a drive around the district or the terrain wherein the farm is located. Circle about slowly in that area probably 5 or 10 miles in every direction. Examine the trees along the roadsides or in the pieces of scattered bush that you find or on the pasturelands. The habit and growth of the trees invariably indicate the well-being of the soil. If the trees are large, straight, handsome, filled with strong, lusty branches and show luxuriant green foliage, then you can be reasonably sure that the soil thereabouts is deep and good, that drainage conditions are right and that the area in general is excellent.

Of course you can even judge this in the winter time when the trees are naked because the shape, structure and formation of the branches is even more apparent then than it would be during the spring, summer or fall.

Make it a point to look at the trees wherever you drive and then at the farm buildings and you'll quickly find that the barns and the homes are reflections of the trees. If the trees are stately, well proportioned and growing well, invariably the barns and homes will be prosperous looking and in a good state of repair.

I've watched this natural phenomenon for probably 25 years and it seldom fails. Where the trees are stunted and of poor thrift, the barns, farmyards and the homes are likewise.

All along the eastern seaboard, extending westward to the Great Lakes area, you will find that Maples, Elms, Oaks, Basswood and Ash are most common—actually in about that order. You'll also see Locusts and Willows in good numbers and, less frequently, the Walnut, Hickory and Beech. In fact, the Beech is really becoming quite scarce— although 25 years ago there were still quite a few of them in the Niagara district.

As you go further north you begin to see Birch, Virginiana Juniper, Red Cedar, Poplar and then Spruce, Pine, Larch and some Balsam . . . and Hemlock and of course White Cedar. The Pines are usually found growing on the poorer terrain. They like the sandy soils that have little or no humus in them. Pines grow almost anywhere as long as it is dry.

Anyway, to conclude my random opinions about the trees indicating the condition of the soil, I want to stress that this rule will seldom fail. In most cases some of the trees like Elm and Oak can be anywhere from 100 to 400 years old and if the soil and growing conditions have been good for that long, then it's a pretty good indication that it should be good even now—or at least it could be brought back to fertility without too much trouble.

Atta Boy Can Destroy

While plants and growing things are my first love, I am, by my own calling, a naturalist . . . and as such, my interests cover anything that forms a part of the natural order of things.

Ants have always intrigued me, not only because they are "social insects" but because they seem to be capable of superhuman deeds and show signs of the ability to think.

The most vicious ant known to modern science is called the Atta Leaf-cutter, Mushroom-grower or Parasol Ant. What makes it even worse for mankind and crops is the fact that he is the best organized of all ants and his destructive potential is tremendous. They claim that this fellow outdoes the Locust when it comes to devastation.

Now this baby is a mean fellow. He doesn't want to bother with the weeds and the natural grasses and crops that can be found anywhere. He likes his crop cultivated. They just step into a tropical plantation by the million and when they are gone the entire area is denuded.

They like it good and hot so they restrict their antics to Central and South America and the southern part of the United States. I'm hoping that we folks in the north don't get too much warm weather or that Florida weather doesn't creep up on us because if it does, so will that lousy Ant.

Now this fella is a real field husbandman and they cultivate underground mushroom farms. The outside worker ants bring in on their heads leaf cuttings and these are used as a mulch in the subterranean caverns. The indoor workers do their chores in bleak darkness, working the beds, fertilizing them, transplanting, weeding—yes, and harvesting the tiny fungus beds, for that is the colony's only food.

Science has striven desperately to combat, wipe out or destroy these ants but so far they haven't been too successful. They dwell in strong, intricately designed forts, seamed with perfectly formed tunnels about an inch wide that interweave through a maze of chambers—each about the size of a small watermelon. The fighting force of these ants can actually slash its way through thick, hard, sinewy shoe leather and get right at the flesh.

It has been established that the Atta Ants test each leaf before working on it by licking it to kill any unwanted bacteria so that the fungus which is used to develop into mushrooms can grow unmolested.

These ants have but one lone individual redeeming feature and that is that a few Indian tribes eat them. Some roast them, others boil them and a few eat them raw and find them delectable, delicious and nutritious. I don't know who it was that tasted them but they compare their flavor favorably with that of well cured bacon.

The same fungus that the Atta uses to grow his mushrooms has been cultivated and they produce mushrooms larger than a dandelion flower. Perhaps we'd like these mushrooms, too.

Some more advanced data should be available soon on this unusual insect . . . But, it all depends on what you call soon. You see the scientists have been working on them now for 25 years and this is all they've learned.

How To Get Rich Quick

I always recall the cartoon I saw back in the old depression days. There was a picture of an old hobo . . . stubble of beard on his face, a holey hat on his head, patched trousers, a worn old jacket and carrying on a stick slung over his shoulder, a bundle of rags.

In this picture he's looking straight at you with a big grin on his face and a hand stretched out saying, "If you're so darn smart, why ain't you rich?"

Well, sure enough, I'm not smart enough to be rich but that doesn't stop me from telling you how to get rich. Isn't it the truth that many a man can advise someone else how to become a success and get rich yet he himself is neither a success nor wealthy. But life's like that.

Now I'm not doing this . . . I'm just telling you to do it. Get yourself a piece of land somewhere here, there or anywhere and plant it out to Christmas trees. The investment is small. The trees to set out only cost a couple of pennies each and in 4 or 5 years you'll have a steady sizeable income.

Scotch Pine is one of the finest of all trees to plant as Christmas trees, chiefly because it sheds few of its needles when cut and usually has a dense neat habit. They only require a bit of shearing once a year and they become compact, handsome specimens. The best strain to plant is the true Riga strain of Scotch Pine . . . and do not set out seedlings, but transplants.

Here's how to do the shaping. The first shearing should be done in June, the second year after planting. The terminal is cut on an angle to 12 inches. This angle cutting allows a new terminal to develop and at the same time permits a new whorl of branches to develop which makes the tree more dense. Also shear the topmost whorl of branches, cutting them back to 4 inches. This is repeated two years later. The following year the lateral branches are again sheared but the terminal is left alone. This produces a tree 6 to 7 feet tall and compact from the first whorl of branches.

While I believe Scotch Pine to be the best and safest investment and also the fastest growing, which means the quickest income-producing, nevertheless there are other kinds that are in demand and do make good trees.

The most popular in the east at least is the Balsam Fir but they are usually found only in native stands because it takes 6 or 7 years before they are ready to cut commercially. Then Norway Spruce, White Spruce, Austrian Pine, Silver Fir, Colorado Blue Spruce and a few Douglas Fir. The Douglas Fir and the Silver Fir are more popular in the west.

Don't fear overcrowding the industry for about 35 million are used annually in the United States and over 10 million of these are imported —*cut* from Canada!

About Planting Roses

Here we get right down to the root of things. . . .

Some years ago I studied the best methods of growing Blueberries and found that the Blueberry root forms a sort of cone. Therefore when the Blueberry bush is put into the soil, the roots should be set on a sort of pear-shaped mound.

This gave splendid results then and now I recommend the same practice when setting a Rose bush in the ground. Form a sort of cone and let the roots spread around it—running down. Don't try to crowd your roots into a small hole. There is plenty of space down below so dig the hole deep enough and wide enough to accommodate the roots properly.

For years and years planters far and wide followed the practice of throwing a handful of fertilizer, bone meal, trash and even grain seeds of various kinds into the hole along with the root. But I warn you against this practice. Put nothing in around the roots except top soil or ordinary garden compost or a mixture of peat moss and garden soil and compost . . . but absolutely nothing else should be put into the hole where the root is being planted. Now, remember, contrary to the advice of the fertilizer man or "whothehellever" else he may be, do not put manure, fertilizer or any other material in the hole or below the hole when planting.

When you have finished planting the Rose bush, be sure at the same time to pack the soil around the roots as firmly as possible with your hands. Don't be afraid to tamp it with your fists or the palms of your hands because you won't get it too tight. Be absolutely sure that there are no air pockets or spaces between the roots and the soil .

Now when you have your Rose roots properly covered, soak the soil down well. This will tend to wash all loose particles of soil around the roots and make it settle firmly.

Do not cut off roots unnecessarily. If you should find some roots that are broken or straggly, they can be removed. But the Rose bush wants all the roots it has.

Now when this part of the job is done, get yourself some loose soil or other mulching material (but nothing beats loose soil) and place it as high up around the bush as possible—even to completely covering it. Yes, don't be a bit afraid of completely covering the Rose plant with loose soil. This mulching treatment is your safest protection against loss and you seldom ever will lose a Rose bush if you follow this practice. Let me stress, you do this whether you plant in the spring or the fall. Now remember that this mulch is to remain around the tops until the roots get established and growth begins.

Come late spring (even though April-May planted) when the buds are beginning to break and growth is starting, remove the mulch to the soil level which means that your bud junction will be setting barely above the level of the good earth. Then you can do any trimming that is required. For Hybrid Tea Roses you only want to leave a few good strong eyes to get the most bloom.

If these instructions are followed carefully, you will have top results with your Roses.

Trees in the Breeze

If you've built or bought your own new home, one thing is sure . . . eventually you're going to plant a tree. Well, you're going to be scurrying about trying to find out the best kind of tree to plant for your individual needs. Now just going up to a sales lot and telling the clerk or salesman there that you want a tree is not going to solve your problem because, remember, when you're planting a tree you want something that's going to be there a long time. It's going to be there as long as you live and longer and therefore it behooves you to think and get the best thing for your purpose.

Let me say this, if you'd come up to me in my younger days—15 or 20 years ago—and told me your problem, I'd probably have looked into my bins and seen the trees of which I had most and said, "Boy, that's the tree for you!" I'd have wrapped it up and held out my hand for $2.00 or $3.00 and you'd have had a tree and I'd have had the money. But whether that would have been the best tree for your needs is another question.

Well, perhaps the other fellow is more inherently honest than I would have been but maybe he ain't. So I'm not going to let you take the chance—I'm going to tell you the best trees for your purpose and I'm not pulling any punches.

If it's a large tree that you want—that is, a tree that eventually grows into a large size—here are the best. I'm not going to give you complete details about them because you can find them all described in the better nursery catalogs. But it is an indication as to which is best and I feel that I'm starting with the first choice on top . . . Pin Oak (Quercus palustris), Red Oak (Quercus borealis), White Oak (Quercus alba), American Elm (Ulmus americana), London Plane Tree (Platanus acerifolia) and the Maidenhair Tree (Ginkgo biloba).

The Beeches are among the finest, if not the most beautiful, of all our shade trees. But they require large areas and are not suited to small city lots. In my own sincere convictions there are no rivals for the beauty and shade giving qualities of the Beech . . . American Beech, European Purple Beech, European Purple Weeping Beech, Copper Beech.

Here are the medium-sized trees . . . Crimson King Maple (Acer platanoides Crimson King), Little-leaf Linden (Tilia cordata), Norway Maple (Acer platanoides), Sugar Maple (Acer saccharum) and Cut-leaved Weeping Birch (Betula pendula laciniata).

Here are the finest small trees . . . and this includes some of those that are appreciated for their flowers . . . Flowering Dogwood (Cornus florida), Hop Hornbeam (Ostrya virginiana), Paul's Scarlet Haw-thorn (Crataegus oxyacantha pauli), Japanese Flowering Cherry (Prunus surrulata kwanzan), Japanese Double Flowering Weeping Cherry (Prunus shidare-sakura), Saucer Magnolia (Magnolia soulan-geana) and Purple Flowering Plum (Prunus Newport).

Contrary to most people's opinion the Flowering Crabs (Malus), while they are very beautiful in bloom, do not make even a half-good small shade tree.

Another thing I'd like to mention is that there is not one poor or doubtful tree listed in the above group so you can buy them where you like but use this list as a guide.

Three Star Discovery

I believe about a year ago I told about some new discovery where it was found that plants made root growth as long as the temperature was above 40 degrees.

True, this discovery was not new to me. I was only waiting for it to be proven because I had believed it for a long time. But to many people it was rather a shock because they believed that the moment fall came and the weather got cold, Mother Nature went to sleep permanently until reawakened by the spring.

That was one of the reasons that I used to urge folks to plant in the fall . . . if possible . . .because I believed that during the milder spells of winter plants would make root growth and development and then be in better shape to move ahead faster in the spring. This is proven in many other ways—especially by those people who have practised for years putting bulbs outdoors—thrusting them underneath coal ashes or mulch to form roots and then bringing them in and forcing them for indoor flowering.

But evidently up until now we've only had half of the answer. The other half turned up suddenly when I was reading an article about soil temperatures at the ground level.

Here's what I learned. Soil bacteria thrive on heat and they work best when the temperature ranges from 90 to 100 degrees. When the temperature goes above 130 degrees they can't work and there is little or no activity. Then as the temperature drops below 100, their effic-iency drops until it gets to 41 degrees. Below 41 degrees all bacterial activity and action ceases.

So now we put the pieces of the puzzle together and we find that the plant roots may be alive even during a frost, but if they can get no food or water, they can't function. But as soon as the temperature rises above 40 degrees they can get a supply of food and water because the bacteria are working and immediately the roots go to work, too.

Now you know not only the why's and the wherefore's but that plants definitely cease their operations when the temperature goes below 40 degrees at the ground level. However, it is important to remember that there are not too many days in the year, even close to the 42nd parallel where the soil temperature at the ground level is below 40 degrees. Therefore roots are growing.

Freedom of the Press

Lately I've been somewhat surprised and even shocked, yes, and impressed by so many letters reaching me, saying that folks have enjoyed Growing Flowers, which is the Quarterly paper I write and publish, more than any paper that they read.

I should feel flattered and honoured and to a degree I am. However, there is a sour note here somewhere. Why should people write and say this to me? After all, let's not fool ourselves, I'm no genius. I just write what I see and think and that's it. I have no special talent or ability and I'm not trying to prove I'm modest either.

So I sat and pondered and pondered and eventually I think I have come up with the answer and here it is. I was writing a little piece the other day—something to do with lawn mowers and I was really saying what I thought about the silly notion of buying a high-powered mower to cut a little plot of grass.

Well, if I were writing this for acceptance by a magazine, there isn't a publication in the world that would buy it because it would offend the sensitive ears of the mower manufacturers and no editor could afford to embarrass or cause grief to one of his advertisers.

So that's the story. Each publication that accepts advertising and lives upon it . . . has a responsibility to its advertisers. After all, the man who pays the piper calls the tune.

Well, then you've got to admit that this does stifle a man's speech and his writing. A dog doesn't bite the hand that feeds it.

It must be admitted that the agricultural or gardening press throughout the world depends very greatly upon the chemical and fertilizer manufacturers for support. Therefore in all sincerity you can't expect that they will tell you that fertilizers are N.G.—even if they believed they were. It's up to you to find out.

So you see in Growing Flowers, because I have no duty to advertisers, I go merrily along saying what I like, about who I like, when I like.

Why Bulbs Rot

At least a few hundred times during the year I'm ripped up the back, yes, and down it too probably, by many of my customers who write me something that goes like this, "Your bulbs are no good and neither are you! I sent for a Caladium and a Gloxinia and I planted them according to your instructions and they didn't come up and when I dug into the soil to see what happened I found a rotten mess. Send back my money at once or I'll report you to the proper authorities. Shame on you for selling such poor stuff!"

Soooooo . . . that will keep John Tobe in his place!

But I'm not the kind of a guy who takes an undeserved tongue lashing lying down or cowering in a corner. If I'm going to go down I'm going down fighting—yes, punching, kicking, scratching in a drag-me-down, devil-may-care, rough and tumble fashion.

Says I, "I sent you good bulbs—sound bulbs—healthy bulbs. If they wern't that way when you got them why in Heck did you keep them?"

O.K.—O.K.—Cool down . . . both of us. The simple, honest, actual truth of the matter is that natural ordinary developments took place.

A bulb without any roots on it has no way to repel water or to use it. Therefore in a short time the water coupled with soil organisms promotes some kind of bacterial action and the bulb in question begins to rot. Therefore it is clear and obvious that until a bulb begins to develop some roots it should not be covered or watered. Now I stress it again. A bulb without roots has no means of utilizing moisture and if planted, covered, and watered it will invariably rot.

Many or most outdoor bulbs can be covered, but water must be given sparingly and good drainage must be provided. For the self-same reason seeds, bulbs and tubers of most any kind often rot in the ground if we strike a few heavy rains soon after planting, whereas seeds and such that have already started and established themselves somewhat before the heavy copious rains came, do extremely well.

So what do you do about it? You take a Caladium or a Gloxinia and just lay it or barely press it into the soil. Give it a drop of water occasionally but as long as it's not covered it won't rot. Soon roots

should develop and when this happens your bulb is ready to be covered
. . . lightly, of course. Then on it goes to leaves and blooms.

I tell you these things. If you'd only read about them in the instructions. But who bothers about instructions!

The Snake Pit

One of my girls raced into the office—out of breath and wild eyed! "Come quick, Mr. Tobe, there's a great big snake out in the storage shed", she said.

Immediately I envisioned a great big boa constrictor, python or asp out there in the storage shed—one by one, sinking his fangs into the legs of my crew and that I would find them all lying about writhing in the agony of death.

I wished at that instant that I had a case of good old Scotch so that I might at least make their last moments pleasant even if I couldn't save them.

But there was no Scotch, Irish or even rye.

Well, I dashed out and grabbed a shovel on my way. When I got there, to my consternation the gals were all standing around in a circle and in the centre there lay a big beautiful garter snake. I honestly think he was 4-5 ft. long and about as thick below the head as a 3/4″ rubber hose but somebody thought that 4-5 ft. was too long for a garter snake, so I better say 3-4 ft. . . . but I still think it was 4-5 ft.!

He lay there quietly and I had a chance to admire his shape and beauty and I'm telling you he was beautiful . . . one stripe down the centre and one stripe along each side. The colors seemed to shine like gold and silver. He looked so cute I could have petted and cuddled him only I just couldn't get around to it for some reason or other.

Someone was shouting, "Kill him—kill him with the shovel" and one of my boys grabbed a shovel and went towards him when I shouted "Stop!"

I said, "Scoop him up with the shovel and see if you can carry him out." He tried but the snake wriggled off.

So I sent him to get a bushel basket and we got him into it and carried him out to the back of the shed and set him free.

"There", I thought to myself, "was a poor homeless snake. He had come to seek shelter in Tobe's nursery storage shed. Why? . . . Because he didn't have a pit to hiss in!"

Brother, Spare Ten Years?

If you can, then grow Eremurus from seed.

No one can deny that it is an outstanding plant and most unusual in many ways. Read on. . . .

The roots of a mature plant look exactly like an octopus. The large swollen purplish pip looks like a bobbing head and the surrounding roots, clustered in all directions about the head, look like the tentacles of a denizen of the deep blue sea.

Well, procure and plant some Eremurus seed. They don't germinate very easily. They need long periods of below freezing weather and will in all probability remain in the soil for two or three years before germinating. You'll probably swear at the seedsman and blame him for his poor seeds and maybe write him a vile nasty letter in the meantime.

Aha, but at last they germinate. Then you only have to wait for about ten years for them to bloom. But ten years passes quickly and then you'll have your flowers.

Now let us go back and watch it from the beginning. The first year all you'll get will be a seedling and it has only a thin grass-like leaf and the poor thing produces but one rootlet which grows straight down just like a radish and it's all finished growing early in the spring. After that the leaf turns brown and you think it's dead but it isn't.

Don't douse it with water at this stage or pour the fertilizer to it. Otherwise you'll drown and burn it. Next year it will be up bright and early and produce a larger leaf than it did the first year and of course the rootlets will grow bigger and better. They'll be sending out side shoots now.

About the third year you should transplant it to another location and be sure to allow enough space for it to grow.

So now that we've got you past the third year, I don't think you'll have much trouble. You've only got about seven more years to go before it blooms.

However in case you are one of these impatient fellows, plants are readily obtainable.

In case I haven't told you, the Eremurus will grow from 4 to 12 feet tall and on top of the spire-like stalk, you will see a cluster of flowers containing hundreds, yes, maybe thousands of star-like, closely growing flowerlets. Yes, sir, they'll stop passers-by dead in their tracks and if you want people to admire your garden, Eremurus will sure do the trick for you.

'Tis the Gospel, those flower clusters will remain in beautiful bloom for four weeks and more—yes, even remaining undamaged through heat and rain. They do not need staking because they're sturdy and can stand on their own legs. Admitted they will sway with the breeze, but they won't break.

Snake Palm

It just happened to be my good fortune (I should have said my misfortune) to come across a most interesting plant a couple of years ago. In fact I recall mentioning something about it in Growing Flowers. This plant suddenly seemed to shoot up one day from a bulb we had set into the greenhouse and practically before your eyes as you watched, this dark spotted stalk with green and hazy skin seemed to emerge from nowhere and before we knew it, we had a beautiful palm-like tree in our midst.

Now I'm going to describe the plant in more detail in a minute or two but what I'm groaning about here is—how do I get mixed up in all these peculiar names and things?

Now this plant first seemed to appear under the name of Hydrosme rivieri. Well, upon checking back and forth I also find that it should be included, was included or has been included in the family of Amorphophallus. So I look up Seymour and here is what he says, "A genus of large leaved herbs of the Arum family, closely resembling Amorphophallus and properly listed under the name". I go to the Royal Horticultural Society's Encyclopedias and they say, under "Hydrosme", "Listed under Amorphophallus". Taylor says, "Only one of them, Hydrosme rivieri, the Snake Palm (it is not a true palm) or Devil's Tongue or Crubee, is occasionally cultivated in the tropical greenhouses under the name of Amorphophallus rivieri".

So in all sincerity and truthfulness, I can't tell you the proper name of this plant. But for the moment, even at the expense of disagreeing with the Royal Horticultural Society's Encyclopedias, let's call it Hydrosme rivieri.

If you want to own about as unusual a plant as is found anywhere, you try this fellow.

When the bulbs get larger, the large blooms will appear before the leaves because the leaves do not develop until the plant is finished flowering.

The flowers are minute but they're crowded on a dense spadix and this spadix is set right in the middle and resembles the Calla Lily very much but it is dark red spotted, carrion-scented and the whole inflorescence is on a stout, fleshy stalk—3 to 4 feet tall.

Well, I might as well add that the name Hydrosme is taken from the Greek and there it refers to the preference of the plant for moisture. Like a rowboat and a baby, it is usually found with a wet bottom.

Mated Plums

For many years it has been a common practice among the orchardists of the Niagara Peninsula not to set an orchard of any one variety of fruit. It was especially advised not to plant solid orchards of Bartlett Pear, Italian Prune, Windsor Cherry or McIntosh Apple . . . of course the reason being that with one variety you would not get cross-pollination. . . . unless it was by accident and therefore you could not expect a good set of fruit. Yet in many cases the solid blocks were set out and I've come across them many times. It usually was due to unsound advice from the nursery salesman but also because of the ignorance on the part of the fruit grower.

I recall being in a large orchard of Shiro Plum at Queenston where this man had not had a crop for the first six years when the orchard was actually at bearing age. He'd scurried about trying to find out what was the matter and of course he eventually found out that they should have been cross-pollinated with another variety and, as a matter of fact, there aren't too many varieties of Plums that will cross-pollinate or fertilize the Shiro.

I recall that the Red June was one variety that was claimed would do the job so he planted a few trees of Red June among the Shiros wherever one died or even if he had to cut one out. But in the meantime it would take 3 to 4 years at least for that Red June to have enough blossoms to do any good. So he went to somebody whom he knew had a few Red June trees and he got some blossoms and hung them in the Shiros and believe it or not, it did an effective job of pollination.

Here is a new note from the provincial apiarist of Nova Scotia. They collect pollen by hand and it's placed in an aperture in front of the beehive exit, so that, when the bees are released in the orchard, they carry the pollen to the blossoms. To test the effectiveness of this method, fluorescent powder was added in experiment at the Ontario Agricultural College at Guelph. This left a trail which could be inspected at night with the aid of an ultra-violet light and gave proof that the pollen from the hive had been distributed as desired.

Incorrect Name!

Do you know the Bartlett Pear? If you haven't tasted its luscious goodness, then you still have a paradise to attain. But of course you have.

My best feed of Bartlett Pears comes just a week or so before they are ready for harvesting. Then I get into an orchard and walk under the trees and here and there I find some of the Pears that have fallen from the trees or some that are about to drop. They have been stung, injured or bruised and then they fell from the tree and landed on the soft sod. I pick them up and eat around the wounds and . . . oh, paradise is mine!

Now if you asked me why in blazes I didn't wait and pick the Pears from the trees and enjoy their luscious goodness without the bruises and such, well, I'd tell you . . . and here is what I would say, I've seldom if ever seen a perfect Bartlett Pear ripe on a tree. The reason is something about the stems—if you wait until they ripen, they fall. So the growers invariably harvest them a week or 10 days before they mature.

Another factor—the canners want them so that they can put them in storage and process them all at one time. So they demand that the growers pick them before they are mature and then put them in storage. They will keep in storage more or less indefinitely—at least, for a long period anyway.

So the truth of the matter is that you seldom ever get a ripe Bartlett Pear on a tree and the ones probably that you buy on the market have been kept in storage and are sold that way. But I'm talking about the occasional ones that I got from a tree. A Bartlett tastes good in most any state but when it's naturally ripened—oh, brother!

So anyway, what I want to tell you is a little bit about the origin of the Bartlett Pear. In Europe it is properly known as Williams' Bon Chretien Pear which may give you the idea that it is of French origin but that is not true. It was first grown in Aldermaston, Berkshire, England. The original tree was found in the garden of a Mr. Wheeler. One John Stair sent grafts of this tree which he found in the garden of Mr. Wheeler when he took over the place, to one Richard Williams, a nurseryman of Turnham, Green, Middlesex, who grew and sold it extensively. It was brought to America in the latter part of the 17th Century and a man by the name of Enoch Bartlett grew some of them and through error or ignorance it was called after him. But this Pear definitely was not originated by him nor did he have anything to do with discovering it.

Credit should be given to John Stair because that Pear really is something that posterity will remember and the originator should be given due merit and credit.

Are You Lime-Conscious?

Every now and then an article appears in one or more of the garden magazines stressing the value and importance of lime in the soil and from then on everybody and his uncle starts off on a rampage of adding packages or bags of lime to their garden plots.

I'm warning you—don't do it! There are "dang" few—yes, very few gardens or farms throughout the country that actually do need lime.

One thing we can stand less of is experts. There are way too many experts and I have heard them time and time again say, "Well, you'll get a better crop of grapes if you get some lime into that soil" . . . "You'd get a better crop of this if you'd get some lime in the soil" . . . "Oh yes, Alfalfa—it needs lime". Well, the truth of the matter is that your soil may need something, but very, very seldom is it lime.

Now let me tell you something about what lime does. It is an absolute fact that lime does have a good effect on soil texture . . . especially the clay soils because it causes this type of soil to become crumbly which is a good characteristic in a soil. But the experts tell you that adding lime to the soil will cause the plant foods in the soil to be released and made available to the plants for feeding.

Sure, it is undeniable that lime does tend to stimulate biochemical reaction and by this means nutrients are released for the use of plants. But, remember, when you make these soluble salts available in great quantities and the plants can't use them quick enough, they're going to be washed away with the first rain and your soil will never get them again. What you're doing is truly impoverishing your own soil in trying to help it.

So that just goes to show you that you can, by indiscriminately using lime, cause your soil to become impoverished. If you feel you must use lime, use it very sparingly but in most cases we would suggest that you add humus content to your soil and you'll probably get the benefits without having the nutrients washed away.

Of course they tell you to use lime to neutralize the soil acidity. Yes, it does do that in a way because it acts as a base or alkali in promoting chemical reaction favorable to soil fertility. But the truth of the matter is that by far the majority of plants grow better in soils that are slightly acid and further, even if your soil is acid, I don't think liming is the way to correct it. Remember that natural manures and organic matter contain a fair amount of lime—that is, calcium —and in decomposing it does to some degree bring down the soil acidity in a natural and proper manner.

If and when you are going to use lime, use the hydrated lime preferably because you'll only need a little over half as much as you would of the ground limestone or chalk to get the same results.

Who's the Murderer?

It is a mystery! It was found dead. No one knew why. It had everything to live for. It had a good home, comfortable surroundings, ideal living conditions and many friends close by. Yet when we viewed it this morning all we saw was the remains—lifeless, still, but standing erect.

A superfluous investigation revealed no cause or effect. Experts were called in and they, too, saw nothing that would indicate the cause of the demise. But something did it. It was in apparent good health just a short time ago when it was purchased from the nursery and planted. Then who was the killer?

The mystery has been and is repeated throughout the world at least thousands of times annually. I'm not talking about trees or plants that die of old age. I'm referring to the newly planted trees that seem to be robust and healthy in every way but yet a week or two after they are planted, they just seem to wilt, dry up, peter out and become totally lifeless.

Now I can't say that it was lack of care or understanding because these deaths happen even among the best and most experienced planters . . . but not as often as they do among the novices and new gardeners. Strange but true, this malady seems to affect only newly planted trees and such.

As is my wont I often ponder these problems until my brow becomes furrowed and resembles not crow's feet but an old fashioned wash board. Sometimes a ray of light shines through and in this case I think I have found what may be the answer. It may save thousands or millions of trees from dying annually—if people will but follow and heed the advice from things that I have learned.

I think the process of osmosis kills most trees. By the application of chemical fertilizers or soils that are too rich in manure, you cause the draining of the life's blood from the tree through the membrane, because in osmosis the life-giving fluids flow from the weaker to the stronger solutions. Therefore if your soil nutrients are much stronger than the nutrients in the tree, they will pull the tree's nutrients out and result in the death of the tree.

My advice to planters for over 20 years has been—If you want to give new plants the finest treatment and the best start possible, then take half peat moss and half top soil and place it about the roots. I still believe that this is the finest planting advice ever given to anyone anywhere by anyone.

Don't let anyone tell you to use fertilizer—either liquid or otherwise —or even manure when setting out a plant. Use nothing but good top soil mixed half and half with peat moss. If this won't make your plants grow, then I know nothing else on earth that will. Don't kill your plants by over-feeding or by over-indulgence or kindness!

Like Quickies?

The other day a friend was in to see me and we were chatting awhile. Then she said to me "You know Mr. Tobe, with all those unkind things you say about commercial fertilizers, I think one of these days those fellows are going to slaughter you."

Of course she was only joking but it did make an impression on my mind. Behind this statement perhaps lies a tale or a moral or something. So I thought that I had best make matters clear so that there would be no misunderstanding, between you and I and the chemical folks. I want to stand up before you all and make this statement— I am positively not against chemical fertilizers. Please remember this and let that not go astray or be lost to you.

However I want to emphasize at the same time and in the same breath that I am 100% for the organic way, the natural way of gardening and farming. I do not believe in "quickies" nor am I interested in giving soil a "shot in the arm". I know what a shot in the arm has done for thousands of dope or drug addicts. Sure it gives them a terriffic lift but then the letdown is catastrophic. Yes, you can also get drugs that give you a feeling of well-being and perk you up like a million dollars. But you and I both have known and seen many people who tried to take the short cut to health by means of pills, do-dads and fads—and where are they now? . . . Pushing up daisies and other plants.

Therefore I'm not a believer in giving the soil any "shot in the arm". What I want to do for my land is build it layer upon layer carefully and properly so that the benefits will accrue for generations to come.

I realize full well that someone can come along to the most fertile farm in the world and ruin it in a few years with improper methods by just taking everything off and putting nothing back. But sound, cultural, natural, organic methods will maintain soil fertility and give bountiful, healthful crops year in and year out endlessly.

So remember, and I reiterate for all to hear, that I am not against commercial fertilizers—It's just that I'm 100% for the organic, natural way of doing things. Further, I am body and soul in favor of doing anything to my land that will make it richer, more productive and more fertile . . . but on a permanent basis.

Right from Wrong

Now this is a true story—even though you're not going to believe it. You're going to say, "Well, Tobe just dreamed this up because he wants to show that the organics are better than chemicals."

I have two neighbors—yes, you can come down to Niagara and

84

I'll introduce you to both of them. One gardens in the old fashioned way and he's a Scotsman and he wouldn't follow any other method as far as I know—and he's not stingy either. The others are a couple of good friends who live in a home with a very, very neat and attractive garden. They buy all the doodads, the chemicals, the sprays, new-fangled ideas and baby their stuff along and while they do have a neat garden, for flowers and plants and growth and health, drop in on my other pal and look at his garden and he uses nothing but straight organic old-fashioned methods.

She uses treated pots, sterilized soil, root promoting hormones, seed disinfectants, bulb purifiers, disease preventors, bug killers, powders to prevent her bulbs and tubers from sprouting, a chemical to prevent damping off, another to prevent the cutworm from cutting off her plants. She has spray guns, tanks, gas masks, special rubber gloves—in fact, she has more paraphernalia than you can find in a chemical lab and an army supply store combined. She has stuff to make her grass grow and other junk to make it stop growing or grow only so tall. Yes, she has everything in the world but a good garden.

But Orkady—his place is a blaze of color in the spring, summer and fall. He drags soil for his plants from the bush, starts planting early, works his garden and really enjoys every second of it, doesn't use fertilizer—at least I've never seen him use any—or other treatments. I think I have seen him use a dust for Roses, but I'm not sure.

These gardens are quite close to each other. They're here to be seen. But if you come down and ask me to show them to you, I won't. If I do, somebody will shoot me because they're still good friends of mine and you wouldn't want me to lose my friends—especially when they're my neighbors.

One does things nature's way and doesn't try to lead, steer or force nature along any path . . . but follows her. The other is doing it the way man would have it done, the way the ads in the newspapers and over the radio and TV tell her to do and the way the scientific fellows would have it. They claim they can make it earlier if you want, later if you prefer, more flowers if you say so, more fruit without seeds if you wish. Tomorrow they'll change your yellow flower to blue if you just say the word or maybe your blue flower into a yellow one if that is your desire.

Actually what they do best is turn the sweet good earth into a barren worthless desert. Yes, they tie things into a knot that probably no one else will be able to untie.

Horse Radish

On my trips to Toronto I usually drop in at a delicatessen shop downtown and pick up a few odds and ends of different things that are not usually obtainable around Niagara. So when I go into this place the owner has the joint strewn with all types of delicatessen including smoked eel, salmon, herring, kippers, ciscoes, Polish sausage, salami, spiced beef, dill pickles, olives, cavier and many other goodies that tickle my salt-and-spice-loving palate and he's very generous with his samples—saying, try this and try that! The shrewd old fox—he knows that once you taste a drop of this or a dram of that, you'll want to take some home and you invariably do. So there is wile and wisdom in his generosity.

As I watch the owner's antics, every now and then a customer comes in and buys some horse-radish and this chap goes over to the machine and sticks the horse-radish root into the grinder and out it comes—strong, fresh, white and ready for use. Then he puts it into a jar and he hands it to the waiting client who in turn pays anywhere from 85c to $1.25 for a small jar of this freshly ground horse-radish.

"Yipes", said I to the fella, "Do you mean to tell me you get up to $1.25 for a chunk of that horse-radish."

"Why, sure", he says, "And it's well worth it, too."

"Well, heck man", I said to him, "We grow the stuff and for $1.00 —why I'll give you enough roots to grow more horse-radish than you'll consume for the rest of your life and you'll be able to eat horse radish every day of the week if you want it."

So he smartly responds, "How about in the winter time?"

"Well, believe it or not", says I, "Even in the winter time, too, because the horse-radish roots even grow during the winter".

Well, to this he takes exception and says that I am as crazy as a hoot owl. I reiterate that I know what I'm talking about—that the horse-radish root actually does make root growth during the milder periods of the winter and if he dug up a chunk of his horse-radish at the first thaw, he could grind it up and have it in the best of condition.

Well, of course this argument doesn't go on while his customers are waiting to buy the stuff and further, I have no intention of trying to put this fellow out of business. But I'm telling you that if you want to have that delicious condiment for meats, fish and other purposes then invest a quarter and you'll have enough horse-radish to supply you with your needs forever and ever because once planted it never dies. Furthermore, it keeps growing stronger and better every year.

You can bet that as soon as my wife reads this article I'll be bugged to bring home some horse-radish and I'll enjoy it, too. But I'll probably have to use a pick to break through the frozen ground—oh, my aching back!

Dwarf Fruit Stocks

Dwarf fruit trees are quite the rage throughout America today and people are demanding them in all varieties of fruit.

Actually and truthfully there are only two kinds of dwarf fruit trees and they are dwarf apple and dwarf pear. The other varieties of dwarf trees are not truly dwarf or, if they are, there is doubt concerning their compatability.

Yet some people offer dwarf cherry, dwarf peach and dwarf plum. But I say, be suspicious.

Now here is a check list so that you can find out whether or not you have been rooked. Generally speaking, a dwarf apple is budded on Malling IX. Dwarf pear is budded on Angers Quince. There actually are dwarfing root stocks of cherry, plum and peach but I have great doubt if any nursery in America is offering stock generally to the trade grafted on these special root stocks. If they are being offered, I don't know where it is and I think I keep fairly close touch with the trade.

Now I can almost hear you say, "Just what are you trying to prove, Friend Tobe?"

Nothing, says I, really nothing. I'm just trying to pass on some information that might be of help to you and prevent you from making a mistake or believing that you're getting something that isn't so.

Here is the list. You may find it valuable some sunny day.

ROOTSTOCKS FOR BUDDING AND GRAFTING USE:

Apple—Malus baccata and also seed of Ben Davis, Delicious and Winesap.

Dwarf Apple—Various East Malling but IX is best.

Apricot and Plum—Prunas cerasifera.

Sweet Cherry—Prunus avium.

Sour Cherry—Prunus mahaleb.

Dwarf Cherry are sometimes budded or grafted to Prunus besseyi, Prunus maritima and Prunus tomentosa.

Dwarf Peach—Prunus glandulosa and Prunus tomentosa.

Pear—Pyrus communis and also Barlett seed.

Dwarf Pear—Angers Quince.

Do You Know Your Nuts?

You don't? Well, I didn't think you did. But that doesn't alter the fact. Me? I know I'm nuts! I've been that way for years and to phrase it aptly—"I'm happy though wacky".

Now the question is—what is a nut? A Brazilnut? A cashew? An almond? A hazelnut? A coconut? A pinion nut? A Chestnut? Some people say they're all nuts but that is not true. Actually speaking, only a few of them are nuts—namely, the walnut, the pecan, the Brazilnut, the hazelnut and the pinion nut.

I've spent time and hours searching through the encyclopedias and the garden dictionaries and when I get finished I'm more confused than I was when I started. I don't know which is a nut and which is not a nut. Seymour says that the Brazilnut, the walnut and the pecan are true nuts. The Columbia Encyclopedia says "No". Other encyclopedias, Taylor's, for example, don't commit themselves as to which is which. I'd say they were smart.

Bailey, on the other hand, who is one of the foremost authorities says that he accepts the meaning of the nut from the common use of the word. So we have confusion between Seymour, Columbia Encyclopedia, Taylor and Bailey.

Now I'm going to the Royal Horticultural Society's Encyclopedia and see what they say. Here's another thing. It claims that the seed borne in a fruit is definitely not a nut. That would eliminate anything like the Almond for example.

So I'm just going to quote you from the various sources and you decide for yourself which is and which is not a nut. I'm certainly not going to get involved in this mess. It's bad enough now. If I got into it, it would be a darn sight worse.

Bailey (botanically): A hard indehiscent one-seeded pericarp arising from a compound ovary.

Bailey (horticulturally): A hard vegetable product—usually a fruit enclosing an edible part within a shell and the edible kernel or meat is released by breaking the integument.

Botanically simplified: A hard, bony one-celled fruit that does not split.

Horticulturally simplified: The fruit of certain trees containing a kernel enclosed in a hard shell.

Royal Horticultural Society: A hard indehiscent fruit and usually containing only one seed.

Indehiscent: Remaining closed at maturity.

Integument: External covering or skin.

Pericarp: Seed vessel of a plant.

Easy Does It — Slow

Seeing that I've taken it upon myself to be your guiding light, instructor, teacher and heaven knows what else let's get together and see what we know about the varied forms of plant reproduction.

First, and probably most important, is the reproduction by means of seeds. This is the true sexual reproduction of the male and female parts and the resulting production of seeds.

However, plants, unlike human beings and animals, have another method of reproduction and that is known as asexual or vegetative. A plant that produces a bulb like a potato or a Dahlia and also produces seed performs both means of reproduction at one and the same time.

While most of the members of the horticultural kingdom are raised by the strict sexual method there are a great many that are propagated by both methods. Yes, there are still a great number that are propagated by purely vegetative means. Let me give a sample. The Lombardy Poplar does not set seed of any kind. Therefore it can be grown only from cuttings.

Now, I mention another means of the vegetative method of reproduction that includes grafting, budding, cuttings, root divisions, root separations and layering. Plants also form bulbs, corms, rhizomes, roots and tubers all of which are the asexual way of reproduction which is entirely different from the standard method of two parent plants getting together and reproducing plants by means of seeds. It must be borne in mind that many plants can be propagated by one, two, or more of these methods as well as producing seeds.

Occasionally in horticultural discussion or reading you will come across the word Clone or Clonal and it is also spelled Clon. This means a named variety of a plant all of whose members have originated from one single plant and are therefore a multiplication of it by entirely vegetative means. In actual truth it means that all of the Elberta Peach trees in the world, for example, are a part of one and the same tree. It's as though we cut a worm in many pieces and each and every piece grew back to normal size and life.

Actually a clone implies an individual whereas seed implies a group of individuals. Now here's the important difference. In plants that are propagated from seed there usually is some variation ranging from slight to something that may be startlingly different—mind you, all from the same plant or plant parents.

But with vegetative reproduction, be it any one of the ones named above, each and every one reproduced in this manner is identical.

Take another example. An African Violet plant gives off seed. If the seed is sown the resulting plants will be similar to a degree and yet practically each and every one will have some minor difference. But remove a leaf and grow a plant from the leaf and you will have identically the same plant.

Honest, I didn't intend to mix you up. I just tried to teach you something.

Aqua Purum

I believe that I've gone on record before as saying that watering is the cause of more deaths in plants than all other causes combined. Now, remember, when I say watering, it could mean too much water and it could mean the lack of water, also.

Really this isn't as simple to track down as it sounds because seldom will anyone admit that they've over-watered or actually allowed a plant to die of thirst. It's just like us humans—we don't take very pleasantly to admitting our shortcomings. But that does not alter the truth—the fact still remains that more plants die because of faulty watering than all other reasons combined.

In truth I have found it almost impossible to convince many gardeners that their plants are over-watered. They would say to me, "Look, I have provided adequate drainage. No water lies at the bottom of the plant."

"Yes", I say, "But feel the soil. Your finger goes through it just as though it was mud. Don't you realize that plants can't breathe if they are kept soggy and plants, like everything else that has life, must have air."

Too much water definitely disorganizes the entire mechanical structure of a plant. Wouldn't your body or my body be disrupted if we were forced to drink a quart of water every hour? Yet it's not quite the same as throwing us in the lake and letting us drown quickly.

Now remember that water evaporates rapidly from the leaf surface of plants and most plants have tremendous leaf surfaces. If the plant gives off more moisture by means of its leaf surface than it can take up then this results in wilting. You have often wondered what wilting was—well, here's a concrete example. In most cases the plant can be restored to health by giving sufficient water and correcting the heavy loss. But in many cases injury results and sometimes eventual death of the plant in question.

Scientifically, the moment that a plant wilts the photosynthesis action stops and does not start again until all conditions get back to normal. When photosynthesis stops in a plant's life, it's almost akin to the stopping of the metabolism of a human being. Then of course it holds true that when a plant can't get water, it also means that it can't get food—and nothing can live without food for very long. This can be readily observed because in time of drought signs of nutrient or chemical deficiencies are clearly discernible.

Invariably when you see bud-drop on your flowering plants, you can be sure as fate it is a case of improper watering. I've noticed some strange things in our fields caused by watering. In years where we have had a lot of rainfall, we find that the resulting crops of bulbs, for example, tend to rot very readily and there's usually great difficulty in getting our bulbs or corms or even seeds to dry properly without a varying amount of loss. In the dry periods you will notice quite distinctly a shrinkage in the size of your crop. That, as I say again, goes for corms, bulbs, fruits or seeds. But they're usually very firm when grown under drought conditions.

Now then we come to the year when we get just perfect or a nice balance. Well, then the crop is plump, clean, sound, healthy, succulent and firm and that is what we call a vintage year. That doesn't only apply to wine.

You Dirty Dogs

On second thought, why should I malign dogs? So help me, even at their vilest, they have never done the likes of this.

Sure, a dog once chewed a button off, and a hole in, one of my friend's best new suits which he'd never yet worn. But he had brought it from the clothes closet and laid it on the bed while he was dressing.

Sure, and once our dog—yes, on a brand new axminster rug—piddled and puddled but good. Probably he was just initiating the rug into the household and that was his way of doing it.

Yes, and I knew another dirty dog who once killed a whole brood of young pullets when they were just about ready to start laying—after the farmer had been spending his days and nights and money raising them to the stage when he could get a little bit of his investment back. This affair happened nigh on to 2 years ago. In the morning my friend went out and was horrified to find the runway strewn with the dead young pullets. Upon examination it was found that each one had been killed by a neat nip on the throat. Expert examination indicated that a dog was the guilty culprit. However, he was totally unprepared when the situation repeated itself the next morning and immediately a search was made throughout the surrounding country for the killer dog. Three or four dogs within a few miles around were looked upon with suspicion but nothing could be proven. So that night he decided to spend a vigil and trap the marauding murderer. The neighborhood local dogs were all eliminated because they were mongrels in most cases without the training that a good bird dog gets and who must have been responsible for this debacle.

So this night he lay from dusk onward underneath the raised chicken house with his sights pinned on the adjoining runway that was closed in with wire netting. He lay there until almost the wee hours of the morning or, at least, until the sun began to streak the sky and he was right on many counts. He knew it wasn't one of the local dogs and he knew it was also most likely a bird dog. The only point that he was wrong on was that it didn't come from out of the country. In fact it came from closeby . . . yes, very closeby—it was his own hunting dog, yes, his own self-trained, tried, true and trusted, well-bred hunting dog. Of course the dog paid for this spree with his life because they claim you can never stop a dog from doing this once he starts. But even this villain wasn't to be compared with the type of dogs I'm talking about.

One of the largest rose-growing nurseries in the United States has the unmitigated gall to cover their rose bushes with a green-dyed chemical wax. These roses are especially prepared and treated and pinpointed for retail marketing in the super-markets, chain stores and other merchandising outlets.

I am not pretending to wear a special badge of virtue. Every nurseryman, large or small, that ever succoured a seedling has sold Roses that have perished or were even ailing—but, at least, you had a gambler's chance because you could see the exact condition it was in upon examination and you didn't need a microscope. It's bad enough to buy Roses at the super-markets, stores or stands where they have to contend with the conditions of exposure, dryness and heat which no Rose wants or should have. A Rose is a tender, living plant at the best and needs all the care that one can give it. But at least you'd have the privilege of examining it and seeing it and if it didn't suit you, you could take your trade elsewhere.

At least when I sell you a Rose and it's dead, you can see it's dead and no one has painted it bright green to fool you or is sticking it into you when your back is turned. If it's a smelly herring, then it looks like one and smells like one. I'm not trying to pawn it off on some poor trusting, unsuspecting soul or would-be-gardener as Shlemile No. 9 or a Night in the Follies Bergere.

This is just a warning for you to guard against these tactics. Watch for these Roses covered with green wax. Come to think of it, after reading this article, I'll bet you got the idea that I'm mad. Ha, ha, ha, ha, ha,—let me you tell you Mister, I sure am! GGRRrrrrrrr!

Pretty Sprite Kitty

I was invited to a little get-together at the home of my niece who had a fruit farm in the township. My wife had gone ahead of me earlier in the day and when I got through some work I had to do at home I drove out there.

As is customary on many farms, they had a large roomy ante-room or whatever you may call it leading into the house, yet being an integral part of the building, so that the man of the house or the hired man could change his clothes or take off his boots out there before entering the house proper. This room is also an entrance to the cellar. Therefore you can come in through the side door or up from the cellar into the ante-room and then into the house. This all seems complicated but anybody who has ever lived on a farm can probably understand it easily.

It was in the early fall and I had my topcoat on. They were all so busy in the house that they forgot to leave the rear light on. I came in the side way and threaded my way along to find the door leading into the house.

You've all seen kittens that insist upon wending their way between your feet and getting tangled up in them. Well, I felt a furry object against my legs and as one does in these cases I cussed audibly because I doggone near crushed the thing under my big feet.

When I got into the house I said to my nephew, "That doggone cat of yours out there almost tripped me. Why don't you train it better?"

"It couldn't have been our cat", said my nephew, pointing down at a furry ball rolled up on the rug in the corner. "Because there's ours right there".

Then suddenly it dawned on everyone just exactly who the cat was as they got a whiff of the odor that was coming off me in waves.

Jimminy, jeepers, jiggers—I had to disrobe there and then and looked cute in my nephew's overalls because he's a few inches taller than I.

Now arose the problem of "how to get that skunk out of the house?" One wise guy suggested I go down and collar it and throw it out by the scruff of the neck—intimating that I couldn't get to smell any worse anyway. I didn't applaud that idea. Well, another but logical

suggestion would be to leave the cellar door and the door leading outside wide open. Then somebody else popped up and said "How will we know if and when the skunk's left without going down and searching for him and taking the big risk of being sprayed again and probably rendering the house unfit for human habitation?"

However, up bobbed one with a real bright idea. "Why not sprinkle some flour on the threshold of both doors? The skunk couldn't possibly leave without making his foot prints in the sands of time."

This was done. We sat and waited for an hour or more. Then we went down and checked and sure enough the paw or foot prints or whatever you want to call them distinctly showed our "pretty kitty" had deserted us. Hallelujah. Glory be!

Weed and Pet Killers

Watch out when you buy chemicals to kill weeds and to do other destructive jobs!

Yes—sure—definitely—I fully realize that there are places where weed killers, no matter how caustic, are sometimes justifiable. I know, for instance, that a parking lot owner has to keep his lot clean and clear of weeds and grasses and, if he can't afford to pave his place, then he's got to resort to some form of chemical weed killer . . . and their needs are quite widespread.

But anyway I just want to point out something for you to watch. You will find that there are even at the present time on the market very, very poisonous weed killers and they recommend that they be spread along walks or paths for schools or other institutions where they will definitely keep the weeds down.

It is no exaggeration to say that some of these chemical caustic weed killers when used will positively prevent growth of any plant life for as much as five years and, even then, I certainly wouldn't want to eat any vegetables that were grown on that land. Take that as sound gospel.

However, to express a thought and to inscribe it on your mind I want to relate a case that indicates the necessity for permanent watchfulness. You know—the price of freedom is eternal vigilance. So be alert.

One of the chemical weed killers on the market was used quite broadly and somebody noticed that the birds around thereabouts were found dead quite regularly. It caused him to wonder, to ponder, to think. Then the light dawned—the poisonous weed killer, the little puddles of water and the dead animals lying in or beside the water pointed out the murderous culprit . . . the weed killer. It was then found that the weed killer was highly toxic and these tiny puddles here and there that could not be prevented after each rainstorm, made a very poisonous drink and animals do need water and they will drink at random—so. . . .

So if you want to protect your pets and such, just be very, very careful when you buy weed killers. Make sure that they're not toxic—especially in the manner I've just related.

Garlic Ain't Gaelic

Either you hate it or you love it. There are few foods known in the annals of mankind that have the distinct supporters and dissenters that garlic does.

If you don't like garlic then I'm sure you must dislike also the people who eat it . . . especially when they get close enough for you to smell their breath. To you folks first-hand garlic is bad enough but second-hand—whoof!

There are more facts and fables about the wonderful benefits of garlic to the human body than probably any other plant in the horticultural kingdom. One thing I know is, as sure as the Lord made green apples, I don't know any sick people who use garlic. Records show that it was well known in China, Egypt and Southern Europe long before the birth of Christ. Its true place of origin is unknown but its medicinal and beneficial values have been known for thousands of years.

Gayland, one of the earliest physicians who practiced from 130-200 B.C. thought very highly of it and called it "the husbandman's treacle".

For many years it was known as, and, as a matter of fact, it still is known as the "poor man's treacle" or cureall.

It is told that garlic was used as a cureall even as recently as World War I. Garlic Oil was actually used as an antiseptic. Among the Italians garlic is a necessity for life and good health. They claim it strengthens the sight and gives a keen sparkle to the eye and it is soothing to the stomach and intestinal tract.

I remember during the flu epidemic we had during the first World War that most foreign children carried bags around their necks. Some of them had garlic in them and others had camphor but I think the use of garlic was quite common in those days to ward off disease. Probably the smell of garlic protected people from any diseases and it's easy to understand why when you realize that the smell will keep anybody at a distance and 'tis in crowds where the disease spreads most rampantly.

Well, I don't know just how good garlic is as a cureall and a medicine but I do know, if used properly and lightly in cooking and salads, it certainly can impart a most delicious flavor to practically anything.

A warning to love birds—If you're going to make love and you've had some garlic, be sure to see that your loved one has some, too.

Seed Starting Vitals

I have learned through the years that the most important single factor in the germination of seed is keeping the seed starting medium at an even, uniform moisture content. Remember, and I stress, that is the most important factor of all in achieving success with the germination of your seed.

Now the second most important factor or principle involved in getting results with the planting of your seed is temperature. It is virtually impossible to provide the varying degrees of temperature required by some seeds. Seeds, or at least the original plants, come from all parts of the world . . . many of them from the Tropics. Well, to simulate the conditions under which each and every one of these plants grew would be practically impossible.

Therefore we have to resort to averages and when plants are known to be difficult or hard to start, they usually are dropped from the lists of seedsmen and nurserymen and the individuals don't plant them either. That is why nowadays there are specialists in every line of horticulture. The truth is that they've learned that they can't grow 50 different crops in a greenhouse at one and the same time. I've learned that to my sorrow over and over again. In fact I'm still learning it.

So in order to get results from your seed, you have to provide the conditions best suited to it. But seeing that's impossible, we do the best we can. However, there's where the temperature matter comes in as the second most important factor. Whatever temperature you do decide to provide, at least it should be uniform—say from 60 to 65 degrees or even from 60 to 70. But you shouldn't allow the temperature

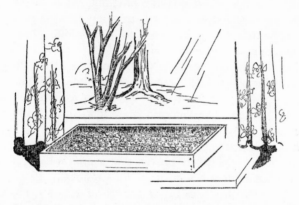

to go either much below or above this. Otherwise you'll probably run into difficulties of varying forms.

We've learned from experience just how important are the proper temperature and humidity conditions. We have a seed-germinating apparatus and, by controlling the temperature and humidity, we can make even a seed with only a remote spark of life grow. In fact if it's at all alive, it will do all right under the conditions we provide because they are the conditions the seed wants.

Well, now that you've provided an even temperature for your seeds, if they've got any life in them most of them will grow. When your seedlings appear and they're between ¼ and ½ inch high, they should be moved to a place where they can get more air, more sun and better still, a little cooler temperature. They don't want it quite so hot—

especially when they're nice and thick in the rows. Remember, too, humus-rich starting medium is almost positive prevention against "damping off".

At this stage the water should be cut down. They shouldn't need as much water as they did before and you must be careful of causing conditions that may lead to disease. But that doesn't mean you should let them get too dry and kill them that way. From here on you should watch them until they're ready to transplant. Then your troubles, in the main, should be over.

Plant Elixir

Yes, every minute, every hour, every day there is something one can learn if one only wants to learn.

For years and years I've been searching for good, sound, foolproof soil mixtures and I've never been able to come up with a solution that was simple. Of course a person is quite safe if, when he wanted some good soil for potting or for growing anything, he went out to a farm that was in good shape and picked up a few bushels of top soil and used it. Well, that would be easy and you would be pretty sure of getting a fairly good rich usable soil.

However, the average individual who putters about his garden or grows a few plants in a little greenhouse or even a few house plants is often quite perturbed or put to a lot of bother to locate a bit of satisfactory soil. You see, like yourself, most folks haven't got a farm to spare every time they want to pot up a plant.

Well, here's something that may once and for all solve this problem. It has been conclusively proven that a mixture of sand and peat moss creates the perfect soil mixture for practically all plants. Tests have shown that it produces better growth and does it more dependably and for less cost than any other mixture that you can concoct.

Now depending on your needs, you can use a 50-50 mixture. This is prescribed for house plants and such but if you want something that is porous then use 75% sand and 25% peat. In all cases you will have a soil mixture that gives you a splendid physical structure.

Up till now, using the above, you've got a good soil mixture but very low fertility. So now to build up your fertility here is the answer. Use either hoof and horn, bone meal or blood meal. This will create sufficient fertility to grow practically any type of plant that you would care to grow.

And I want to tell you this. These organic fertilizers are long lasting. You don't have to add to them every other day or so like you would with some of the chemical fertilizers.

Depending upon the type of plant that you're going to grow, the amount of organic fertilizer used varies from one pound to ten pounds per cubic yard of the mixture. This you can decide yourself by testing. But you can't go wrong either way—a little more or less can't get you into trouble.

Now put this down. Note it carefully. Place it somewhere where you can get it because this may be the most useful thing that you ever come across for helping you grow good plants without worry or bother.

Poor Northerners

Many, many folks in the northern latitudes feel so terribly sorry for themselves because they claim that they are unable to grow so many of the choice horticultural items and, to be bold about it, I don't feel a bit sorry for them. Too dang often have I heard the wail, "Oh, we can't grow this and I'd like it" and "We can't grow that but it would be very nice" and "I tried this once but it didn't grow". The actual truth of the matter is that they can grow almost limitless subjects but they don't grow them for the simple reason that they haven't tried or that someone has failed and spread the word that it won't grow here or there. Believe me, the failure was not always, in fact very seldom, due to northern climate or latitude.

On my visit to Alaska a couple of years ago, travelling through the Yukon Territory, which once I had believed to be a barren frozen wasteland, I found that the flora was much broader than I ever dared hope or imagine. Now I spent a good many hours on various occasions going through the bush and around the lakes to see the various types of vegetation that could be found and I was astounded to learn that the variation was probably as great as it is in Southern Ontario and I might even say that they even have a more varied vegetation without fear of contradiction.

Probably the reason that this tremendous variation of horticultural subjects is growing there so well is because up there nature hasn't heard about this business of not being able to grow it or that it's too far north. By chance a seed just fell and grew—it didn't know it wasn't supposed to.

Right at the present time on the shores of Lake Ontario we are growing Azaleas, Rhododendrons, Holly, Boxwood, Blue Hydrangeas, Redbud and this year we're going to try the Mimosa Tree—that is, the Albizzia.

My advice and suggestion to you folks who dream about growing many of these luxurious, connoisseur's items that you have eyed for years and years after you have seen them growing around Florida, Georgia and Virginia is to try them. You may be pleasantly surprised. Give them a little bit of extra care and use your head for the first season or so and you may get the surprise of your life and also you may be the first one in your part of the country to grow that specialized item.

Dare to do it and succeed!

Osmosis in Process

For y'ars and y'ars I've been teaching you, my children, various little things about seeds, plants and growing things. Well, the time has come when I must tell you a little bit more. I must lead you deeper into the woods and I must tell you the truth so I beg you to listen.

Osmosis—what is it? To make it sound even more complicated, it is also referred to as the process of Osmosis which actually is the absorption of one liquid into another.

How does it concern you and plants, you ask. That is a reasonable question and I'm going to do my best to explain it simply and as quickly as possible. Somewhere down close to the roots of a tree or a plant there is a thin diaphragm that separates the contents or the juices or sap that flows in the root from that which flows above. That is called the "permeable membrane".

Now this flow, contrary to normal expectations, is not from the denser to the lighter but from the lighter to the denser. In this manner soil solution carrying plant food in weak solution is absorbed through the walls of the root hairs because it is not so concentrated as the liquid sap under the root cells.

Now you may ask a more important question—where does the process of Osmosis concern the average Joe who gardens in a limited way? So I will get down to definite cases. I just stated that the liquid soil solutions or nutrients will flow from the lighter to the denser. Therefore, if you make soil conditions more concentrated or richer, you are actually doing damage or harm to your plant because it will drain the solution or the nutrients from the plant. That's why it is vitally important to supply manure, fertilizer or nutrients that are readily soluble to your soil in small but steady quantities to get best results. If you give it an overdose, instead of helping your plant, it will drain the vital juices and sap from it and perhaps kill it.

By feeding in small quantities you will prevent the soil solution around the fine roots from becoming more concentrated than the liquid in the roots. If this should happen, the process would be

100

reversed and the plant would starve for the want of food even though it is surrounded abundantly.

Here I want you to listen carefully. It is important to note that the Osmotic process is at least in part, if not greatly, responsible for the ascent or descent of sap—often referred to as root pressure.

So you see, if you bear with me, Osmosis is probably the answer to most crop fatalities or even the failure of your plant to grow—and you perhaps wondered why.

About Plenty and Hunger

I'm sitting here musing about plants and things when a strange thought comes to my mind, "Why is it that folks who nurture and feed their plants and water them to perfection don't get the flowers that some other folks get?"

Well, you know the scientists say that a flower is a neglected leaf on a plant and that is why, always, the flowers seem to come from the terminal buds where the leaves don't get much nourishment and are treated like step-children. Therefore, they turn into flowers.

No, don't laugh and snort derisively . . . because that's what the plant scientists tell us. I'm not a plant scientist, so therefore I'm not telling you. I'm just repeating what I've read and heard and learned.

This only goes to illustrate that probably the most blooms are had from plants that are more or less starved or hungry. Well, it's true as far as people are concerned. The starved nations or the hungry nations seem to be having all the children. The rich get richer and fatter and the poor get skinny and have children. Good compensation? Fun, anyway!

Believe it or not, from my years of toying with nature I've found that there really isn't much difference between a human being and a plant. In many ways the human being is smarter or seems to know more than a plant. On the other hand, I can show you many, many instances—yes, likely hundreds of them—where plants are obviously much more intelligent, capable and move more in the right path than human beings do.

You know it's not the well nourished fellow, the rich guy or the chap that's brought up in the home of comfort that hops out and climbs Mount Everest or seeks to find a new country in the frozen north nor does he cross oceans on a small rigger or row boat to try to found a new empire. They usually stick close to the native hearth and warm their "tootsies" on a cool night around the fire.

You know luxury, comfort and plenty usually sound or ring the death knell of enterprise and ambition. So why should you expect plants to be different? Well, the moral is—don't overnourish a plant, don't build up your soil too highly—because if you do, your plants will get lazy and they won't give you the fruit and the flowers.

Now again perhaps this goes against the grain for everything you've ever learned or read. That I cannot help. I am only telling you what I learn as I go along. Take or leave it! (Damn, Old Tobe, the iconoclast.)

Why Plants Die

No matter how many reasons I or anyone else can give, you can be certain that there are other legitimate reasons too.

Perhaps if we could perform an autopsy on a plant the same as the medicos do on a human we might in each case pinpoint the actual cause of death. Sure the medical boys are smart. They say McDuff died of a heart attack but they don't tell you what brought about that heart attack. It is far more important once a person is dead to know what brought about his death or caused it so we can help others stay alive.

So when analyzing the demise of a plant it is not very smart to say the plant died from chlorosis or an attack of mealy bug. Basically something went wrong with the plant's organism that led to the other thing.

Being ignorant in this instance I'm going to confine myself to the general broad applications of the sort of indirect things that cause a plant to die.

Here we go:
1. Borers or insects in your soil.
2. Neglect.
3. Dust clogging the pores.
4. Insufficient water.
5. Drowning (overwatering).
6. Leaching or lack of vital nutrients.
7. Chilling and cold draughts.
8. Dryness (lack of humidity).
9. Soil too acid.
10. Soil too alkaline.
11. Too warm.
12. Too cold.
13. Improper drainage.
14. Lack of sunlight.

15. Over fertilization.
16. Too much sunlight.
17. Fumes (gas, coal or oil).
18. Too much fluorine or chlorine in the water.
19. Spray injury.

Usually if a plant has perfect drainage it is difficult to over-water. Some plants form a root ball and then when you water it just runs down the sides and out of the pot without penetrating the root ball and actually the plant may die of lack of water.

Another common cause of disaster with plants is the over-enthusiastic gardener who this week gives them water and plant food every day and probably next week will forget the plants exist and not give them a drop of either. This type of catch-as-catch-can attention is usually deadly to plants.

With all the bad news above it is still a fact that plants are easy to grow and care for. Just like babies you know . . . even though the hospitals have a lot of sick ones there are still millions of beautiful bouncing babies about.

I'm At It Again

You know a man no longer has many places where he can go for peace and solitude and to be alone. He can't find it in his house with the kids, radio and TV blaring like the trumpets at Jericho. So where can a man go besides the far, far north?

Sure, I'll tell you where . . . to his garden! A garden is still a man's sanctuary where he can indulge in good healthful honest toil in clean unhurried work and exercise—where he can, by means of his own hands, head and back feed himself as a man ought to be fed—with good natural foods . . . where peace, quiet, sanity, safety and, yes, security can still be found.

Mebee, if we're lucky, we can keep the X-ray, the atom bomb, the chemicals, the fluorinated water and chemically treated foods the "heck" out of there.

So far I haven't recognized or noticed the great advances that chemical science has made in agriculture. In my opinion it has subtracted rather than added anything to the benefit of the soil or mankind.

An intelligent individual will begin to ask questions. "Where science has made so many advances and inroads in many walks of life and fields of endeavour why has so little been done on the land?"

Well, the answer is really simple when you look into it. Scientists, just like you and me and everyone else, have got to eat. So, if they told you that a natural compost-treated soil is much better in every way than chemical fertilizer-treated soil, that isn't going to put any bread in their bellies or bucks in their cash registers. I've sort of found out that the lab boys can find almost anything they look for excepting, of course, the cure for cancer.

Now, for instance, if they discovered how wonderful organic soil is for the health of mankind, what would that get them? . . . A pocket full of dirt! But, on the other hand, if they find out that a certain chemical will do such and such to this or that, why they just put on a great big campaign in the newspapers, over TV and the radio with a fanfare and splurge that just dazzles the eyes and everybody is out buying this new wonderful chemical that performs these miracles and the cash registers ring a ding-dong merry tune.

You see the larger chemical corporations set up projects at the universities to find out certain things and when they come up with the answer that suits them, they emblazen it throughout the country. If the answer doesn't suit them they just throw it in the ash can and nobody knows anything about it.

Yes, the reports that may show the organic fertilizer way is the best are chucked into the incinerator—yes, I said incinerator—not the waste-basket. They don't want to keep it in the wastepaper basket because it might turn up. But in the incinerator, it's burned and destroyed forever.

Well, I guess when I was born and even when the world was born, we depended upon Mother Nature. I think I'll place my faith in her still for as long as I live anyway. The chemical boys may have a better way—I don't know—I'm ignorant—but I have a little sense of loyalty to my Maker and, to the old lady who looks after me. "I'm sticking with you." . . . That was that popular song, wasn't it—"I'm sticking with you-oo-oo".

Kill Nil

"Kill first and ask questions later" seems to be the general theme by which many children in the cities are raised.

I've noticed that when the city kids come out to the country, if they see an ant or a fly or a worm or a bug, they want to step on it and crush it. Perhaps this would be understandable if he was a fruit grower's son. He would seek to crush a caterpillar or any other insect for fear it would multiply by the million and ruin the crop of fruit.

By far and large the children that are raised in the country are not killers of animal life. Sure, as they grow older, they probably will go out shooting rabbits but they don't destroy them wantonly. At least

104

they can use what they kill as food or perhaps make use of the skin. Sometimes the rabbits are hunted because they damage orchards. Occasionally, too, they'll shoot a marauding skunk—I mean the four legged kind that swipe chickens.

Now I'm not taking sides either way, justifying it or not. But I do take exception to folks who believe in the adage . . . Let's kill it first and find out what it is after!

Don't teach your children to fear and destroy animal or insect life. After all is said and done, there are so few, if any, vicious or poisonous animals and insects in our country that we should be told about the many splendid benefits that these other animals bring to us.

Of course I'm not expecting you to teach your children to love and fondle a pet snake, a mud turtle or a ground hog. But honestly, it wouldn't be such a bad idea if you did—long as it wasn't a rattler or a snapping turtle.

But these animals, as well as bees, dragon-flies, bats, skunks and squirrels are actually beneficial to man in one or many ways.

I've been racking my brain as best I can to find out how a rabbit benefits mankind but so far I haven't come up with an answer. So I'll have to consult a wiser and older authority than myself (I know —let's say he eats weeds.)

But at least if you can't teach your children or your grand-children to love animal life and nature, at least show them why they shouldn't kill animals and insects.

Recipe for Long Life

Forget your years! Act as though you were going to live forever. Work, plot, plan, think—not in terms of minutes or days but in weeks, months and years—yes, as far in advance as you possibly can.

There's old Bill McLeod. When I first came to Niagara about thirty years ago, he was driving the rural mail in an old jalopy—one of those 1914 Model T Fords. How he got around those bumpy roads, especially during the winter, was the miracle of miracles. But he managed to make it.

He was an old man then—at least, by my standards. Remember this was thirty years ago and he was probably in his late 50's. One day as he dropped off the mail in my mail box on the farm he asked me about Black Walnut Trees. He wanted to know the price of them and how they grew and what age they were and when they started to bear and about their timber qualities. You see it had been just a few days ago that a buyer from across the river had been over scouting this part of the country for old walnut logs and also the roots or burls or whatever it was they wanted and he had met old McLeod and told him what he was looking for. So that gave McLeod an idea.

When McLeod was asking me these questions about the Black Walnut trees, I remember distinctly quoting him a price on them and giving him what information I had and I said, "Well, the trees start to bear in about 8 or 10 years and they yield quite a few bushels per tree." I didn't know where he'd market them but I guess there was a market for the wonderful meat of the Black Walnuts.

"Oh," he said, "I'm not interested in the nuts. It's the trees for timber I want."

I said, "Trees for timber? Why, it will take 25 years to get trees suitable for logging."

"Yea", he said, "That's what I figured—that's what I figured."

Well, this became a standard joke around this part of the country —McLeod, somewhere around 60 years of age, planting Walnut trees for logging purposes. Heck, it was so utterly ridiculous that it didn't even bear repeating. But yet, as I said, it was a heck of a good joke.

Well, the fact is that Old McLeod is still alive. Yep, that's right. He's about 90 years old and he's in pretty good shape, too. He has his faculties. I haven't seen him lately but I presume he's planting out some new Walnut trees for logging in 25 years. I guess he'll be cutting the others now if he hasn't already started to cut them.

So you see a man never knows. He wasn't counting on them for nuts which would take 10 years . . . No, siree, there was nothing short sighted about McLeod. He was planting them for timber in 25 or 30 years. You see that man really had vision, foresight and courage. He

deserved to live and he did something about living. He had a goal and he marched straight towards that goal—and, doggone it, he reached it, too. Now, he's going beyond it for a new goal that he's set up. Can you claim anything of determinative nature to compare with that? No, you can't. I know "doggone" well you can't. But if you could and if you did any of these things, you'd probably live to be as old as McLeod and maybe stay just as healthy.

Plan ahead—look ahead—then you'll have something to live for and a doggone good reason to guard your health and well-being. A purpose to live and stay alive for is the finest and lowest priced insurance policy in the world.

Wrap yourself in interesting and absorbing work, business, occupation, endeavour or activity and you will be alive to get it done. Don't let your family or friends prevent you from being busy. Their sympathies are MURDER.

About Bargain Lawn Seed

If you're going to plant a lawn today, tomorrow or some day in the future or if you know of someone who's going to plant a lawn, please listen to me.   Read this article carefully because it may save you some money and, what is even more important, it may save you a lot of grief and probably will aid in giving you a more beautiful and more permanent lawn.

To begin with, no product is better than the reputation of the man who makes or sells it. For almost a quarter of a century I've been selling seed and seed mixtures to the Canadian public. One of my chief items has been grass seed. In order to satisfy my customers and also keep peace with my soul, I've honestly given the best values in grass seed that I know how to give. I spent a lot of time learning and studying the best grasses, the best mixtures—considering climatic and other conditions. When at last I did come up with the formulas, I believed that they were the best offered by anybody anywhere—irrespective of price. That held true almost twenty years ago and it holds true even more so today because I've learned and made a lot of comparisons in the meantime.

Nowadays the laws in both Canada and the United States do much to protect the buyer of most products against unscrupulous business men and that is good. But it could still be better. I don't mean the law doesn't go far enough because no law can protect a man against himself and I don't ask that the law be made instruments to protect people against their natural greed and foolishness.

When you buy a mixture in Canada the government makes the seedsman specify clearly on the package the grade of the mixture. That is, in order to state that our grass seed mixture is No. 1, we must meet certain definite conditions but I do admit that there is an awful lot of leeway in these requirements and you can get a poor, a fair and a good mixture all with the No. 1 brand on them. Therefore the fact that it is No. 1 mixture does not necessarily mean that it is a good mixture or that it is adaptable to your soil conditions. What would be better is that if the law stipulated that the contents must be indicated clearly on the package.

Now I understand in the United States that a regulation somewhat similar to this exists at the present time but even that cannot guard the purchaser against the unscrupulous dealer or someone who is definitely trying to mislead the public. And, believe it or not, this is often done.

Preaching Jack

I've often wondered just what kind of sermon Jack-in-the-Pulpit preaches. Then it seemed to me that he could preach but one kind of sermon—the sermon that he knew best—of the forest, the woods, the trees, the flowers, the birds, the bees, the rivulets, the streams, the sun, the stars, the rain and the snow and the animals—the rabbits, the squirrels and the groundhogs or woodchucks and bats . . . that he lived with.

He could tell of the many adventures, of the multitudinous things that occur and the things that he sees and does, the life that he leads—simple, clean, true and pure. That is what Jack does with every moment of his life and as I see him there preaching his sermon I feel that he is lecturing in the wrong place because he should be out in the cities telling the folks just what they're missing.

You see if I come to him and hear him and see him in the woods, nothing is gained because I know, understand and love the woodlands and nature paths. I know the woods and love them and thus his sermon is wasted upon me. But if he could get out onto the sidewalks in the cities and tell the folks of the beauties by which he is surrounded and of the goodness to be found right here he would be preaching a sermon to an appreciative eager audience.

On the other hand perhaps he is telling us, those of us who frequent the woods, to carry his message to those who are less fortunate than we and bring them out to the country to see the beauty, the grandeur, the peace and the loveliness of the woods and forest.

Truly that must be the sermon that Jack-in-the-Pulpit preaches.

Perhaps he tells of the advance of civilization, of the fast dying forests, of the disappearing beauties of nature, of increased tempo of modern living and the toll that it takes in human life. Perhaps he tells of the encroachment of the cities and the subdivisions and that he and his friends the Trilliums, the Bloodroots, the Solomon's Seals, Dogwood, Columbine, Pussy Willows, Hepaticas, Lady Slippers, Butter and Eggs, Gentians and the many other native plants are being squeezed further and further north until they will reach the end of their tether where they will no longer be able to grow and thrive. Perhaps he sings a warning. Let us heed, let us help, let us preserve him and those that surround him.

Tree Size Facts

Ah, how often have I said it and I will say it again and again and again . . . Do not plant overgrown, large or extra large heavy trees, plants, shrubs, evergreens or any other planting material.

The finest plant known to the horticultural world is the young vigorous plant. Invariably they grow better, start earlier and give better results than the bigger fellows. Don't try to plant the biggest plant you can get. Otherwise results will not be what you expect.

It has been conclusively proven that if a one or two year tree were planted alongside a three or four year tree, the younger tree will produce its crop sooner, will produce better crops and probably even better fruit. So therefore, remember, there is no advantage whatsoever in planting great big overgrown trees.

Broadly speaking, the success that you derive from your planting depends far more upon the care and the attention given the tree than the size.

Remember that the nursery is the place to propagate and start young plants and trees. It is not the place to keep them for continued growth. That is your job.

Never judge a tree by its size. Now by this I don't mean that you should purchase or have someone send you undeveloped, dwarfed or stunted stock. What you want is thrifty clean, well rooted plants of good size, good quality and filled with stamina and vitality. But don't for heavens sake, make the mistake of believing that the biggest tree or plant is the best one. It's just as true with plants as it is with humans—the biggest and fattest man or woman is by no means better than the slender, wiry or stocky fellow.

Ancient History

Well, seeing you're studying things about horticulture, I think it is only fair to know a little bit about its history. So let me tell you the story of a man who is known as the Father of Botany. He was one Theophrastus—a Greek.

He was born in the year 370 B.C. which was evidently in Homer's day—on an island known as Lesbos but later it was called Mytilene I'm not going to enter into the story here about Lesbos but that makes fabulous reading. Look into it some day, boys. You'll like it.

Well, it appears as though Theophrastus, along with Aristotle, became a disciple of Plato in Athens and when dear old Plato died, Theophrastus continued his studies under Aristotle. They evidently were not just master and pupil but sincere, devoted friends.

When Aristotle died, he gave to Theophrastus his exceptionally fine library along with his own manuscripts and the botanic garden which Aristotle had established in Athens.

Theophrastus was a very prolific writer and it is said that he wrote over 225 treatises of which his two botanical works are the most oustanding.

He didn't live to be quite as old as Methuselah but he did reach the ripe old age of 107.

If you take into consideration the fact that this man lived over 2300 years ago and that most of his writings are still authentic and that he gave the names to many, many of our plants which they still hold, you'll have to admit that we don't have anyone to share his top honors in the botanical field.

Evidently Theophrastus travelled very little in his lifetime. He got all his information from classical and contemporaneous sources. But he was an original thinker and he dreamed up the names and the ideas by himself. He knew all about the times of fruiting and flowering and the effects of drought and moisture. His works deal with over 450 species—covering practically the entire horizon of plant life.

He had a tremendous inquisitiveness. His power of observation was unbelievable because he ferretted out the minute structure of fruits, flowers, foliage, roots, stems and tendrils. He knew all about the structure of seeds, the way they were made up, about their germination —yes, and about the way seedlings and plants behave.

So come on, folks! Get interested in gardening and botany and see if you can't live to be 107, too.

Botany is the classic science and the oldest branch of natural history.

Remember, botanists, gardeners, horticulturists, farmers, fruit growers and such, if anyone asks you what you do for a living, tell them you practice applied botany. (Like a doctor practices medicine and, if practice makes perfect, how long will it take till they're perfect.)

The Sure Road To Health

For a long time now I've had the conviction and belief that practically each and every one of man's illnesses, diseases or difficulties with his body are caused by nutritional deficiencies or you can call them dietary deficiencies. I'd say deficiencies of actual elements.

Well, here's a report that was taken some time ago from the periodical, Clinical Medicine. "Blood pressure studies made by N. S. Davis and E. F. Poser suggested that essential hypertension may be due to chronical minimal dietary deficiencies. Working on this theory, these investigators administered ascorbic acid in doses of 333 mg. three times a day to patients with high or rising blood pressures. It was found that the administration of one gram of Vitamin C daily to patients, even those with well-established hypertension, caused a marked lowering of blood pressure levels together with subjective relief in many cases."

It has been definitely established that the body contains at least seventeen distinctly different mineral elements. I claim that eventually study will prove that the human body requires and contains more. Well, these elements come to us primarily or almost entirely from the soil. That is, the foods that are grown in the soil that contains these elements are eaten and utilized by the body in the way it needs them.

But bear in mind that these minerals can only be absorbed by the body cells in an organic or colloid condition. The body has no means at its disposal of absorbing or using these elements in their crude and relatively massive forms. Therefore they must be put into the colloid state which is referred to or defined as the fourth state of matter. Then too it is almost infinitesimally small and in subdivision.

111

This means that the elements are picked up by the tiny fibre root-lets of a plant, taken into the plant, and then divided into minute quan-tities. Then the human eats them and these elements are dispersed or distributed throughout the body as required and this maintains health and good living.

This, I hope, is as clear as the sound of a bell.

Aha, Red Russians Too

One of the greatest mistakes the human being makes is to judge things too much by appearance. Yes, man just about gauges every-thing according to how it looks. If the appearance of it suits his eye, then he thinks it's good for his stomach. Boy, sometimes he's so wrong— in fact, he's dead wrong—and often he dies for it.

Now you know and I know and we all know that the best looking girl is not the best wife, the best housekeeper, the best nurse—in fact, she's usually not the best of anything. Yet that's where the man goes when he wants to get himself a wife—the poor sap!

Of course they've said for ages that beauty is only skin-deep but unfortunately it's the poor man who gets skinned when he picks a beautiful girl as his wife.

Now take in tomatoes, everybody wants rich, red, ripe tomatoes. Yet there are two or three wonderful, marvelous varieties that are golden colored. They are better than any red variety that was ever grown or created. Yet the demand for them is almost nil.

Last year I had one of these yellow varieties. It was called Sun Ray and Mr. and Mrs. Nobody nowhere ever tasted a better tomato. It looked good, it was firm, it was beautiful inside and it was marvelous to eat. Yet whoever heard of it? . . . Probably nobody but myself and a few other so-called connoisseurs or searchers.

Now let's hop to apples. Go into the chain stores or supermarkets or any market and you'll see buyer after buyer buy the apples strictly on color. Now everybody knows the wonderful Spy apple. Well, the true Spy apple is not red in color. It's somewhat streaked but at the best there's very little red in a Spy apple. Yet everybody, yes every-body throughout the world who ever ate an apple knows that the quality of the Spy apple is unexcelled. There is no better apple.

Now there is a red Spy apple on the market but it is not a Spy— definitely not a Spy. It is an apple that looks like a Spy but it doesn't taste much like one. In fact it is much inferior in quality. It has the good red color and they are sold as Red Spy. But the Spy apple is still the streaked apple with very little red on it.

When we buy Plums at the market . . . without a shadow of a doubt every one of us selects the nice big red Plums. But boy, oh boy, time after time and year after year what a disappointment. They're sour, the pits cling, the flesh is soft or soggy or tough. There isn't one redeeming feature about them. But the color caught our eye and we stupidly followed the color line.

Well, I could go on and give you a hundred more examples but it still wouldn't prove anything to you. You'll probably go on buying red tomatoes, red apples, red plums, red meat and probably kiss girls with red cheeks and red lips and what's worse—so will I!

Moanin' Low!

Today I'm feeling sorry for myself. It's just one of those moods and one of those days. You've felt sorry for yourself haven't you at different times? Did I stop you? . . . No! So today is my turn. I feel sorry for myself.

Why? . . . Well, I'll tell you! It just occurred to me that I've got the world's toughest job. The diplomat, the policeman, the factory worker, the soldiers, the sailors, the airmen—nobody has a job as tough as mine. Aha, and you thought my job was easy—that I had a cinch—that mine was the sweetest and most pleasant job in the world because I deal with plants. How wrong can you be!

So before you run off and think that I'm just kidding you, I'm going to get down to details. Just hold, sit tight and listen!

Stupidly, many years ago, I began to feature advertisements in the newspapers throughout Canada that would appeal and attract folks who had never gardened before. I would say that 75% of the people who write to me every year never grew a plant in their life. Yes, yes —most of them are as innocent about the ways and means of gardening as an angel is about original sin.

"So what?" you say. So what! They make just every mistake in the book. They take my good healthy plants and plant them upside down and then write me a letter saying why don't they grow and my plants are not good.

You think I'm kidding! Well, I swear it's true. They plant cactus-type plants, that like it nice and dry, in soggy soil and they put Blueberries and Christmas Rose in sand where they never get a bit of moisture. They leave their Gladiolus, Dahlias and Canna bulbs outdoors to freeze and they dig up their Tulips and Daffodils. They sow a lawn —putting the seed in good and thick. They get a hose with a good sharp stream of water and wash the whole works down the drain. Then they write to me and say my grass seed is no good and it didn't grow.

I know what you're thinking . . . you're thinking that this is all a tall tale, a figment of my imagination or a huge big lie or exaggeration. But I'm telling you each and every instance is true. Now, I can just hear you saying gleefully, "Well, why don't you instruct them? Why don't you give them bulletins and literature that will teach them how to do it right?"

Now I scream! . . . Can you hear me? The nursery is crawling with instructions on how to do everything. We send bulletins to everybody every time, but listen—who is so naive as to even read instructions?— Who can be so simple minded as to need them? I'm the only guy who reads the instructions that I write and I read them when I write them. Directions are something for "joiks" and half-wits.

They do the impossible—these folks. They blame everybody and everything except the person who is responsible and do you know who he is? Themselves—you! Yes, just you—toodle-oo-doo. Sweet you. Pardon me, I got the writing mixed up with my singing.

So now you see the story. Most seed and nursery houses don't make any great attempt to attract beginners, but I, smart Tobe—I do and I really go after them—and then boy, they really go after me. Poor me! Woe is me!

The Origin of Species

Good natural animal fertilizer has been harder and harder to procure each year. It's got to the stage now that out here on the farm some of us think more of a load of manure than we do of our families.

We don't have any cattle on the nursery. We do use a horse but I stable her down at my brother's and the dividends accrue to him because of the care and attention he must give old Dobbin.

So necessity dictates and we have to buy the manure. Each and every year we spread 100 tons over the nursery acres. It is preferred to get the stuff in during the winter and spread it when the ground is frozen and the manure spreader can get about fairly easily. But sometimes we get loads of manure in in late spring and this happened last April. It seems that the fellow who hauls manure has contracts with various organizations calling for him to lift the manure and clean out certain premises at certain specific times. So he has to haul spring, summer, fall and winter.

So one balmy May morning he pulled in with a steaming high-piled

114

load of this stuff and dropped it on one of the front fields. We got the manure spreader and loaded it on and spread it over this front piece of land—and let me tell you, brother, this stuff was ripe . . . the wind was in our favor and we really got a noseful. To me the odor was strongly nitrogeneous but not unpleasant. I would say the odor was invigorating if I wasn't afraid of contradiction by some of my female readers.

To tell the truth this load was a little rank and the atmosphere for many millions of cubic feet roundabout was permeated or polluted with its fragrance.

At last it was spread and in places it was probably a couple of inches thick.

A car pulled up and a customer came over. I didn't know the man but he walked to where I was standing and he held a handkerchief over his nose. When he reached within earshot, I said, "What's the matter, fella? Got a cold?"

He took the handkerchief away from the front of his nose long enough to gasp, "Whew—it's awful." He was as pale as a ghost and he really looked sick. I expected him to pitch his dinner ten or twenty feet in front of him any second. He was walking very daintily and stepping even more carefully to avoid putting his feet into it. So far he hadn't lit on anything to worry about. (It's a pity he hadn't slipped and landed in it—kerflop!)

"What do you put this horrible stuff out on your land for?" he said.

"Well," said I, "I intended to plant a lot of vegetables on this piece. I'm going to use it as my trial grounds for my vegetable patch and it will soon grow some wonderful corn and taters".

I took a look at him, and his eyes, or what of them I could see above the handkerchief, were wide in amazement and horror and he removed the protective linen mask long enough to gulp and gasp and stammered, shaking his head, "You wouldn't eat anything grown with that!"

Truth Shames Satan

Sometimes I wonder—I wonder whether it pays to tell folks the truth and give them sound advice.

Yes, I mean actually what I say here. There's not much sense in wasting my time and giving my efforts if folks won't believe me anyway.

What am I wailing about, you say. Well, it's this. Invariably folks ask my advice about the best type of upright evergreen to use in a foundation planting.

115

Really the selection is decidedly limited when it comes to upright evergreens, especially of the prim formal types. You can either have Swedish Juniper, American Pyramidal Arborvitae, Clipped Upright Yew or the upright growing Hicks Yew. Now there also is the Clipped Boxwood but they're not hardy in all parts of Canada. Then you have the upright Virginiana types but these are not too good where you want them clipped. They're best allowed to grow naturally.

So there we remain with the choice of four . . . Swedish Juniper Pyramid Arborvitae, Clipped Upright Yew and Hicks. There isn't any doubt about it that the Swedish is the most attractive and also the neatest in growing habit but of what use is paradise if no one can get there? Look about you. See if you can find anyone who has a good looking Swedish Juniper except at the nurseries. It just seems they won't do well in the northern latitudes. Maybe they do all right down south but not here. Yet because of their attractiveness and beauty everybody wants them. But again I repeat—they won't survive.

Next is the Pyramid Arborvitae. When in good growth and condition it's a mighty attractive piece of evergreen furniture. But it, too is subject to the vagaries of the weather and seldom does one encounter a Pyramid Arborvitae that has been growing in a location for more than 4 or 5 years.

Again, I say—what good is paradise if you can't get there?

So what does that leave us? One redeemer remains . . . the Hick's Yew. This doggone thing doesn't look like anything until it's 5 or 6 years old and then it becomes very attractive, bushy and erect with deep, deep green foliage. You can clip it, hack it, buffet it, smack it— it takes it all in its stride. Yes, they'll live probably longer than you or I. So why seek further when this is your "Eureka"?

The Clipped Upright Yew possesses all the good qualities of the Hick's but there is one factor . . . you have to keep it clipped!

That's it folks. That's the advice I give people when they come to the nursery. But what do they buy? Guess! You guessed it—you're as right as a right angled triangle. Everybody buys the Swedish Juniper and the Pyramid Arborvitae. That's how much faith they have in my advice. Bless their beating old hearts!

Bafflin' Baffin

It was my good fortune last summer to have a visit from our very good friend, Dorothy Robinson—the miss who teaches school way way up in the north—in fact, she taught in the most northernly school

Yes, these colonies are state-owned. Anyone, irrespective of his financial rating, class, creed, color or what-have-you, can rent one of these plots and the entire rental fee is 5 pounds a year approximately. Those who want larger or fancier houses of course can have them for a little extra. But in each case these houses contain all modern facilities—bedrooms, dinettes, sitting rooms, sleeping bunks for the children, up-to-date kitchenettes, bathrooms and of course sanitary conveniences, lighting and heating just as you would find in the best city homes.

Then there are nice prizes for the best gardens and there is real keen competition. Each group of colony gardens have their own little community and they lead a happy, ideal, communal existence. There are facilities for the group to have dances and other forms of amusement and also a space for festivals and garden club meetings, shopping centres and meeting places.

It is also possible to buy these homes and the sum is approximately $250.00. Many young Danish couples make one bold attempt to save and skimp until they can get enough to buy one of these places and then they enjoy the beauty of living in the country as well as the health and pleasure that gardening and outdoor activities give them.

Oh, Really Now, O'Reilly

I had to go out to the field a few days ago and on my way back I noticed there was a well dressed man waiting for me . . . and he was standing beside the manure pile. I noticed this starkly for two reasons. One was because he was almost the exact height of the manure pile—about 6 feet. Second, I wondered what the H--- a well dressed city-slicker was doing standing there and I thought, "How can he stand it?"

As I got closer I recognized him as my packaging salesman—an Irisher by the name of O'Reilly.

"What are you doing standing beside that outfit?" I said, "Doesn't the smell of it make you sick?"

"Sick, my neck", he replied, "I love it!" and he inhaled deeply and completely, closing his eyes as he did as though he were in a trance.

I looked at him suspiciously, trying to figure out what kind of a stunt he was pulling and I said, "Probably when you leave here you'll bring up last week's dinner but you're being brave just now."

"Naw" he said, "I love it. I was born on a farm and lived on a farm until I was about 15. I loved every day of it and long for it even now. I wouldn't be selling this stuff if I had my way. I'd be back there on the land where I belong. But you know how it is. I'm married and the closest my wife ever gets to a farm is when the milk man delivers a pint of milk and some butter . . . and that's as close as she ever wants to get to one."

"Well", I said, "If you went up north you could find yourself a squaw. From what I gather they have no aversions to farming—at least not yet!"

In my humble opinion, ladies and gentlemen, that in a neat pack age sums up the real reason why most men forsake the land. They give up doing the things their hearts and souls want to do. They scuttle their hopes and their aspirations and their dreams. Most women nowa days just won't live on the land. But hail, doff your hats and bend low to the occasional woman who still is willing to follow her man to the good earth.

On the other hand, can we blame those women who refuse to partake of the heavy burdens of farming? Are they being selfish or are the men selfish who want them to sell themselves to the drudgery of the land? You all can best answer this question for yourselves.

Many A Mickle Makes A Muckle

Are you the kind of an hombre that's thrift-minded . . . the kind that sort of wants to make a buck, save a buck and earn a buck? Well, if you're that kind of a man then I've got just the thing for you. Yes, by this method you can cut living costs, beat high prices, protect your home and save money.

How? No, no, you don't need a farm but you do need a good back-yard. In it you can have your own orchard wherein you grow some fruit, berries and then a good vegetable garden. Yes, it is an absolute fact that you can save up to $500 a year by growing your own fruits and vegetables. Naturally the bigger your family, the more you save—in truth, the more you need to save nowadays with a big family.

You'll probably save five times your investment the first year, especially if you grow a good stock of vegetables and then go into the small fruits. It will take 3 or 4 years before you get your money back on fruit trees but once they're planted they'll last you for a life-time. So you see that's a mighty, mighty good investment.

For instance, if you planted Rhubarb roots, next year you'd have Rhubarb. You'd get more value from it the first year than the price you paid for the root to begin with and you'd have beautiful fresh Rhubarb to start with. Yes, for less than the price that you would pay for one Rhubarb feed you will own your own Rhubarb probably for the rest of your life. The same applies to Asparagus. You go out and you pay 30c or 40c a pound for Asparagus. Well, for 40c you can have yourself about 10 roots and those roots will bear crops for you bigger and better every year for 20 long yielding years.

Say, how stupid can you get? What are you waiting for? Why don't you hurry up and get that garden planted? If you planted a horseradish root in the spring, by fall you'd be able to make all the horseradish you could eat—yes sir, and probably all your neighbors could eat, too. You know how long it will be there? Say, it will be there long after you're gone. No fooling—and I hope you're around for a heap long time too.

My Shield

Each and every one of us should have an aim in life. If not an aim, at least a philosophy or a rule book by which we live.

I've heard of and read various men's philosophy in life. So I thought that here I'd like to outline a little bit of my own philosophy. Maybe you'll like it and maybe you won't. Here it is for better or worse.

I believe in the Golden Rule. I believe in helping my fellow man to the best of my ability. I will not tell any man he is right when I know he is wrong. I believe in admitting my errors and transgressions. My loyalty to my friends will not diminish nor will I desert them because they have erred—but I'll not deny their error—and defend them and love them in spite of it.

I believe in living by the natural laws of the universe and I will not desert nature. I believe that the good Lord has endowed me with a set of organs which I require to live and I will not knowingly part with any organ in my body. In the event of an accident or dismemberment, this law is naturally waived.

I believe that a man should enjoy life to the utmost because we're a short time alive and a long time dead. But this joy in life must not be at the expense of any other human being. I further believe in enjoying all of life's pleasures—partaking of all of the things that life offers . . . all in moderation—none to excess.

I resolve never to be pompous or haughty. But on the other hand I will not be so humble as to allow anyone to walk over me or use me as a footstool.

I resolve to always face the truth and never to fool or hoodwink anyone and this means starting with myself. I believe in fighting for what I believe is just and right. If I fail to accept the challenge, then I have failed and no longer deserve the respect of my fellow man.

I believe that the system under which we live in this country is the best system offered by any nation or peoples in the civilized world. If I knew of better ways I would do all in my power to encourage my friends, neighbors and the peoples of my country to adopt them.

About Azaleas

I want to tell you a little bit about indoor Azaleas. There are two terms used in connection with these plants that you should know something about. First is "indica" or commonly referred to as Belgian Azalea.

Now this is actually supposed to be a Rhododendron, properly Rhododendron indicum. This has been crossed with many other species and varieties to give us the present Indicum Azalea. Mind you, the actual Rhododendron indicum is a late flowering type—most unlike the Indica Azalea that we use today for early flowering.

This species is actually a native of India and many varieties were introduced into Europe and the United States in the early 1800's from Japan. The great proportion of the breeding work on the Azalea was done in Belgium. It seems that the Belgians adopted this variety and have done a tremendous job in research, cross breeding and cultivation of this floriferous, colorful plant. Eventually they came up with what is now known as a Belgian Azalea or Indica.

Now the other type of Azalea that is in common use by the florist trade throughout America, yes, and even throughout the world is the Kurumes. They too, are true Rhododendrons descended from the Rhododendron obtusum japonicum. This was a native of Japan and bears the name Kurume because most of the finest varieties were developed around and near the city of Kurume.

This variety of Azalea was grown in that part of Japan for many, many years but, as it is a more or less isolated location, this wonderful Azalea never really became popular until early in the century when a man by the name of E. H. Wilson brought it to America in 1916.

The Kurume Azaleas are extremely dwarf in habit, very twiggy, compact and bloom exceptionally well when small. They're easy to force and simple to propagate from cuttings in sand and peat. They are generally used for forcing as pot plants. Not very many of them are grown outdoors, especially in the northern latitudes.

There are two kinds of Indicas. One is used for early and the other for late blooming. The early varieties are usually forced for Christnas or mid-winter, whereas the late ones are used for Easter, Mother's Day and early spring.

The outdoor Azalea is something quite different—much taller in growing habit and is known as Azalea mollis.

Why Soil Mulch Roses?

My fat face is red. Just finished expounding my theory about shallow planting when someone meekly asked me, "Well, how about Roses about which you advise they be mulched up 4, 5 or 6 inches or even completely covered with loose soil?"

Hold the lashes, folks. Don't beat me till I'm proven guilty. Let me emphasize there is a difference between planting deep and mulching shallow or deep.

I am a strong advocate of mulching in all phases but I still state there is a difference between deep planting and mulching.

In the first place I advise the mulching of Roses with loose soil only for late fall and early spring . . . not during the active growing period. Further, I stress this chiefly with Roses only because it seems that the bacterial action of the soil induces growth to Roses.

Now probably I'm a nut about this but here's my luny theory. An H.T. Rose, for example, is budded on a Multiflora root stock. True, they are both of the same family but fairly widely apart just the same.

The union between these two for some reason or other never seems to be one of these complete blood relationships. There is, I would say, a little incompatibility and this is evidenced by the many failures and the dying off of the top.

In dealing with Roses you will learn that it is the top that dies off while the root still remains strong and virile. In most plants when the top dies along goes the root too, but not with budded roses. So this lends evidence to my theory that it's sort of a step-son arrangement and that the root stock isn't so concerned about feeding, nourishing and taking care of the distant relative on top.

I can just hear the Multiflora rootstock. "So what if I don't feed him so well? If he dies I'll shoot out some of my own kin. They're tougher and they'll stand the going a lot better than those weak panty-waist Hybrid Teas anyway".

Therefore, come back with me to the basis of my philosophy. When soil is placed against the top and the graft of the Hybrid Tea Rose

127

. . . The Rose seems to revel in the fact that it is in contact with the good earth on its own and responds cheerfully and vigorously. But it is a positive proven fact that Roses do do better when mulched with soil until active growth starts.

Go ahead—say I'm as crazy as a loon . . . I'm happy that way!

Joy Killers

Ah, woe betide me—I moan—I groan—it seems they just won't leave Mother Nature alone. Soon they'll be interfering with our practices of procreation because they're already doing just that with flowers.

Without fear of contradiction I can say that in Holland they raise the largest proportion of all the Cyclamen seed in the world. Let me explain that Cyclamen is one of the most popular plants for Christmas and, I dare say, millions and millions of plants are grown. Practically all of them are started from seed. Thus, fresh crops of seed in huge quantities are required every year to meet the demand for this trade.

Well, it got so that the Dutch growers just couldn't depend upon the bees to give them proper pollination of the flowers to enable them to set seed. There was too much money invested in their crop to take a chance on something going wrong and resulting in no seed. So the very ingenious Dutch seed breeders came up with a new idea. They created an artificial bee.

The old method consisted of collecting the pollen of the flower on the thumbnail and carefully transferring this to the flower stigma with the aid of a camelhair brush.

As I've explained, this left too much to chance and the canny Dutch found a safer way, even if it means cheating the bee out of his fun and the flower out of its sexual orgy.

This artificial bee is a tiny electrical contraption which consists of a long flexible needle with an eye at the end and this is placed over the stamen. Then a slight electrical current which is given by a tiny battery vibrates the needle, thus shaking the pollen loose, yet not in any way damaging the flower. This work of pollination is usually done on a warm sunny day, mainly in the afternoon when the temperature in the greenhouse is quite high. At these times the best results and highest germination can be obtained.

Then they wait a week or ten days after the pollination process. If the work is done properly the flowers will start to drop their petals. This indicates that effective pollination has taken place.

Those plants which have not been fertilized can then be given the treatment over again.

In this way maximum results can be obtained every time without risk of missing.

A Pruning Chart for Roses

Follow these instructions carefully and you will get better results than you have ever had before from your Roses.

BUSH ROSES which include Hybrid Teas, Hybrid Perpetuals . . . As soon as danger of late frost has passed in the spring trim the rose bush back quite drastically. Of course remove all the weak, immature growth, damaged branches and such first. Then cut everything back to within two or three eyes of the base and about ¼ of an inch above the last eye and be sure that this last eye is facing outwards—not inwards. This will tend to give you a more open bush . . . better, larger and more colorful blooms.

HYBRID POLYANTHAS, DWARF POLYANTHAS, FLORIBUNDAS . . . For the first season cut the main stems back to within about 4 eyes from the base but in the following years limit your pruning to removing weak, broken, damaged or injured branches and cutting the rest of the bush back to approximately half its height.

CLIMBERS . . . For the first season little or no pruning should be done. Give your plant every chance to grow. Of course, if there is any unripened wood or poor weak growth, remove it too. But otherwise do no pruning the first season on your climbing Roses.

Never cut Climbers back drastically, no matter how vigorous they grow because if you do you may tend to create a reversion of the plant to a bush form and it will lose its climbing habit.

In order to keep your Climbing Rose in good condition and make for more and longer periods of bloom each year a few of the heavier branches should be cut back to about 15 inches from the ground. This will promote new growth and insure you a continuous supply of Roses.

I have seen good results obtained by pruning Roses in mid-summer—not later than mid-August. But don't trim too drastically at this time.

RAMBLERS . . . Trim back the newly planted Roses about 2/3 of their entire length—leaving about 8 or 9 eyes. Remember, this is only for the first season. For the future remove only the old wood and any weak shoots and do this as soon as flowering is finished. This will leave the new growth untouched, in good condition and eager to bloom the following year.

Wooden Buttons

If you walk out about two miles on the Lakeshore Road from Niagara, on the lake side, you will see an old, old, old Buttonwood tree. This species is properly known as Platanus acerifolia. It is also called the London Plane tree and sometimes Sycamore—not to be confused with the Sycamore of the Bible which is Ficus Sycamorus.

This is the tree that has the very, very unusual bark. I always describe it as being piebald or mottled. There are patches of silver and grey and other colors running up and down, along and around the tree from the base right up to the smallest limbs. This bark shreds or peels off, giving the tree a distinctive character unknown to any other tree.

These are long lived trees. I recall, some years ago at Niagara when they were restoring old Fort George they wanted to rebuild the fort as it stood in its pristine state about 200 years ago. So they located a tree of similar species, size and appearance and by means of heavy tree moving equipment, transferred it to its new location. This one landscape lifting or shifting job alone cost in excess of $5,000. It lived or I should say struggled, for two or three years and eventually gave up the ghost and died. That was a costly, I shouldn't say blunder, but it was a costly attempt.

Well, anyway, to get back to our original tree. You'll find it there . . . an old tree and a sturdy tree with an enormous girth. The strange thing about it is that it is mostly dead. Ninety per cent of its branches have either died or been killed for some reason or other. The dead branches still reach into the sky in profound supplication. But this tree struggles valiantly to live. It has shot out some leaves and a few branches on only one section of the entire tree. There you see it struggling so desperately to retain this little bit of life. I hope it makes it. I pray, that next year it is alive and that it will grow and bring forth new branches all around and regain its health and vitality.

It actually would be a tragedy to lose this wonderful old tree. Though 'tis covered with bumps, contusions, carbuncles and spavins, that remind one of a crockety old faithful horse bearing these hard knobs and usage signs, still it is a majestic specimen. No doubt about it, it was there when the Indians roamed and lived in its environs. It could be that many of the bumps and injuries came from their arrows or tomahawk cuts.

On other occasions I thought of the old barnacled tree as resembling an old female dinosaur with these buttons all over it that looked like teats.

No matter what I tell you about this or how I describe it, it will be inadequate. You couldn't visualize it until you got out here and saw it for yourself.

Discover These Roses

The time has come for us to talk about Climbing Roses.

Seldom does one read anywhere any information about this very talented or gifted member of the Rose family.

There are very few flowers in creation that give as much beauty, animation, and vividness to the landscape as one individual climbing Rose bush. They have so many uses. Their application is so wide and so varied that one could talk about them almost endlessly.

Probably the only Climbing Roses that have wide general acquaintance or acceptance are Paul's Scarlet, Blaze which is almost similar, New Dawn which is a pinkish-white, Dubloons, a sort of a yellow, and of course the old fashioned Dorothy Perkins in white, pink or even red. Probably that would be the extent of most people's knowledge of Climbing Roses.

Actually Dorothy Perkins should not have been mentioned in the same category as the others because its true habit is rambling rather than climbing, which means it spreads right and left rather than growing erect like the others.

But there's a new, vast field of Climbing Roses that to most people is unknown, unexplored and untried. Still that branch contains more generous beauty, more loveliness and profusion of bloom than the older types of Climbing Roses. Here I'm referring to Climbing Hybrid Teas. Actually they have attained a vigorous habit of growth that ranks them with the Climbers. No, it won't climb twelve or fifteen feet like some of the Climbing Roses will but it will climb or grow robustly to a height of 8 to 10 feet. The important thing is the quality, substance and coloring of these roses is so much better, so much more beautiful and finer than that of the other Roses that, in truth, it is well worth having even though the others may climb with greater vigor and alacrity.

Now in these Climbing Roses you have the finest quality of the Hybrid Teas for, in truth, they are in body, soul and fibre true Hybrid Teas. They're not one bit inferior to the best of the Hybrid Teas. Only they do grow more rampantly, and give you a greater profusion of flowers.

Therefore the scope now of Climbing Roses has been so enlarged as to be as wide as the horizon. Don't be afraid, jump into the field and select yourself some Climbing Roses that have these qualities I have outlined. Treat yourself to the best.

They have been lying asleep and neglected for too long. Step into the breech and enjoy their wholesome beauty, magnificent fragrance and enchantment.

How To Plant A Rose

Attention!—This is significant—more important than you probably realize—because it is in the planting of the Rose that you spell its life and bloom or its growth or doom.

Start off by mixing yourself some top soil and peat moss—that is remove the top soil from the spot you're going to dig and mix it half and half with peat. The rest of the depth of your hole put aside and, when your Rose is planted, you'll put this on top because we want the good top soil that is mixed with the peat to come in contact with the roots of the Rose. Be sure to do this.

When you're planting your Rose spread the roots in the hole and sift this mixture of soil and peat around it, covering slowly but absolutely firmly. This firming of the soil mixture around the roots is a prime necessity.

Here I offer my advice concerning the depth or planting level. The juncture of the graft and the root stock should just barely be covered with soil. It shouldn't be very much below the ground level—just barely covered so that the root and bud juncture is in direct contact with the soil and has the benefit of the soil bacterial action.

After you have finished planting firmly, mound soil up around the Rose as high as you can—yes, 5, 6, 8 or 10 inches high—a perfect mound even if it means covering the Rose until its nose doesn't even stick out. Allow this loose soil to remain around the Rose right up until the middle of May. Then and then only remove this soil mulch and do your trimming or pruning.

If the above planting technique on Roses is followed you won't lose one Rose out of 100 and if you don't follow it your losses will be much, much heavier. Remember this.

Let me add to the above—do not use fertilizer of any kind when setting out Roses. What you do after the Rose has become established is your own business but do not use fertilizer of any kind—organic or inorganic—when planting.

Peat moss mixed 50-50 with soil is the ideal planting medium.

Live and Learn

I was visiting with some friends the other day when one of them said to me . . .

"Well, now that many folks have begun to appreciate your writing and you've become a full fledged author with a couple of books to your credit, why not retire from the toil and drudgery of running a farm, greenhouse and nursery and devote yourself exclusively to writing?"

Boy, that speech made me feel like a million dollars. My spine just tingled with pride. My head floated in the air. I felt so good that I tried to reach around to my back to pat myself and to tell myself what a great guy I was.

I was going to shout three cheers and sing "He's a Jolly Good Fellow" when a horrible, horrible thought entered my head and I realized that that vision could never come true. My life could never be a life of pleasure-bent idleness.

I'm glad I realized it before retiring to stud and then having to learn the hard way that that was not the life for me.

All day long, practically every day, whether I'm working in the field, showing a customer around, puttering in the greenhouse or dictating in the office, I meet people and folks seek me out. Oft I'm "A fur piece in the hinterland" at the back "40" and there someone looms up who has walked all the way back a good half mile to flush me out.

Sometimes they catch me by surprise. Often I'm in the act of doing something or other and I'm awfully happy it . . . weren't a lady. Please remember chums, you should always whistle or hum a nice loud tune if you ever come out to find me at the back "40" . . . sort of sound a warnin'.

But the fact is that each and every day I meet folks, new folks, different folks, old ones, young ones, handsome ones, homely ones, thin-railed ones and pot-bellied ones. I talk to them and they talk to me and from these conversations I glean most of the tales I write.

Besides this there are a thousand and one chores that I have to do practically every day and in the act of doing them I learn something or recall an incident or something happens. This gives me a vessel into which to pour out my heart and soul.

Then if I were to devote myself to writing I would lose all that, and that is my inspiration, my life's blood, my very existence. So I guess you'll still find me here next month, next year and perhaps ten years from now, too, if the Good Lord is willin' and I'm deservin'.

Don't Water Your Lawn

Watering your lawn is not the answer to a beautiful well cared for, attractive lawn.

You don't believe me! Well, I didn't think you would because this statement is so revolutionary that I don't expect that very many people will accept it. Yet I can offer proof of my allegations.

Yes, sirree, I contend that the best lawns are not the ones that are watered the most. I contend that a lawn which means a carpet of grass on a piece of good soil, yes, on soil in good health and good tilth should not require watering more than once in 10 to 14 days.

If that is true, and I contend that it is, then nature usually provides a rain in our latitude once every two weeks. It is seldom that a fortnight will go by without some form of rainfall and if my premise is true then lawns seldom, if ever, need watering.

I will go along with you in that if we have a drought period when no rain falls for two weeks, and continues on for a period, that a good soaking would certainly be beneficial and of help to your grass.

But even without water for two or three weeks with your soil in good tilth and a good thick carpet of grass, your lawn should not be in a condition where it would be suffering.

I know what you're thinking to yourself, "Why, heck, if I didn't water my lawn every three or four days during summer, the darn thing would burn up."

Well, listen fella, if yours is the kind of a lawn that will burn up if it isn't watered for three or four days then it better burn up and it should burn up. You don't want that kind of a lawn and you certainly neglected both your grass and your soil if you are dependent upon that much water—or if you've made it dependent upon that much water.

No doubt if you have a lawn in a very sandy soil, it will require watering every day anyway during the hot period because as quick as you put water on it, it will either drain away or the sun will absorb it so you're really not helping it much to begin with. On the other hand if the lawn is good and thick and the soil is rich the sun's rays won't penetrate to the roots and harm it because a thick matting protects it. Then, of course, a humus laden soil won't allow the heat and the sun's rays to penetrate too quickly. Therefore your grass roots will live in comparative safety and happiness and they in turn will give a lovely green color to the leaves . . . which is the grass and your emerald carpet.

Sure enough, if your lawn is the kind of a lawn that has been built up on sand and doused with chemical fertilizers that only give stimulation without building up either the roots or the soil or anything else,, then probably you need to water it every day and maybe more often. But if you have followed the instructions or the convictions that I've tried to instil into you by creating a decent soil by means of a compost heap or peat moss or manure or other natural fertilizers, your lawn can and will do better without watering.

Let nature water your lawn!

Now while I'm on the subject a very important factor about maintaining the tilth in lawns is, cut your grass before it gets too long and leave the grass cuttings right where they fall. Cut it often, cut a little bit at a time and leave the clippings where they fall. They won't be unsightly. The only time they are unsightly is when they're long and then it looks as though you've got a hay crop on top of your grass— if that's the situation, buy a cow and get some milk, cream and cheese out of the deal!

Hidden Fragrance

I came into the office that night. The pleasing wholesome fragrance struck me clearly. It was about 1.30 a.m. What was I doing at the office at 1.30 in the morning? . . . Well, I'll tell you.

My wife had been out playing bridge and she got back about 12.30. So the kettle was put on and we had a cup of tea and by then it was 1 o'clock. The wife asked if I was going to bed and I said, "No, I'm going to sit up for another few minutes to finish up some work."

Then suddenly I remembered. (It was the 20th day of September and that was about the coldest Sept. 20th since records have been kept). The radio had warned in the morning and many times during the day that the thermometer was going to tumble that night, and I had started the stoker fed heating system. Hallo . . . quickly I realized that the hopper of coal would not last all night if the temperature dropped to 32 or below. So, lest the wife think that I had run off with a beautiful buxom blonde (I can dream, can't I?), I called up to her and told her I was going out to the nursery.

Well, it takes only about 7 or 8 minutes to cover the 5½ miles to the nursery. When I opened the door to the office a very pleasant odor struck me. I couldn't think what it was. I put on the lights and looked around . . . nothing there that would cause that pleasant odor! Then I walked into the bathroom and there I saw a handful of flowers that someone had stuck into a glass of water.

It was the Night Blooming Jasmine . . . a plant which in growing habit and the shape of the leaves resembles the Gardenia, except that the leaves are larger and it is much more robust. The flowers are but small. They're a long tube about an inch in length with a star-shaped single-eyed bloom at the end and white, but there are thousands of them on a plant and the perfume is simply wonderful. I don't know of anything that smells as pleasant or as sweet and every flower on each stem was open. There were hundreds and hundreds of them.

When I got back to work at 8 o'clock in the morning all of the flowers were closed tight, coiled up like a piece of paper rolled up. Now I know why it is called the Night Blooming Jasmine.

It's funny . . . I've had that plant on the premises for 3 or 4 years but in the back greenhouse mixed up with hundreds of other plants, and it was never noticed. But the minute the flowers were cut and put into a glass of water by themselves . . . then it really showed its true character.

Rise An' Shine

Have you ever been up at dawn and actually watched the sun rise in the east?

Maybe you won't believe this, but on the other hand, if you stop and think perhaps you will. I'll wager that not one person in a hundred has ever stood facing the east and watched the sun rise as it breaks above the horizon on a sunny summer morn . . . yes, or even in the spring, fall or winter.

No, it's not because we're lazy although that could be part of the answer—but because we're so busy, busy doing this, that and the other thing and probably nothing. But we don't get enough sleep as it is and therefore to waste a perfectly good few hours sleep just watching the old sun rise sounds ridiculous and foolish.

Well, sure we know Old Sol will rise in the east without us standing there to watch. Ah, shucks, the sunrise isn't very important but, doggone it, it would be awfully important if it didn't rise one day. Besides it's awfully important that it rise—at least to me and probably to many others like me.

Of what use would it be to tell you how glorious it is . . . how utterly fantastic and fabulous? You wouldn't understand. Unless you have actually witnessed the creation of a new day you couldn't believe it.

But let me try to phrase my feelings as I watch the dawn. I stand awed, humbled, tragically puny and worthless. There all the truths and realities of creation rise before me—slowly, deliberately, magnificently. 'Tis the bliss of creation, combining the thrill of action and the splendor of beauty.

Hist, yesterday was but an illusion—something that really never existed. It is only now . . . today that matters!

Ah, but today . . . today well and intensely lived becomes the joy of creation. Yesterday and tomorrow justly are illusions and visions. But today is here—we must find happiness, contentment and hope.

Even as this fresh day is being born one thinks of the morrow but it is but a vision that will blossom and burst into a blaze of bloom ere long.

Now back to my sun-up. It is life . . . and life is to be lived in any guise . . . a sparrow or a bird of paradise, a mole or an elephant, a beggar or a king. Each one should live life to its utmost, enjoy every instant, every breath until the sands of time run out.

The Beauty of a Rose

Have you ever tried to describe or to define the loveliness of a Rose? If you haven't, lend an ear and see what I can do.

It is a flower whose matchless beauty rivals the sun for majesty of brightness. Its grace, its form, its rapturous elegance have beguiled man for countless centuries. Its texture, its symmetry combine nature's lightest touch with its grandest image. There is no work of art, no matter in which field you search, that could give anything that matches the sublime beauty of a Rose.

Is there anything, flower or creation of any kind, that can equal the coloring, the hues, the tints, the shades that are to be found in this glorious flower? It has freshness, splendour, dignity and ornamentation. It has the blush of a virgin, the incomparable excellence of shining youth.

Remember a Rose is not only a Rose when 'tis full blown, but examine it in bud . . . as the tightly contained gemmule begins to swell and slowly open, one sees promise of things to come—heart warming anticipation, so fine, so sublime like the glow of tender childhood.

Was not a maiden's blush borrowed from the Rose?

Now here I've said all these glorious things about the flower and yet I've never even mentioned fragrance. The perfume of a Rose

137

overcomes men's minds. It mesmerizes their senses. It creates love and rapture—it exhilarates—it uplifts—it exudes a sense of well-being and contentment. It is not only the flower of the beloved but also the flower of those who would be loved and, too, of those that do the wooing.

Yet the scent of a Rose is never overpowering, never too brazen or too bold, but always soft and sweet and when the dew is on a Rose then Heaven has done its utmost to give mankind its grandest flower and scent. It is flowerdom at perfection. It has superlative form, bathed in diamond studded drops of dew—lavished upon it by nature to the Nth degree.

'Tis the glory of the earth—the pride of the sun! The Epitome of Nature!

Ha, Ha! . . . Surprise, Not Laughter

A pert young miss walked into the office a few days ago and said, "Mr. Tobe, have you ever heard of the term 'ha-ha' and do you know what it is?"

"Why, yes ma'am," I said, "I sure do and if you'll take a seat for a moment I'll be glad to tell you all about it."

She did and here's what I told her. It seems that the "ha-ha" is an English creation. Evidently it came to light in the fertile mind of an English landscape man. Probably you know that the English country scenes are the most beautiful or enchanting scenes found anywhere in the world. For sheer beauty, hominess and pastoral charm it's hard to beat the English countryside.

Now unless you have some domestic animals around a country estate you would never know it was a country estate. Grass, a house and a few trees do not constitute a lovely natural country setting. There must be animals in it. But if you've got animals like cows, horses, goats, pigs, chickens, and such then they'll wander all over your lawn and in all probabilities stay as close to the house as possible . . . and that wouldn't be very nice. It's bad enough to have to push a cow or a pig out of your way when you want to get from one place to another but if you trod on a soft, squashy, squeegy mess your feeling would not be one of exultation and delight. So the domestic animals have got to be kept out.

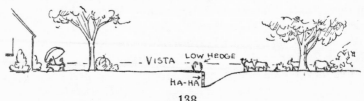

Of course you could use a fence but at best, most fences become unsightly and there's a lot of up-keep concerned with them, too, apart from the restricted confined atmosphere they create. Besides, these larger animals like horses and cows have a habit of just busting them down, too, and probably horses, goats or even a cow might leap them.

No, you've got to have something better than this. You want the animals in view but under control for the perfect country setting so this bright boy (there's an argument as to who he was—some folks say it was a landscape genius called Capability Brown and other people say it was Humphrey Repton, a well known landscape designer) really came up with a 'humdinger' of an idea. He dug a ditch along the boundary separating what he wanted to be the home grounds and the part where he wished to confine the animals.

Now this ditch had a sheer wall coming down from the home side from 5 to 6 feet deep and then from here on it angled up like a ramp —something like a right angled triangle. This meant that it was an impassable barrier which the animals could not overcome and yet was not noticeable or apparent until you came up to it. Thus, from all sides and directions the scene appears to be one of continuous expanding beauty—no fences and yet the cattle stay where they belong and all is serene.

It actually is a form of boundary, sunken wall or ditch below the ground level. How the name came about can easily be conjectured. Probably someone who marvelled at the control and wonderful habits of the animals in keeping to their own premises, was walking jauntily and suddenly came upon this ditch and I can just hear him ejaculate —"Ha-ha!"

Likeable Lichens

I never quite understood the value or the significance of Lichens on a tree. Now I'm told that the appearance of Lichens on trunks and branches of trees indicates evidence of a pure atmosphere. They claim that you seldom if ever, see Lichens growing on the trees in the city.

Can't recall that I ever have seen Lichens on trees in the city and what's more, I'll say that I seldom, if ever, saw Lichens on trees in the country either. Unless one goes pretty well into the deep bush, at least hereabouts, one cannot find Lichens on the trees.

Anyway, Lichens are actually a combination of algae and fungii. No, they are not parasites nor do they prevent air from getting into the trunk of the tree and cause mildew and other troubles.

Now I don't know whether Lichens are particularly attractive on trees. I think that some folks would regard them as being unsightly.

Whenever I've seen Lichens growing on trees I felt there was something wrong with either the tree or the air circulation and even considered the problem of a moisture condition. From now on I'm going to pay a little more attention to the Lichens on the trees. I've gathered Lichen moss for years and we've used it for covering the wires that show up on the Ming trees that we used to make.

If you really want to see Lichens on trees go down to the coastal areas of California where you have a dense foggy atmosphere almost continuously (when it isn't raining). You also see it very noticeably around Tillamook in Oregon where they get more rain than they do anywhere else in America I think.

Boy, the luxuriousness of the foliage down there is hard to imagine unless you've actually seen it. Lichens thrive in a great variety of kinds, colors and tones.

Lure of the Land

I heard this story and it struck a sort of vibrant cord in my make-up. It sort of made me feel smiles all over.

It's about Tolstoy, the famous Russian writer and philosopher. He came across a peasant plowing in the fields. He watched him for some time. Then when the peasant approached him guiding his plow, he

waved him to a halt and said, "If you knew that you were to die tomorrow what would you do now?"

The peasant wiped the sweat from his hot brow, looked straight at Tolstoy and replied, "I would plow".

I don't know if you ever felt the peaceful assurance that comes with working on the land. How can one explain something that exists only in spirit? . . . something intangible? . . . something that one cannot feel with the hands?

When I've got bundles of bills to pay and no money to pay them with, when there are hundreds of orders to ship and I can't get them shipped, when there are hundreds of things to do and I can't get them done, I can always find comfort, yes, and peace too by sitting on the tractor and plowing or disk-harrowing a field. The earth doesn't have any smell or odor yet we say when the plow throws open a furrow it smells good, invigorating, like life being recreated.

When I tell my crew that I'd rather work in the fields than do anything else in the world they look at each other knowingly and smirk or smile in obvious disbelief. They think it's malarky to kid them or the unsuspecting public. Little do they know that it is the simple, unadulterated truth. I'd sooner work on the land spring, summer and fall and, if possible even in the winter than do anything else in the world. Perhaps you understand.

Gardiner was a Gardener

A chap by the name of Richard Gardiner of Shrewsbury in Shropshire was, I gather, the first seedsman and nurseryman. At least he's the first guy who ever had the courage or audacity or whatever you might call it to print a catalog.

Way back 350 years ago he put out a little book of 39 pages devoted exclusively to vegetables. Now this fellow really wasn't a seedsman by profession. He was a linen-draper but he liked to garden and he took to selling vegetables and vegetable seeds and eventually he published what is supposed to be the first seed catalog on record. It was "imprinted" at London by the firm of Edward Allde for Edward White and the establishment was located at "the little North doore of Paules at the Sign of the Gunne, 1603".

You see—even in those days seedsmen and nurserymen were considered to be nasty individuals—"the great and abominable falsehoods of those stories of people which sell Garden seedes", and considered "Many thousand poundes are robbed yearley from the Common

Wealth by those Caterpillers," whom he advised to "have a care to sell in reason and conscience."

His favourite "kitchin" garden items were obviously lettuce and carrots. It wasn't that he liked carrots so much but he felt, "Carrets are good to be eaten with salt fish. Therefore sowe Carrets in your Gardens, and humbly praise God for them, as for a singular and great blessing; so this much for the use and benefit had in the commonwealth by Carrets. Admit if it should please God that any City or towne should be besieged with the Enemy, what better provision for the greatest number of people can bee, than every garden to be sufficiently planted with Carrets?"

You know I sort of like this guy Gardiner, I wish I could learn more about him. He was quite a boy. He'd fit well into our modern way of things.

Become A Famed Hybridizer

How would you like to cross-breed your own African Violets and raise some sensational, new, glamorous, wonderful, stupendous and amazing plants? Who knows?—Perhaps you'll even get a yellow one out of it but I doubt it.

Now here's how you do it. Follow me carefully and don't get lost. The African Violet flower contains 2 pollen sacks that face each other and by all appearances seem to be stuck together. Carefully cut these 2 yellow sacks from the bloom, hold them over a piece of white paper and pull them apart. From the pollen sacks grains finer than dust will scatter over the paper. Put a crease in the paper and shake all the pollen into the crease. Then get yourself a glass phial, vial or test tube with a cork in it and shake the pollen into this container.

Then get yourself a very, very fine paint brush . . . they usually say a camel's hair brush, and brush the pollen grains that you have gathered into the stigmas that you want to cross-pollinate on the other flower. In case you don't know what a stigma is, it is the top of the fine threadlike appendages like an antenna that sticks up well above the pollen sacks.

Now this is no job for folks who haven't got patience but it is so rewarding that you will be happier and more pleasant to live with if you partake of this hobby.

In order to be sure that you get pure crosses we advise this procedure. First decide on the plants that you want to breed together. For instance if you have a red one and a white one and you want a cross between the two just as soon as the buds appear on your plants cover them with a piece of polyethelene or cellophane bag. This will prevent chance pollination.

Then follow the procedure outlined above, removing the bag from the plant only long enough to effect the breeding process by means of the brush.

Now when you become famous and are known universally as a great hybridizer, remember old Tobe down in Niagara taught you how to do it.

Atomic Gardening

If you believe all the advertisements you read in the magazines and newspapers you'll get to the state where you'll visualize yourself in a garden bedecked with flowers, trees, fragrant scents, a lawn shaved to a fraction of an inch of the desired heights, no insects or bugs, no fungus or disease.

Well, you can imagine yourself just sitting there and doing nothing. That's Paradise I'm told. If it is, you can have it. I'll take the other place.

Is that what everybody wants out of life? . . . A garden where you just sit on your fanny and breathe in the surrounding beauties? That's not my type of gardening. If the sign of a weed appears there, you just squirt it with P.X.T. Then you dust off your hands and that's finished. If that beautiful flower appears to be fading you give it a shot of A.T.Z. and the flower is again as fresh as it was the first day it opened. Then if a bug should attack your favourite vegetable you release your special atom exterminator and your food is safe from that marauder but probably is filled with death-dealing atomic rays. If you look up at the sky and say, "no, no rain today", you press a button and a beautiful light Heavenly rain begins to fall from concealed pipes. Of course your grass won't grow more than an inch and three quarters because you've used that marvelous new growth inhibitor. You don't have to dig because that was done away with, oh, long ago. You just drop a few bits of Kilicum on your soil, turn on the sprinkler and your soil is as soft and textury as a baby's face. You plant your seeds perfectly prepared and pelletted. In fact, you don't plant them. You just drop them into appointed places and they grow.

There's only one thing missing. They haven't got anything thought up yet to harvest your crop and to eat it for you . . . but be patient, that will come. Push Button Gardening is wonderful!

Careful How You Say It

I have discovered the beauty of Episcias and I want to share my discovery and pleasure with you.

I started growing them about four years ago. I brought in 100 plants on three occasions and lost every one of them. No one, not even the rankest amateur, could reach a record like that. I gave them up.

Then I went to visit a friendly competitor of mine one day and she had one of them growing. It was beautiful. She said it was the easiest thing to grow she had in the place. I was ashamed to tell her how poorly I had fared so I resolved to try again and now we have more Episcias and more varieties than anyone in America.

My trouble was chiefly that the plants were chilled enroute and a chill spells death to these plants. They will stand almost anything else . . . heat, humidity, sunshine, most any type of soil, but not the cold. They do best, however, when the soil is damp and the surroundings hot and humid.

The soil in which we grow them is almost pure peat mixed with compost and sand.

You have heard of them probably as the Flame Violet and that name is very appropriate, but I found there are other colors besides red. Now, mind you, this red is a real red or scarlet, not like the plum or wishy-washy reds you find in African Violets. So far, in African Violets, a half decent red has never been discovered and some folks are betting it never will.

At first I didn't think they bloomed as profusely as African Violets but I have changed my mind. I think in a given period you will have more flowers on Episcias than on African Violets.

The foliage of an Episcia is far superior to that of an African Violet. There isn't any comparison. In my opinion, and I say it with a full understanding of what I am saying, it is one of the finest foliated plants that I have ever seen—in texture, quality, color, sheen and loveliness. It is pretty hard to find its superior.

I have checked through the horticultural books and none of them list more than five varieties. I don't know why or how but we have

6 distinct varieties. Two of them are light green but in one of them the foliage is very shiny and has a silver cast. Both have real red flowers.

Then we have two with deep green foliage and silver or phosphorescent skeleton-like etchings along the veins. Both have orchid blue flowers that rival an orchid, for exquisite daintiness. The flowers last but a few days but then there are others opening or ready to open. Each individual flower is a jewel. You will appreciate it very much.

Now the other two varieties I have never seen bloom. One is supposed to have a yellow flower so I am waiting and I will tell you about it as soon as mine eyes have beheld that joyful sight.

There are coming on the market shortly some new varieties grown from hybridized seed. Watch for some sensational offerings.

'Tis A Fairy Tale Come True

It brought joy into my heart and maybe it will do the same for you.

A rose is a lovely thing. Even the plainest Rose is still a thing of gracious beauty and loveliness.

When we come to Hybrid Teas there we see Roses in their full glory . . . graceful shape, glorious colors, divine fragrance and a freshness that rivals the rising bursting sun. I know of no flower that exceeds the Rose in beauty.

Do you like the huge full-petalled Roses? Or do you like the medium, slender, graceful ones? Ah, but there is another—the Fairy Rose as it is best known—but it is also called Midget, Dwarf and Alpine.

Now look, we're talking about true Roses—not just a relative or a kinsman but a true rose. It is every bit as much a Rose as the Hybrid Tea, the Moss or the Centifolia.

You know there's something about a diminutive person that accentuates cuteness and beauty. You know of girls—the big ones have to act like ladies always, whereas the little girls can do most anything and get away with murder because of their size. They can say things and do things that are considered cute, whereas if a big girl did it you'd think she was a clown. So it seems that beauty is intensified when it is small and it's just like that with the Fairy Rose.

Now a true miniature Rose must not exceed 12 inches in height and the flowers cannot be any larger than 25¢ pieces.

Here's a distinct advantage that the Fairy Rose has over all other Roses . . . Its flowering fashion—it blooms continuously from May till the end of October—yes, and longer, too. You can use them in so many different places in your garden and what a remarkable potted plant they make.

Now let me tell you something about their origin. They're supposed to be a dwarfed variety of the well known China Rose and the true proper name is Rosa Chinensis minima. It was first grown in England in 1815 and a drawing of it appeared in Curtis's Botanical Magazine. Another one was reported in 1821 and still another in 1837, and isn't it strange that for the next 100 years there was little or no word heard of these Dwarf Roses?

Then along came a Frenchman—a soldier by the name of Major Roulet and he found a tiny pink Rose growing in a pot in a home in a Swiss village. The owner claimed that this tiny Rose had survived the avalanche that had destroyed a nearby village where many of these tiny Roses could be found. He went about having the variety propagated and it was called Rosa Rouletti.

The Fairy Rose is easier to grow than most Roses. They do like open sunny locations but do quite well in partial shade. Do not plant them close to a hedge or wall. They like a nice rich loam and they'll do well in clay but just give them plenty of humus. For a rock garden they are unsurpassed. Isn't that one of the troubles most folks with a rockery have in that they cannot maintain a succession of bloom during the summer and early fall? Well the Fairy Rose takes care of that situation to perfection.

You can use these little Roses in beds and borders and as edging plants. They look splendid planted in the proximity of a garden ornament. They like very little pruning . . . just a matter of removing the older and worn wood in the early spring.

You can grow them indoors during the winter and they'll flower freely for you. They like lots of light and a temperature of 55 to 60 degrees and they'll respond to liquid manure.

If you haven't had one of these beauties then I envy the joy that can and will be yours.

From Late August Till November

Most of us don't realize it but folks living in the northeast part of the North American continent see colors that are found nowhere else in the world. I have learned that the gorgeous fall colorings that are found in Eastern Canada and in the New England and Northeastern States cannot be duplicated anywhere else on the globe.

Frankly, I believe that we do not appreciate our fall beauty. Sure we have nice springs and summers too and lots of beautiful flowers

I doubt if I've ever met a person who said they liked a skunk.

I believe skunks and snakes are the two most misunderstood animals n the world. Of the two I guess I would sooner take the skunk, smell ind all, yet a snake is a clean, quiet, beneficial animal too.

Actually they're both helpful to man. In fact they're among the nost beneficial animals of all. They're natural enemies because a kunk will kill a snake if he can.

Upon examining the stomach of a skunk found killed on the high-vay it was found that his innards were chuckfull of adult grasshoppers. There were more than 300 lawnleapers in his stomach at the time. During the period of the year when grasshoppers are most plentiful hese polecats live almost exclusively on a diet of these hoppers. They atch most of them during the night when they lie still in the grass. don't know how the cats locate them but they do and the hoppers an't get away because the cool evenings sort of render them immobile.

Of course I don't expect you city folks to like skunks. They really an't do you much good but they can and do benefit your friend the armer and I've never seen a farmer run around the country hunting kunks. Occasionally if a skunk insists on being a marauder and de-nands a luxurious chicken-a-la-king diet then friend farmer goes a gun-toting hunting for the guilty skunk and fills him full of buckshot.

I should mention here that skunks devour mice galore—field mice, neadow mice, baby mice, etc.

Don't regard nature's controls lightly. If it weren't for skunks and nakes the damage to field crops by mice and other animals would run o staggering figures and here it concerns you in the fact that you'd bay a heck of a lot more for your groceries. So every time you go into a supermarket to buy your heaping baskets full of groceries say to your-self, "Nice skunky, nice skunky, nice skunky—if it weren't for you I'd be paying a lot more for these 'vittles' ".

The Difference is Astounding

A friend of mine asked me if I could come down to their home and ake a look at their evergreen planting and give them some advice. I lon't get a chance to do this very often but this was a special friend ind it was close to home so I got there.

What I saw was what had been a few years ago a beautiful plant-ing . . . but it had outgrown its setting and drastic action was needed.

This house was a one storey affair, built rather low . . . a white house with bevel siding, on a small lot.

"Well", I said, "My advice is to pull the whole works out. Just leave those 2 Picea Conicas and 2 Mugho Pines at the edges of the entrance and I'll suggest a variety of material that will not outgrow its surroundings for at least 10 years".

"Now", I said, "if you'll root these things out tomorrow morning, then get out to the nursery, you can have the new material in within an hour because only 12 Evergreens are required altogether."

This was done and the transformation was like magic . . . actually astounding and bewildering. From gawky, sprawling, misplaced Evergreens there was now a neat, tidy and beautiful arrangement that blended the grounds and the house into a beautiful picture of harmony and naturalness.

If you don't believe me, I ask you to come out some day and I'll drive you down to this new creation and let you be the judge. This planting is well worth seeing. I'm not going to tell you what I took out but here's what I put in its place . . . Hicks' Yew at the corners, then a Brevifolia Yew, followed by a Hemlock, then a dwarf Birds Nest Spruce and then as the "piece de resistance" a Dwarf Spreading Kosters Blue Spruce and, of course, there were the Dwarf Picea Conicas that are cone-shaped and the Mugho Pine that were left there, too.

Now if you know of a finer Evergreen planting for a small home I challenge you to show it to me.

The Story of the Silk Worm

'Tis a fabulous tale.

This tiny insignificant insect has been kept working, building clothes for human beings, for 5,000 years. It is the world's greatest and oldest slave traffic.

In its native state it was found in the Himalayas but if these enslaved silkworms were put back in their native habitat they would quickly starve or perish because man has done everything for them for so many years that they would not know how to look after themselves.

Strange to relate also, it is no longer found anywhere in the world in its native state. By man it is protected against heat, cold, rain, snow and disease and fed by hand.

This is the fellow that feeds on Mulberry leaves. During its short life cycle it eats more than 4,500 times its weight.

The eggs, smaller than the head of a pin, are artificially hatched.

During the season that the Mulberry leaves are feeding the larvae, the worm increases in size so fast that 8 weeks after hatching it has grown to be 2 inches long. In 45 days the silk-worm reaches maturity.

When the larva is full grown it stops eating and hunts an elevated place to spin its cocoon. There, in the rearing house, brushwood branches are provided. In order to prevent the spinning of double cocoons ample space is provided to eliminate crowding.

In 3 to 4 days the insects complete their thick, oval, white or grayish cocoons which measure slightly under an inch in length. For commercial use the cocoons are collected and the pupa killed by dropping the cocoon in boiling water. Sometimes they're placed in a hot oven. In this way the bursting of the shell by the fully developed moth is prevented.

Then the thread is unwound and often one measures more than 1,000 feet in length.

Now, let's go back and look at those that haven't been cooked, but are kept for breeding. In the pupal stage it has fasted for more than 2 weeks but as soon as it develops into a moth the insect's first desire is for a mate and not for food as one might expect. Amid a wild, rapid vibrating of wings, but yet with all 6 feet on the ground, the cocky little male starts out on its final adventure. A strut brings him to a waiting female. During the mating period neither of the lovers eat, nor will they ever eat again.

In its adult form the male silkworm moth is a delicately beautiful object of nature—winged and perfect in every way. Actually the silkworm, although it has perfectly well constructed wings, does not fly. It has been so pampered by man that it has lost its strength and need for flight. This, of course, is an advantage to the commercial grower for they do not have to watch the silkworm as it doesn't roam about and can be easily handled.

The female silkworm lays about 300 smooth white-yellow eggs which are deposited on a mulberry leaf. After this she lives only a day or two.

Everything has been done to breed the silkworm to the highest stage of productivity with the least amount of effort. It is now harmoniously adapted to unrestrained captivity . . . breeds readily and the young mature quickly . . . all this has been accomplished by breeding many races of silkworms. Breeders have even improved various strains for color, quantity and quality. In China the silkworm moths have produced as much as 100,000,000 lbs. of raw silk in one year.

Wonders Never Cease

It looks as though the art of agriculture, horticulture, farming or whatever you might call it has reached the end of its tether. No, I'm not kidding. I'm being quite serious and truthful.

There's a magazine I read called "World Crops". It's a good magazine—strictly on the up and up—and it reports the happenings and developments of agriculture in every country of the world. In it they had an article describing a miracle machine and this machine is now being used in Texas. It is reported and it is borne out that the machine cuts the work of the old farmer by 90%. In other words it can do in a month what the average farmer does in a whole year.

Here I'm going to give you some of the pertinent facts about this wonderful machine. It is called a Wonsover and is diesel operated, but is not self-propelled—being drawn by a tractor. The various implements are put into operation through a portable panel of electric switches which are attached to the towing vehicle and controlled by the driver.

It is 24 feet long and combines the following: plough, harrow, conditioner, seeder and fertilizer—all in one single operation. As an example, this machine planted one complete acre of potatoes in a single operation that required only 20 minutes. Now if this operation were done by standard methods it would have taken approximately 3 days.

At the front of the machine are 2 bins—one for lime or fertilizer or both and the other for chemicals to kill weeds or insects. By flicking a switch the machine spreads these uniformily over the ground.

Behind comes the rotary blades that dig, toss and mix the soil and the chemicals spread in front. This is all done to a depth of 10 inches. The soil is broken up in the process to a fluffy consistency. Another blade levels the soil.

Then a sub-soiler bores down as deep as 25 inches to help improve the distribution of moisture. Now behind the sub-soiler is a seed bay and apparatus which drops the seed in proper quantities and at the required spacing and the fertilizer can be applied at the same time.

An arrangement on wheels at the end of the machine packs down the soil over the seed. The wheels have a notched pattern in their tread which prevents erosion and retains moisture.

Then the last contraption is an outfit that sprays the area prepared, tilled and seeded with a weed killer to prevent freshly blown weed seeds from germinating.

This outfit can move at a speed of 5 to 15 miles an hour. Now there's one additional advantage this machine has. It even uses the

healthier, happier and handsomer. Now I'm pretty happy and I'm pretty healthy but handsomer—that's what I could stand being—but good.

So they gets my buck and I gets me a couple of packages of so-called tea. I follows their directions and brews me up a concoction and I taste it and it's good! It looks like tea, it smells like tea and even tastes like tea except that it has a little better bouquet and a more exhilarating effect. I've noticed lately that all the gals are shinny-ing up to me. So therefore I know I must be getting handsomer, too.

So I went and searched for some information about this tea and here's what I found out. The South American Indians were the first to discover that this miracle herb gave them added strength and en-durance. When the Spanish explorers came to America they tried it and also felt its invigorating and strengthening effects. It's been used for centuries by the natives, the gauchos of the Pampas and the settlers.

Jeepers, today it is distributed all over the world. They claim with authority that it is more stimulating than tea or coffee and contains a heck of a lot less tannin than either of these beverages.

Stay! This is very important. Yerba Mate contains more chloro-phyll than either green or black tea. You know that's the stuff that makes your breath "kissing sweet" and if you're going to be handsomer then this is what you need.

Searching further, I find that authorities claim that this tea produces mental exhilaration, body comfort and refreshment, but, please let me emphasize, with no subsequent organic or physical destruction. It is a first class stimulant for the muscles, nerves and brain. It facili-tates digestion without affecting the heart or disturbing sleep, because of its soothing effect on the nervous system.

Here's an interesting item about it too.

They say Yerba Mate has properties that lessen the sense of hunger without the fattening elements. Under stress and strain Yerba Mate can be used temporarily as a substitute for solid foods.

Ah-ha—how do you make it? Well, it's made just like ordinary Chinese Tea. It can be served hot or iced. You can sweeten it if you like but use honey, rather than sugar. You can flavor it with a dash of cinnamon or lemon. I like mine neat (not tidy).

We Tangle With Epiphyte

Well, according to the diction book this actually means "a plant that grows on other plants". But the word is also broadened to include all air plants or tree perchers.

According to the botanists, an epiphytic plant is an air plant or organism with unusual root systems, not readily adapted to deep or other penetrations. These often have thick, fleshy, white, corky, light roots.

For sure these air plants or epiphytes are quite common in the tropical areas but are extremely scarce in the Temperate Zones.

Here's an important note that you want to get into your head. Actually an epiphytic plant lives on another plant but it does not live from the other plant. It is positively in no way a parasite. It accepts nothing and takes nothing from its host, but an address or a fixed abode.

Actually speaking, this plant is in a better position to provide for itself than is its host. Why? . . . Because upon it has been bestowed the extremely rare power to create or get food and water from the air.

If you imagine that this is a mean feat, stop and consider—see if you can find another plant or group of plants on the face of the earth that have this God-given power. I might add that the only other plants of my aquaintaince in this category are a few Bromeliads.

Hie yourself to the jungle. The closest jungle we can find is that which is located in Central America. That is where Orchids are found in great abundance and variety. Orchids are seldom, if ever found on the jungle floor—although conditions on the jungle floor are ideal for many, many plants. The reason is that the Orchid requires light and in that impenetrable jungle, light is something that the plants on the ground seldom get. So that is the chief reason that this plant perches on a limb or tree as high up as it can get.

Invariably you will find them growing in areas where the humid, moist breezes come off the ocean and they can absorb as much moisture as they want. Some of the finest Orchids are found where the rainfall or heavy mists are almost continuous. There are few places in the world where this condition prevails. I know it happens down in Ecuador anyway.

In the tropical parts of the world you'll find Orchids perched on telegraph poles, on wires and even in the eaves of homes.

Now to the ways and means of this special power or apparatus . . . Science has given it the name of velamen. This is the white or greenish outer covering of the aerial roots of many of our tree-perching Orchids and other Epiphytes. This velamen has the rare faculty of being able to condense, absorb and use the atmospheric moisture and turn it into the required food and drink for the plant. The word "velamen" actually means "a membrane like a veil or a curtain". What a veil or curtain that is!

The Epiphytes don't seem to want the direct light. It is the filtered or indirect light that they get through the trees that suits them best.

Their roots are known to grow upwards as well as downwards where they can cling and get a firmer hold on another limb or branch to increase the security of their position.

The Epiphyte usually has other means of protecting itself and storing food. As well as thick roots, they often have bulbs, pseudo bulbs and thick heavy leaves.

The roots often have a contact with the humus-containing medium or the humus itself but seldom do these aerial roots ever live in or contact the soil.

Plant Explorers

Without getting involved too deeply I am going to tell you a little about the fellows who search for plants. These are the fellows who are chiefly responsible for the introduction of all those wonderful plants that we know today.

Of course you all know that most of the plants, in fact the best of the horticultural material that has been introduced and that we use in America and the west generally, came from China. The rest of Asia is also very notable in their contribution of good plants. I'm afraid the contributions of the rest of the world all together don't even closely stack up against the contributions of China and Asia alone.

I think that Robert Fortune was the greatest of all the plant explorers. You see when he did it, it was something new and he did risk his life with practically every step that he took in China. White people at that time were "persona non grata".

So here in one quick list I'm going to give you the names of the explorers, the country of their birth and the area in which they travelled or explored, and some of the plants which they are credited with discovering:

1. Robert Fortune (Scotland) travelled in China—Abelia, Deutzia, Forsythia, Jasmine, Honeysuckle, Bleeding Heart, Chinese Holly.
2. Ernest H. Wilson (England) travelled in China, Japan, Korea, Formosa, South Africa, Australia, New Zealand and India—Kolkwitzia, Dove Tree, Regal Lily, Buddleia, Korean Box.
3. George Forrest (Scotland) travelled in China—Fairy Primrose, Chinese Gentian, Yunnan Crab, Forrestii Fir.
4. Reginald Farrer (England) travelled in China and Burma—Farrer Aster, Viburnum fragrans, Farrer Gentian, Fountain Buddleia.
5. Frank Nickolas Meyer (Holland) travelled in China, Manchuria,

Korea, Caucasus, Turkestan, Siberia—Chinese Elm, Actinidia, Cherry Laurel, Chinese Hawthorn.

6. David Fairchild (United States) travelled in Dutch East Indies, South Seas, Japan, China, Africa, Australia, New Zealand, West Indies, South America and Central America—Soy Bean (Japan), Tung Oil Tree, Dates, Nectarine, Rhodes Grass, Flowering Cherries.

7. James Veitch (England)—Because he was a nurseryman and an able business man, the writers give little information about him. I am delving further.

8. Jos. Rock (Austria) travelled in Burma, Assam, Siam, China—Chaulmoogra Tree (2 kinds), Drooping Anemone, Lilium Davidi, Incarvillea.

9. F. Kingdon Ward (England) travelled in China and Tibet—Wintergreen, Cotoneaster, Mecanopsis betonicifolia baileyi (Blue Poppy), Ward Rhododendron, Campanula calcicola.

You will note that two of them were Scotsmen, four of them were English and there was one Austrian, one American and one Dutchman to make up the list.

I know this list is not complete and probably I'm leaving out a lot of mighty good men. But these folks are the ones who discovered most of the plants that we know of today.

The thing I'd like to do more than anything on earth is travel about the world hunting in more or less inaccessible places for new and wonderful plants for everybody.

Horticultural Benefactors

Let's know something of our friendly but misunderstood animals.

Yes, even the lowly rattlesnake is a great controller of rodents and insects. It is estimated that a snake on a farm is worth $40.00 annually as a pest destroyer.

Of course we know that the skunk eats his own weight several times a week in crop-destroying moths, grasshoppers, slugs, grubs, snails, gophers and mice but he does eat a few berries and vegetables and occasionally he likes a chicken dinner. But he earns this many times over. It is also established that a skunk never kills for fun. It's only to appease his hunger.

Bats, much as we fear or dislike them, are about one of the most harmless animals on the earth. They have never been known to attack a human being. They feed entirely on the night-flying insects which they capture in flight. It is stated that they will eat half their weight in insects in one day. They have ravenous appetities and a great portion of their food is made up of mosquitoes. I'm cheering for the bats!

Old Mr. Toad everybody knows and sees, and many fear, although I can't understand why. He really does a good job of keeping down the insect population. Sure he's not very handsome and has got warts all over him but that's no reason to dislike and mistreat him. It is estimated that he eats well over 10,000 garden insects in one summer. He does all this by means of a long flat sticky tongue which he lashes out like an elastic band and catches cut worms, chinch bugs, grubs, caterpillars, mosquitoes, potato bugs, beetles, spiders, ants and other pests. They even brought toads from Argentina to Florida to help combat the sugar cane beetle and the toad licked that situation up in a hurry to everyone's satisfaction.

Moles are generally misunderstood animals. I know for a fact that gardeners as a rule don't like them because they seem to burrow holes in the most unlikely places and obviously in their path they cut roots, but the fact is that they're burrowing and seeking for food which happens to be our insect pests. So what if they do cut off a couple of roots now and then? They're doing a lot less damage than the insect would do. A mole, too, eats more than his weight in bugs in a single day and his choicest foods are Japanese beetles, coddling moths, cut-worms and other available pests. It is definitely stated that moles do not eat plants.

Of course there are a lot of lizards that eat bugs and worms and things but we don't have many of these fellows in our woods.

Well, we better mention a couple of beneficial insects. First comes the Dragon-fly. He's the fellow that dives like a jet bomber and I can't visualize any insect being fast enough to get away from him. They do say that he is the strongest and fastest flyer of all insects and I believe it. This is important—he is positively in no way harmful to human beings but he is other insects' No. 1 enemy—eating mosquitoes, gnats and flies as well as other insects that fly high. I've seen the Dragon-fly work over a pond and the speed at which he catches his prey is astonishing.

Well, we'll just have to mention here, too, that the Praying Mantis (some call it "preying") was called the Devil's Horse. He's harmless to humans but he certainly is deadly to practically all types of other insects. His nut-cracker or pincher-like parts crush and dissect anything in the insect world. He gets up hungry in the morning and never stops eating and probably goes to bed hungry, too.

He wouldn't stop eating even then except that he can't see in the dark. He eats only other insects and this goes on from the time he is born in the early spring until he perishes in the fall. He's really a valuable fellow to have around your garden.

Be A Cactus "Egspert"

I've been checking and double checking on ways and means of growing a wide variety of Cactus from seed.

You know, Cactus is one of the most fascinating sectors of the horticultural field. Most folks think of them only as the types one sees pictured in the desert or the tiny plants often seen in pots with the prickly spines stuck all over them. Admittedly many members of the Cactus family are like this but the range is so wide that one can find plants of practically every description in the Cactus family—yes, even plants with leaves, some that climb, some that must be kept watered continuously, others that can't stand the heat and the sun. I know this may shatter your illusions about Cactus yet everything I said above is true.

When I was down in Arizona I sought out a desert botanical garden that had more than 10,000 different kinds of cactus. It has the finest and broadest collection of Cactus to be found anywhere in the world. There were not only weird, unique, grotesque and frightening species of plants among them, but there were many whose beauty would stagger the most broadened horticulturists.

So here if you'll follow me I will tell you how to get best results in growing them from seeds and also how to keep them so that they will grow and be healthy and continue to thrive.

Now you can use various mediums for sowing but here is what we'd suggest—fine vermiculite. This is very much like sand except that the

capillary action is better. Therefore it will not dry out as quickly as sand, and yet give you the desired drainage.

If you're going to grow them in pots, make sure that the Vermiculite is at least ½ in. below the pot level. Sprinkle your seed on the surface. You could actually use a salt shaker or one with bigger holes if your seeds are larger. Wet this down thoroughly and then cover with a sheet of brown paper. Always use lukewarm water when watering. Now it is absolutely essential that the pot be set level. Otherwise there will be a drifting and the seed will wind up in one corner causing poor germination, overcrowding and mildew troubles.

Many varieties of Cactus seed will germinate within 10 to 30 days. But other varieties will take 3 months and a few a full year.

Continued watering may sometimes cause moss to appear and grow. Well, this is a bigger problem sometimes than you imagine. Of course you can easily stir up the Vermiculite, sand or soil, whichever you happen to be using, but if you did, in all probability you would destroy or damage some seeds that were lying beneath. Therefore, we rule out this practice. The logical thing to do if moss appears is to use a regular weed killer in very small quantities but care should be exercised.

As the seedings show growth and develop they should be potted up or planted in a flat or bed in a mixture made up as follows: On the bed put gravel, stones, or broken pottery. Next place a couple of inches of good, rich sandy loam. On top of this put a layer of sand. This combination will create the ideal condition in which your Cactus will thrive.

To the casual observer it will appear as though the Cactus is growing in pure sand but you will know that it is being well nurtured by a rich sandy loam soil underneath. The gravel, stones or broken pottery on the bottom provide the perfect drainage which Cactus must have.

Bargain Lawns

It is generally conceded that Kentucky Blue Grass is one of the finest all round lawn seeds that can be used anywhere in the Temperate Zone of the world. Kentucky Blue Grass truthfully deserves this popularity because it is good and of course it also makes a wonderful pasture and meadow grass. At various times, depending on crop conditions, Kentucky Blue Grass will vary in price from $33.00 per 100 lbs. to $100.00 per 100 lbs. Well, when it's at its low price, there is not much need or desire on the part of the dealers to make substitutes, but when it reaches a high price, and it has been high for the past four or five years, then some dealers or unscrupulous people scurry about for substitutes.

Now there is a grass called Kentucky 31 Fescue. Remember that name well because it has no resemblance or relationship with good old reliable Kentucky Blue Grass. It is a Fescue Grass and I'll describe it to you. It's a tall Fescue, primarily a pasture and soil conserving plant. It is sometimes used for hay which is coarse and not too palatable. Animals will eat it during the winter but they'll eat most anything else in preference to it. It has been used to prevent animals from bloating. When they're out feeding in the field they'll eat themselves full of Ladino Clover, Alfalfa and other leguminous grasses which have a tendency to cause bloating. But an animal is smart enough that if you put some of this Kentucky 31 Fescue grass close-by, they'll eat enough of it to prevent them from bloating and killing themselves.

Here I've given you a little idea about this grass and one thing I should mention, too, is that it has a very bad habit of bunching—especially as it gets older and you'll find it one horrible mess when you've got to cut it. Then you'll cuss not only the guy who sold it to you, who deserves to be cussed, but you'll cuss yourself for being sucker enough to plant it to begin with.

Well, because its name can be easily confused with Kentucky Blue Grass one of the large chain stores in the country bought this grass and had it put into a mixture and, of course, they're relying upon the word Kentucky to sell it and undoubtedly it will sell it. Without trying to make a hero of myself, I deplore this action but I'm also mentioning it to you to show you that you can depend upon your local seedsman and nurseryman. I'm quite convinced in my own heart and soul that a man whom you meet and makes his own mixtures would never do that to you.

Sure, I'm concerned about what I put into my grass seed mixtures. Why? . . . Because if the seed doesn't work out you know where I live. You can either drive out, phone or write to me and you can tell me what you think of me. Don't misunderstand me. In the many years that I've been in the business many folks have told me what they think of me and it wasn't always good. But I'm still here prospering a little bit, which goes to prove that perhaps I haven't fooled all of the people all of the time.

You know when you buy something in a chain store that isn't so good and you go there with a complaint, the fellow that you complain to says, "I'm sorry but I don't know anything about it. I didn't do it. I'll write to head office and let them know and see what they say."

So you see he can pass the buck beautifully and I can assure you that they're some of the best buck-passers that ever passed a buck and they get smarter and better and more experienced at it every day. On the other hand, if that should happen to me and you came out, who am I going to pass the buck to? . . . My uncle? My wife? You just try to pass the buck to my wife and see what will happen to you. Grr-rr!

So no, Buddy, I've got enough trouble without looking for it and I'm the guy who's gotta catch the devil! So I'm playing it straight and close to my chest, too.

Get The Lead Out

I don't think I ever told you the tale about the man who worked for me some years ago. This man honestly and truly worked harder avoiding work than any man I ever had doing his work.

The strangest part of it all is that he worked for me on three different occasions and it was only on the last stint that I found out that he spent his days avoiding work, and, boy, he kept busy at it, too.

Later it dawned on me why he never remained with me for any great length of time. He worked for a few weeks and then he would say that he had to go elsewhere for some reason or other and the next year he'd be back again and such.

I discovered that he worked at different places all along. He was smarter than most people because he knew he could not continue working in one spot for any length of time without being found out. On the third hiring, the time I managed to find out about him, I happened to be looking out of the window of our two storey packing shed and this gives me a commanding view of the entire rear end of the farm. It's really a splendid view. The front windows face the lake and the sight of the water and the surrounding country is panoramic. It is a view that is dream-inspiring and extremely attractive. Yes, in any season, spring, summer, fall or winter, I go up and drink in this picture every day at least once. ·

Anyway this spring day I was gazing out the rear window overlooking the farm and I saw this man appear driving the horse and wagon. This was some years ago when we still had horses. He was going out to the back to load up a batch of nursery stock to bring to the shed. He sat on the wagon, slapped the reins and the horse began to move. Then he suddenly jerked the horse to a stop, jumped off the rig, adjusted the horse's collar, jumped back on the rig, picked up the reins, called "Giddyap" and went along. He didn't go twenty paces until he stopped and leapt off the wagon. This time he began to fasten the hames strap to the shafts. He got them straightened away by lugging, pushing and pulling the horse, pulling the strap and then tapped it, looked it over, stood back and appraised it, jumped on the wagon and set off again. He didn't go another twenty paces when he was off again. This time he was doing something with the horse's belly band. I don't know what he was fixing. He tightened this and pulled that. This took another four or five minutes. Again he stepped back and appraised it from both sides and then climbed on the wagon again and off he went.

Well, this manoeuvring took place all the way out as my eye followed him. I didn't know whether to be mad or laugh but it was certainly an unusual sight. But the fact remains clear and undimmed that he started at 8 o'clock to pick up a load. He never got back with his first batch of trees until exactly noon. Actually this operation should have taken 30 minutes and it took him four solid hours.

From then on I began to watch him and it is almost unbelievable the things that the man would do and the ground he would cover in a day without accomplishing anything.

Of course I let him go at the end of the week but not before I carefully watched him and marvelled at his ingenuity. I still don't know where a man could learn all this. It must have been in many countries. He was not a Canadian. He couldn't have learned it all in Canada. He might have learned some of it here because he was in the army in Canada too. He was an old soldier and probably learned it in the various armies.

But man, oh man, I repeat, he worked harder avoiding work than any man I ever knew. He could swing the lead better than any lion could swing his tail!

Pheasant Story

We decided to break up that piece of sod, bush, bracken or whatever you want to call it that we've been letting go to pot for about 10 years. Yes, it was about 10 to 12 years ago that we planted it to Locust and other shade trees and we dug them slowly as we needed them for sales. Eventually a bunch of them got too big for sales so we chopped them down and from the remains the "doggone" Locusts shot up all over and if you walked down the rows or into the fields, you practically had your clothes ripped from your body by the "daggerish" Black Locust thorns.

Critically we'd been eyeing the field for a long time with the idea of getting rid of the Locusts. Well, today was the day! We went in with the tractor and I didn't think the Old Ford would do it but it did. Row after row was turned over. There were some good sized trees in there, too, and I didn't think it would make it but it got through.

Well, every now and then we'd come across a big stump that was lying in the way left from the previous ones that we'd dug up out there. Then we'd up and roll it out of the way—when I say we, I mean Alex and myself.

We stopped to move this one big heavy trunk and both of us were rolling it with our back and feet braced the best way we knew and it gave . . . when suddenly a litter of big fat field mice ran for cover. Gosh, they were plump and healthy looking—really and truly they were. They must love that Niagara country.

Now, this went on a while and we only had about 3 more rounds to make in the field to get done with it when we came across another stump and there was a hole beside it where it had been uprooted. So we went about trying to move it . . . when suddenly there was a flurry, a swoosh, a rush and a pheasant took to the sky right in front of us and we both nearly took a fit. We were so frightened because we didn't know what in heck it was that was coming out of the ground. We thought probably a geyser was exploding right under our noses.

Well, then we looked under and around—then our eyes lighted on the pheasant's nest and in it were eggs. We counted 13 pheasant eggs and of course the hen had been sitting on them and they were warm. Young Bill, our neighbour's boy, was just close by. As a matter of fact, he'd been darn close by because with his tractor he'd been helping us get out of the mud holes we got into. Every time we'd get stuck we'd call for him and he'd come over and hitch up a series of chains from tractor to tractor and yank us out.

Bill came over now and said, "Look, I've got a settin' hen. We've got her sitting on a batch of eggs. So how about me putting these pheasant eggs under her?"

Well, that's exactly what he did and that's where the pheasant eggs are at the moment of writing. Now, won't that old hen be surprised when she sees those little chicks grow into pheasants with beautiful

plumage. I'll bet that old rooster that lives around there is going to be awfully jealous and he's going to wonder what's been happening—and perhaps do a little snooping and investigating.

I should mention that the pheasant eggs reminded me a lot of robin's eggs. They were just about as blue as a robin's egg except that they were two or three times larger. The pheasant's egg is quite a bit smaller than a hen's egg. Otherwise they look very similar. The nest of the pheasant, of course, was right on the ground and made mostly of hay. That's what it looked like to me—and pretty good hay, too. And there were feathers lining it here and there and also some little pieces of sticks that the mother pheasant must have got together for the nest. Apart from that, the nest was like any other nest.

I'll be waiting to see what happens to those eggs. I hope they hatch into pheasants and grow up to be nice birds—I'll shoot the first hunter who tries to shoot them—sure as shootin'!

Let's Take A Peek At Achimenes

Most people never heard of the plant—yet it has been known for well over 100 years and there are about 30 species. Most of them come from tropical America.

They're related to the Gloxinia, African Violet and Episcia and require the same general cultural treatment.

An important thing to remember about them is that they do not like the cold. They must be kept warm and comfortable at all times. They like a lot of moisture. In fact they want continued moisture. Never let them dry out but don't keep them soggy wet either.

They can be had in bloom any time from February onwards and continue right through the summer. A friend of mine counted as many as 86 open flowers on one plant. This lady planted a box 8 x 24 inches and there were 562 open blooms at one time and this continued daily during the blooming period.

After they have finished blooming, water is withheld until the tops die off. Then the bulb can be lifted again and the process started anew.

The flowers have short tubes but with a wide lip and the color range is broad . . . creamy white, blue, pink, deeper shades of red and purple. The Hybrid varieties have flowers that measure several inches across.

They require a temperature of about 70 degrees and try to keep them at this or warmer. They prefer 75% shade but want free circulation.

170

But did you know that there's a separate silk strand for every kernel on every ear of corn?

Now don't scream blue murder when you receive the bulbs and you find them to be tiny things—because that's the way nature grows them. The propagator is not responsible. It is true that the finest things come in small parcels. And this applies to Achimenes.

This is one plant that will bloom every day for 6 months . . . yes, literally, with thousands of lovely flowers from April till October.

Achimenes grow from seeds, corms, the scales from the corms and cuttings. It takes about three weeks for the bulbs to begin to sprout. They do well grown as a hanging plant or if you want them to grow straight up, aid them by means of small canes or sticks.

Bet You Didn't Know!

For years and years and years—ever since I was a wee boy—I've watched the corn stalks grow, the ears form and these silky tassels hang from the tops. Perhaps you have, too.

Bunt And Make First

I'm going to make your mouths water. I'm going to talk to you about ginger-bread. Do you smell it? I can almost taste it.

It's a lost art. One just doesn't see gingerbread any more. Do you wonder why? Well, there's a reason and a mighty good reason.

Back about a hundred or two hundred years ago gingerbread was very, very popular and its popularity was not only deserved but essential. Life is like that—we've all learned that necessity is the mother of invention—well gingerbread was conceived, brought to life and reared by old mother necessity herself.

At that time a very serious fungus was causing smut disease in wheat. This disease was and is known as bunt.

In some bad years in those days almost half the grain would be lost and even in a good season many crops had enough "bunt" to give the detested violet discoloration and characteristic smell to the flour.

Now they tried to put this affected flour to some use and therefore and thereby gingerbread was born. For you see when this "tainted" flour was highly flavored with ginger and molasses and made into nice shapes the taste of the "bunt" could not be noticed. No one could detect the smell and color of "bunt" under such a heavy disguise.

So you see gingerbread was actually a means of using unpalatable flour. I feel like the miserable old cuss who told the kids there was no Santa Claus, so he wouldn't have to buy them any Christmas presents.

I hope this doesn't break your old heart and disillusion you about the nostalgic flavor of gingerbread.

Nice Girls Love A (T) Tar

Those of you who love the Rose, its perfume or fragrance, hop aboard with me for a journey to Bulgaria. There is found the world's largest supplier of Rose Oil which is the basis of Attar of Roses and this in turn is one of the most valuable basic ingredients of the world's perfume industry.

We're travelling in Bulgaria during the summer and there we meet a continual shuffling, plodding stream of donkeys. On their backs are loaded bags—each bag containing thousands and tens of thousands of Roses . . . yes, the flowers or petals of Roses. They are wending their way to the nationally owned distilleries where these rose petals are taken.

There the rose oil is extracted under steam pressure and supplied to the world at large. An ounce of this fluid is worth more than $15.00 and the distilleries are under constant police supervision. It is estimated that in order to make one pound of Rose Oil, three-quarters of a million rose flowers are required. Just think—to make one pound of this oil the flowers of three-quarters of a million roses are used.

The Rose that is used in making attar is usually the Rosa damascena or Damascus Rose. This is the one that has been used for centuries. However, Rosa centifolia or the Cabbage Rose is also used and it closely rivals the Damascus Rose for quality.

The word "Attar" is rather a conglomeration of names. The one most often used is "Otto" or "Ottar". Both are actually common. In fact 50 years ago the other names were more common than the word "Attar".

Attar is described according to the dictionary as a volatile, highly fragrant essential oil. The word "Attar" comes from the Persian "Attar" meaning essence.

It requires 250 pounds of petals to make one ounce of attar. And to get 250 pounds of petals takes a few acres of Roses.

They Work For Free

Here's something every gardener wants and really needs.

With the help situation tough and everyone needing assistance, here are some helpers that will work for next to nothing. Now who couldn't use some extra help around the garden? Well, that's where these fellows do their best work. In fact they take to work in the garden like a duck to water.

No, actually you don't have to feed them. If you had a dog or cat you'd have to go out and buy milk and some of that especially prepared food for it but these workers actually aren't particular and they provide their own food.

In a compost heap or manure there are actually billions of tiny laboring micro-organisms and they really work. You see they haven't learned yet about recreation, sports, beer parlors, vacations and such and my advice to you is to get them working for you soon before they learn about the A.F.L. and the C.I.O. Once these fellows get to them you can bet on it the first thing they'll do is stop working 24 hours a day and then they'll want a raise in pay and won't work Saturdays and Sundays.

Getting grimmer all the time . . . I suggest that you get these boys to work right away and it's easy. Just get that compost heap humming and some manure and these fellows will be in there working for all they're worth. Yes, it's these teeming billions of tiny micro-organisms that turn a heap of weeds and garden refuse into sweet smelling, healthy, friable soil and what's more, they'll create a balance to your soil that most worn out plots are sadly lacking.

So it will mean better crops and better health. Aren't bugs wonderful?

New Seed Starter

I try to keep my readers up to date on the things that happen in the horticultural world so here is something that is really new.

A new chemical was discovered in Italy which stimulates the germination of seeds. It is called Aleuronin and was first extracted from cell layers just beneath the seed coat of wheat grains in 1953 by an Italian scientist, E. Perini.

Aleuronin is found in minute quantities in practically all seeds and experiments seem to indicate that it is responsible for the starting off of the germination process. Further, it was found that Aleuronin when bound with chemicals like Cobalt was much more active than in its pure form.

When used in germination tests with wheat a 1% solution of Aleuronin-Cobalt created active germination after 12 hours and the seedlings maintained their advantage over the control seeds which did not start to germinate fully after 72 hours.

There is much enthusiasm over the future use of Aleuronin by scientists and horticulturists alike, particularly as it has been found that it also increases the activities of rooting hormones and may eventually be used as an aid to rooting cuttings as well as to budding and grafting.

There is no reason why Aleuronin should not assist in obtaining earlier blooming of flower bulbs.

Apart from the chemical significance and the important part it may play in the future the fact that Aleuronin has been discovered tells us something about the mechanism of seed starting.

'Tis The Soil That Counts

You know you won't have much trouble if you keep your plants healthy. Yes, that's an absolute fact.

You know in humans when you see a weak, sickly, undernourished child you may note he gets every disease in circulation, but not very much seems to bother the husky robust lad.

Probably if you got down to the root of things you'd find that the sickly boy was very fussy about what he ate. In fact you'd probably find that he didn't eat much of anything and when he did take a

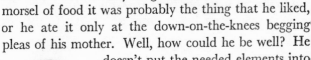

morsel of food it was probably the thing that he liked, or he ate it only at the down-on-the-knees begging pleas of his mother. Well, how could he be well? He doesn't put the needed elements into his body to nurture, build and protect it. Then again the kid that's active, robust and healthy eats everything in sight and no one has to coax him. He eats because he's hungry and loves food. No, I'm not suggesting that he needs to be pot-bellied and flabby either.

Well, the same goes for your plants. You give them a nutritious, proper soil, good drainage, ample water, comfortable conditions and your plants won't be bothered with many insects, if any. I can prove this time and time again.

You know it might do you good some time to actually grow some things in good soil and some of the same things in a poor soil. Then watch the developments.

The greatest favor that you can do your plants is keep them healthy and this is easy if you grow them in a well balanced soil.

England Expects

A handsome couple with a cute youngster drove into the nursery and asked if they could look around. "Sure", I said, "Go ahead, make yourself at home and cut yourself a piece of cake".

After a few minutes they came over to me and said they'd like to get a few things . . . I got them what they wanted and they paid me. I was rather struck by the fact that their accent clearly and distinctly indicated that they were fresh off the boat from dear old Blighty. It isn't often that one hears the cockney accent so far from Bowbells.

As they were leaving I said to the lady, "Would you like us to put you on our mailing list to receive our Growing Flowers Catalog? Would you give me your name, please?"

"Charles Pinchott", I repeated after her, "and the address?"

"No, no", said the lady, "The name is not Charles Pinchott—It's Snodgrass."

Puzzled, I said, "Well, where in blazes did I get the idea that you said Charles Pinchott?"

"Pshaw", said the lady, "when you mentioned Growing Flowers I thought you were referring to the issue that I had in my hand and I was saying to you 'child's pinched it'."

Merion Is Tarryin'

Tsk, tsk, tsk! Well, well, well—another meteor falls.

Just received a report that Merion Bluegrass has been removed from the recommended list of the Kentucky Agricultural Experiment Station and here is the story.

Merion Bluegrass was hailed as the answer to a maiden's prayer for lawns and was said to be the most colossal discovery in grasses of modern times. In 1954 it was attacked by, and proved susceptible to a smut fungus. In 1955, under test, Merion Bluegrass succumbed to a strain of rust. The research workers also report that this variety apparently has a high susceptibility to these two agents.

Therefore, the fact that it is able to produce a low growing, dense, sod-type grass that stands mowing well, is of no great consequence. After all it is better to be a live dog than a dead lion.

You'll remember that just a few years ago Merion Bluegrass sold for as much as $7.00 a pound. This year it was selling for $3.50 to $5.00.

Actually this variety of grass was tested for 12 years before it was released.

Now here let me go a step further. When the Merion was attacked by rust in 1955, the stand was killed out completely, whereas adjoining fields of plain common ordinary Bluegrass were hardly affected at all.

The main difference between the Kentucky Bluegrass and Merion Bluegrass is that Merion is lighter in color and does produce a lower growing plant.

This is another vital case in point . . . Don't make a mad rush for the new stuff.

Bulb Has Bud

Verily, the flower bud is in the bulb.

When you buy a tulip, a daffodil, a hyacinth, an amaryllis, or any bulb for that matter, the flower bud is already formed but lying dormant within the bulb.

All that's required is suitable conditions for the flower to appear so that you can enjoy its beauty and loveliness.

As a matter of fact, the soil doesn't have to be rich because nature has provided the food for the flower so that it will be nourished even without further feeding. After the bulb has bloomed for you, the next year's bulb and flower are formed during the summer . . . and they are the ones that need the feeding.

All this is a preamble to tell you that you can't miss when you plant bulbs. The flowers have just got to come and you can't stop them. They will come in spite of you.

Now if you want to stop them from blooming the simplest and most common method is to give them poor drainage. Then they will decay and rot and by spring you will have neither bulb nor flower.

Now that is about the only way I know of, short of not planting them at all, to prevent a bulb from flowering.

So hear ye, hear ye, all you who would have gay flowers in the spring. Plant bulbs and they are positively sure to bloom if you give them adequate drainage.

Tobe's "Eppytaff"

On my tombstone when I go
Please inscribe this tale of woe—
"He died before his time and age
Because he thought he was a sage.
He ate but foods from balanced soil;
He ne'er allowed his blood to boil.
Ne'er touched food with chemicals tainted
Nor fruits or girls with skins apainted;
Drank no water with fluorine
His garden doused with PU-R-ine;
Went early to bed and was quick to rise
But it never a bit did make him wise.
Well, the truth must be known—the devil's got him . . .
One of the chemical boys done up and shot him!"

Capillary Depth

Here is a little chart that may prove of interest and, yes, perhaps be of great use some sunny day. So put it where you will be able to locate it.

Often we're concerned about the capillary action of soil. Of course, it is understandable that the capillary action or water-drawing powers of any soil will vary according to its consistency or physical structure.

So this little chart should be of educational value anyway. Now this chart refers of course to the distance that the soil will draw water from below the root level of the plants.

For Heavy Loam—The capillary action works for 32 inches.
Sandy Loam—28 inches.
Coarse Sand—Only 14 inches.

I've never been able to find the distances when I needed them. Often I told people to be sure to have a high or a low water table for their plants but I couldn't tell them just what I meant by high and what I meant by low.

Well, evidently a low water table wouldn't be of much use in the case of sand, whereas for heavy loam it would be fine because it could draw for a depth of 32 inches.

Anyway I hope this is of some help to you. You don't often get a chance to pick up information of this type. So I thought I'd make it available to you.

Running Amok

When you read about genes, chromosomes, heredity and mutations, it is apt to get confusing, not only for the layman but even for the fella that's somewhat steeped in the horticultural holocaust.

But here's a description that's rather apt and fitting and probably explains more in a few words than a scientist or a lawyer could explain in a volume.

"When a gene in a plant's hereditary life's cycle feels an individualistic urge, right there and then begins the creation of a mutation."

Neigh, Neigh

I came home from the nursery one day last spring. I had been working hard. Besides the 101 tasks around the nursery there was quite a bit of office detail that had to be attended to and before the evening was finished I was on the tractor. One piece had to be plowed, another piece had to be disked and there were a bunch of furrows that had to be opened in readiness for planting.

Tired, weary, sweaty and dirty, when I got home I didn't bother changing my attire. I just stuck my hands under the water tap to

hose off some of the loose dirt and sat down to eat. There on my plate was a raw potato.

"What is the meaning of this?" I said to my wife.

"Well", she says, "You work like a horse, you smell like a horse and with that long face you even look like a horse . . . so I've reached the conclusion you should eat like a horse, too."

Now I didn't say so at the time but I thought she showed horse sense.

Early Annuals

There are always a few of us who want to beat the gun and get off to an early start. I can't say that I am one of those fellows but maybe you are . . . so I'm just dropping a hint here about sowing annuals outdoors in the fall or early winter so that you will have lots of lovely blooms early. You see it is an absolute fact that where these hardy annuals are sown in this manner, you will get blooms much quicker than you can in any other way with the exception of starting them in flats in a greenhouse or indoors.

Now, in order to achieve results by this method, you've got to guard against one fact and that is to be sure to sow where the seeds won't wash away with the first rain or melting snow.

One word of caution—don't sow too early in the fall as the seed might germinate and begin to grow if we should get a few warm days.

Anyway, here is the list and, remember, if you sow them in the fall or early winter, you will get blooms actually weeks ahead of our regular method.

Bachelor's Buttons, Annual Poppy, Calendula, Balsam, Calliopsis, Candytuft, Cleome, Four O'Clock, California Poppy, Cosmos, Petunias, Nigella, Larkspur, Gaillardia, Sweet Alyssum, Snapdragon, Nicotiana, Sweet Peas and Portulaca.

Now to treat the Sweet Peas right, put them in before the ground freezes and cover them with some compost, straw, hay or other mulching material.

Well, now that you've done it, I know—I know—that you're going to have lots and lots of blooms much earlier next summer.

It's Only Money

I've had complaints of various kinds before in my life, but I struck what was a most unusual one the other day. I was going through the bills that had accumulated in the cash register from our door sales and I noticed that one of them was a refund and on it was written "Plant returned—$3.95 refunded—because of bad wife".

So I began to ask questions and I found that this nice pleasant man had come to the nursery and selected himself a beautiful Rhododendron. There were at least 15 beautiful large buds on it ready to bloom. He thought it would make an excellent gift for his wife and when I say that he selected it carefully, I mean just that. According to what I heard, he went through practically every plant in the slat shed, before he found one that met his discriminative taste. Then he made sure that they wrapped it carefully for him and he took it home.

The next day he was back and asked if he could have his money refunded. This was promptly done and as he was leaving he lamented, "I bring it back because I have bad wife."

She evidently didn't appreciate the plant as a token of his esteem. She thought that $3.95 in the coin of the realm looked a lot better.

It's just a matter of opinion.

Not Sun Worshippers

A flowering house plant that will thrive in the shade or semi-shade is more or less of a rarity, but still, there are a few old standbys, so I'm going to tell you about them. Then, whenever you run into a situation that requires a flowering plant for shade, you'll have the answer.

Here they are: African Violets, Gloxinias, Impatiens sultani, Fuchsia, Tuberous rooted Begonias, Fibrous rooted Begonias, Episcias, and Gardenias.

$2 + 2 = 4; 3 + 1 = 4$

A friend of mine who has a large garden was looking for a new gardener. She paid good wages and was a kind, considerate employer. So when folks around town heard that she needed a man, she had a lot of good applicants.

From these applicants she selected a husky, strapping youth—much to the surprise of folks in town who knew him to be very lazy. When asked how she made her selection she said that she had personally interviewed all the applicants and she liked this young man's viewpoint.

After a couple of months the youth no longer worked with her and I asked her what had happened. She said that she had hired him because of the way he expressed his love for gardening but after finding him loafing on the job on 3 or 4 occasions she had to dismiss him.

"You know", she said, "I was taken in by him. Yet he told me the truth. I just didn't recognize it."

"I don't quite understand that. Would you explain it in a little more detail?" I asked.

"Well," she said, "when I interviewed him he told me that he liked doing nothing better than gardening and I found to my sorrow, that he meant just that!"

Shade of the Old Hawthorn Tree

If you ever come within hailing distance of Niagara-on-the-Lake during the summer, drive out of town on the Lakeshore Road. Stop at the One Mile Creek and there on the north side you'll see a bunch of Hawthorn trees. They sort of form a canopy or big tent at this area by the side of the creek and you can find shelter, peace and comfort under their spreading arms.

The trees are so dense in this location and the branches so closely woven and interlaced that you'd wonder that even the rain could penetrate. If you know the Hawthorn you'll understand just how close together they can grow.

You can walk or crawl underneath their branches, spread a blanket and rest or you can plan a picnic thereunder. Evidently I'm not the first one who has thought of this idea because the area is fairly well levelled which means that some folks have been using it for exactly that purpose.

Nowadays whenever anyone sees a Hawthorn tree he gets the brush killer to work to destroy them. Well, I hope they don't destroy these because not only are they a landmark, not only do they offer shelter and beauty but they are still a relic of bygone days and I hope they remain for many years to come.

To Be Had Where 'Tis Found

You know how folks laugh at and belittle the average soil found in the city. Probably I've laughed and derided it too at times.

When I am in Toronto I often take a stroll down along Front Street where the choo-choos cross and one hears the hustle-bustle of the transportation industry. Believe it or not there's quite a variety of wild flowers that can be found growing there on the banks.

This day I saw a very attractive Phlox. I'll be doggoned if it didn't look as good as some of the named varieties that we have. So I decided to dig it up. I looked in the pocket of my car and I found a tablespoon that either the wife or one of the kids had left there and a polyethelene bag that had evidently contained some fruit. So armed with these I crawled under the railing and began to dig up my plant.

Begorra, I was astounded! The soil was not only black and rich-looking but it was richly humus-laden, nutrient-filled and gritty which improved the drainage. I wondered how come this soil was in such good tilth. I couldn't figure it out. Well, eventually I decided that for many years the wild flowers had been growing there, actually taking nothing out, and the city dust and smoke from the engines was continually settling and being held by the leaves. After 50 years or more of this no wonder the soil was in good shape.

Ideal for Orchids

Henry Teuscher, the famed curator of the Montreal Botanical Garden, was recently down in Venezuela searching for rare plants and Orchids.

He mentions that in one section where Orchids grew abundantly it rained every afternoon between 2 and 3 o'clock as if timed by a clock, sometimes with considerable violence.

A cool fog usually descended first from the tops of the mountains which were always covered by clouds. This occurrence could be observed particularly well from the glassed-in veranda of the biological station. The fog came drifting down from one side and, like a drawn curtain, shut out the vista of lake and mountains.

This is the kind of weather that Orchids love—copious quantities of water in the atmosphere and yet they are set either high up in a tree, on a rock or some place where the water just runs off and the roots can breathe and not be drowned.

We learned this a couple of years ago and seldom ever lose an Orchid plant now. We give them lots of water, but make sure that it just rolls away. That way they respond to being hung up.

Orchid growing is real easy . . . and they are such unusual, rapturously beautiful specimens when in bloom.

Very Important

Here's a little bit of advice that will help you get good results with at least one phase of your gardening.

When you've got a planting or transplanting job to do if it is at all possible, select a cloudy, muggy day and water your plants thoroughly with a weak solution of liquid manure.

You'll be amazed at the growth your plants will make, and you'll cut losses to the vanishing point.

Smell Ain't Everything

When first I came across the word "Eureka" I wondered how it originated and I found that it meant "I have found it."

Every year we have a fellow who comes down to visit me and take my order for and supply us with the manure that I need for our fields. We usually buy cow manure because we understand or believe it to be better than any other.

When this fellow walks into our office I'm always reminded of the word "Eureka" only we say it this way, "You reek a . . . cow manure."

I'm glad to have him come along though—smell and all—because I don't know where else we'd get the darn stuff, and believe me, it's really a necessity.

I recall shortly after he had brought us the first few loads last fall, we brought a few wheelbarrows full into the greenhouse and mixed it in with the existing soil in the benches and for a few days there was a very strong aroma arising from the beds. Then I recall that a lady came in and asked permission to visit the greenhouse. She didn't stay there very long but came into the office with a handkerchief over her nose. Assuming that the place always smelled this way she asked the girls how they could stand it. Well, I don't think the girls liked it very much either but the plants love it and they show it too.

If Only It Could Cook!

Did you know that there is a grass that reaches a height of 120 feet? No, I'm not referring to Seaweed that might grow on the ocean's bottom and reach the surface. No, this is a grass that is common in the Orient.

Now this grass supplies a grain that looks like rice and it is used for food and drink, honey, fruit-like apples which are baked, sprouts which are cooked and served as a vegetable, beer brewed from the seeds, pickles are made from the vinegar-soaked nuts, and candy from the sprouts cooked in sugar.

They make raincoats out of its leaves—yes, and umbrellas too and delicate sweets are also wrapped in its leaves. When the grass is mature it is used as water pipe, making boats, masts, life preservers, nets, hats, wickerwork, candlesticks, pails, phonograph needles, chopsticks, flutes, swords, art work, pens, spoons, bottles, bird cages, canes, wheelbarrows, blowguns, bows and arrows, fans, ropes, pipestems, kites, brooms, agricultural implements, bridges . . . yes, and even houses and furniture.

This plant is known to grow as much as an inch an hour in the moist, hot climate.

Perhaps you've guessed it. This common Oriental grass is bamboo. It is considered one of the most useful of all the plants bestowed upon mankind by nature.

Home Buster-Upper

Got a complaint from a man the other day and this is the gist of his letter:

"Tobe, I'm coming down to Niagara to blow your brains out."

When I read that part I stopped and laughed like heck and I had a good mind to write to the guy and say, "Brains . . . that's the nicest thing anybody has said about me in years."

Bub, you can't blow out or drive out something somebody doesn't have. Act your age and be sensible. Would I be a nurseryman if I had brains?

"O.K., fella", I said, "Come down and see if you can find them and if you find them you've got my permission to blow them out because if I had any brains and didn't use them any better than I have, I deserve to lose them."

"But what have I done to you to make you want to blow out something I don't have?" I wondered.

He continued, "Tobe, you old sinner, you're ruining my life. That Growing Flowers thing you send out—as soon as it reaches my house my wife forgets her father and mother, her children and her husband and just sits down on the chesterfield and reads Growing Flowers till it's finished. The animals, the children and I don't get fed, the beds don't get made, everything goes to rack and ruin and that, says I, is justification for blowing your brains out."

No Soft Soap Here

The insect killer manufacturers are not going to like me very much, but maybe the soap fellows will for telling you this. Who knows, they may even put me on a soap opera as a hero riding a white steed. Boy, wouldn't I look classy in that outfit?

Did you ever hear of old Fels Naphtha? Well, it's a soap and its pretty good when it comes to killing insects. Here's what it did when used as a spray . . . killed several kinds of aphids, also killed young San Jose scale, oyster shell scale and euonymus scale; murdered lace bugs on Rhododendrons; devastated spider mite on Hemlocks and rendered "hors de combat" the larvae of elm leaf beetle.

Now I don't know what other insects this sudsy monster may slay, but the next time you have some insect problems, before you rush to the corner insecticide sales station with a fist full of money, reach up and get yourself a bar of good old Fels Naphtha for a couple of dimes. By the quantities you use a bar of Fels Naphtha will last about 6 years. That's providing you use it regularly. You take 1 tablespoon of soap and 2 gallons of water. Dissolve the soap in warm water and you're in business.

You'll find it works pretty good, never clogs your sprayer or nozzle and probably it will keep you clean in the bargain.

I'll bet you didn't know what they used that stuff for before . . . for washing of course! Now we use detergents.

Color Means Nothing

I know this is going to break your heart, folks, but if it is, grab a chair, relax and survive the shock. It better be done quick and get it over with.

Like most of us you've probably always been taught to believe that black soil means a rich soil. As a true matter of fact I always hear people express themselves about soil and say, "I want some of that good black dirt".

For some unknown reason when we talk about soil the words rich and black are synonymous. I won't deny that many rich soils are black, yet most of the good soils I know are brown or even green.

Swamp mucks are practically always black yet the soil from such locations is usually leached and barren of all its valuable nutrient content.

It is an actual fact that many unscrupulous dealers who have sold so-called loam and black dirt actually use some type of coloring material to color the soil and make it look black, or rich if you would have it. A man was complaining to me not too long ago that the nice rich black soil that he had bought was now a nice red clay. Rain had come along in the meantime and washed away the black soot or dye or whatever it was.

185

Now don't think that I'm giving you an isolated case or I am stretching the truth because the points I'm making are actual and factual. So, remember, black soil doesn't necessarily mean good soil or rich soil.

And Happy Landing

Without much doubt you've heard of the expression that goes like this, "You should only drop dead!" Or maybe you've heard it as just plain "Drop dead".

Well, that isn't a very tender or pleasant sort of wish for anyone and I've been trying to dig up the origin of this most unusual expression. Truly it bodes no one any good.

Well, after much searching I came upon this story. It appears that in the early days of trans-Atlantic flying there was a stewardess on a certain plane and on board with her was a very nervous passenger. He had a big bottle of liquor with him and every few minutes he would take a big suck at the bottle. By the time they were nearly half way across he was rather "tight" and instead of remaining comfortably and safely seated in his chair, he insisted upon prowling or staggering up and down the aisle—much to the disconcernment and

consternation of the stewardess. Well, on one occasion as she was walking up the aisle to give some coffee to one of her passengers this inebriated character insisted upon getting up. He staggered and fell against the stewardess, knocking the tray of cups and coffee flying and breaking the dishes and spilling coffee on everybody.

The stewardess very politely and painfully began to pick up the pieces and generally tried to clear and mop up things. Then she glanced up at the passenger who caused the trouble, and in a subtle, yet most pleasant voice, said to him, "I wish you'd go out for a little walk".

Black Is Not White

Yes, who would believe that the word blackmail is of agrarian origin? Strange it is and true, too.

Even back before the 17th Century much of the farm land in Scotland was owned by English noblemen. Sure, they were absentee landlords and they charged their tenants very high rents. This rent was termed "mail" and it was stipulated that the payment be made in silver. As we all know silver is not always available, and the farmer who could not raise the money in the white metal was allowed to pay in the produce from his land and cattle. This of course caused the values to differentiate very badly and the term "blackmail" as compared to "white mail" was used to indicate that payment was being made in something other than silver.

Of course this led to various pressing of the farmer for more and more of his produce, especially when he couldn't produce the silver. So this term began to be called "blackmail" to indicate an advantage that one held over another and, thus, was exacting a very high tribute.

Today the word "blackmail" has come to mean an actual bribe paid a person holding a distinct advantage over another . . . or had I better say a victim.

Safe, Sure, Mildew Cure

Here's something that may sometime be of value to you. Often plants are affected with mildew. If this should ever happen to any of your plants don't run around looking for a cure or spend a lot of money at a drug or chemist's shop.

Make up a spray by using 1 lb. of washing soda, 1/4 lb. soft soap in 5 gals. of water. This will give you effective control in most cases of mildew.

Tennyson Said

"Any man that walks the mead
   In bud, or blade, or bloom may find
   A meaning suited to his mind."

Some years ago a very dear friend of mine passed away. He died when he was quite young. He wasn't even forty years old. It was a terrible shock to his wife and two children. I didn't know what to say or just what a man is supposed to utter under these conditions.

So I wrote to her and somehow this little verse seemed to come to mind and I sent it off. Some time later—in fact a long time later—the widow told me that these few words had comforted her more than anything she'd seen or heard at that time and thanked me for it.

So I'm going to quote this little verse. Perhaps some time you may find a need for it, too. If you do, use it with my blessings.

"Who are we, to judge,
   Of those who pass
   Beyond the Great Divide?
   Perhaps there
   They wait for us,
   And for our souls provide."

Lo! Let's Lift Loads

Much has been said and written about making things better for those who follow us—making man's burdens lighter—preparing the way. Politicians and sages have echoed these sentiments for countless centuries . . . Let us make things better for those who follow us.

Sorry, folks, but I must disagree. I don't think that we're helping either our children or our grand-children by making the road easier for them to travel. In fact, I am convinced that we do them an injustice and harm by making things easier for them.

After all is said and done, good steel cannot be made without a crucible—without putting it through the grueling tests and workouts that are required—heating to white heat, cooling, re-heating, etc. Good steel is no accident and good men are no accident either. They must be built layer upon layer, character upon character, strength upon strength and it is burden upon burden that does it.

Sure, it's a mighty nice thought . . . to make things easier for the man that will follow us and we think its ennobling and we feel uplifted even at the thought. But, believe me, I do not think that we are doing the man who is going to follow us one little favor by making things easier for him. We are simply justifying our greed!

Don't destroy their heritage! Leave it as we found it. Cut the bull about light loads and stop cutting their forests and killing off the wildlife and drying up their streams. Preserve and protect their natural heritage—don't waste or destroy their future—that is the best way to help those who will follow us.

Add to Adage

We all know that the Giant Sequoias are considered to be the largest living things on earth. Yet their seeds are so tiny that one ounce can produce almost 7,000 trees.

So the next time you hear about some mighty Oaks from little acorns growing, remember that the Giant Sequoia, the largest living thing on earth grows from something not much bigger than a molecule.

Don't Be A Greeny

The only horses that we see today are those that run races at the Woodbine or some of the other tracks throughout Canada and the United States. Righto, they still have them in the grand old merry-go-round, too. Yet not more than a few years ago—just less than 20 years—horses were found on practically every farm and used to do practically all of the heavy work.

Now, while they have been used on the farm only for the past hundred years more or less, horses have been used and domesticated by mankind for thousands of years. Yet I repeat, only for the past century or so have they been put to work on the farm.

Before that the work on the farm was left to oxen and an ox as you know, is a rather stupid animal—slow to learn and often vicious too. So when oxen were offered for sale, anyone who bought one wanted to make sure the ox had been completely broken-in and domesticated. Therefore it was not of any use to offer him a young one.

You see, they could tell their ages by their horns. When their horns were young or green, which means they were soft and undeveloped or immature, no one wanted them. If such an ox were offered to a farmer he would shake his head and say, "No, sir, I don't want a greenhorn" meaning that he didn't want a young ox because the older ones were bad enough to handle and a young one would spell only a lot of grief and woe.

So that's how the term "greenhorn" started and now it means, in our language, practically anything or anybody who is new at something, or untrained.

To the contrary, however, one with a green thumb means someone who has a special knack, experience or know-how to make most any plant grow and thrive.

Don't Do It

Read an interesting report recently and it deals somewhat with an old pet peeve of mine . . . deep planting.

Some folks aren't satisfied unless they've buried a plant and I just don't mean the roots but the trunk and the top too. Nature intended that the roots of a plant be below the ground and the rest of it above and if you plant deeply you defeat nature's avowed purpose.

For example, take most of the nut trees like Black Walnut and English Walnut. They are known to have very few roots but a long thick strong tap root. That is nature's way of providing herself with a means of getting into the earth deeply if she wants to. Whether it be in search of deeply hidden minerals, water, or for anchorage purposes when nature wants that which is hidden deeply in the soil it will send the roots down for it . . . and don't you ever suffer under the delusion that nature doesn't know how to get what it wants.

You have seen those Cypress knees as they are called. Well, that's nature's improvised means of a tree living in water like a fish and yet breathing fresh air. The knees protrude above the water while the roots are buried beneath it. One of the chief reasons that we are unable to grow Rhododendrons successfully . . . or Azaleas and Kalmias (Mountain Laurel) . . . is that invariably we set them too deep and the plants just don't like it and show their contempt by losing their foliage, not giving any bloom or just plain kicking the bucket.

Go out into the bush and examine the trees. If you find them planted deeply, write me a letter and blast the blazes out of me.

Don't plant deep!

Incredible But Factual

Lest you get the idea that farming is losing its importance, I want to give a run-down on some pertinent data that will stress and definitely fix in your mind the great importance or the vital role that farming plays in the economy of our present world (Whatta mess).

These figures quoted are for the United States but, as you can bet, they are just about equally significant in Canada and Great Britain. A survey made by the University of California shows that farm production in the United States is 75% greater today than it was in 1910, although the acreage has remained practically identical.

In 1910, 35% of the population of the United States was engaged in farming in one form or another. Today, startling to relate, this figure is only 13.5%.

Further, let me emphasize, that 25% of all the business firms in the United States are engaged in either marketing, processing, manufacturing, or distributing farm products and goods made chiefly from these crops from our good earth.

Amazing—but absolutely true!

Yes, while only 13.5% of the entire population produces not only the food for the entire 100%, but also food that is exported to practically all nations of the world, there's still a great over-abundance.

Don't Stand Still

We can learn from nature. Human beings, if they want to exist, should learn something from plants. That is—they must be amenable to changes.

The world has existed for many, many eons, periods or ages—I don't know what to call it. But it has existed a long, long time. It is obvious that physical conditions on the globe are changing. They practically undergo some form of change every day.

Well, the plants also must change to meet the physical conditions of the world in climate and such. If they don't make these changes or adapt themselves, they perish. How do we know? . . . Well, the fossil remains dating back thousands and even millions of years, distinctly show those plants that couldn't or wouldn't adapt themselves to present conditions or changing conditions, perished and no longer exist.

So that is a warning to you, fella. Keep time with the world as it is and not as you would want it to be. Then you'll be just O.K. If not, you're a dead duck. A million years from now you'll just be an old fossil, you poor prune—so don't be a stick in the mud—get on!

Laugh Clown Laugh

In one of the Canadian farm magazines under the heading of "Horticulture", there was an article written by one of its columnists and here is what he says: "Many of the flowers, shrubs and vegetables that our grandparents planted would be as much out of place today, in the modern garden, as the old woodstoves are out of place in our up-to-date kitchen or the Model T on our super-highways."

Now perhaps you agree with him but I sure don't. I'll admit that the research and lab boys have come up with some fairly good items in recent years, but 99% of all the plants for beauty and food that are used today were in existence 100 years ago.

A short time back in a discussion with an up and coming gardener, I offered him $25.00 if he could name me 10 species of plants that were unknown 100 years ago. He could only name one. I suggested that he carry the offer back to the gardening school and let the same stand to any member of the staff or students. But I haven't heard anything from them so I presume I have no takers.

Now I know full well that there are more than that number of plants that have been discovered in the past 100 years, but they'd have to do a lot of searching to find them. Offhand I know the following plants that were unknown 100 years ago: St. Paulia, Episcia, Kolkwitzia, Hypoestis sanguinolenta, Pilea cadierei . . . but they were just undiscovered not uncreated.

So I'll still stick with the old timers. I think if we walked into a garden 100 years old, and all other things being the same, we'd never notice the difference. I don't think that horticulture has progressed that far in any category with the exception of farm machinery.

Home Beauty is Easy

I've been asked on occasions for tips and advice on landscaping. Well, I can sum up the substance of landscaping—in a few words and if you'll follow them, you'll never go wrong and always have beautiful surroundings about your home.

Do not seek to ornate or to make a great display with your planting. Just try to simulate natural surroundings and unspoiled beauty. Don't try to do a better job than nature does in her own way. That is the total sum and substance of succesful landscaping. Simplicity is the keynote!

Room For All? I Hope

There's quite a bit in the news lately about fats causing coronary heart conditions. Milk has been looked upon with suspicion as have all animal fats.

Well, if you like your milk and yet don't want to take the risk of dropping dead from a heart attack, you can move down to the South Pacific. There on an island called Ifalik you will find the solution to your problem. Go to your Coconut Tree. Find the Coconut flowers [and they're ever present], cut their stems and a juice will run out freely. It is called "hachi" or toddy and it is an unfermented sap.

Gosh, way down in Ifalik the natives have one chore and one chore only—twice daily—morning and evening. They do their milking. Actually it is like milking a cow. Each man has a particular tree or trees and gathers this sweet nutritious sap which takes the place of milk. When served fresh it is a main item of diet for the children. It can be fermented and then makes a good drink for the men.

Gangway, lemme go. I'm on my way! Cheerio, farewell, goodbye —to Ifalik for me—one chore a day. No thrombosis, wow! Paradise on earth! You don't have to die to go to heaven.

Strawberry News

For a hundred years or more the standard practice or method of planting Strawberries in this area, or should I say in the entire east, has been the matted row system.

By this means you usually set the plants two feet apart in the row and the rows are 4½ feet apart. Then you allow about 10 runners each for each mother plant and this forms a matted row about 18 inches wide.

Now for the hill system, the plants are set in 3 rows with 12 inches between plants and also between the rows with a 30 inch alley between every third row. In this system all runners are removed after two week intervals.

From a test conducted during the 1955 season in New York State, which incidentally was one of the hottest and driest seasons on record, here is what happened! Under the hill system all varieties produced considerably more fruit than those in the matted rows. This was especially true from the irrigated plots.

Now there appeared to be no difference in the size of the berries under the two systems but the yield in the matted rows as compared to the hill system was phenomenal—yes, actually unbelievable—there were so many more berries on the hill system than on the matted rows.

So you listen, you fellows who grow strawberries. The smart thing to do is to grow them according to the hill system.

In the test mentioned, please bear in mind that six entirely different varieties of Strawberries were tested and in each case the hill system very greatly outyielded the matted row system.

Also, both systems were tested with and without irrigation, but the results were still as mentioned.

Gayest of Color

A Caladium is just about the world's easiest bulb to grow if only you will use your head.

To begin with, I don't know whether to call it a bulb, a tuber, a root or a thing-a-ma-jig. No matter, it looks just like a chunk of hard blue clay, no sign of life in it anywhere. But there is one important thing to look for and that is, that the silly thing, whatever it may be, is firm and sound, not mushy or hollow.

Zounds! There is no doubt about it. A Caladium leaf is one of horticulture's gayest spectacles. They vary in color from pink to innumerable tints of red, white, and green . . . or fantastic combinations of all those colors and many, many more.

Bear in mind that they want partial shade, whether indoors or out. They must have a super abundance of moisture during the growing season and the warmer it is the better they like it. When growing, it is smart to feed them dashes of Liquid Manure.

They will stay in leaf up to eight months. Then they should be rested off.

Never cover the bulbs when you plant them. Just set them on the surface of the soil and give them a little bit of water now and then . . . then, when you see roots or shoots, plant them properly.

By cricky, they are a cinch!

---❖---

Remember that many of the best of the modern types of Roses are prone to set seed heavily and they start to set it quite early in the blooming season.

Unless you like to see these pods which are sort of attractive, too, covering your plant in mid-summer, I would urge you to remove the Roses as they wilt, thus preventing the plant from going to seed.

Remember that when seed begins to set, you will have no more blooms for that season because the plant will be busy doing the job it is intended to do and that is set seed and procreate. It will not be interested in producing any more flowers from then on . . . Really quite natural and understandable.

194

How Sweet Are Our Cherries?

I've discovered something new about Sweet Cherries.

There isn't much doubt about it. Cherries are about the trickiest of all fruit trees, or any tree for that matter, to get started. They are hard and they are difficult. Years of experience has taught us that about 50% of all the Cherry Trees planted each and every year die the first year. This mortality can be reduced.

But for certain, Cherries positively do require dry feet. If they're planted where water will lie you can be sure that your Cherry will die. Yet, strange as it may sound, the roots of the Cherry must be kept slightly damp or moist. They must have some humidity. So I strongly recommend a good mixture of peat and earth be placed around the roots of the Sweet Cherry trees when they're planted.

Now this self same mixture of soil and peat will definitely benefit every tree when planting and give a higher degree of livability, as well as more growth and healthier growth to your tree. Therefore it is beneficial to all of them but positively almost a necessity when you're planting a Sweet Cherry. So please bear this in mind and you will cut down your losses on your Sweet Cherries.

Don't Miss Pieris

Sometimes I think that you folks don't pay any more attention to my talking than you would to a jackass braying. Don't you dare say it! I know what you're thinking—"There is a great deal of similarity between them".

But for a year or two now I've been telling you in my own glib way something about that wonderful Pieris japonica or Andromeda, as it is sometimes called. Now this is a beautiful, hardy little plant. It has flowers on it or some color 12 months of the year and I do believe, so help me, that it will grow in Aklavik or in Tuktoyaktuk. I haven't found a place yet where it freezes out or is even damaged by the cold.

It's a broad leafed evergreen and has beautiful lily-of-the-valley-like flowers in profusion in the early spring. Then they open up later, the foliage changes color and sort of has some kind of a seed pod like a corn tassel after that. In the fall the colors vary from crimson to scarlet and green and bronze.

It's a low-growing, attractive evergreen shrub. The ones we have here at the nursery are about 12-15" tall and wide—yet neat and compact in habit.

When all aspects are considered, you'll have a tough time finding a better garden subject than this Pieris. I should also mention that it will do well in the shade, semi-shade or even a lot of shade and it will also do well in the sun. It's not too fussy about soil but it definitely prefers it to be acid. So use plenty of peat moss or leaf mould around the roots when planting.

Dear Old Mulberry

What do you know about the Mulberry tree? Somehow or other this seems to be a neglected variety of fruit and, really and truly, it merits consideration and planting by every gardener.

If you like the mild fruit which is produced by the millions on the young trees, this in itself is good enough reason for planting a Mulberry. But even if you didn't like the fruit, the birds love them and you'll have birds around your garden like nowhere else on earth.

Now leaving these two factors out, the foliage of the Mulberry is good. It is a very light green—quite unusual and different from the rest of the green usually found in a garden. Another very, very nice thing about a Mulberry is that the leaves stay on the tree—they're just about the last to shed their leaves and they do so very reluctantly in late, late fall or early winter.

In ancient times the Mulberry tree was called Sapientissima arborum and the literal translation of it would sound like "The Wise Tree". Well, the reason it was called that was because it never opened a bud until it was sure that the last frost had gone. But on the other hand, another ancient writer said—it was the delight of the young and the first harbinger of happy fruit time. Why?—Because its fruit was the first to mature and that is no lie or exaggeration.

I've written about the Mulberry before and I'll probably write about it again and the reason is simple . . . it's a good tree, gives good fruit and enormous quantities. Besides that, it's a good shade tree to have around. I don't know why else I would be chortling its praises so highly.

The Anvil Chorus

Rose Chafers have been the bane of the Rose grower's existence for many, many years and yet even today no proper or sure preventive or anything to keep the chafers from the Rose bushes has ever been found.

So that you will know your enemy, here's the chafer's portrait. He's also known as the Hessian bug or Rose Beetle. He's lean, lanky, long legged and clumsy, not over ½ in. long and of a resin yellow color. He chomps away at buds or opened flowers, devouring the flower clean into the heart. There are few known sprays or insecticides that can frighten or stop him.

An old rosarian used to tell me that the best way to stop chafer devastation was to catch him and put him twixt an anvil and hammer.

Hand-pick 'em if they appear and dump them into a container of kerosene.

Here's another suggestion that may give splendid results and maybe you'd be smart if you adopted it. You'll find it will give remarkable control against chafers.

Get some moth balls, the ordinary kind you buy in drug stores, or the ordinary flakes of napthalene. Put them into an old sock and push a stake down in among your Roses and suspend this bag containing the moth balls from the stake. Somehow or other when the odor of the naphthalene permeates the atmosphere round about the roses the "Rose Chafer" won't come around. Could be he is repelled or nauseated—I don't know what happens, but he doesn't like the smell of the moth balls and he leaves the Roses alone.

It's well worth trying and here may be a simple effective cure for Rose Chafers. If it works, wonderful—if it doesn't . . . so you lost a few scents!

Flying Roots

Often you come across the term "aerial roots". Now probably you know what an aerial root is. For many years I thought an aerial root was the kind of root that grows from climbing plants and I didn't know whether it was a root or a ways or means of climbing. Actually this is an aerial root, but there is another kind of aerial root probably just as important and yet it performs a somewhat different function.

Correctly any root that appears above the ground level is properly called an aerial root. Besides the Ivies where they are most common, you also see them on plants like Philodendrons.

Now the other aerial roots are found on plants of an epiphytic nature—mainly Orchids. I find at the greenhouse here that the aerial roots on the various Orchids seem to be climbing all over. You see them almost at the soil level—you see them half way up—and then you see them also right at the extreme tips of the plants. I guess you would just say that the aerial roots shoot out all over or any place.

There is a good reason for this. These roots are perfectly and admirably suited for the function that they are to perform—namely, absorbing atmospheric moisture as well as for catching holds, stabilizing or firming the position of the plant.

The Winner!

Sometimes you folks may come across a quiz program or someone who asks you the question like "How many types of *flowerless* plants can you name?"

So just in case that should happen to you, rather than see you lose $64,000, I'm going to tell you the answer so that you won't be stuck.

Here they are. I'm not saying this is all of them. This is just giving you a partial list or, at least, it's all the ones I know . . . Ferns, Fern allies, Fungi, Mosses, Liverworts, Sea Weeds and Lichens.

Manure and Music

I can just visualize what's going to happen when Petrillo and the musicians' union read the heading above. They're going to marshal their forces, come together and parade down to Tobe's emporium in Niagara-on-the-Lake and tear it apart shred by shred until not one grain of sand remains on top of another.

To a shop keeper the cling of a cash register is music to his ears. Didn't some great opera writer compose one of the great songs of the ages from the clang, clang, clang of a blacksmith's hammer on an anvil? Didn't someone here or there bang out a song about the hoof-beat of horses? Isn't there a piano piece about a kitten on the keys—and a bee buzzin'—and a glow worm glowing? Well, then just so there is music in manure, too.

"Why?" you ask . . . Well, simply because it was handled by a pitch fork.

Now let's be realistic for a moment. Isn't it true that a pitch fork should be used for determining pitch for musicians? In the dictionary under the term "tuning fork" it says clearly and distinctly—giving a tone or a certain pitch. Under the word "pitch" the dictionary says—one set to a key note or the elevation of a key or note of a tune; to pitch a tune; to fix or set the tune of.

A farmer uses a pitch fork for pitching hay on or off a hay-rack or from the loft to the manger . . . or manure out of the barn or onto the spreader. Well, probably the musicians' sensitive souls were insulted and they wouldn't use the proper word which would be pitch fork because it is used by the lowly farmer. So they got a new word— tuning fork. But you know that the proper word for a tuning fork is a pitch fork . . . I've done my pitchin' for now!

Everything is Rosy

Almost everybody at some time or other uses the phrase "A bed of Roses".

There is an old, old legend that goes back to the Grecian Sybarites. For magnificence and luxury they excelled all of Great Ancient Greece. These citizens of Sybaris were devoted adherents and followers of the Great God Pan. And old Panny Boy was the God of Revelry—you know the poem, "There was the sound of revelry by night" only there it was morning, noon and night. He lorded over wine and gaiety as well. He was the sort of "Good-time Charlie" of today. Those Sybarites certainly followed Old God Pan when he was having fun because they loved their fun too. They never missed an opportunity for a party or a celebration—just like some of my friends.

Some gay young blade at one time dreamed up the idea of sleeping in a bed of roses. They would have the petals and the flowers plucked from thousands of plants and strewn thickly onto a couch and it was the ultimate in luxury and pleasure for them to lie in this wonderful cozy, fragrant, invigorating bed. Can you imagine the softness, beauty, delicacy and the perfume that would emanate from such surroundings?—I'll have to try it some day. Of course they were very careful to see that no thorns were mixed up with these lovely flowers.

So nowadays when we want to emphasize the fact that life is a picnic or has reached the ultimate in pleasure and cushyness, we say "A bed of Roses". To him the world and life are "A bed of Roses".

Top Ranking Gardener

You've heard it said that cleanliness is next to godliness. That isn't true. Of course the reason they said it is because they wanted to encourage people to be clean for hygienic purposes and for their health. So they picked up the slogan saying that cleanliness is next to godliness in order that all devout and true believers would adopt clean habits which is very, very good.

But the truth of the matter is, and let me emphasize, that gardening is next to godliness. Ask anyone who has ever gardened. He knows this full well. Then, of course, when you're finished gardening you've got to wash up and get clean. So then after gardening, cleanliness is next to godliness.

I must tell you here, too, if you do not already know, that God himself was the world's first gardener and he still is today the world's greatest gardener without any doubt or contradiction. Proof is readily available. He created the Garden of Eden and then he set Adam up in business to live there. No one can deny the excellence of his handiwork, nor his generosity and magnanimity. So, remember, God was the first gardener and when you join the fraternity of gardeners, you join the most exalted, most wonderful and yet the most humble profession and occupation on the face of God's good earth.

It was Bacon who said that gardening is the purest of human pleasures. He also said that of all the professions gardening is the greatest

You know we can learn many vital lessons from our garden and one of them is to appreciate the simple things that surround us so abundantly and to be content with the world as it is and find peace of mind.

I Find A Pearl

Barley is a well known food and plant to some people and other people know little or nothing about it. I've always partaken of barley soup and we're very fond of it at our home. I've noticed that they called it pearl barley when you bought it in the shops. Of course in thinking about it, I felt that it was called pearl barley because the seed grains probably resembled tiny pearls.

But that didn't satisfy me, so one day I thought I'd delve into the matter and see what the dictionary and encyclopedia said and of course the first couple of dictionaries I looked in didn't even list pearl barley They said barley, but they didn't say anything about a pearl. So I began to search and eventually here is what I found.

Pearling is the process of stripping the outer husks from the grain. So then the stuff we buy in the grocery stores is actually pearled barley —but for short they call it pearl.

The kind of barley we eat is properly known as Hordeum sativum.

While I was at it, I thought I'd go right through with it and here's something else I found. Barley water is good for many allergies. It is also beneficial for stomach ulcers, for gastritis, colitis and insomnia.

Actually this stuff we drink and call beer is barley water plus the barley carbohydrates rendered soluble by the malt enzymes.

That reminds me of a poem I studied of Tennyson's many, many years ago about the Lady of Shallot or something . . . "On either side of the river lie the fields of barley and of rye".

Blimey, Limey . . . A Rose Tree

Whenever someone writes to me or comes to the nursery and says he wants to get some Rose trees, I know at once, and I'm right in 99 cases out of 100, that the party is an Englishman, or of English descent. Why?—you ask . . . Well, because the English seem to be the only people on God's earth to call Rose bushes Rose trees. I don't know why they do this but it's still done. It's the custom in England, evidently, that Roses, as we know them, are called by the English, Rose trees.

Now that's absolutely incorrect because a Rose may be many things but a Rose tree in its natural state has never ever been found. It may be a bush, it may be a shrub, it may be a climber, but it's never a tree.

Yes, yes, I know that you and others have seen Rose trees. But these are Roses grafted on the stems that have been trained for years to grow erect and the Rose is grafted on top of it. It is not a true tree in its natural state. It is the concoction of man.

It is usually grafted on a rootstock of Rosa rugosa or Rosa canina which are vigorous growers and therefore one can get a stem 3 to 6 feet tall for grafting.

I thought for a while that maybe they called the Hybrid Tea Rose a tree because they were more slender in habit and were not as bushy or as hefty growing as the Mosses and the botanical types of Roses which can be found growing quite abundantly in Britain.

Anyway the English call them Rose trees and Rose tree is not correct. Now just watch the "heck" I'm going to catch from the English folks across the length and breadth of the nation as well as overseas.

Tree Full of Tulips

Everybody, and I do mean everybody, loves the Magnolia. An awful lot of folks call them just plain Tulip Trees because of their large tulip-shaped flowers, but Magnolia is the correct name. Soulangeana is the pinkish one and then Soulangeana nigra is the dark or purplish one.

Whichever you buy, they are very, very lovely. And these, too, can be grown in most places in the country although, where the sections get cold, they'll probably need a fair amount of protection.

But the strange thing about them . . . We find that no matter where you plant them during the first year or two, they will freeze back rather drastically—sometimes right to the ground—but next spring sees them coming up and going to town. About the second or third year, this freezing back seems to stop and they go ahead like crazy. I can't explain this action unless it's one of the few plants that takes an extra year or so to become acclimatized to the colder parts or the cold winters.

I've seen lots of them around Toronto and quite a few of them within 50 miles north of Toronto and they do quite well. But I think you must bear in mind that it takes a little bit of gentle handling for the first year or two. But, gee whiz, something with such beauty is worth a little effort, a bit of time and a spot of care.

Remember, this is a tree that is covered completely with thousands of huge flowers bigger than any tulip you've ever seen and it's completely bedecked—I mean right from top to bottom. There are no leaves on the plant and the flowers look so strange and unusual without leaves, but that's the way it is. Then after the flowers have finished, the leaves come and it becomes an attractive tree for shade or specimen.

Direct from the Kremlin

Here's a rather cute idea that comes from Russia. It may be worth considering. It seems to have possibilities even for the home gardener as well as for the commercial grower.

"The Institute for Agricultural Machines at Moscow has constructed a machine which lays one foot wide strips of special impregnated paper and covers this with a thin layer of soil after it has punched holes in the paper at pre-determined distances through which a few seeds are dropped. It is claimed that this paper mulch speeds up germination and prevents the development of weeds."

Hybrid Vigour

'Tis high time for you to learn and know a little bit about this business of hybrids.

It seems that everything is hybrid nowadays. It started with corn, then it was Cucumbers, Tomatoes and Petunias, African Violets and now most everything is hybrid. It seems as though if it isn't a hybrid, it isn't any good. Of course that's not true.

You have a perfect right to ask questions to find out what "hybrid" means. So if you will pull up your socks and be still for a minute, I'll tell you.

Hybridization means the crossing of two distinct inbred lines to bring about what is known as hybrid vigour. To begin with the parents are selected and isolated. Then they are self-fertilized for five, six or more years until they become genetically pure or what is known as homozygous. Due to the inbreeding for five or six generations, a definite decline takes place in the yield, resistance, height, vigour and other factors. Eventually the plants become very uniform in their weakness or debility.

Now after this has been done, these two inbred plants are grown together and cross-fertilization is encouraged. The resulting seed is called an F_1 generation by cross-fertilization.

Now in order to have the seed do this each and every time, new seed must be produced in identically the same manner every year. The resulting seed cannot be sown and produce the same result.

You see after a plant parent has been allowed to become inbred and then two inbred lines are crossed, a sort of explosion or terrific impact takes place and the yield, the size, the power and the strength of the resulting cross is in most cases phenomenal as has been proven in Corn and in other horticultural items.

Watering

Watch your step when watering. Bear in mind that plants in the hot summer, with temperatures from 80 to 100 degrees, hit by hose water at 50 to 60, get an awful shock.

Remember that most city waters are cooled and they're kept cool. This is not good for your plants. It can cause serious set backs and perhaps kill some of them.

Therefore, it is a good practice to confine your watering to the early hours of the morning or the evening when the temperatures of the air and water are somewhat similar.

Billy Shakespeare and I

Probably you will doubt the veracity of this statement I'm going to make but nevertheless, like all things I tell you, it is true . . . Billy Shakespeare and I had something in common.

Way back some time in the years around 1700, William Shakespeare planted a Mulberry tree in his native town of Stratford-upon-Avon. Unfortunately this tree was cut down in 1759 much to the chagrin and disgrace of the community.

Ten years later, when David Garrick, the famed British actor, was visiting the birthplace of Shakespeare, he was extended the freedom of the town and presented with a beautifully carved casket and a goblet made from the wood of that Mulberry tree.

On the occasion of the Shakespearian Jubilee, Garrick, holding a cup in his hand, sang a song which he composed himself and it goes as follows:

"Behold this fair goblet, 'twas carved from the tree
Which, O my sweet Shakespeare, was planted by thee:
As a relic I kiss it, and bow at the shrine:
What comes from thy hand must be ever divine!
All shall yield to the Mulberry tree:
Bend to the blest Mulberry:
Matchless was he who planted thee;
And thou like him immortal shall be."

It is also a fact that a Mulberry tree was planted by John Milton, the famous blind poet and one of the greatest poets in the English language, too, in the garden of Christ College, Cambridge. But each succeeding gardener from that time onward has regarded that Mulberry tree as his own personal charge and the Mulberry tree has done well. Even the smallest twig that falls from that tree is reverently and carefully treasured.

Fertile is Fruitful

The word "fertilization" in dealing with horticultural plants usually has two meanings. One—the act of cross-pollination . . . and the other —to add humus, manure or fertilizer of some sort to the soil. So let it be said here and now and clearly understood that, generally speaking, fertilization is used in two distinct senses in horticulture.

Now we come to a further complication. The words pollination and fertilization are used synonymously. I doubt very much if the average gardener or horticulturist would even attempt to distinguish in meaning between these two words and in truth I have yet to find a horticulturist whom I questioned about this who knows the actual answer. So without giving you a chance to show your ignorance or your great fund of knowledge, I am going to tell you the difference between pollination and fertilization.

Fertilization refers to the actual union of male and female germ cells within the ovule. This clearly and definitely indicates that fertilization is a biological process, depending upon pollination yet being entirely distinct from it. The actual dictionary meaning of the word "fertilize" is to make fertile or render fruitful or impregnate.

Now pollination is purely a mechanical means of pollen movement. It is better described by saying that it is a conveyance of pollen from the anther to the stigma of a flower. To describe the actual word "pollen" one might say that it is the fertilizing powder in the cells of the anthers of flowers.

The process of pollination is usually assisted by insects, wind, water and presumably many other means that nature might contrive to gain its ends. Many flowers are fitted or prepared for self-pollination without assistance from outside sources but, broadly speaking, nature prefers that her children cross-breed. It is said that nature abhors inbreeding and will do most anything to prevent it.

Clem for Short

I don't know whether you pronounce it Clem'atis or Clema'tis, but it makes no never-you-mind. It is also known as Virgin's Bower.

Anyway I'm very fond of this plant and I doubt if there is a more attractive climbing plant in existence—at least for the northern latitudes. One exceptionally fine feature about the Clematis is the fact that it extends its blooming season right into September, October and even November and you can have these beautiful, gay colored flowers practically until the snow flies in the fall.

Clematis is from the Greek and it means "slender vine" which is a good description.

Many people find Clematis hard to grow. I can't understand this because here at the nursery they grow like nothing, without any care, trouble, worry or work.

Some good authorities suggest that they be planted with pure sand piled all around the stem. It seems that they don't want bacterial action around the woody part and sand is comparatively free from soil bacteria. I've known for years that Clematis do resent deep planting. They're practically sure to die if you plant them down very deep. They should be set practically on the surface. Just protect or cover the roots with soil or mulch.

So it seems that the sand placed on top and around the stem of the plant doesn't cause bacterial action and the plants seem to thrive.

So from now on you can get good results with your plantings of Clematis by keeping the stems free of soil. Remember, plant shallow and keep some sand around the top to sort of keep the woody part dry.

They like a cool, rich, moist soil on the limy side—and excellent drainage.

Do You Know The Hoya?

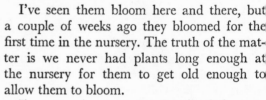

I've seen them bloom here and there, but a couple of weeks ago they bloomed for the first time in the nursery. The truth of the matter is we never had plants long enough at the nursery for them to get old enough to allow them to bloom.

I'm not going to try to describe it because I've been describing plant flowers for years, and to try and tell you of its beauty is absolutely ridiculous. How can one tell of beauty that is bewildering, inspiring, amazing and astounding? One just can't—that's all.

The Hoya is a long lived plant. It's quite common to see plants 10, 20 and 30 years old and their growth can be twined round and round, covering the walls of a room completely. It has good foliage, the leaves being thick, leathery and glossy.

They used to call it the Wax plant. The flowers are actually perfect white stars with another perfectly formed pink star in the centre. To me they always represented a diadem. The greatest jeweller in the world could not match the beauty, the form or the setting of these beautiful flowers in their natural cluster.

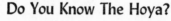

When selecting a floral bouquet or a potted plant for someone who is sick or a chronic invalid, stay away from the white flowers. Bring them something gay and colorful . . . yellow, pink, blue, red, scarlet, but not white. You see, white has a definite association with funerals and death, and some people may connect them and feel depressed. So stay away from the white potted plants and flowers for the sick room. Try to lend an air of brightness and cheer.

Breeding is Fun

The Mulberry tree has been a source of some irritation to me over the years. The one I have in my yard and the ones I see growing along the railway tracks in Niagara bear prodigious crops of lovely delectable berries and so I tell my friends to plant a Mulberry and they, too, will have berries. A good many of them planted them and they are 3, 4, 5 and 6 years old and still no fruit.

Now every indication seems to be that they should bear young. As a matter of fact I've had them bearing some fruit in the nursery rows out here.

Well, after 15 or 20 years, I think I've come up with the answer. I'm not sure but listen . . .

When a Mulberry tree gets old enough to bear flowers, all the early flowers or the flowers of its youth are pistilate or female flowers. But the young trees seldom if ever, carry any male flowers. That means that with the one type of flower only, the Mulberry cannot set its fruit unless it receives some pollen from another tree that has male flowers.

But as the tree grows older, more and more staminate flowers begin to appear and then we get the setting of the fruit. Remember, this is only my theory, but I believe there is sound basis for it. It's also to remind you that nature abhors inbreeding and does everything in her power to encourage cross-breeding, which she prefers.

You see nature would prefer cross-breeding, but if cross-breeding is not available it will accept inter-pollination and thereby the staminate flowers are brought into being.

Silence is Golden

You don't see too many birds in the cities any more and the chief reason is that they can't find enough to eat.

I remember years ago watching a little starving sparrow. It flew about until it could no longer fly very much—looking for food. Then it hopped here and there, but on the hard sidewalks and roads there were no worms and she couldn't dig into the soil because there wasn't any. So the poor little sparrow was slowly dying of starvation.

But suddenly, lo and behold, an old pedlar came by with a wagon and a horse and as good fortune would have it, the horse performed its act of nature there and then and dropped its excess cargo. The poor little sparrow could barely hop to the pile of luscious food. 'Twas indeed manna from Heaven. It had a good meal and it grew strong and could fly once again.

The voice that was stilled began to chirp, then a little louder—louder—louder—yes, until it reached a high crescendo that could only be brought about by good food and health.

Suddenly a hawk flying way, way up in the sky heard the sound and song of the sparrow and swooped down in a flash and with one fell swoop, swoosh—devoured the poor little sparrow. Good-bye, you chirpy, twerpy, sparrow!

Now there is a moral to this story and heed it well, my friends, lest the same thing happen to you. When you're full of that stuff, keep your mouth shut!

Mike or Riza

Here comes your botanical lesson for the day.

I'm sorry. Forgive me. Will you allow me to paraphrase the famous poet who said something like this,

"I slept and dreamt that life was beauty.

I woke and found that life was snooty."

Unfortunately I can't sugarcoat this harsh pill.

Do you know what "mycorrhiza" is? I guess you would plum pronounce it as though you were saying "Mike", "or" and then "Riza" . . . Mycorrhiza.

Scientists have not decided whether this is a bad hombre or a good one. You know science isn't as "hep to the jive" as are the "hepsters" or "hepcats" who can recognize a good guy from a bad guy in the westerns and on the screen in a split second. I think we ought to take lessons from these youngsters.

I don't know how long mycorrhiza has been known. It is commonly recognized as a root fungi and its connection with roots of plants is known as the mycorrhizal association. Now there are two main types of mycorrhiza. One is the endotrophic and the other the ectrotrophic.

Mycorrhizas are believed to constitute an example of a symbiotic association of mutual benefit.

Some scientists, however, state that they are merely examples of limited parasitic attacks.

Now we're not taking sides in this dispute with the scientists. Let the scientists look after themselves. They started this mess so let them get themselves out as best they can.

But no matter what the relationship between the plant and the fungus, it is absolutely clear that in most cases the plant benefits from the association. For example, in some varieties of Pine the presence of mycorrhizal fungus has been shown to be vital for the healthy development of young trees. Often a plant is starving for nitrogen and can obtain none because there is very little in the ground. So the mycorrhiza is made available to the tree or plant roots which otherwise might have died for the lack of this element.

In many cases the nitrogen content of the soil is so slow that the ordinary plant roots could never hope to pick it up. But by means of the mycorrhiza, it is able to ferret out even the tiniest trace of nitrogen in the soil, bring it forth and accumulate it in sufficient quantities so the plant can use it and benefit from it.

Glad We Are

The earliest records that I can find of the cultivation of Gladiolus is in 1596. Gerard, the famed English botanist and herbalist, cultivated them in his garden. He called them Corn Flag. Obviously it

was the Gladiolus byzantinus. Then they were considered quite common and not greatly esteemed. They began to be better known in about 1760 when one John Milton listed over 30 species—many of which he raised from seed which he got from the Cape of Good Hope. From then on they seemed to make greater progress and you see what we've got now!

Red Heads are Cute

Often, ever so often, I'm asked about Red Barberry for a hedge and from my reply, folks usually stay away from it and that really causes me a little hurt because I'm very fond of the plant and it does do a really fine job and should be used far more widely than it is.

Because of my unfortunate habit of speaking the truth when asked a question, I probably do myself and maybe Red Leaf Barberry an injustice. I tell folks this . . . If you want a very colorful hedge, this is it. On the other hand, if you want a very thick dense hedge, then you have to ask yourself a few questions. One is—Is there going to be ample sunlight? This plant is a waste of time and money if you don't have an open, sunny location because Red Barberry does its best and shows its true beauty only when there is adequate sunlight.

Then, it must be allowed to grow at least 3 feet tall. If shorter, you are going to have to do a lot of clipping and that won't allow the plant to show its true loveliness either. And remember, the Red Leaf Barberry is quite prickly and you have to be prepared to face the consequences if you happen to back into it accidentally.

Yes, mum, it is a nice plant, a good grower with luxurious color but it must have the conditions that I have outlined if you want to get to know its true fascination.

To my way of thinking, it is the most attractive, graceful and alluring hedge plant where only a short distance like 25 to 50 feet is required. Where a large expanse is to be covered, I don't think it would be advisable to use it . . . in fact I'd say don't ever. Switch over to Privet or something of that nature. But where short spans are needed, I think Red Barberry would do an admirable job for you.

Trees Save Souls

"If a house of peace you would erect
Then let nature be your architect."

All of us during some period of our lifetime have burned a tree or used wood for a fire. Surely you must have used wood for a table, to build a house or even to trim your doors and windows. You might even have used wood in the form of a birch rod or maybe you were flogged with a part of a tree yourself.

Now if you want to prevent being paddled in the hereafter, then plant a few trees to compensate for those you have cut down and aided and abetted in wrecking. 'Tis a debt you owe to the coming generation—your child, your grand-children.

For the mere effort of planting a couple of trees you'll be able to stand erect on Judgment Day and say, "I made the old world a better place, a healthier place in which to live. I helped conserve water to improve irrigation, to benefit the soil. I planted a tree." . . . And your puny chest will swell up like that of a bull frog.

While you're doing it, plant a good one. An Oak will be there for hundreds of years after you are gone. Make it a few and perhaps when you go "Home" the "Boss Man" will skip or erase a couple of those "bloomers" you pulled and thought you were getting away with. But he'll have them down good and clear on that day of reckoning. Perhaps if he sees in the distance a cluster of trees you planted he'll be merciful.

So now instead of Tobe the horticulturist, it's becoming Tobe the Soul-saver. The big thing is—make sure that you're not one of those "ginks" who made starvation and Hell and Brimstone one step closer!

Hybridize the Blueberry Tree

Fellows, here's your chance to attain fame and fortune . . . well, fame anyway. I've never known anybody to make a fortune in the horticultural business—at least not in Canada.

This Blueberry tree (that's what I dubbed it some years ago and the name seems to be sticking) is truly an Amelanchier. Out west they call them Saskatoons and it's also known as the Serviceberry and by many other names.

This berry really is good fruit. It's a nice tree, too. Well, now if somebody would go to the trouble of planting a few thousand seeds, lining up the seedlings and then selecting from these seedlings the ones that bear the best fruit and repeating this process for about two or three generations, then you'd really have the finest berry . . . and in tree form. What's more it will bear big crops. I'm sure it would be as popular as Cherries and, yes, maybe even as good.

So why not start yourself a proposition, eh? I'm a little too old for that now. I want a young fellow who has got two or three generations ahead of him because it will take 15 or 20 years to accomplish any worthwhile notable results.

But the promise is there. It would surely bring you fame and probably your name would be known forevermore.

You think 20 years is a lifetime—that's just what the judge and jury say. But in a garden or on the farm a man has just got the hang of the ropes and he needs 20 or 30 years more to round out some of his work. That's why you live longer on the land—there's so much that's gotta be done and it takes time! . . . And the big, good, kind Shepherd takes that into consideration and makes appropriate provision accordingly.

Natural Nitrogen

One hears so much about how plants can take nitrogen from the air and put it into the soil that needs it so badly—in fact, that's about the only way the soil can get supplies of essential nitrogen.

It was about 75 years ago that a German scientist by the name of Nobbe discovered that the small nodules found on the roots of leguminous plants contained bacteria that took nitrogen from the air and transferred it to the plant. This discovery was hailed as one of the greatest of the age and it was . . . because from then on we knew that legumes were nitrogen-gathering by means of the bacteria.

It seems that the bacteria live in the tubercles formed upon the roots of the various leguminous plants such as Red Clover, Sweet Clover

Alfalfa, Peas, Beans and other vegetables. If you haven't seen them, dig up an Asparagus Plant and you'll quickly see what I'm talking about. These tubercles are actually the homes of the bacteria.

Actually the legumes themselves—now, get this straight—have no power whatsoever by themselves to draw nitrogen from the air. But these tiny bacteria that are housed within have the power to absorb and free nitrogen and cause it to combine with other elements to form nitrates or other assimilative compounds ideally suited for plant food.

It has also been proven conclusively that as a rule, different species of bacteria work for different species of legumes.

So now you know how leguminous plants bring nitrogen into the soil.

Man You Were

Probably you heard me sound off some time ago about manure and why it was called manure rather than any one of many other things. Well, now I can really and truly tell you why it's called manure—and incidentally it has nothing whatsoever to do with the origin of the word "man", for which I am very grateful. Yet it has much to do with man as we know it.

You know the word "manoeuvre" which was frequently used during the war days. It means sort of sleight of hand or something akin to it. Well, that word is derived entirely from the French and the French incidentally, took it from two different words—the first one was an old word "manu" meaning hand and the other word was the common word for work "oeuvre". Well, when you combine them it makes "manoeuvre".

Many hundreds of years ago the tillers of the soil discovered that they must put something back into the soil. They realized in those good old days that spreading animal manure on the land was the most important function of the field husbandman. Therefore, the handwork of preparing the soil was regarded as being of prime importance. As the versatility and value of manure was learned in Great Britain, the English adopted the French word "manoeuvre—to manure" because they, too, felt and knew its value.

I only wish we had enough sense to realize that vital fact today. It seems as though man working with soil or a combination of manual labor with soil is manure.

Notwithstanding this, a friend of mine writes and tells me that he has a way of expressing the description of the various types of manure to be used. Here is what he calls them—horsh, cowsh, pigsh, goatsh —guano droppings are birdsh—sounds like a silver-barked tree.

213

Green Tears

Do you know the Baby's Tears?

I recall that the first time I saw the name in print I thought they were selling "baby steers" and it looked like an ad that a butcher put out.

It is properly called Helxine Soleirolii and one of its not often used but common names is Mind-your-own-business. Some folks call it Paddy's Wig. I call it Elusive Tiddly-Winks because the little leaves remind me of tiddly-winks and the plant will grow exceptionally well for a period and suddenly it will be gone and you wonder what happened to it.

The best place to grow it is in a semi-shaded location. We grow it underneath the benches or anywhere where it gets some shade and it thrives and grows and grows. It will make a mat as thick as 3 or 4 inches and cover any area as densly as vegetatively possible.

I ripped a chunk off the one in the greenhouse a while ago and in shape it resembled the hide of an animal. Truthfully it looked like the skin of a lamb except it was green. It's a pity it wouldn't stand a little more abuse. Otherwise you could use it as a green rug in your living room. This is no exaggeration—you can rip it from any place where it's established just like you could a bear rug.

Now I understand there are two other varieties of this same plant —one with golden leaves and the other with silver leaves. I'd very much like to get hold of these. In fact, I'm going to try.

White vs. Blue

There seems to be a fair amount of confusion between these two species of conifers.

Actually there is little cause for perplexity because there is a big difference between them. But some folks, when they are thinking of a Spruce Tree, say Silver or Blue or White and they sort of all mean the same thing.

Well, let me explain the difference between them. In the first place the White Fir is properly known as Abies concolor. It is a beautful tree that is found growing native through the entire west of North America. Its shape is better than the Colorado Blue Spruce (Picea pungens glauca) and its needles are slightly longer. Whereas the Colorado Blue Spruce has its most prominent blueness at the tips, the Concolor Fir is sort of steel blue, whitish or silvery throughout the tree. The Blue Spruce's branches droop and hang down, especially as the tree grows older, whereas the Fir tree's branches stand out erect

Both of these trees retain their limbs right down to the ground almost permanently.

Either of these trees is an asset to any landscape but what I'm attempting to do here is clearly establish the difference between the Colorado Blue Spruce and the Silver Fir. Most of the trees that you know and think of as Silver Fir are, in reality, the Colorado Blue Spruce or the grafted variety—Kosters Blue Spruce. The Kosters is the one that is high priced because it has to be grafted and it takes at least 7 years before you have a specimen worth selling. So if you are asked to pay $10.00 for an 18 inch specimen that is 7 or 8 years old, don't think that you are being robbed.

Straw for Strawberries

It has long been the custom of Strawberry growers to place layers of straw between the rows and among the plants. This has a twofold purpose. It keeps the hanging fruit clean, prevents rot and, to some extent, prevents damage from slugs and other injuries.

Some growers straw their plants in the fall as a sort of winter protection. Others put the straw down early in the spring. They use from 1 to 1½ tons to an acre.

Now here's an interesting point and something worth watching, when strawing Strawberries. Do not use oat straw, because it soon becomes rusty and will impart an unpleasant flavor to the berries. Other straws seem to be satisfactory.

No Hot Air

Did you know that trees are actually nature's air conditioners?

Without the protective shade of leaves and foliage offered by our native trees, a house can become an actual hot-box during the summer and not only would it be impossible to live in the house not shaded with trees during the day but it would take so long at night for it to cool off that sleeping would become impossible.

When you are planting trees for ultimate shade and comfort and beauty, take into consideration the fact that they should not be set on the east side because it's not the morning sun than can cause you any great difficulty or trouble. The morning sun is welcome in most cases. But it's the afternoon sun that you've got to worry about and it's the one that during June, July and August can cause your home to feel like the inside of a furnace. So set your trees where they will shade the west walls of your home and in that way you have the finest protective and comforting influence that one can possibly have around a home.

Remember, a good tall, spreading tree will cool the upstairs as well as the downstairs. You see, here is where there is a great advantage in having deciduous trees rather than evergreen trees because in the fall and winter and maybe early spring you want that sunshine and therefore your tree will be denuded and you will get that warmth when you want it and get the shade and protection when it is needed too.

Among the best trees for this purpose I'd recommend Oak, Crimson King or Norway Maple, Linden, or Basswood, Sycamore Maple, Ginkgo.

Not Fortunes

Quite some time ago I was talking about the Kolkwitzia plant and, of course, you've heard me describe it as the loveliest flowering shrub in creation. And from everything I've seen in the past 25 years, there is nothing that would induce me to change my mind. Yes, I still believe that the Kolkwitzia is the most beautiful flowering shrub in the horticultural kingdom.

It's a slender shrub with a graceful, arching, elegant habit of growth. It reaches a height of probably 6 to 8 feet when fully matured and a spread of almost as much. The flowers are sort of tubular with a very lovely fragrance and with a white to pinkish cast.

The flowers just cover the plant from stem to stern and from leeward to windward or fore and aft or whatever other description a sailor might use. It is not a rampant grower and doesn't grow quickly either. It takes about 3 years in the nursery to get a decent sized plant. Usually we send out 2 year plants and while they are not very big, they usually grow if given a fair amount of care and watchfulness.

I remember, when first writing about Kolkwitzia, I mentioned that it was discovered by Robert Fortune. In fact, I thought I read where he had seen it somewhere in China. But I could never get this established and no matter how I searched or where I searched through all the encyclopedias and garden dictionaries and such, nowhere did anyone tell me when the Kolkwitzia was discovered or by whom. But eventually I tracked it down and believe me, it took a lot of digging, too. I found that it was discovered by a man called Frank N. Meyer who was a plant discoverer of no mean note. I understand he was connected with the United States Department of Agriculture and did some remarkable work on plant exploring throughout the world. I probably will tell you more about this man later.

216

Smooth Skin Nectarine

Have you ever tasted a Nectarine? If you haven't, then you have a very, very pleasant taste sensation in store for yourself.

They're not very plentiful and they're not available generally. It's a shame, too, because a Nectarine is every bit as hardy as a Peach and they should be far more widely known and appreciated.

To the best of my knowledge and belief, a Nectarine is nothing else but a Peach without fuzz. Now you know how annoying some people find Peach fuzz. Peach pickers and those working in the packing sheds with Peaches certainly get itchy noses and when I was a youngster, they used to say that an itchy nose meant that you were going to kiss a fool. Well, certainly those gals working in the Peach orchards must have done an awful lot of fool-kissing in their day.

Maybe you didn't know it but Nectarines have been known for over 2,000 years and they are actually considered of finer flavor and texture than Peaches. A most unusual phenomenon takes place concerning Peach and Nectarine in that Peaches occasionally appear on Nectarine trees and Nectarines occasionally appear an Peach trees.

This phenomenon is not due to cross-pollination because this rarity takes place in the absence of either tree.

Darwin, who carefully studied and investigated the situation, could reach no positive conclusion but felt it was due to bud mutation or bud sports.

Now I've heard folks for years and years say, "Gosh, wouldn't it be nice if Peaches didn't have any fuzz on them!"

Well, a Nectarine is a fuzzless Peach. I promise that you'll like them and you'll enjoy the tree and the fruit and probably you'll be the only person within miles around who owns one of them.

South of the Border

I was just reading the other day something very, very interesting and new about Mexico—something I never knew or believed before and here it is.

There are more species of plants and animals in Mexico than can be found in any other individual country in the world. That's a pretty broad statement, but the writer is a man who should know—he's a Doctor of Science.

The reason given is, in addition to being quite a large country, it has greater variations of climate than can be found in most other countries and I guess that's true.

So just remember that almost a stone's throw from us, we have a country that has more species of plants and animals than any other country in the world. It's worth knowing.

We ought to go down there and do some searching for plants and I've been told that there are hundreds and perhaps thousands of varieties of plants that have never been discovered or identified.

Got some spare spondulix to sponsor an expedition? Barkis is willin'.

Wasps Study Anatomy

How else could a wasp unerringly shoot its venom into the abdomen of each victim? As you know, most insects have segmented bodies and at a certain segment, definite nerve centres are located.

The wasp, in order to use its victim for its full intent and purpose, must locate it, inject its venom at precisely the right point and then capture and retain its victim alive so that the body will not decay. That is why the venom only paralyzes the prey and thus it remains fresh so that it can be host for the larvae of the wasp to feed on and mature in the way that nature intended.

The ganglion or nerve centre of the insect is located in different insects in various parts of the body or in different segments. But the wasp knows the exact segment where that nerve centre is located for it shoots its venom in the right place and never misses.

Now I would comment to this that the wasps probably study only insect anatomy. They don't know the first thing about human anatomy because I've been stung on the posterior on many occasions and I don't know what benefit they expected to derive from that. I think 'tis assinine!

Evergreens and Water

Here is some advice about growing evergreens successfully.

Never allow an evergreen to go into the winter in a dry condition.

As a general rule, especially in the northern part of America, it is very seldom that we do not have sufficient fall rains. As a matter of fact, they are usually quite abundant. But I have known the occasional year when the fall rains were scarce.

In years like this you'd be very wise to give your evergreens a good watering. Don't do it too late. Probably October is about the right time. Just make sure that when the freeze-up comes your plants have had plenty of moisture around the roots. Of course, I am sure you will know enough to provide good drainage.

Now, while this applies to evergreens in general, it has been proven that it is most important for newly planted evergreens. Just remember it. Of course, it applies to broad leaved evergreens as well as to the needle type.

The chief reason for providing this water is so that the tree can absorb and hold all of the moisture it can. You see, during the sunny, mild days when the air is balmy and below freezing, the foliage gives off moisture and being frozen below the ground, the tree cannot replenish the exuded water—thus, causing serious injury.

Do You Know Hopalong?

It was a stormy day in early spring. Things had been very busy and at last when evening did come, I was really ready to go home.

I had my arms filled with odds, ends, doodads and parcels to lug home with me. Some were stuck under my chin and I barely could open the door. When I did, I looked down at the floor and there sat a toad and as the door opened he hopped into the office.

I stood there gaping at him in genuine surprise and I couldn't help saying, "What brings you here . . . of all places?"

Then I pondered and the reason for this visit was clear. He had evidently started his trek from the margins of the pond perhaps a mile or so away and in his slow, halting, hopping travel he'd heard motorists stop residents and ask them where Mr. Tobe lived and they pointed out the nursery.

So here he was. He had come to visit Mr. Tobe but he thought they said Toad and felt that it was a logical place to visit.

❖

Often it is necessary to fertilize a plant while in bloom. As a matter of fact many plants when in flower would very much appreciate some fertilization. Well, the way to do it is not with chemical fertilizer or by disturbing the plant. Get some liquid manure and water it with it regularly. You'll maintain your flowers longer, better and with improved color. Try it—it works like magic!

You Will Like This

Get to know the Passion Flower.

You know it's an amazingly beautiful flower —one that attracts wide interest and yet is easy to grow. It is a tendril climbing vine of graceful slender habit.

Each flower is 4 to 5 inches wide with a circle of deep red petals and sepals from which the characteristic Passion Flower "fringe" hangs. The flower structure is most unusual and thought to be emblematic of the crucifixion.

It grows easily and quickly from seed and the flowers are found in white, blue and purple. It prefers cool conditions and a fibrous loamy soil with leafmold. When in good growth feed with liquid manure.

Oh yes, the flowers are followed by egg shaped yellow fruits.

They Still Do It

Here's some really big news about grass seed. Agronomists tell us that 40 plants of Kentucky Bluegrass to a square foot gives perfect coverage and is all that is required to make a rich luxuriant lawn. Please remember what I said—40 plants to the square foot.

Get this, these same agronomists or lawn seed experts recommended using one pound of grass seed for every 250 square ft. of lawn. It is known that there are approximately 2,177,000 seeds to a pound. Therefore we are planting at least 8,708 seeds to the square foot to get 40 plants.

Yet, many landscape men and gardeners insist upon planting, yes, 10 lbs. or more to 1,000 square feet. So that you may see and judge the true merits of the case for yourself we have quoted the above reliable figures.

I've battled the landscape men and gardeners on the topic for years, but they still insist on sowing grass seed like snow covers the ground.

Acres and Acres

The word "acre" many years ago in England actually meant the amount of land which a yoke of oxen could plough in one full day.

That is the interpretation as it was in the 13th Century and defined by English law.

Yet, if we go back to the Babylonian, we find that in those days the word "agar" meant "watered land".

It is known that the word "acre" has been used in English for 800 years.

Another fact that is strange to note, is that in Ireland and in Scotland the size of an acre differs from the acre that is termed and measured both in England and in America.

The word was originally used in English to indicate any cultivated field regardless of size and it was only in the 13th Century that English law defined it as a definite area.

Roses for Prodigious Bloom

If you want Roses that bloom practically continually and profusely from June till late fall, then plant Polyanthas. Now they may lack the exultant fragrance and cutting qualities that the Hybrid Teas possess, but for every bloom you'll get on a Hybrid Tea you'll probably have 25 on a Polyantha.

In bud, and as they gradually open, you'll find them as exquisite as the finest Rose that grows.

They grow quite vigorous and bushy and are ideal in beds or for hedges. There is a broad selection of color that will satisfy even the most fastidious.

Plant these with confidence that you will have a grand show of beautiful flowers.

They are definitely more resistant to mildew than are other Roses.

Deserved Cognomen

The Christmas Cactus really deserves its name. Of course it is also called Crab Cactus, Lobster Cactus and properly known as Zygocactus truncatus—quite a chunk of a name for a plant isn't it?

Why I say that this plant really deserves its name is because I recall on the 24th of December last year I happened to be looking at our plant and there I saw a few huge buds ready to open the next day. Yes, on Christmas Day they were open and a succession of bloom continued from that day on well into the month of January.

Truly the Christmas Cactus is not only beautiful and long lived, but it actually does bloom for Christmas.

It is a native of Brazil, prefers a richer more humusy soil than most Cactus and is comparatively easy to grow. It is of drooping or hanging habit. A large plant, when in good condition, will give hundreds of huge red blooms.

Red + White = Pink

Here is a bit of advice for those of you who are interested in plant breeding.

Remove the stamens from a flower before it is fully developed. Then take the pollen from another flower of the same species and put it in the place where the stamen was removed or in the pistil. In this way you are preventing this flower from producing seed from its own stamen and pistil. This process is referred to as emasculation.

For example, if the stamen were removed from a flower that was red and you brought the pollen to this plant from a flower that was white the possibility is that you will get a wide range of pinks from the resulting seeds. You will also get some whites and also some reds, but you will get a varying degree of pink shades, whereas if you allowed the original pistil and stamen to complete the fertilization, all you would get would be the original red.

Now remember that the resulting seedlings, whatever they may be will actually be your own creation. Isn't plant breeding wonderful

My Darling Daughter

Did you know that the words "milk maid" and "daughter" are practically synonymous?

Begorra, yes, 'tis true! Way back hundreds and hundreds of years, the Anglo Saxons used to call a "dohtor" one who did the milking.

It is taken from the ancient Sanskrit "duh", to milk. As a matter of fact, then too as it is even now in most families the work of milking fell to the feminine members of the family—in most cases, the daughters. Gradually the word spread from the milkmaid to the female members of the family.

Yes, the word was used in England even before the time of Shakespeare. A daughter—one who milks.

Again the Good Earth

Did it ever occur to you that plant life supports every other type of life in God's great universe? I know you probably realized that plant life supports man, but remember, it also supports animals as well as our complete marine life—that is, our fish and the inhabitants of the sea.

Somehow or other most of us usually think that fish live off the water. A fat lot they'd get there! But the fact is that in the water float populations of microscopic plants known as Diatoma and these are there in unbelievable, unlimited, uncountable numbers and these vegetable plants form the food of practically the entire population of the animals that live in the sea.

The sea actually supports a tremendous abundance of vegetation along practically all of its margins and as far below the surface as light can penetrate and, believe it or not, it also supports vegetative growth a way, way out in the sea, many, many miles from land. That's where this floating population of microscopic plants is found.

So remember it is plant life that supports the sea animals too.

Easy to be a Good Cook

The secret of cooking, especially with vegetables, means cooking them fresh. The sooner a vegetable is cooked and eaten after being culled from your garden the better it will taste and the more health it will give to your body. Remember this, do not depend upon others —shops or markets—for your supply of vegetables.

Grow your own. Have the fun of seeing the seeds sprout and the plants lift themselves out of the earth. Eventually you will reap the harvest and enjoy a grand treat and, of course, do much to encourage good health and benefit your body.

Try it once and see for yourself the difference and you will never willingly do without fresh vegetables from your own garden whenever possible.

King Cole (Slaw)

Do we realize that cabbage is a wonderful food and has many, many virtues?

In this instance let's go to Cato, the famed Roman statesman, philosopher and horticulturist, for his opinions on this splendid food. He claims that the wild cabbage was the best.

He believed that it surpassed all other vegetables in food value. It could be eaten cooked, raw or dipped in vinegar. It aids digestion and is a mild safe laxative. He continued that cabbage makes a good poultice for wounds and cleans and heals all types of sores painlessly, will soften open boils, will cleanse suppurating wounds and tumours and heal them better than any other medicines. It should be applied as a poultice and renewed twice a day. It alleviates headaches and eye ache.

He recommends that it be eaten on an empty stomach for best results. It is said that an apple a day keeps the doctor away, but a head of cabbage now and then will do away with doctors forever.

O! Canada

Do you know the official provincial flower of our ten provinces? If you don't, take note. You should know them.

British Columbia—Flowering Dogwood; Alberta—Wild Rose; Saskatchewan—Prairie Lily; Manitoba—Wild Crocus; Ontario—Trillium; Quebec—Wild Blue Flag; Nova Scotia—Trailing Arbutus; New Brunswick—Purple Violet; Prince Edward Island—Showy Lady's Slipper; Newfoundland—Pitcher Plant.

I'd like to relate here that 'twas Nova Scotia who first took the lead in adopting a floral emblem. In 1901 the Trailing Arbutus was selected as Nova Scotia's own plant.

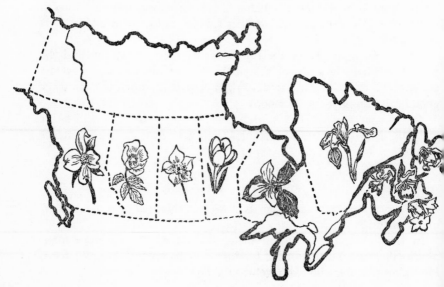

The Gracie Fields' Plant

Did you ever see an Aspidistra flower? Probably you never knew it flowered or never heard of it flowering. But it does flower. In fact

there are no plants in the flowering group of plants throughout the world that do not flower. But their ways and means of flowering are unusual and sometimes they are quite inconspicuous and are never seen.

The Aspidistra flowers at soil level and there is a very logical reason for its flowering at soil level because the plant depends upon snails, slugs and other inhabitants of the soil for pollination. You see—to each its own!

Green Grow Burns

If you've ever been down along the banks of the Rio Grande River, you would know that they refer to white men or Americans as "gringos". Practically every Mexican when he refers to an American will say "gringo".

Well, the way this originated dates back to the time of the Mexican war. When the American soldiers invaded Mexico a song written by Bobby Burns was popular at that time and the song went something like this—"Green grow the rushes-o". The soldiers at that time just loved that song and they sang it over and over and over again, until it rang or clanged in the ears of the Mexican people.

The words that stuck in their crops were "Green grow" and they corrupted that to sound "Gringo" and that is the way the Americans came to be called Gringos by the Mexicans.

Clever Fellow

I received a letter a little while ago from a woman away up north, who told me that they had a way of burning logs in their stoves so as to create the least amount of work for her, because, she said, her man was away a good deal of the time and she had to find some means of getting wood and heat.

So they would have the logs cut in 4 foot lengths to save work, and then stick one end into the fire. But as the log burned, she could keep pushing it further into the flame. Then she would get heat and they wouldn't have to cut the logs up. So I thought that was a very clever idea on the part of this man, I can tell you that.

Well, another woman I know and to whom I wrote and told this, wrote back and said, "My husband, he was much smarter. He didn't take any chances on things happening and being in difficulties. He protected me against anything like not having any uncut wood around during the winter when a woman really needs a fire. He left me in really good straights—he taught me how to use a buck-saw."

When is a Cactus not a Cactus?

The answer is—when it's not a succulent because all Cactus are succulents, but not all succulents are Cactus. Remember that!

In order for a plant to belong to the Cactus family, it must possess five characteristics. Now don't go off and say that a Cactus is a plant that can live without water or is drought-resistant. Don't chirp up and say that a plant, to be a Cactus, must have prickles or stickers. And don't tell anyone that a Cactus is a plant that grows on the desert, because there are plants that are not Cactus, yet fit each and every one of the above descriptions.

Now here are the five characteristics: (1) Cactus are all perennials. (2) In the seedling stage every Cactus must have two or more seed-leaves. (3) The fruit of the Cactus is a one-celled berry with no divisions between the seeds. (4) The flowers of the Cactus are always borne above the fruit. (5) To be a true Cactus, it must have aeroles from which the spines or leaves, new joints and the flowers grow. Yes, I said leaves because some varieties of Cactus do actually have leaves.

226

Remember, these five principles and you'll never be fooled about a Cactus.

Eve's Apple, Says I

You've all used the term "Adam's Apple" and I know that you know what it is, but I'm going to tell you anyway. It is that sort of swelling or enlargement at the throat that is found in every man.

Legend has it that when Adam took the bite of that apple, when Eve seduced him, the good Lord, in order to emphasize his sin, made the bite that he took stick in his throat and thus leave its mark forever upon him and his progeny.

Of course it's not fair for me to judge, and who would quarrel with posterity? But the fact remains that the person who did the seducing doesn't bear any sign of the crime. She got off Scot-free and she's still pulling the same stunts, whereas the poor gullible man . . . he bears the imprint forever more.

Anyway, it's definitely not Eve's apple—it's Adam's apple—now!

Why I Am Blue

I just read a letter in one of the garden pages of a magazine, where someone asked how to change the color of his Hydrangeas from pink to blue. The expert went on to explain how it was done.

Well, I just want to make it clear to you that all Hydrangeas cannot be changed in color. The only one, to my knowledge and belief, that can be changed or does change its color is the Hortensis variety —commonly known or called the Blue Hydrangea.

If the soil is not acid or runs to the alkaline, its flowers will be pink or violet. Where the soil is acid the color will be blue. As the acidity is increased the flower becomes bluer until it is the deep beautiful blue that we know so well.

Remember, as far as I know the P.G. or A.G. Hydrangea cannot be changed to blue no matter how much the soil acidity is increased or diminished.

The Hortensis variety is the one that reacts like litmus paper.

———❖———

When the weather man says you're in for a real killing frost, probably in October, why not dig up some of those Salvias that have been gaily decorating the front of your house and put them in pots and bring them indoors? They'll probably give you three, four or five weeks of continuous lovely scarlet blooms. Try it—you've nothing to lose!

Dare Face the Truth

Look me square in the eye and answer me! I'm going to ask you a pretty pertinent question and I expect a bold clear answer. It is a fact, is it not, that the produce of the farm and sea is the complete, total and entire means of a human being's sustenance? Now stop, reason, think. As of yet and now the food that we get from the toil of the farmer and from the nets of the fishermen from the sea, makes up entirely the food that we eat.

Therefore it is entirely organic or created by nature in its own way by growth and development.

Then why, oh, why, when we seek remedies for our aches, our ills, our pains and our mishaps should we go to medicines that are not organic, that are not natural and that are manufactured from chemicals?

Is it not reasonable and understandable that we should go to the same source for our cures as we do for our foods which permit us to live? Think and answer the question yourself.

Drat the Reds

It has been recently discovered by Russian plant physiologists that carbon dioxide, which is an essential ingredient for assimilation, is not gathered only from the air by the plant.

In these experiments the plant was prevented from getting the carbon-dioxide that is required from the air and soon the plant took measures to procure the required carbon-dioxide from the soil. That is, the plant roots began the search for ways and means of finding the carbon-dioxide in the soil and making it available to the plant.

Up until now, of course, it was generally believed that the only way that the plant could get carbon-dioxide was from the air and this discovery which comes from the Russians as mentioned, certainly will mean that changes must be made in our textbooks.

Rain is Good

One of these days when you've got nothing else to do with your time, get a couple of gallons of rainwater, by some manner or means and test two plants. Feed rainwater to one plant and tap water to the other. Give them the same conditions, the same treatment, the same amounts and everything else alike and see what happens. I have a silly notion that you'd find the rainwater plant much healthier, better and lovelier in a few months than the other.

Try it and write back and call me a liar. I predict you'll have better foliage and better flowers with fewer difficulties of every type.

I just think this is so because I've seen the results at times from watering with ordinary rainwater.

Robbers on the Farm

Quite often we sow chestnuts and other large edible seeds in our fields and in the spring we wonder why they haven't germinated and grown.

Of course, if a squirrel or a mouse or a crow learned or accidently found where these nuts were, sure as fate they'd go right up the row and eat or steal every one of them.

You'd wonder how they could do the job so thoroughly because not one would be left.

Now they've come out with a protection against this occurrence. You can coat the seed with tar oil or paraffin before sowing. Somehow this seems to deter the animals.

The only other way we know of is to stand around day and night with a shotgun . . . this is not very practical, though.

Unafraid O' Shade

This problem keeps turning up time after time, year after year, season after season.

It's like this. A customer writes in and says, "I've got a shaded spot in my garden. Hardly anything will grow there. I'd like to have some color there this summer. Can you tell me what would do well there?"

So I ponders, I thinks, I seeks, I hunts and this is what I write. "Well, if you want to get some color in a hurry and you don't want to spend much money and it's shady and nothing else grows there, get yourself a packet of seed of each of these annuals and you'll be happy forever more . . . at least while they're blooming—Schizanthus, Cornflower, Myosotis, Pansy, Sweet Alyssum, Balsam, Nicotiana, Periwinkle, Lobelia and Anchusa.

Here are a few good shrubs that will grow under these conditions too—Azalea, Rhododendrons, Barberries, Pieris Japonica, Kerria, Boxwood and Mahonia. While I'm at it, try these perennials for the same purpose—Hosta Lilies, Coreopsis, Columbine, Hardy Ferns, Bleeding Hearts, Aster, Lily of the Valley, Day Lilies, Coral Bells, Plantain Lily, Campanula and Aconitum.

Single not Bachelor

I'd like to call your attention to a little bit of pertinent information.

You will note that all the Double Tuberous Rooted Begonia plants will produce some single flowers throughout their flowering season. This is another example that nature cannot be denied because the double flowers are invariably male flowers or staminate and they produce only pollen and are incapable of setting seed, whereas, the single flowers are female or pistillate and they are the only ones that can produce seed. Therefore, the Begonia must have some single flowers if it's going to be perpetuated.

Isn't nature something!

Lamb, Julep, Wrigley

Do you have Mint in your garden?

You know the dang stuff has a million uses and it's so easy to grow. A sprig goes dandy with some cocktails and you can't beat it with lamb. Many folks use it for seasoning in cooking.

All you have to do is plant it once and it will be there for a lifetime. It will grow in the most barren soils.

So why not get yourself a plant of each and have them around for now and ever more? The most popular kinds are Spearmint and Peppermint, but you can also get Applemint. The Applemint is a little more attractive in growth and habit.

Buy yourself a couple of old auto tubes, mix spearmint with it, chop it up and the result will be similar to the gum you get nowadays.

Queenly is the Word

Do you have Regal Lilies in your garden?

In the mad rush of growing annuals and perennnials and such I've noticed that the planting of Lilies has sort of been neglected.

For a garden subject I'd doubt if you can name a plant that is more attractive, more stately and elegant than the fabulous Regal Lily. Most subjects are subdued by its beauty and quality.

If your garden does not have a good supply of Lilies then you are cheating yourself out of one of the finest things that can be grown. We grow about 5,000 of them here every year and to walk among them is a thrill that's hard to describe.

They're an easy subject requiring little care and definitely no pampering. Just make sure that they're planted where the drainage is good. They like a fairly rich soil and they'll bloom for you year in and year out and last almost forever.

Heavenly Body

In he comes on a late Saturday afternoon, striding towards me . . . "I wanna get me a Jupiter Tree—like so", he says, moving his hands up and down in the shape of a pyramid.

"A Jupiter Tree", I repeated. "You don't mean a Jupiter Tree because Jupiter is a planet".

"Huh, huh", he nods. " That's right—I wanna plant it."

Well, what can you do with a guy like that? Of course you have to understand that in the nursery business many of the folks who come to you for advice and to make purchases don't know too much about plants and trees. In fact, some of them are fledglings—having never planted a seed, shrub or cutting in their lives. So it's natural that they won't talk like botanists or horticulturists.

Still it would be better if they came to you and said, "I don't know beans about planting. What do you suggest or what do you advise?" Instead of telling me that they want a Jupiter tree.

Sabina Juniper

This is a low-growing Juniper but with a slightly more erect habit than the Pfitzer. I usually refer to it as being vase-shaped. It is spreading, dense, with short, straight, tuffted branches. It grows to a height of about 4 feet at maturity.

This evergreen is native to the lower Alps in Southern Europe and is also found in Greece, Spain, the Pyrenees and generally in the mountain regions.

It has blackish-purple or dark violet berries just about the size of currants which cover the plant in the fall and the bloom on the berries is quite attractive.

It is one of the oldest ornamental evergreens known and it has definitely been in use very close to 500 years. It was mentioned by Turner in his "Names of Herbs" which was written 420 years ago. The berries are believed to have definite medicinal qualities.

The planting of this fine evergreen shrub was once prohibited in France.

Along with the Pfitzer it makes a splendid landscape arrangement for foundation or wherever a medium, semi-spreading evergreen shrub is required.

Flowering Dogwood

'Tis a fickle heart is mine. 'Twas but a little while ago it was doing hand-springs because of the beauty of the lovely pink blossoms of the Apricot. How I esteemed its bold heart, its bravery and its courage because it came into bloom before spring had really arrived and while winter was still holding a tight grip upon us. I could not help but admire its delicate yet staunch charm.

But today, just a few weeks later, my heart is fluttering like a butterfly's wing for I saw for the first time this spring the flowers of the Dogwood . . . Ah, rapture—Oh, tender elegance—My epitome of loveliness. You speak volumes as you bedeck the bare branches with exquisite beauty . . . hide their bleak nakedness until nature's raiment, the leaves, can appear.

Dogwoods belong in every naturalistic setting—in every enchanted woodland. They are admirably suited for the wild flower garden. They want soils that drain well, but that don't remain soggy and yet never completely dry out. They are well suited to be planted along creek banks and seek locations that are rich in natural organic material.

Undoubtedly there are more beautiful trees in the world than you, Oh, Dogwood . . . but none has captured and enraptured my soul like you.

Know the Leucothoe

Properly 'tis called Leucothoe catesbaei.

Now I don't know what it sounds like to you but to me it sounds like one of Charles Boyer's love scenes in the bedroom.

This is an exceptionally fine broad-leaved evergreen that grows where there is little sunlight. It is one of the few plants in creation that really does well in dense shade and it is covered with splendid lily-of-the-valley like flowers. Later a reddish-bronze foliage throughout the entire winter contrasts with other evergreens—making a splendid showing even through the dark days of winter.

Of course it is exciting, too, for flower arrangements.

'Tis a close relative of Pieris japonica. Don't miss this little gem!

Spray Feeding

If you have been thinking of using the liquid fertilizers that are applied by spraying, my advice is don't.

I've been checking on the experiments conducted in Ohio to test whether these foliar sprays benefit the plants. There is nothing to indicate that this type of fertilization is of any value.

If the plants are not in need of fertilization, then fertilizing them in this manner is of little or no use. On the other hand if the plants are in need of fertilization, the quantities that they would normally require could not be met by a few gallons of liquid fertilizer spray—only a small portion of which might get into the plant's blood stream.

So don't be too eager to jump into this type of fertilization. The proof so far indicates that it is not worthwhile.

On The Bum

Bet you a cookie it will shock you to learn that the word "hobo" is of definite horticultural origin.

In the early days when the west was being settled, there was a tremendous shortage of men to work the land. Good wages and the wide demand for help caused a great supply. Men came from all over . . . an army of field-workers was created and they went about selling their labor to the highest bidder . . . eventually they grew into quite a sizeable army.

Well, as the farm machinery began to be invented and introduced, there were fewer and fewer of these wandering laborers needed and thus they became jobless. As they had no money to buy food, they became beggars and tramps—or better still, as we know them today, hobos.

You see the name originally meant "a hoe boy" and hobo today means "a man who bums for a living, going from place to place getting hand-outs."

233

Sawdust O.K.

Lately there has been quite a bit of to do about sawdust being used as a mulch and as a soil improver.

Reports of experiments from all parts of Canada and the United States indicate that sawdust is a wonderful material for mulching and for soil improving. It does improve the soil over a period of years. But it does not decompose quickly enough to give immediate results.

However, using lots of sawdust in your soil may bring about a problem. You see it actually takes away the nitrogen for use in its own decomposition that the plants need for themselves. That's why experimental stations recommend the addition of some nitrogen fertilizer when using large quantities of sawdust. So when you use big quantities of sawdust for a mulch and soil improver, add 7 to 8 pounds of ammonium sulphate to each cubic yard—thoroughly mixed with the soil. This means 2½ pounds per bushel of sawdust.

Tickle Me Timothy

One never knows wherein lies fascination and a thrill.

A while ago a customer inquired if we could supply him with some Western Catalpa seed. We said we could and he sent along his order.

This was during the summer and we waited until the pods were hanging from the Catalpa trees and then we pulled them off and opened them up to get the customer his seed.

But what did we find inside the beanpod, as I call it? (One of the ones I had was exactly 16 inches long.)

In the botanical books the fruit is described as a very long, cylindrical capsule separating into two valves with numerous, small, oblong, compressed seeds bearing a tuft of white hair on each end.

He's quite right . . . it is a capsule—cylindrical in form. But I don't agree that it separates into two valves because we had to cut the ones we had to get the seed out.

When the pods were fresh they could not be cracked by squeezing them. So I sliced right down the full length with a sharp knife. I did the same thing on the opposite side so that they separated and opened up—showing the nut, the fruit or whatever you call it. It was exactly the same shape and almost the same size as the outer shell and it was nothing but a mealy pulp.

So I looked about to find the seed. I thought perhaps it was in the pulp but upon checking the pulp and dissecting it as best I could, it revealed nothing.

Then picking up the pod or shell again and examining the inside of it closely, I found what appeared to be scales adhering to the pod or husk and in checking these scales with a sharp-pointed knife, they came loose. Actually it looked like an inner bark. But they came apart and each one looked like a small propeller blade and the black spot in the centre indicated where the seed was.

Here the encyclopedia was quite correct. They were small oblong compressed seeds, bearing a tuft of white hair on each end.

Actually the seeds lay around the inner part of the pod like a very thin, fine, membranous lining.

There was more joy and fascination in examining the fruit of that Catalpa than in a bottle of rye, a trip to the race track, a game of poker or even a T.V. show and it's free for anyone. Pay heed you suckers or chumps who are always short of money.

Too Lush Grass

Those of you who have always advocated the natural ways of doing things and the avoidance of chemical fertilizers on the soil will take heart from the following quotation.

"The intensive cultivation of pasture herbage with fertilizers is sometimes blamed for serious disorders in the health of grazing animals. In some parts of Europe 'grass tetany' is seriously incident and it would seem to occur when animals start grazing on new and lush pastures. Hypomagnesaemia is said to be on the increase in Britain and veterinary opinion has sometimes attributed this to a lowering of magnesium content in herbage caused through the raising of other mineral nutrients".

This quotation is from a very fine publication called "World Crops" and appears on Page 49 of the February, 1956, issue.

Seeing is Believing

In this horticultural business, a guy could go nuts easy—effortlessly and without even trying.

In fact I'm succeeding in encompassing this condition without even knowing it.

In practically every science, art or industry in the world there is, somewhere along the line, one supreme authority. In horticulture every gardener, every landscape man and every guy who turns over a clod of dirt is an expert, an authority, an unimpeachable source, a seventh son of a seventh son.

For example, today I happened to be looking up the data and facts and such concerning a plant called Medicago echinus. These are old world plants naturalized in North America, named from Media—the country of supposed origin. The fruit is a spirally twisted, unsplitting pod—sometimes smooth but also spiny. And each one of these peculiar pods contains 1 to 10 seeds.

So I turned to Bailey. He's supposed to be tops. He'd never even heard of the thing. He doesn't even list it. And the thing has only been known for a couple of thousand years.

So I dig into the Royal Horticultural Society dictionary of gardening and, lo and behold, I found it. But then something twitches in my eye and I can't find Medicago sativa which is nothing else but our common old Alfalfa. They don't list it! Imagine . . . That good fodder—the elixir of a horse's life—unlisted by the Royal Horticultural Society! Tsk! Tsk! Tsk!

So evidently Bailey is mad at one and Mr. Royal Horticulture is mad at the other.

However, in looking up the supplement of the Royal Horticultural Society, I notice they've got good old Medicago sativa or Alfalfa listed there.

Then I also notice that they don't list Medicago lupulina, which is one of the original Shamrocks. But Bailey has that one and the Royal Horticultural Society has forgotten it. It's not even listed in their supplement.

So between these two encyclopedias and a few others, like Paxton, Louden, Johnson, Gray, Green, etc., that I have to meander and check through, I've become a "mugwump". You don't know what a "mugwump" is? A "mugwump" is a guy who sits on a fence with his "mug" on one side and his "wump" on the other, and I'm telling you, I've become an expert at it, too. . . you can't tell my "mug" from my "wump".

Now this all came about because I was checking up on Medicago echinus which is also known as Calvary Flower. It's an annual that grows about 6 inches high with yellow flowers in sort of clusters. Somebody in some remote part of the Dominion wrote and asked me if I could get this plant for him so I started to make inquiries throughout my various sources.

No one in America listed it or knew of it, so I skipped to Europe. There, out of the hundreds of botanic gardens, I found two of them that listed it in their plant lists. So I wrote and asked them if they could send me a few seeds. I got a letter from one telling us they had lost their plants in the interim and didn't have any seeds and they wish they could get a few seeds themselves to start it over again. A few days later I got a few seeds in from Copenhagen, of all places. I said that I got a few seeds in but what I meant was I got a few pods in.

These pods looked like and were shaped like an acorn except that they were covered with spines. The spines were quite sharp—nothing that would hurt a man's hand, but for a woman's tender hand, it might cause trouble.

So I toyed and played with this little nut or acorn or whatever you might call it—husk. And Gerda said, "I guess I'll send two or three of these seeds or berries out." She was handling or toying with one, too.

I said, "No, don't do that. I want to examine it a little closer. I think the seeds are inside and probably there is more than one."

She was under the impression that probably they should be planted in the husk. I didn't agree so I got hold of one and tried to squash it —hoping it would crack like the shell of a nut. But it didn't so I began to pull at the ends and suddenly it popped like a spiral or spring and I began to pull at one end and the thing untwined. As I began to pull and unwind it, tiny, shiny, hard coated, black seeds began to pop out of it . . . first one, then another and another.

By the time I got finished uncoiling the thing there were almost a dozen seeds that came out and then I let go of the end and the thing just sprang back into place. I guess if stretched out and uncoiled the thing would measure probably 6 or 8 inches long. As it sat, it was probably only ½ inch broad.

But as I held the husk in my hand after, I really was impressed by the wonders of nature. If any man on this green earth of ours needs proof that there is a greater power than he around, tell him to get a seed pod of Medicago echinus and uncoil it and feel it and examine it.

Of course he doesn't have to go to Medicago echinus . . . just try a common Milkweed pod! We can locate that much easier—and be even more amazed!

Favorite Posy

Glad I'm not the only man in creation who appreciates some of our weeds . . . or am I?

I've always admired the Chicory when it was in bloom during the late summer or fall—yes, it's even prettier than the sky. And where, oh, where, oh, where can you get a better yellow than you see in the Goldenrod or in my favorite Dandelion? Now take these and some of those Asters you see around after mid-summer and the Wild Phlox and you've got a combination that's pretty hard to beat.

237

I don't know why I particularly appreciate these plants but maybe it's because I do quite a bit of walking and they do brighten my day and my horizon and help me feel chipper and happy. You see they're growing without coaxing, care, attention or worry. They give their all and get little or nothing in return.

Confusion or Order

Most of you have heard of the term "Orchid Cactus". Now this definitely refers to a type of Cactus called Epiphyllum hybrids.

Actually there is no similarity or relationship between Orchids and these Epiphyllums or Orchid Cactus. The only remote connection between them might be taken from the fact that they both have extremely beautiful flowers and also that they have Epiphytic traits in many cases.

In the event that you don't know what an Epiphytic plant is this will give me a chance to show off my superior knowledge by telling you that it is a plant that grows on another plant but yet is not a parasite. It also means that it is a plant that derives its sustenance from the air. Now to put it all in simple parlance— an Epiphytic plant is a plant that lives almost entirely on air.

Let's get on with the cleaning up of the confusion. The name Epiphyllum is a new term—actually having been used in the United States for less than 35 years and it replaces the old term, Phyllocactus, which has been used for over 100 years and is still used in Europe and other parts of the world.

There is also a term called Phyllocereus but this refers to a definite intergeneric hybrid—actually an Epiphyllum crossed with Heliocereus.

Now while we're talking about Epiphytic Cacti, you all know the widely distributed and much loved Christmas Cactus. Well, the Christmas Cactus is listed properly under Zygocactus and is called a Zygocactus by the botanists as of the present time. However, according to the best information that I'm able to find or locate, this Christmas Cactus is not a Zygocactus for the simple obvious reason that its flower is not Zygomorphic.

Again, a Zygomorphic flower, according to the dictionary, is one that has a set of flowers that are divisible into similar halves on one plant or it could be said that they must be bi-laterally symmetrical and, if the flower is not bilaterally symmetrical, it cannot be Zygomorphic and the Christmas Cactus is definitely not Zygomorphic and therefore does not belong in that category. But it is placed in that category and the plant is called Zygocactus truncatus although there are many variations of this interesting plant.

So if you are clear on the subject, and I have done my best to confuse you under the pretext of teaching you something, I should add here that Zygocactus does have irregular flowers of Fuchsia-pink which have a short tube and a 4 to 5 ridged ovary with large scales. The flowers when they first appear are usually slightly hooded with the petals opening wide on the second day.

Chlorosis Means S.O.S.

I don't talk too much about plant diseases because if your soil is well balanced and you give your plants half decent conditions, you won't be bothered too much with them.

I find here in our establishment that we're seldom, if ever, bothered with diseases. In the first place, we don't use commercial fertilizer and, second, we use sprays only very, very occasionally. As a matter of fact, the only spray I use at the present time is an Aerosol Electric Sprayer in the greenhouse probably 3 or 4 times a year. We try to keep our land in good condition. We don't over-manure but we add regular quantities of animal manures to maintain the tilth of our soil.

My ordinary experience has been that when farmers, nurserymen or gardeners grow the same crop three and four years and longer in the same place, even with the addition of fertilizer or manure, they will run into trouble. Therefore the old, old idea of crop rotation was sound then and is just as sound today.

Roses are a notable example in this instance. Now I'm not pretending to know the technical or scientific details because I am not a scientist or a technician. But after 4 or 5 years Roses in the same bed will tend to become difficult to handle. There will be diseases and mildew and mineral deficiencies will become apparent. All these things will make it difficult to grow Roses because you are maintaining a rose bed continuously in one location.

Now you may tell me that I am off my rocker because you have seen Roses that have bloomed continuously in one location for 25 years — or 50 or even know of them being there 100 years. I'll agree with you but that's an individual Rose. If you'll show me a Rose *bed* that has been growing and doing famously in one location for 25 or more years, then I'll pay heed and check and double check my thinking.

But let's get on with our topic. I want to tell you a little bit about Chlorosis. If you notice that some of your plants become pale green or almost white, watch out because you're in for trouble. Your plants are probably suffering from the disease called Chlorosis.

Now, this disease, as would any deficiency disease, definitely weakens the plant and causes poor growth. Your plant will not survive too long unless something is done about it.

In soils where there is a high content of calcium, chalk or limestone, the soil would be alkaline and Chlorosis is quite common in such locations. Actually the plants are suffering from too much alkalinity in this instance.

Of course, where you know this is the trouble, its very easy to correct. All you have to do is add liberal quantities of Peat Moss mixed in around the soil close to the roots. With next season's growth the condition will have disappeared and your plants will probably be thriving.

Plants that suffer this way in alkaline soils are usually plants that prefer soil acidity so the condition can also be remedied by moving the plants into another location and putting in plants there that like those alkaline conditions.

The word "Chlorosis" comes from the Greek and actually means "making green".

Pathologically speaking, it is called the "green sickness". But in botany it is usually referred to as a disease that causes plants to lose their green color or parts that are normally of another color to turn green.

In any event it usually or always indicates a mineral deficiency. So in this case the plant by its color definitely tells you that something is wrong . . . "Please help me!"

Grafters Note

Here is a very interesting note for folks who do any budding or grafting.

The age at which young apple trees begin producing has been found to be directly associated with the source of budwood used. This is separate and apart from the types of rootstock used. Trees grown from buds taken from a bearing tree came into flower two years earlier than trees propagated from buds taken from young non-bearing trees.

Own Your Own

In this little tale I don't think I'm going to tell you anything you didn't know before. But even if you do know it, it bears repeating.

It is considered to be a fact that Peaches, more than any other fruit grown, improve greatly in quality if allowed to naturally ripen on the tree.

I'm not trying to be melodramatic when I say that folks who have only eaten Peaches that have ripened en route or picked when green have never ever tasted the pure wholesome sweetness and lusciousness of a tree ripened Peach.

'Pon ma soul, the Peach crop, even at its best, is a precarious crop to handle. Most of the late Peaches, for example, if allowed to ripen on the tree would never remain there that long. The winds, storms and gales would blow them off.

You should be in some of these orchards when the late August or early September gales are blowing. The trees take a terrific beating. You'd wonder there's a tree left—let alone any fruit. You see, a Peach tree is heavily laden with foliage, apart from the fruit, and the wind just whips around there like all get out—and it can wreak havoc in a few short minutes and it invariably happens, practically every year, either the latter part of August or early September . . . come these wild gales.

Now, too, the bulk of the Peach crop is harvested in late August and early September and it's nothing unusual to find in the larger plantings dozens or even hundreds of broken, crippled trees strewn about the orchard after one of these severe storms.

Of course in the city you don't feel their effects nor see the result of these things . . . although occasionally I guess you do, too, in one way or another.

Let it be said here and now that in all fairness the grower would prefer to pick tree-ripened Peaches but that isn't possible. In the first place if he could leave them on the tree until they were ripe, when he picked them every finger mark and bruise would show up clearly at that stage of maturity and you wouldn't buy the "darn stuff".

Another factor . . . It takes two or three days, at the least, for the fruit to reach its destination and marketing place and this must be taken into consideration when the fruit is harvested.

Then, too, the fruit will gain in weight and size more in the last two or three days than it does in any other period of its development. So you see it would pay him to leave them on the trees.

On good authority it was estimated that in a 40 acre Peach orchard the gain of volume in 1 day would amount to a full carload of Peaches—that is, at the optimum point.

The net and positive result of all this is that you should plant your own fruit trees—especially Peaches, but all other fruits as well. Have your own and you won't be worried about marketing and quality and such because you'll have the best fruit that money could buy right in your own backyard.

Fuchsia Fruits

Sounds like a cobbler with a mouth full of tacks . . . sneezing.

Did you ever see the fruit of a Fuchsia tree?

In the first place, did you know that the Fuchsia plants of the greenhouse are trees in their native clime?

Now, if you were a native of Central or South America or even New Zealand, you would probably have seen the fruit on these trees. But if you're not, then I doubt very much if you've ever seen the fruit of a Fuchsia. For that matter—did you even know that the Fuchsia tree ever had any fruit?

To start, let's be realistic about this. Up until two days ago I didn't know that a Fuchsia had fruit, either—that is, it never occurred to me. I know if a plant bears flowers, it usually has a fruit of some kind or another . . . unless the flowers are sterile which is the case with a plant like Viburnum opulus sterilis and many others.

But generally and broadly speaking, in the horticultural world, if a plant has a flower, you can rely upon it having a seed or fruit.

Gerda was watering the greenhouse on Saturday afternoon just prior to taking our leave of the nursery. I happened to be walking through when she hailed me and said, "Here is something interesting, Mr. Tobe. Look at this!"

Lo and behold, upon examination I see a Fuchsia plant with two, three or four blooms on it and behind them, where blooms had appeared previously, there hung three fruits. They were very much like a Cherry. In fact, in color and texture, they were almost identical to our Sweet Cherries grown throughout the Niagara district.

One difference was that they were individual—not in clusters or bunches—and, secondly, they were elongated rather than completely round or spherical.

This was the only time I had ever seen a Fuchsia fruit in the greenhouse and we have grown many, many thousands of Fuchsia plants.

Upon checking the encyclopedias, I find that Fuchsias seldom, if ever, bear fruit under glass. Perhaps they act like the "Reluctant Dragon"—not willing to give their all under forced or captive conditions.

Nevertheless, I moved the one Fuchsia plant aside so that it wouldn't be bruised or woman-handled about so that I might be able to show it to some other folks like you.

About My "Langwitch"

A lady came in to see me one afternoon. She was a nice, fine, charming person, really and truly—mild mannered and delightful—every inch a lady. She was a dear soul. She came from Brockville and it was a gift to talk to her.

In the course of our conversation, she said, "I do enjoy your Growing Flowers very much but I wish you would use less slang."

I smiled and then walked up close to her and looked straight into her eyes and said, "Would you want me to pretend to be somebody or something that I am not? Should I change the language that I know and use for something that I might find in the dictionaries or hear spoken at "pink teas" which I do not attend?"

You see the language I write is the language I speak and it's the only language I know.

Another thing, I speak the language that I use in my daily conversation. I repeat the language that people use when speaking to me. Perhaps that is what makes Growing Flowers different to other papers. There is no attempt at sham or pretention.

I'm an ordinary country hick even though I was born in the city. I plow, I harrow, I sow seeds—Yes, I really do! And I know the language that the men and women in the country use—at least, I know that best. I know the other language, too, but that isn't the language I love.

So I write in the language that I feel and that moves about me. I do remove some of the obscene or rather bad swear words that some folks use. But, all in all, I just repeat the plain ordinary language of my country.

Now another thing, maybe it would be an idea and it certainly would be easy to remove the slang expressions if it would serve any useful purpose.

On the other hand, you may not recognize it if I did that. You know I don't think my voice would sound the same if it were smeared with honey.

A Tree Will Make You Free

Everyone in this wide world of ours is continually seeking independence.

Independence has a variety of meanings—depending on each individual's own interpretation. To some people it means freedom from worry. To others it means freedom from work. Then, without doubt, to some it means that they can tell their boss to go to Hell.

But by far and large I think independence generally means that a human being is seeking a shortcut out of his worries, cares, problems and troubles. And in some cases perhaps he wants to be free to do what he wants, when and where he wants.

You must admit that not too many people reach independence. In fact, few people ever know true independence and I believe that it is not even desirable . . . because history has proven that mankind is not mentally and socially prepared for true freedom and independence. What they really mean is financial independence.

Well, here is a way you can in a few years, with a small investment, more or less create for yourself financial independence. Now follow me carefully. I'm going to tell you the whole story and the true story.

It appears that the demand for Christmas trees is an ever increasing one. Between eight and ten million Christmas trees were shipped from Canada last year into the United States. Now the Canadian market itself consumes a few million Christmas trees and that added to the demand from the United States will probably run the requirements of Christmas trees every year to between 12 to 15 million.

That's a lot of trees and, granted that quite a few of them are cut from the natural stands of timber in various parts of the country, it is a fact that we are coming to rely more and more upon the planted tracts. Every year one has to go farther, farther into the backwoods and off the beaten path to cut from natural stands. That source is actually drying up or becoming too costly to operate. What with stumpage, cutting, dragging out, hauling, loading, transporting and shipping, depending on natural tracts is becoming almost prohibitive.

Now whether you have a couple of acres or 50 or 100 acres, you can start growing Christmas Trees. The three usual spacings are 3 x 3, 4 x 4, 5 x 5. This would mean 4,840, 2,722 and 1,742 trees per acre. Therefore by planting an acre at a time you can have 2,000 to 4,000 trees to cut every year. If you maintain a planting scheme of that type, and with trees running around $1.00 each, wholesale, you can see what the possibilities are for a good living after the trees are four or five years old.

The most popular Christmas Tree of all is the Scotch Pine. It is easiest to grow, makes the nicest shape and form and is most preferred by the American trade. The other popular and most planted varieties are Colorado Spruce, Douglas Fir, Austrian Pine, White Spruce, Norway Spruce and Balsam Fir.

An important factor to remember is that the Christmas Trees, especially the Pines, do best on sandy land which in most cases is wasted and not suitable for most other crops. Thus you can utilize waste land that can be had cheaply.

244

Remember that Pines grow much faster than Spruce and hold their needles much longer and appear fresher and more attractive for weeks, and even months, after they are cut.

So let's examine it again . . . Canada requires approximately 3,000,000 trees per year. The United States requires upwards of 30,000,000 trees per year. Granted that the Canadian market can only supply a portion of the American demand, it means that there is an actual need for approximately 15,000,000 Christmas Trees annually. This is a market that has never been fully supplied, the buyers are relying more and more on properly grown Christmas Trees and it appears that the demand for Christmas Trees is an ever increasing one. Therefore, Christmas Tree farming is at the present moment a very real and profitable enterprise.

Now I'm not trying to tell you that there is no work or grief and that growing Christmas Trees is a cinch. But I am trying to tell you that compared to most other enterprises, this is a really hot item. Only a small investment is required and it is well worth investigating. You don't have to start in a big way. Even if you had a plot of land that enabled you to cut but a few hundred trees a year, you could get the retail price for them which is from $2.00 to $3.00 for a nice tree.

You start by planting a few hundred every year and then about the 4th year you would begin to cut and this could be continued—planting a batch and cutting a batch. You would have the privilege of selling your trees wholesale or retail.

I Talk About Rex

This Begonia is said to be the king of foliage plants. No, I'm not going to crown anybody nor am I going to beat the drums for something without merit. But I will tell you quite candidly that the foliage of some of the varieties of Rex Begonias is fabulous—to say the least.

The variations in the leaves of the Rex Begonia are so unusual and so wide that they dazzle and confuse even the experts when they come to name or typify them. They have a metallic lustre that no other plant possesses and distinct zonal colorations of silver, gold, red, scarlet, rose, silver-edged and combinations of these, too. Some of them are so deeply colored that they border on black.

There are varieties of these leaves that actually look as though an artist had painted them with all types of metallic inks. As if this were not sufficient to give it fame, the wide variation of shapes of the leaves is really something worth noting. Of course I have not yet referred to anything concerning the texture of these leaves which also is exceptional to feel and touch. Some are like velvet, others like silk and still others like ribbed cloths and velour and satins.

If treated right, they live forever and ever but don't let me tell you or make you believe that they are the easiest things in the world to grow because they are not. But those who will pay a little attention and learn their needs can grow them as easy as "licking a lollipop".

One of the first things they've got to have is lots of humidity. If your house is dry and kept dry, then spare yourself the trouble of trying to grow these wonderful plants. They want shade and prefer the shade. Yes, they do too. They'll color up beautifully in the bright light but they won't do well. They do respond to good rich soil. You can't make it too good for them. They want good drainage as usual, but the the the best soil for them is usually made up of good old compost, sand and peat. Don't let the soil ever become dry as they are gross feeders—liquid manure is best.

In case you want to propagate them and go into the nursery business as competitors to us, well, here is how to do it. Lay the leaf face down and cut through the main veins with a good sharp knife. Then carefully lay it face up on some damp sand. We usually try to keep the leaf tight down in one way or another so that it will root quicker and easier. Wherever it is cut new plants will develop.

So the story is—if you can provide them with a neat shaded spot, lots of humidity and good rich soil, you should have no trouble growing Rex Begonias that will rival the colors and hues we expect to find in the "Happy Hunting Grounds."

How Little We Know!

Perhaps you wonder why the horticultural folk don't do so well on the $64,000 or other questions. Well, this may give you some idea.

Take the Orchids, for example . . . and what an example! They are quite a large horticultural family—in fact, one of the largest.

Prior to 1940 more than 15,000 different species of Orchids alone were known and recorded. You will gather that one man couldn't possibly know even a fragment of all the Orchids—their full proper names, descriptions, native habitat and cultural requirements . . . let alone all the rest of the many hundreds of thousands of plants in the horticultural kingdom.

So you see why Old Tobe says, when it comes to horticulture, there are no such things as experts. Believe me, my children, and I re-affirm—there really is no such thing as a horticultural expert!

Of course since 1940 new hybrids were created and new regions were explored—each contributing its share of new Orchid species. Way back in 1907 just one single expedition in New Guinea that lasted 2 years brought to light over 1,100 new species and it is fair to assume that there were at least that many more right in the same location that remained undiscovered and unnamed . . . waiting for you or I to dig further.

Now, while I'm talking about Orchids, I might as well tell you that they are found everywhere except in the extreme Arctic regions and the great deserts. Eighty-five per cent of them are native to tropical and sub-tropical areas. But they prefer the mountainous districts where they are found in great profusion and variety.

If you ever went up to Greenland, believe it or not, you would find a few varieties of Orchids growing there. I might also mention that to a great extent, or almost exclusively, the Epiphytical Orchids are found in the Tropics or Semi-Tropics, whereas the Terrestrial type are found in the temperate and colder regions of the world.

Another interesting feature about Orchids is that the pollen, unlike that of other plants, is not a powder but forms tiny, sticky balls.

Have you ever come across the word Orchis and didn't know what it was or referred to? I'll bet you many of the sharp horticulturists don't know this. Orchis is actually a genus of about 80 species of Terrestrial Orchids found in temperate Europe, Asia, North Africa, America and the Mascarene Islands.

Would you like to know how the word Orchis got its name? Well, in Greek the word Orchis means "testiculate"—referring to the two oblong, ball-like tubers found in many of the species or because many of its roots are in the shape of testicles or nuts.

Do You Like Asparagus?

Well, it's not surprising that you do. As a matter of fact, Asparagus has been a delicacy for mankind for more than 3,000 years.

Yes, if you go back to the time of Cato, the elder, in 234 B.C., you'll find that he wrote an article on farming and mentions Asparagus and tells you how to grow it. And would you believe it? . . . The methods and ways of growing Asparagus back in 234 B.C. are practically identical with the methods used today. So either they were "doggone" smart people back in them days or we haven't learned very much.

In those days he suggests fertilizing with sheep manure. Well, that holds good today, too. But of course horse manure, cow manure or any other animal manure would be just as good—or would it? It would be a lot better than commercial fertilizers anyway.

Asparagus is also lauded very highly by another Latin writer by the name of Columela. He was also a specialist—That is, he wrote mostly about agricultural matters. He was alive in the 1st Century A.D.

In the early days in England they used to call Asparagus "Sparrow Grass" and today they say only the uneducated people call it "Sparrow Grass" . . . so be careful how *you* say it. . . . Well, here's what I call it—"Asper-gus".

It doesn't make a bit of difference what you call it. There is no better vegetable or green grown in our land or any land than dear old Asparagus. One of the good things about it is that is is so easy to grow.

You set out the nice, well rooted pips early in the spring and then you don't cut it for a year. Then you can cut it the second year or the third year and from then on for 20 years. Just imagine—by planting it once, you can cut it for 20 long years or more. Now where, oh, where, can you get a greater rate of interest for your investment?

By planting a hundred or two of Asparagus pips you will have enough to grace your breakfast table or as a vegetable with other courses from early May until July every year—and if you're smart, you'll also have lots to can up so that you can continually enjoy it summer, fall, winter and spring.

Need I plead with you to do what is best for you?

Hazel the Witch

I've often wondered how the Witch Hazel got its name. Which Hazel are we talking about?

It seems that the plant was named because treasure seekers used its branches to make divining rods.

60 Down — 40 To Go

What can a man do with convictions or beliefs that are a part of his soul? Stifle them? Kill them? Restrain them? Or allow them expression and manifestation?

A man can't continually go about shouting everything he thinks and believes through all the years because soon he would be labelled a fool, and indeed, a fool he would be.

But on the other hand, after an idea or a conviction has tried to emerge from a man's conscience and he still keeps the hatch battened down on it, I'm afraid this is not right and an explosion may occur physically or mentally—or the inspiration will die ere 'tis born.

Going back more than 20 long years, I've had the feeling that all of the elements that I learned about when I was a boy studying chemistry have a meaning to a man. I don't just mean that they are written in the text books and therefore have some significance. I'm referring to a man's everyday life. I contend that each and every one of the elements forms a basic part of man's existence.

I don't mean that Heaven created iron for man to make cannons or nitrogen for man to make gunpowder or uranium for man to make "deathnicks". No, I suggest for use by vegetative and animal life.

For too, too many long years have horticultural scientists played around with the three major elements which they claimed were the main parts of the agricultural development of mankind . . . namely, nitrogen, phosphorous and potash . . . and ignored or misunderstood the value of and need for the others.

Of course now we realize that many of the minor elements also play a vitally important part in agriculture and in man's survival.

But, no, I'm not content with adding a few more, and maybe later on a few more elements, and accepting that as satisfactory. It is my feeling that all of the elements—yes, the whole list of more than 100 —play a part in animal and vegetable life of the universe . . . and that genuine, bountiful health cannot be had without all of the elements taking their role. Some, it is granted, we use in large quantities and some are required in lesser amounts and still others in infinitesimal degrees. But even these insignificant particles play a vital part in the health of plant and animal life.

In these infinitesimal quantities of elements, in my humble but profound opinion, lies the cure of the most dreaded diseases known to man.

Most of the elements we get into our systems by means of the food we consume. Some we breathe into our lungs and bloodstream. Then, too, there are those that permeate through our pores from the rays of the sun and other planets. And last, but not least, there are the elements we take into our bodies by contact with the good earth itself —when working in our gardens, walking barefoot or even when we kneel in humble supplication and prayer . . . Pray your way to good health—Roll up your skirts and trousers, get on your bended knees, you sinners, and pray often and long!

It is my sincere conviction that many of these vital elements are denied us and therefore keep us in poor health because of the heavy shoes, the sidewalks, the pavement and the other things and ways that keep us from contacting the good earth directly with some parts of our bodies.

Perhaps that is why devout gardeners live longer than most segments of our population. It has always been my contention that folks who have direct contact with the land live longer than any other group of society. Refute this if you can!

I Saw A Redwood Die

I saw a Redwood fall . . . it was *not* an inspiring sight! I was not thrilled. In fact it was sad and depressing. As I watched it thunder down the mountainside I felt for a moment as though civilization itself was crumbling before my very eyes. There but a short time ago had stood this giant Redwood—a symbol of nature's permanence—fully 200 feet tall, in robust health and perfect well being. Now I stood on a ridge and viewed its corpse as it lay still beneath my feet. Man had done his work well.

The destruction of a Sequoia is no mean undertaking. The executioner must study his job and he does not do it alone. Here is how the job is accomplished.

First the men cut a few incisions in the tree with the old-fashioned axe and from this foothold a scaffold is erected. Then they go round to the other side of the tree and make a few good sized nicks with the axe so that the blade of the saw can dig right into the wood—not bark or cambium.

Now with the power tools, they cut a chunk out of the tree to a depth of 2 or 3 feet. Then they make another cut above it but at an angle and remove a long narrow wedge. This will cause the tree to fall in the desired direction. Then they go around to the other side where they have built their platform and begin the work of sawing—by power, of course.

The cutters had penetrated deeply into the tree. As the last sinews of its red heartwood were being cut the tree began to sway slightly and then it leaned towards the side where it was undercut. It swayed and then wavered—still holding on to those few life-sustaining inches that were not cut and which the woodsman's saw never cuts.

Then as it began to lean farther over, it seemed to hold—to clutch

—to grab— just like a drowning man—and the earth shook as though an earthquake had struck as the huge tree tugged on its roots to help keep it from falling . . . then it was all over! The last few sinews snapped and down hurtled the noble specimen—trying to take its roots and surrounding acres with it.

As the tree rolled down the mountainside the smaller Pines and Firs (which here would be giants) in its path were felled like nine pins. When the tree finally landed at the foot of the mountain it raised a cloud of dust that could be compared only with the sight caused by an atomic explosion—at least, so I imagine . . . never having witnessed an atomic explosion.

Can you share my feeling? This tree . . . this memorable part of antiquity was about 2500 years old. It stood by thro' the rise and fall of Rome. It was but young when mighty Caesar ruled the earth. It was there growing when Christ was born—yes, and Confucius and Gautama, too.

The Redwoods are one of nature's most permanent and indestructible creations. They are mere striplings until they reach the age of 300 years and then life begins for them. Insects, storms, the elements and, yes, even fire cannot harm them. They laugh at lightning. Evidently the thick impenetrable bark insulates the tree both against lightning and fire. They are without doubt the grandest living things on earth.

This 200 foot tree yielded more than 60,000 feet of good lumber and that was why it was felled. Thank Heaven, now organizations have been formed throughout the United States to protect and prevent the destruction of these miraculous specimens of God's grandeur. There are still a few privately owned groves and, of course, the owners can do with them as they please.

These trees, you see, have nothing else to fear . . . no, nothing but the machinations of man and perhaps the eruption of a volcano or an earthquake. Yes, only man is their mortal enemy. Man and his axe or his saw are the only things that can destroy them. But even these have only reduced very few of these colossi. Evidently they must be highly favored in the eyes of the Lord . . . and no wonder!

These great, grand specimens of nature's handiwork are found only in California and a small part of Oregon. Remember, they are native to no other part of the world.

It was my privilege to see a petrified Redwood tree some years ago and it thrilled me more to view this solid stone tree which had lain in its lava bed for many thousands of years (the scientists say millions) than it did to see a living tree die. The petrified tree was per-

fect in every way. Every fissure was clearly marked. Think of it . . .
a colossal tree of solid rock!

Which End is Up?

I'm asked that question about bulbs and tubers at least a thousand
times a year and, to be quite blunt about it, I don't know the answer.

Now in a Begonia, the side with the depression is usually the upside.
In a Gloxina, the part with the hair is usually the downside and the
part that is more or less shiny without the hair is the upside.

In a Canna, you look for the reddish sort of enlarged or alive-like
looking pip. In a Calla, you've got to use a microscope to see if you
can see the swelling of one of the sides where it might indicate something is starting to grow. Actually there is no way to tell when it is
completely dormant. In a Caladium, it's even worse. There isn't
the faintest sign or indication of which side is upside, downside or
sideways.

Talking about Peonies, of course there is always an eye and that
helps. In Bleeding Heart there is also usually a bit of growth, practically any time of the year but still it can be tricky. With a dormant Phlox plant the black coarse roots indicate which end is down.
Take an Eremurus, the thick fleshy pip indicates the upside. Again, in
the Crown Imperial, it's not easy but there is usually a depression in
the part that is to be up. It's usually a good sized bulb and it has
a very fetid odor. It smells like a ripe skunk.

Looking at an Anemone, you let the bulbs soak in water for 48
hours and then you've got to do a little guessing although the shiny
part is usually the part I place up. With Ranunculus, the fact that
there are sort of claws and the claws go down is the way you know
which end goes into the earth for the root.

In most bulbs usually the pointed part is up and the flatter part is
down. So that's that!

How about a little digression for a few minutes . . . .

Every town has its "character" or "characters" and dear old Niagara is no exception—except, of course, that we may have a few more
characters than any other community of its size in Canada.

Some of the "characters" are from the upper status of society and
some of the medium status and then again there are others who are
lower down on the social sliding scale.

As I said before, Niagara has a little more than its share and of
course you gathered that I meant the upper strata—naturally.

I passed by the chief constable one day as he was wrestling with one of our characters who was lying out on the sidewalk dead drunk. He wanted to get the character on his feet so that he could take him in his car and haul him to the gaol. There he was prodding his foot into the rear of the drunk, saying, "Come on now, Bill. Get up—get up!"

And this time the inebriated one managed to get as far as his knees, but his hands were still on the ground and so was his head. Again the sharp bawling came, "Get up, you lazy drunk. Get up!"

This time you could hear a noise coming from the lips or mouth or the throat of the drunk, saying, "I . . . I . . . wanna . . . I wanna get up . . .but which way is . . . *up?*"

As it stands I've only helped muddle you up so far in this lesson but just the other day I was stymied when a woman asked me about a Sweet Potato that she said she wanted to grow. She understands they make beautiful plants and she wanted to know which side to plant up and which side to place in the water.

Well, lucky for me and for her, too, my education re Sweet Potatoes has not been sadly neglected and I could tell her that it didn't make any difference which side she placed up or down because the downside would grow roots and the upside would grow tops. Even if you laid it sideways, the middle section would grow roots if it were touching soil or water and it wouldn't matter whether it were upside or downside. Then, too, if you cut it in half, the part imbedded in soil or touching water would grow roots and the upper part—stems, leaves and flowers.

Evidently in some plants it is a matter of light and darkness and sun and moisture that decides which way the roots go.

Don't look to me for a lot of details and explanations. I've told you a thousand times that I'm not an expert and this proves it.

Penny Saved is Earned

What kind of fertilizer will I use?

Nearly every time that somebody comes out here and buys a plant, no matter whether it's indoor, outdoor, seed, bulb or tree, they always somewhere along the line ask that question.

In days gone by I'd sort of see red but nowadays I see a light instead. And I calmly reply, "None, please."

"If and when", I continue, "you buy plants elsewhere and they advise you to use fertilizer, chemical, organic or otherwise, then go ahead and use it. That's your business but on my plants don't use anything, please."

"That's funny . . . how will it grow?" they ask me.

"Well", I reply, "If your soil is so badly in need of nourishment and other conditioning that it won't grow anything, then the injection of a bit of fertilizer isn't going to do it a heck of a lot of good. On the other hand, if your soil is natural, ordinary garden soil as is found in most places in our good country, then it will be able to support the plants in question."

To begin with, let me emphasize that I am in the plant business. I am a nurseryman and a seedsman. I am not in the fertilizer business and, while selling fertilizers might make a little extra profit for me, I don't see why I should ballyhoo up someone else's product for the sake of making him some money to the detriment of my customer's pocketbook and maybe his soil.

Shush, don't blast at me. I'm not even telling him to use organic fertilizer. Sure, if the soil is impoverished, something has to be done. But in most cases I have not found the soil impoverished. Most of the soil in this country is comparatively good, as yet.

If you have a garden and you wish to maintain your soil fertility, then I say to you, "Use compost continually." That is, replenish the soil as it bears its crops and you will retain its tilth and well being "for aye".

Now I'll go further. In my humble opinion most soils that are run down are not deficient in mineral content. They are deficient in humus content. The minerals are there. It's just that the plant roots are unable to use them without a satisfactory humus content. Therefore if you feel you must add something to your soil when you plant, then I'd say unto you, "Add Peat Moss. Then you know you can't be wrong."

If you're one of those duffers who must add something (You're probably so big hearted that you feel you've got to do something for everybody—even your soil) buy yourself a bag or bale of Peat Moss and add it to your soil. So instead of spending $4.00, $5.00 or $6.00 on a bag of fertilizer, spend $1.00 for a bag of Peat Moss and you'll be treating your plants royally.

Now remember, don't feel that it's necessary to add fertilizer every time you plant anything. I decry it—I bemoan it—I warn against it—and, what's more important, never ever when planting trees or plants put fertilizer in and around the roots unless you intend to kill them or prove that your nurseryman sold you poor plants.

When your plants have become established, I think it's a good idea to incorporate mulches, manures, or, better still, compost. Then if you want to use fertilizers, chemical or otherwise, then go ahead and use them. Boys must be boys and every dog must have his day.

I have contended for years that the application of chemical fertilizers when planting has killed more plants than they make grow. If you want good plants and you want them to grow well, treat them as we request. You'll be happy and we'll be kicking our heels in the air, too.

Pugnacious Plants

This is about plants—you'd never know!

This is the "fighting" department because it deals with hydrophytes, xerophytes, halophytes and mesophytes. However, it sounds like a "hallowed mess of fights".

Well, the first one—hydrophytes—refers to water plants as the name would indicate. Among it are included water lilies, cat-tails and iris. They are adapted to an excessive amount of water and are found in wet places. They may be submerged or have floating leaves or immersed but have roots in saturated soil.

They often have leaf structures to resist evaporation to help them keep from drying out when water is ice cold or frozen.

The problem of these plants is to live in the water yet breathe air because they don't have gills like fish.

They usually have a poorly developed conducting system.

They have large air spaces in their tissues—especially the underwater organs—to facilitate internal passage of air to assure an uninterrupted supply.

All right—now let's deal with dry plants . . . the xerophytes . . . for example, pine, oleander, cactus, succulents. These are plants of the arid regions, sand and rocky soils and they include most of the plants that are called epiphytes (still more fights).

Their problem is to store water and prevent evaporation. Therefore, they have been provided with thick skin, waxy, sticky or hairy mucilaginous juice, great reduction of leaf surface, rolling leaf blades so that the stomata or breathing spores are on the inner surface, fleshy underground stems, bulbs and fleshy roots that store water beneath the surface of the soil. They are adapted to a limited water supply.

Next we come to the saline plants or the halophytes. They are plants that have learned to live in locations where there is an excessive quantity of mineral salts. Plants of this group are Salicornia, Suaedo, Obione, Molinia and Empetrum.

They are adapted to soils with an excess of mineral salts—usually salts or soda. They are found along sea coasts, in coastal marshes and round salt lakes or springs.

The problem of this type of plant is to get sufficient water without killing itself by absorbing excessive quantities of harmful minerals. Therefore its structure is in some way similar to the xerophytes—reduced leaf surface, mucilaginous juice, hard or thick skin. This enables them to stay alive until they can replenish their supply of fresh sweet water.

So far as can be determined they do not have special organs or means of changing the mineral conditions of the water. A state of physiological drought exists—that is, lots of water (like in Coleridge's "Ancient Mariner" . . . Water, water, everywhere, Nor any drop to drink) but absorption by the roots is difficult so plants can suffer from drought.

Now we come to the mesophytes or middle plants. They seem to be in between the hydrophytes and the xerophytes. Maples, elms, basswood and most of our good deciduous trees are in this group.

They require a sufficient supply of water but definitely not an excess. They just want ordinary conditions—not too dry and not too wet.

Now those found in the tropical forests have broad thin leaf blades to allow water to be quickly evaporated and need no special protection against excessive transpiration. They grow only where they are never water-logged or allowed to become too dry. They are the normal land plants. Practically all deciduous trees are mesophytes.

Plants must adapt themselves to change or be exterminated because the earth's physical features are constantly changing.

Thus their problem is to maintain equality or normal conditions—not too much water or too little.

All this is actually a study of ecology—the adaption of plants to their surroundings.

Vulgar Forsythia

I wouldn't have planted one in my garden—no, sir, not me! Why that cheap, common, little twerp—just everybody had it. It was growing in everybody's backyard and was included in everyone's garden or landscape scene—along fences and corners—shady and sunny—wet and dry. Wherever I went the vulgar Forsythia was a sore in the eye. It grew in the hills and the dells and on the sand or in the clay and on the marsh or the highway.

Well, for me, I didn't want any part of it. Yes, I was pleased at my resistance—or, as some people might call it, jackass stubbornness! Then came that day in early spring—how well I remember! 'Twas bleak, dismal and miserable and it had been like this for days. The wet sleet was falling, making me more miserable than I was. As I walked along the street (I had to be out—I had an errand to do that had to be done and therefore I couldn't seek shelter at home) there in the distance I noticed a glow—a brightness. It was cheery and pleasant in this dismal atmosphere—like the dove on the ark. I wondered what it was and tried to figure it out but I couldn't even come close to the answer.

When I came up to it, there it was—a small Forsythia bush completely covered, including every tiny branch and twig, with lovely golden, glowing flowers. Ah, I felt sheepish and ashamed. The Forsythia is sort of an emblem of hope. It believes in the calendar. When the calendar says spring is here, the Forsythia springs into bloom. Though the weather man may break faith with us who live on this good earth, the Forsythia believes him and stays out in bloom—not pulling back in fear like some others are wont to do.

Sure, it's all right for the calendar to tell us spring is here. It hangs up on the wall in comfort, peace and ease. It doesn't have to go out and brave the weather that it tells you is so delightful. Yes, and the calendar doesn't have to be exposed with its bare face hanging out to catch the full force of a March wind and the sharp sleet and the snow and the slush.

Of course that's spring. You occasionally see a bright gleam of sunlight, too. But the Forsythia, it braves the elements. Spring is spring—the calendar said so and it must know—it wouldn't tell a lie!

So those glorious, golden, glistening flowers remained for days and days and weeks and weeks. But eventually spring at last did come in earnest . . . as the Forsythia knew all along.

> Blessings on you
> little golden bells
> For 'tis a tale of faith
> your courage tells.

Robert Fortune first found the shrub growing in China in what was called the "Grotto Garden" of a Chinese mandarin. Later in his wanderings in the interior he discovered it growing naturally in the mountains of Chekiang. Fortune tells of his joy at finding it "where I thought it even more ornamental in its natural state amongst the hedges than when cultivated in the fairy gardens of the mandarins."

It bears the name of a great man—one who has done more for the improvement of fruit culture than any other man of his time and all time . . . William Forsyth, who was curator of the botanic gardens at

Chelsea. Robert Fortune was appointed to this post on his return from China.

Through the years it has been crossed and re-crossed and now there are varying forms, shapes, habits and blooming periods of the old fashioned shrub. Each has its own qualities but all have the brave beauty and hardiness of the original.

Shyly I tell—Today I have four or five Forsythia bushes planted along my fence line, dividing my property from my neighbor's.

Oh, happy am I that I saw the light! Come to me, my common vulgar Forsythia—let me press you to my heart. I love you!

P.S. Vulgar has many meanings but the one here suited is "belonging to the common people".

Leaves Come Atumblin' Down

When old gal nature throws caution to the winds and decides to have one last glorious fling, we say, "Look, the country is aglow with these gorgeous autumn tints. Ho, there, gaze on those colorful Maples!"

Then . . . "Why do leaves change color in the fall?"

I'll bet you've asked, or have been asked, that question countless times. I'll bet you further that you weren't able to give a legitimate or logical answer.

Well, Brother Tobe is going to see that you won't be embarrassed any further about this because from now on you'll be able to tell people just what brings about this change of color to the leaves in the fall.

Yes, days, weeks and even months before the leaves begin to drop from the trees they are making preparation for this big event. You know it just doesn't happen by accident.

Right at the base of the leaf stem or, as it is called, petiole—a thin-walled layer of cells begins to take shape. This layer of cells creates a weak spot and this is called the abciss layer where the petiole will finally break away from the twig.

Now while this event is taking place, a corky layer of cells is beginning to develop between the thin-walled cells and the twig itself. This means that eventually when the leaf falls, there will be no open incision, contusion or wound.

So when all of these preparatory goings on and doings are completed or, should I say, when the abciss layer is all set and ready, the leaf is still attached to the twig by means of veins or strands of vascular tissue which go right through the abciss layer and hold on to the outer covering of cells which is called the epidermis.

It is clear to see that this is a very unreliable sort of support because a good strong blast of wind or a heavy rainfall will cause the leaves to go tumbling down . . . but they's a-ready and a-willin'.

'Tis gospel—the change in the color of the leaves is not due in any way to frost or weather conditions. It is strictly the result of chemical changes that take place within the maturing leaf. In the summer time the leaves are green because of the presence of pigment chlorophyll which is found in the cells. But there are also present at the same time yellow pigments which are not ordinarily seen during the summer because they are disguised by the green chlorophyll. At this time the chlorophyll that is used up or destroyed is made up again and replaced.

As we come close to fall and the changes around the petiole begin to take place preparing for the shedding of the leaf, this chlorophyll which is used up can no longer be replenished or replaced. . . . Thus, the yellow and other colors become apparent and visible.

When you see those beautiful reds and purples in the leaves, they are caused by a chemical substance known as anthocyans which are prevalent in the sap of the cells. While this ingredient may be available at all times in the leaf in greater or lesser amounts, it usually becomes apparent only in the spring or fall. Only when the temperatures are comparatively low are these anthocyans formed—caused by a large supply of sugar which is present at these times in the sap cells.

In the summer when growth is rapid and things are moving swiftly for trees, the sugars are used up or quickly transformed and therefore there is no accumulation of this material in the leaf. But with the coming of the fall the process is slowed up and sugars begin to accumulate in fairly large quantities.

The extent of the red or blue in the leaf depends on the acidity or alkalinity of the cell sap and therefore the variations in color that one can see are endless.

Now you know the why's and wherefore's of the grand beauty that we enjoy in the fall.

Go Far Afield

Nature despises inbreeding! "How do you know?"—you may well ask. Well, from what I've seen, heard, watched and learned, I'm quite convinced that this is an honest statement.

As a matter of fact, nature, from time immemorial, has done everything in her power to prevent inbreeding by her children, whether they be plants or animals.

You know the story about the female mice maturing a few days before the male mice which means the former go off in search of mates and this prevents inbreeding between brother and sister.

Well, that is the story of nature almost all the way down the line. But occasionally something goes wrong or some condition arises where nature hasn't been able to guard against it and . . . inbreeding occurs.

Let's look at one thing at a time. For instance . . . you'll notice that an Apple tree lives to be, yes, easily over 100 years if left alone and in good tilth . . . much longer; so will a Pear tree. I'm not too sure about Cherries—the sweet ones. I do know that I've seen trees that looked to be 100 years old anyway—huge trees that bore 100 or more baskets of fruit. Now Plum trees are comparatively short lived— around 20 years. The Sour Cherry is somewhat the same. Peach trees are the shortest lived of all—somewhere around 15 years, under good conditions.

Now let's go back again. Apple, Pear, Plum and Sweet Cherry trees all require pollination in order to set fruit. In other words they lack the power to fertilize themselves and therefore you must have two trees of different varieties of the same fruit in order to get a crop. But when you go to the Sour Cherry and the Peach, you will find in most cases that they are capable of self-pollination and in most cases do pollinate themselves. There is only one variety of Peach that I know that requires cross-pollination and that is the old J. H. Hale. As far as Plum is concerned, there have been quite a few varieties of Plum that are self-fertile but most of them do require cross-pollination.

Now further, once a Cherry, Pear or an Apple tree becomes established, it will live for a long time. They're not bothered too much by disease. That is the tree itself I'm talking about—not the fruit. But you take the Peach. It is short lived and never ever reaches 30 years in good health and a few years ago it was estimated that the average life of a Peach tree was less than 8 years. Sour Cherries, too, don't live long. Their life span would probably stretch to 25 but they're not long lived in any event and they also are subject to a lot of diseases and viruses that play havoc with them. Plum trees, by and large, are not long lived either but longer than the Peach by far and better than the Sour Cherry. Some varieties of Plum are subject to Black Knot and this is usually deadly.

So there is your picture. Those varieties of fruit that inbreed are sickly and short lived. The ones that depend upon cross-pollination are long lived and healthy. The conclusion that I draw is that there is strength, vigor and long life in crossing and there's weakness, disease and death with inbreeding. Look around you and see how true it is in life, too. I'm sure the same pattern is followed in the flowers, where you will find that the cross-pollinated items are larger, stronger, more fruitful, more vigorous and of greater durability.

Mum's the Word!

Hop back to 1940. Would you believe it? . . . Then there were few, if any, of our garden Mums being grown in this part of the country or even in all of Canada. They were considered unsuitable for our northern climate because we didn't have a long enough season for them to bloom and then most of them didn't live over the winter. Those scarce, brave few that were grown in those days were a far cry from the lovely, gorgeous colors, shapes and forms that we have today.

So actually in this short span of 17 years, the garden Chrysanthemum has come from nowhere to be the leading fall blooming plant and flower in Canada—yes, and throughout America.

You can grow them successfully in the east, west, the plains and the central part of Canada as well as you can in the northern latitudes. I know what I'm talking about because I've seen them growing and I have received hundreds of letters to prove it besides.

They do prefer a light sandy loam that is well drained. Now I would recommend that they be planted where they can receive the full sun but let me also stress the fact that they will grow in partial shade.

But there is something else to remember. If your plants are grown in a shady location, the more shade they get, the taller your plants will become. They don't grow as tall in the sun.

Where there is danger of early frost, why not have some burlap bags or even some heavy paper ready to cover them with? In this way you will get by the one or two early frosts and probably have blooms for another month or more. This little extra effort is ever so much worthwhile.

It is important to remember that Mums are heavy feeders. They like a lot of manure or compost and I would certainly incorporate it as much as I could with my soil before planting. It has been noticed that when plants are grown in poor soil that the stems become very woody and they do not last very long—for cutting especially. But if grown in rich soil, the plants are more or less succulent and they do have long keeping qualities as any of you who have grown them will know.

The time to plant them is in the late spring or early summer when the danger of frost has passed. Rooted cuttings or separated divisions should always be used.

Much as we believe that many or most varieties of Chrysanthemums are hardy and, by allowing them to stay out in our fields, we have proven it, yet we do recommend that where there is any doubt in the matter or even if you just want to be sure, lift them in the late fall and put them in shallow boxes, leaving a fair amount of the original soil around them. Then place them in a cold frame or in an unheated shed or down in your cellar. The temperature should be kept anywhere from 32 to 45 and they'll remain in good shape.

Just give them an occasional watering so that they will never be completely dried out.

Come spring . . . separate them individually and start over again and you'll have hundreds where you just had a few before.

Fabulous Flowers

For some reason or other I haven't urged my readers to grow Gloxinias. Probably in my subconscious self I had a reason. I didn't want to share their luxuriant startling beauty with everyone.

But now that I've conquered my subconscious I want to urge you one and all to enjoy the blessings and sublime beauty of these wonderful, wonderful subjects.

I think that some of the horticultural big-wigs have labelled the Gloxinia as one of nature's finest items for a pot plant. They haven't said that it was the closest to perfect of any house plant in the world, but I do.

No, you don't have to be a horticultural genius to grow them. All you need is the requisite for life—common sense.

An unusual feature about this plant is that it can be grown from tubers, leaves, cuttings or seeds. All plants are propagated from one or more of these methods but few can be grown in all of these ways.

I'm not going to attempt to describe their beauty to you because if you haven't seen one, shame on you! It's high time that you did. But I will say that some of the stunning, crinkly, beautiful, variegated, silky sheen flowers measure 5 inches across and it's not a bit unusual for a plant to have 25 flowers open at one time. The color range is as broad as the horizon. They are long, tubular and deep throated.

It takes about 3½ months to get them to bloom from tubers and about 6 months to get flowers from seed. They like a well drained, coarse, rich, friable soil. African Violet soil is perfect.

When planting tubers don't stick them in the soil and cover them because you'll probably rot them if you do. Just press them slightly into the soil, water occasionally, keep them in semi-shade until growth starts and then give them lots of water and a good amount of sunlight. They like to be kept warm—around 70 degrees. Eight months a year Gloxinias can take all the sun they can get but they should be shaded from the hot summer sun. They require a lot more light than African Violets.

There are very few insects that attack Gloxinias. Just keep the soil and plant in nice condition and you'll have no trouble. You can water from the top but don't spray the leaves any more than you can help. Any plant with hairy leaves doesn't like water on them.

Quick temperature changes, overwatering and draughts are things to be avoided. When the plants have flowered for a good long period they should be rested off.

Now you know as much about Gloxinias as I do.

Tobe Tells all About Amaryllis

Have you had failures in trying to grow Amaryllis? You needn't have because the culture of Amaryllis is quite simple.

There are, however, a few main points that differentiate quite drastically from the accepted manner of doing things and these are the things to watch for. Then you will have no trouble growing Amaryllis successfully.

To begin with, get a pot that is not glazed. They prefer the plain, old fashioned pots. Make sure the pot is large enough to allow 1 inch clearance all around the bulb. Then, of course, as usual put some broken crockery or pebbles in the bottom so that the holes will not get plugged up with soil.

Yes, Amaryllis must have a light, airy soil—that is, one that will not pack or stick closely together. Sand, leaf mould or peat moss mixed with the average good garden soil should be perfect for growing Amaryllis.

You can buy bulbs with or without roots. For easier handling by the grower for shipping, packing and storing, the roots are usually trimmed off. If you have one that has a lot of roots, just let the roots hang until you sprinkle some soil around them and the bulb is sitting naturally on soil with the roots imbedded prior. Never press the bulb into the soil. Just work the soil up and around the lower part only. Do not cover more than the lower quarter at this stage.

Well, after the bulb has started active growth and you can see the leaves, then you can firm the bulb into place and sprinkle some more soil around it—building it up a little higher than it was originally. At least 2/3 of the bulb should be *exposed* above the soil level.

Now Amaryllis do thrive on a fair amount of water but under no circumstances whatsoever must the soil be kept saturated.

Here is something contrary to most people's accepted theories and beliefs and that is—do not water from below. The Amaryllis bulbs want water from the soil working downwards. This is important—and the Amaryllis pot or bulb should never stand in water.

There are two things that will tend to prevent an Amaryllis bulb from flowering and I attribute 90% of all failures with Amaryllis bulbs to one or both of these factors. They are that the bulb or pot was kept too wet or they were not kept warm enough. The Amaryllis will not flower satisfactorily unless the soil and the room in which they are kept are warm—warmer than most plants prefer to have it—65 degrees or better.

For indoor growing, which is the case when you are raising them in a pot, you want to select the warmest place in the house. Most experts warn against setting flower pots on radiators but in this case, this is the place for them because they will love it and thrive under those conditions. But remember, don't let your soil in the pot completely dry out because if you do, then you'll be in trouble.

If you maintain proper moisture and heat and other conditions, you should have flowers in approximately 8 weeks from the potting up of your Amaryllis bulbs. If you potted up your bulbs in the latter days of October or early November, you should have blooms by the time Christmas rolls around.

Keep the bulb growing on even after it has flowered to give the bulb a chance to produce sufficient food so that it will be ready to bloom again the following year. Next year's failure can be caused at this time.

As soon as the frost-free weather arrives you can put your Amaryllis outdoors. When fall comes, the bulbs should be dug up and water withheld. This will get the bulbs ready for blooming or forcing again in a short while.

Remember, do not allow your Amaryllis to be chilled. If you do, you won't have any flowers.

Bella Bella

I was visiting my daughter a few weeks ago and I noticed she had created a very novel arrangement of a plant that I had given to her.

I thought it would be interesting to some of you folks and might give you ideas as to how to handle an unusual item.

I had never seen anything like it before anywhere and it was an original idea, as far as I know.

There on a bookcase sat a Palm about 18 inches high, growing and looking very, very luxuriant. Now these are, generally speaking, more or less difficult items to raise and I was surprised at its vitality, color and look of well-being.

She had this plant growing in a brandy glass. You might even call it a brandy tumbler. It's one of these huge glasses with a flanged base. I actually believe that the proper term is "brandy snifter". This was an exceptionally large one and would probably hold two

quarts of water or beer (because nobody could dare tackle that much brandy).

Evidently this acted somewhat like the original wardian case and created the root conditions, at least, that this plant loved. Perhaps it closely simulated its natural conditions.

Nevertheless everything about the plant looked in such admirable condition. It had four or five strong, sturdy green stems completely covered with leaves . . . the frond-like leaves of the Palm . . . and they were glossy and long and springy.

It was surely the healthiest looking Palm I'd seen anywhere—including the ones I saw growing in California. I've never been to the South Seas and don't know what they look like there. But it was certainly a virile, luxuriant-looking affair.

Well, this may be an idea for you and will perhaps serve in helping you grow a Palm to perfection. Everybody seems to want one but most are a bit leery of them. The first thing to do is get one of these big brandy snifters—and don't fill it with brandy. Just put your plants in it with a base of peat moss and soil and I think that should keep it thriving for a more or less indefinite period. If you must feed it, use a little liquid manure. If you use a good rich compost to start with, you shouldn't require any additions for a long time. Place a few bits of rock and other small ornaments here and there about the base for added effect.

I might mention here, too, that the proper name of the Neanthe Bella Palm, which is the Palm that I am describing, is Chamaedorea elegans.

Green Grow Sir!

Actually how many different kinds of vegetables do you use regularly in your own home? . . . either for cooking or eating raw?

You know that eating raw vegetables is considered to be one of the healthiest eating habits yet known to man. Yes, I fully realize that there are people who suffer from allergies or other disorders who cannot, or are not supposed to, eat raw vegetables according to the doctor's orders. But these circumstances are indeed rare or unusual and of course are definitely caused by some deficiency, probably due to omission of raw vegetables in the diet in the first place.

I like to wander around the foreign sections of Toronto and keep my eyes open for the types of vegetables and other eatables that these people eat. It's a fact that every nation or people have their own preferences and likes and dislikes. Among them are fruits and vegetables and also culinary dishes that most of us have never heard of.

It is bad enough that we consume such large quantities of animal fats in our regular diet without using it for frying, cooking or baking and other ways. I am sure you realize that 'tis not by mere chance that the olive oil consuming people (Italians, French, Greeks, Spaniards) suffer less from the various heart ailments than the heavy animal fat using nations like the Scandinavian, British, American and Canadians.

Well, here are some of the vegetables that I bring home with me . . . Celeriac, Kohlrabi, Black-skinned Radish, Broccoli, Chinese Celery-Cabbage or Lettuce, Whiteclump Radish, Chinese Greens, Fennel and Endive.

Celeriac actually tastes like and is closely related to Celery except you eat the root instead of the stalk. Kohlrabi tastes something like a Cabbage or a member of the Cabbage family except that it has a finer, milder flavor. You can cook it when it gets large or eat it raw. The Black Radish is actually a winter Radish. It is quite strong and pungent. It is very delicious and if you enjoy Horseradish, you will love slices of this Black Radish.

Broccoli you should all know. It is a very delicious vegetable and also a member of the Cabbage family. Chinese Cabbage is seen and sold in many of the better stores and also in the foreign sections. It is definitely better than any lettuce you've ever eaten. It's not as stringy and tough as Celery and far more pleasing in flavor than Cabbage. Another thing, it's just as easy to grow as any vegetable in creation and you get big heavy large heads. They require no special handling or blanching.

Then if you like mild Radish, that White-clump Radish is a honey. You slice it and eat it with a bit of salt, if you like, or you can cut it into salads. It is exceptionally good and, as I said, if you like a milder Radish, this is perfect.

Too, there is the Chinese Green that I've only eaten cooked. The stalk is very white and smooth textured, very much like Celery, except that it is not ribbed. The leaf part resembles Spinach. Now I don't know what it actually is. I've been trying to track down its proper name by the descriptions and for a moment I think it's Mustard—then I think it's Collard—and then I think it's Swiss Chard. But I don't know which it is. I'm going to find out by hook or by crook eventually and I'll tell you about it. I can tell you this . . . when cooked, it is a marvellous, fine tasting vegetable.

So if these vegetables were added to the ones you already do eat, probably like Tomatoes, Cucumbers, Celery, Lettuce, Cabbage, Brussels Sprouts, Potatoes, Carrots, Turnips, Spinach, etc., you would have a good broad variety for your table and, believe me, the good it would do your health by means of balancing your diet would amaze you.

If you're having little health difficulties of various natures, try balancing up your diet by adding some of these lesser known, but splendid vegetables.

Whatever you do, don't miss the Celeriac and Kohlrabi which, incidentally, I call "Cold Rabbit".

How to Grow Cyclamens

Easy, of course—
but you've got to know how.

Cyclamen is a remarkably popular plant come the Yuletide season.

No one can deny that its popularity is well deserved. There are few, if any house plants, especially at that time of the year, that flower more prodigiously than an old reliable Cyclamen.

Indeed, now that you've got one, I had best tell you how to tend it. First, they like it bright and sunny but they don't want the heat that is usually found with the sun. They want it where it is cool. A little spot where the daytime temperature flits between 55 and 65 is just what the doctor ordered for them.

If you want to move them where it is warmer for special occasions go ahead and do so but put them back where the woollen underwear is necessary as soon as you can. That is where they are happiest.

They are not gross feeders but a handout every two weeks with Liquid Manure will have them nodding their dainty heads and saying "thank you" and showing their appreciation by hundreds of new buds springing up all over the place.

They can stand a copious water supply but even at the expense of sounding monotonous, I'll say once more, "See that it drains away".

Carry-on Flower

Bet you think that fragrance is nature's only means of attracting scent-conscious insects to flowers and thus achieving pollination.

Love is not the only thing that makes the wheels of life revolve. Food, come to think of it, is important also.

Think now—if you were lost, wandering in the desert, which would be of greater value—love making or food and water?

Without question age would make some difference in the choice that would be made. At 16 love would be the choice. At 50 food and drink would be preferred.

There's a lonely plant growing out there on the desert and a million years of trial and error have taught it that there are more important things than smelling sweet and elegant. It desperately needs insects for pollination. It just can't do the job itself and outside help must be rallied. But how?

Nature's ingenuity is unconfined. Anything and everything that lives on the desert must eat and food is scarce and hard to come by.

So this plant uses the odor of food—strong smelling so that it will carry to attract the insect upon whom it depends for its life.

Further, without any tests, and speaking strictly empirically, I'd bet my boots that a putrid stink carries a lot farther and lasts a lot longer than a sweet perfume.

After all, the jackals and the sea gulls are sort of garbage disposal units, whereas a bear likes sweet berries and fresh meat. Some animals will eat only the food that others have caught or brought down and yet again others must catch theirs on the wing or not eat at all. Just as in humans and animals there are among plants variations, likes, dislikes and tastes, too.

Way down in Arizona on the desert one day I came across a huge Stapelia. It's also known as Star Flower and, better still, as Carrion Flower. It had the largest flower I had ever seen anywhere. Truly, the flower was as large as a good big pitcher and somewhat shaped like one. The flower was wonderful, unique, strange, beautiful—but, oh, what an odor—vile! It smelled exactly like carrion.

Probably the Stapelia could have prepared a much better odor but there where it grows it found that the odor of carrion attracted more insects or the insects that would do the job it needed done. Therefore it simulated the odor of carrion.

What good would it do a skunk to expel an odor like that of Roses? Ain't nature wonderful!

Growing Hyacinths

Let me first get you off to a proper start. Usually there are two grades of Hyacinth bulbs. The top grade or the huge bulbs are best for early forcing but if you want bulbs to grow outdoors, then you're as well off with the 16 or 17 centimeter bulbs which are medium sized. Of course for growing outdoors you don't need any special technique. Plant them just as you would Tulips or Daffodils.

However, most Hyacinths are purchased for forcing indoors where we want a little bit of color and fragrance and beauty during the duller parts of the year. Now when you get them they should be potted up. Put one of the large bulbs to a four inch pot, two bulbs to a five inch pot or three bulbs to a six inch pot. Make sure that the top half inch of the bulb protrudes above the soil. No special soil mixture is required—just ordinary garden soil is plenty good enough.

Most bulbs of course have their flowering buds already formed inside and Hyacinth bulbs are no exception.

Now put them in a dark place where the temperature is not above

50 degrees and a little lower would be all right. You can put them in a cellar, cover them with straw or hay, or even outdoors covered with cinders or sand. Of course if you can keep the temperature controlled, then that's so much better. But on the other hand, it won't harm them if the temperature varies some—as long as they don't get too warm.

They should be kept in this condition until the roots are fully developed and the top begins to show about one inch of growth.

The earliest you can possibly get Hyacinths to flower would be about the 1st of January and for this purpose, they should be potted up by October 1. If you are going to flower them that early, they should be taken out by the latter part of November and kept at a temperature ranging between 65 and 70 degrees. They should be kept covered with paper until the shoots begin to grow. Just a few days is usually ample.

Then they are kept at about 60 degrees until they begin to show flower. Well, as soon as they begin to show color the temperature should be dropped to about 50 degrees. This will make them firm, sound and hard.

Naturally the later you want them to flower, the less time is required and the less difficulty is encountered.

The Weeping Willow's Secret

It appears that the Weeping Willow was not known to the western world prior to the year 1700—at least, not much before that anyway.

I think it was Pope who made first mention of the Willow but it is a fact that it was cultivated at Hampton Court as far back as 1692.

One day Pope received a gift of figs that was brought from the East and these were contained in a basket made of green willow twigs. When he was eating the figs, he noticed that one of the twigs had put forth a shoot. This he planted in his garden at Twickenham. It took hold and grew readily and luxuriantly and this is said to be the original stock from which most of the Weeping Willows known throughout the west were originated. It is indeed unfortunate that this tree was cut down about 50 years ago.

Pope's successor at Twickenham, one Sir William Stanhope, sent cuttings of this original Willow into most parts of Europe and in particular—to the Empress of Russia in the year 1789.

Hark, lest you get confused . . . I'm not talking about the Pope —but one Alexander Pope, a famous English poet and author.

It is a fact that there is a Weeping Willow planted over the grave of

Napoleon at St. Helena. So even if no one else mourns the passing of Napoleon, the understanding Willow weeps for him.

The Willow grows most anywhere but prefers any place where it can get a good supply of moisture and where the weather doesn't get too cold or too hot. Actually its true home seems to be the marshy flat, low-lying lands and meadows bordering the Euphrates and its tributaries. It is a fact that the Willows still grow along the banks of the Euphrates just as luxuriantly and as beautifully as they did in the days of the Bible.

Pretty Doll

'Tis time to talk about the Dahlia . . . so pay heed. What do you know about it?

Actually this flower was named in honor of a man by the name of Dahl who was a Swedish botanist and was at that time well known to every horticulturist.

Records would indicate that it was first imported or brought to France in 1789 and actually it remained in that country and was highly cultivated there up until 1814. Then it began to spread into other countries—Germany, Denmark and then to England.

The Dahlia is a native of Mexico and Central America.

Maybe you didn't know this but if grown indoors, it will actually flourish and bloom for about 8 months. Maybe you should be growing some of them indoors. But you'd better have a lot of room because they do grow to be "whoppers".

To my mind the Dahlia gives the largest flowers that are grown in America. I can't tell offhand any flower that will attain or reach the size of a well cared for Dahlia. I know that botanically speaking there are larger flowers but I doubt if any are grown in our gardens or are even remotely as beautiful.

So honours to the Dahlia!

Many Flowered Vine

When you want a hardy flowering climbing vine, I doubt if you can do any better than planting a Clematis.

The Jackmanii (purple) is without doubt one of the most beautiful and prodigious flowerful climbing vines that can be grown in the northern latitude.

They prefer locations that get at least 6 hours of sunshine a day and they want a soil that is loamy and rich with spendid drainage. Clematis do best if given a support on which to climb.

A good mulch around the base of the plants to keep them sort of cool and damp during the hot summer months is what will please them best. We'd suggest a mulch about two or three inches deep and at least a foot or fifteen inches in diameter. They don't like to be dry at any time and the mulch will prevent this from happening even during the hot dry periods in the summer.

For fall and winter protection we'd recommend mounding up four, five or six inches or even a foot around the base of the plant with just good loose soil—that's all.

They don't require much pruning in the spring. We'd suggest leaving them at least 18 inches above the ground level. This pruning should be done just before the new leaves start to grow.

Clematis is sometimes subject to wilt and when you set out a new plant and it wilts back, don't despair. In most cases a new shoot will start to grow from the base of the plant if it is kept in nice humid conditions. As it grows older it becomes immune to this wilt disease and you'll have no further trouble.

But remember, the drainage must be good and put on that coating of mulch for the summer.

Songs About Roses

How many songs do you know about the Rose?

I'm sure each and every one of us know a few—some probably quite a few. And maybe here or there we'll find a more nimble-minded fellow who will know a great many.

Here are a few that I remember: Roses Are Shining in Picardy; Rose, Fairest Rose; Rose of Tralee; Moonlight and Roses; Only a Rose; A Rose in Her Hair; The Last Rose of Summer; I'll Bring You a Red, Red Rose; The Rose That Grows on No Man's Land; The River of the Roses; Sweet Rosy O'Grady.

'Tis Not To Reason Why!

After wandering around Europe for a couple of months and observing the types of flora that are grown there, I was puzzled and mystified.

In Germany and in Denmark I saw marvelous specimens of the Baccata Yew, which is considered the most beautiful of all Yews and one of the loveliest Evergreens grown anywhere.

Very few of us in the northern latitudes of America have ever seen a really fine specimen of this tree. As a matter of fact there is a golden-leaved one, too, which is even more attractive.

Can you just imagine a tree similar in shape to a Lombardy Poplar except that it is a stately luxuriant Evergreen? Then you have some idea as to the appearance of the Baccata Yew. It's commonly called the English Yew.

Way back many hundreds of years ago in merry old England the boughs of the Yew tree were used to make bows and they made wonderful bows, too. The bigwigs in England had Yews planted in the cemeteries where they knew they would grow undisturbed. Then, whenever a cause arose or a battle or war was impending, they went out to the cemeteries or burial grounds and lopped off limbs from the good old Yew trees and made bows and arrows.

Now that's supposed to be an actual fact so don't snicker.

You know the English are smart. They think years and years ahead. As a matter of fact, they tell me that the English planted Oak trees continually so that they would have good timbers to build those wonderful ships. You remember the old song, "Hearts of oak are our ships—Hearts of oak are our men". But you can be sure that their heads weren't made of oak.

Let's hop back to my travels. I also saw splendid specimens of various Cypress, Hollies, Rhododendrons and I don't know how many other things—I can't recall them all at the moment. But in every case they were growing luxuriantly and I know that their climate at times and places is colder and harsher than ours.

Says I to myself, "What's the gimmick? Why can they grow them there . . . and here, where we have the protection of the Great Lakes and in some cases the Atlantic and other instances the Pacific Ocean, we can't grow them?"

So I began to do some cogitating and I think I've come up with at least some of the answers. You see we have hot summers and long days and in all likelihood the plants that I have mentioned cannot stand so much sun and so much heat. Then, too, I think they get more rainfall there than we do here because we can go from the latter part of June until September, almost with narry a drop of rain . . . or at least not enough to wet my balding dome.

That seems to be part of the answer.

Then I found out that during the winter, up in these latitudes, they have very long nights and cloudy days so that for days on end they hardly see the sun. Well, that doesn't happen very often in the northern part of North America. We have lots of sun even through the more or less dismal winter days.

I have found, for example, one of the things that definitely does play havoc with our evergreens here . . . The ground is frozen solid perhaps six inches below, a foot below or even in the colder sections of the country probably a foot or two below soil level. Well, then we get a bright sunny day. The sun pours down on the evergreens—especially the broad-leaved types—and what happens? . . . The call goes forth from the leaves down to the root for some sap because the sun is taking out the moisture from the leaves at a terrific rate. Sure the sun takes it out but the root is frozen solid and it's dead to all intents and purposes. It cannot replenish the moisture that is being evaporated or given off by the leaves. The result—devastation.

Course I'm not an expert as I am wont to say time and time again but that seems like simple, common logic to my old befuddled head. What do you think?

'Tis A Tree, Too

Did you know that a Fuchsia can be grown year after year?

I've seen them grown outdoors on tall stems covered with masses of beautiful drooping flowers. After they have been outdoors all summer long and have displayed their beautiful flowers they can be lifted before frost and brought indoors. By December water should be withheld . . . not entirely but just a drop or two given. Then they should be repotted.

Now pruning . . . cut off about 50% of the plant. Then put it in a cool shady spot and continue to give just a little bit of water until the middle of March. Then return it to open light, water freely and it should start to go ahead for you beautifully.

It takes about 5 to 6 weeks for the plant to start blooming again. During the summer the Fuchsia will do better if given partial shade.

A Daisy . . . Lazy . . . Crazy

This corn I'm going to talk about is not only lazy—it's crazy.

Shortly after I came back from Europe I walked into the fields and there I spied some corn that was lying on the ground. I tried to straighten it up but it wouldn't straighten up.

So I went in to Gerda and said, "You must have had a devilish storm out here to knock your corn down like that."

She shrugged her shoulders and answered, "What corn?—What storm? We haven't had a storm here. Why, it hasn't hardly rained since you left."

"Come and I'll show you," I snapped and led and she followed me out.

"There," I barked, pointing down at the corn sprawled all over the ground, "Look right there. What do you think caused that?"

Then I noticed a smile spreading over her face and I asked, "What's the big joke?"

"Don't you remember?" she said, "That's that Lazy Corn seed you got from some place or other and told me to plant."

"Well, I'll be a horn-swaggled, old seadog," I chortled, "Let me take a good look at that thing now."

So down on my knees I dropped and began to root about. I found that the first shoots or stalks grow straight up but every one after that just seems to get tired and grows along the ground—yes, right flat on the ground. And they can't be straightened out either. They spring right back. In every way they're healthy, sound stalks with good ears and leaves. Some of the stalks were as thick as a baseball bat. But they're just tired or lazy or who knows? . . . maybe crazy.

I have an idea you'll like them and probably you'll want to lie down beside them on a hot summer's day and be lazy, too. It will be fun!

Do You Need A Couch?

I deplore waste—whether it be of money, goods, food or anything else. Therefore I hate to see folks wasting their money on fertilizers and other soil improvers where they are not needed.

It is the beginners in the gardening field who really throw their money away. The man or woman who has been gardening for a few years quickly learns that all soils are not in need of fertilizer.

So let me recount a few things. To begin with, hard clay soils are seldom, if ever, helped by fertilizer. Sandy soils are never helped by fertilizer, and normal soils—they just don't need any fertilizer.

A hard clay soil needs humus to make it lighter and more friable so that water, air, sun and heat can penetrate and make things grow. It usually has all the nutrients in it that it needs. So why add more?

A sandy soil needs humus and lots of it if it's going to be in good tilth and health.

Before you go out and buy yourself some fertilizer, ask yourself some questions or, at least, discuss it with someone or get advice somewhere . . . for I contend that in most cases soils do not need fertilizer and adding fertilizer will in no way help it . . . but it can do harm. It's just throwing money down the drain.

If you are genuinely concerned about your soil and want to improve it, I'm going to outline briefly the best ways to do it. One is by means of compost. Two, by the sludge that one can pick up free of charge from the sewage disposal plants in practically all of the larger cities. Three, animal manures. Four, by the addition of Peat Moss. Five, by leguminous or other green crops turned in to make natural fertilizer. Six, sawdust and other organic wastes used as a mulch or turned under.

Land sakes alive, if you haven't got enough there to work with without spending your money on "guk", then you need a psychiatrist —not a bag of fertilizer.

Youth and Old Age

There is a tremendous variation in the ages to which trees live. For example, some of the varieties of Birches are considered old when they reach 40 years, whereas a Sequoia when it reaches 3,000 years of age may be said to be in its prime.

There are Junipers known to have lived to be 2,000 years of age and Oaks, 1,500. Yes, and even the Sugar Maple has been known to live 500 years and the Elm is in about the same category.

Like us humans, trees when young are virile, strong and healthy but as they get older the infirmities of age crop up here and there and usually they suffer for somewhat the same reasons as man does. The same things that cause death in a man will cause death to a tree—cold, malnutrition, disease, drought, fire, drowning or lack of sunlight.

One thing—man has a great advantage over a tree in that he can choose or move his environment or abode, whereas the tree can't. Wherever the wind or the rain or whatever it is carried the seed, there it must remain for better or worse.

As the tree gets older it begins to have difficulty with respiration. It then finds it not so easy taking in sufficient food and energy to promote wide growth and a multitude of shoots. It begins to make fewer and fewer wood cells each succeeding year and the sickly, dead or dying branches begin to increase in number as the years go by.

Then the power to recuperate after an injury begins to slow down. I remember when I'd stub my toe when I was a youngster—a real good wack up against the cement gutter—and the blood would squirt out like water out of a water pistol—and the gash would be clean across the entire toe and it seemed to be open a foot. But in 48 hours there was hardly a sign of the wound. Today if I prick myself with a pin, I have to bandage it and be careful with it for about 3 or 4 days and I'm scared to death of infection, too.

Well, it's just like that with the old trees. When a young one gets a cut, it's hardly made when the healing process begins and in a short time the bark has already encroached upon the spot where the cut was made. But now it seems that they never heal completely —as you have no doubt noticed.

Now the leaves no longer have their usual vigor and vitality. They gradually become smaller. How I remember the leaves shot out by young trees. If they were compared side by side you would hardly believe that they are from the same species. You seldom, if ever, see a young tree broken or uprooted by wind or tempest but every time through the winter and fall that the breezes blow a gale and I hear the . . . WOOOoooooo0OOOoooooo . . . and the whistling of the wind, I know that tomorrow the orchards will be strewn with branches and the streets will be covered with debris and probably the power lines will be snapped and there will be no electricity for our breakfast in the morning. Of course this is nature's pruning process but there is nothing to prune in a young tree. It holds on and cares for every one of its shoots.

Well, right about here is when a man could do a little thinking. A 40-year Birch is old, a 40-year Oak is just a fledgling and for size and shade, the Oak will probably be every bit as good as the Birch. A 10-year old Poplar may be a little larger than a 10-year old Elm but in another 15 years the Poplar will be old and ready to fold, whereas the Elm would be but a "babe in arms"—yet displaying its charms.

Each kind of tree plays its part. Some have a lesser role and others have a greater but each of them is essential—for the earth's purposes.

About Manna

According to the Bible it was produced by God for the people of Israel when they were wandering in the wilderness prior to entering the Holy Land.

I have been trying to track down the true Biblical Manna—but 'tain't easy. But I'm having lots of fun and I am going to submit my findings to you and you can decide what is right and what is wrong and which you will accept. I am only presenting the case. You will be the judge.

We will open our case with a tree known as the European Flowering Ash, properly Fraxinus ornus. The sap is procured somewhat similar to the way in which we tap Maple trees . . . by cutting into the bark. However the exudation is very concentrated and is good to eat in its original state. But it can be dissolved in water to make a less concentrated food or drink. Often the Manna oozes out of the bark without effort by itself and appears on branches as small, snowy-white, flaky balls.

This tree is found in Italy and in other parts of Europe, over to Greece, Turkey and Asia Minor.

Next we come to the Manna Tree, properly Alhagi maurorum. Only this time it is not a real tree but a shrub that grows to a height of 2 to 3 feet. A honey-like sap exudes from the leaves and branches, becoming hard at night and constituting Manna.

During the very hot weather and the high winds that are usual on the steppes, the rootstock—plant and all—is often blown out by the wind and carried long distances. This Manna food is supposed to be in the form of roundish, hard, dry tears—varying in size from that of a mustard seed to that of a coriander. They are of an amber color, sweet to taste and with the odor of senna.

Now there is what is known as Tamarisk Manna, properly Tamarix gallica mannifera, which exudes from its slender branches during June and July a food in the form of honey-like globules. In the cool of the early morning they harden and are found in a firm solid state. This Manna does not come about because of a natural condition but is actually the result of a sting by an insect that punctures the bark of the Tamarix. The insect is known as Coccus manniparus.

Another Manna created by the puncture of an insect, during August, is that formed on the twigs of two varieties of Oak—Quercus vallonia and Quercus persica.

We find there is also a Manna obtained from the scrapings of branches or stems of Astragalus florulentus or adscendens . . . both Old World plants that are seldom mentioned even in horticultural literature. I might mention that the Loco Weed of the United States is in this family, too.

Also suggested is a species of Lichens of the genus Lecanora, still found over large areas of the barren plains and mountains in the widely varying sections of West Asia and North Africa. These produce edible manna-like protuberances.

Then there is an algae of the genus Nostoc which grows rapidly on moist ground like a mushroom or tiny puffball. It is both pleasant tasting and palatable.

There are two other suggestions—a plant called Pyrus glabra whose fruit very much resembles the Oak Manna in appearance. Last but not least is a group of Australian plants. They are Eucalyptus and the nutriment is found on the leaves of Eucalyptus viminalis, E. gunnii rubida and E. pulverulents.

The Fraxinus ornus gives its fruit in July and August. The Alhagi, in July. The Tamarix, in June and July. The Astragalus, in August. The Oak Manna, also in August.

After careful consideration and weighing the matters involved, the experts seem to give the nod to the Tamarix gallica mannifera as being the true Manna—the one that the Children of Israel found on the ground in the morning for six consecutive days during their wanderings in the wilderness.

But you are in a position to make your own decision and whatever it is, I doubt if anyone will dispute it—especially since the experts do not all agree among themselves.

Wild Man Tobe

Whenever I hear or read of a new plant, I try at once to get some seeds, bulbs or plants of it so that I can, for my own satisfaction, see how it looks.

Nothing in the world intrigues me more than waiting for a plant that I have never seen before to sprout, grow into leaf or come into bloom.

A while ago I received a shipment of various bulbs and odds and ends from Africa. I didn't have time to give them the study they deserved. But I did look them over and shortly after that I went on my trip to Europe.

Now I recall that in Denmark we got to Copenhagen very late and while hunting for our place of lodging for the night, or I should say early morning, I came across a florist's shop that was lit up. In the centre of the window was a spike that stuck out of a pot and at the end of the spike was a huge red ball.

I flew to it like a moth to a flame and jam-stopped the car and rushed over to look at it and there I found a most unusual plant. The women were grumbling and I could hear such talks of an insurrection—"Of all the crazy goons", one of them said, "A guy going out to look at plants at 2 o'clock in the morning!" . . . "He's a loon", said the other . . . "Loony as a hoot owl", they agreed.

Thus I was dragged away . . . But I made a mental note of where this shop was and got back into the car, amid some very unpleasant remarks, and drove to our abode.

Well, in the morning I had nothing else on my mind but that red-hot ball and I went down to the shop and found it. I went inside and asked the lady what it was.

"I don't know", she said, "It's something new we got in. But I

can't tell you its name and the boss isn't in now." So she couldn't do anything for me and this conversation took place in Pidgin English and Cuckoo Danish.

Later we went down town in Copenhagen and wandered about the shops, restaurants, beer gardens and Tivoli . . . then suddenly—there it was again—the same plant in another florist's shop.

I didn't waste a moment. I hiked right in and asked the clerk if she could tell us the name of it. She called a man out and he shrugged his shoulders and said that he didn't know what it was. The man who knew the names of all the plants was away on his holidays. Then of course they didn't speak very good English and he mumbled something about some name he thought it was which I couldn't understand. I didn't even think it worth writing down because it didn't sound like anything on earth that I had ever heard of or knew of.

I looked at it, admired it, felt it—but left it with a feeling of frustration.

No, sir, I didn't forget the plant but there was nothing I could do about it. But I made up my mind that I'd look it up or make inquiries about it when I got back home.

Well, about 3 days later I was in Heidelburg walking down a street, a very narrow street incidentally, right near the university. There was my plant again . . . and I marched quickly into the tiny shop and there was an old man who ran it who couldn't speak very good English and I couldn't speak very good German—but I spoke enough to make him understand that I wanted to know the name of that plant.

He went and rummaged about and dug up something and came back with it written on a piece of paper . . . and it was Haemanthus multiflorus.

Aha, now I was happy! I'd seen my plant again and it was a really unusual, beautiful, large specimen and I had its proper name.

When he told me the name or showed it to me, somehow I recognized the name and it had a familiar ring to it but that was all.

O.K.—after that I saw thousands of plants or millions of them in all parts of the continent.

Let's go—just hop a lot of things . . . I'm back home—I rush to the office—I'm there to say hello to the girls and then I dash into the greenhouse. What is the first thing to greet me? . . . Yes, my friends, an Haemanthus. This was one of the bulbs that I brought in from South Africa and there they were in full bloom and were they gorgeous!

I tried to describe them and the closest I could, would be by calling them "a ball of fire"—"red hot Cactus"—or "flaming porcupine" . . . Maybe the "whirling red headed dervish."

Now if you can just imagine this perfect sphere about 7 or 8 inches in diameter with red hot spikes sticking out all over it, that's exactly what this looks like.

Granted—there may be more beautiful plants and there may be lovelier plants and things that "have more on the ball" . . . but there isn't a more outstanding plant grown in creation than this Haemanthus multiflorus.

So there it is—I travelled all over Europe and ran around like a wild man hunting the name of it and I've got the "doggone" thing growing in my greenhouse.

Grass Widow—Hay, Hay

Come summer and the kids get their holidays from school, then a man's thoughts begin to sail into the distant woodlands where holidays, peace, serenity, comfort and natural beauty take over the picture.

Judging by the antics of my friends, it seems that they drool all winter long and spring waiting for the time to come when the kids can get out of school and they can take their usual holidays in the country for the summer.

Of course in most cases the men-folk stay home and tend to business or go to the office or to work and just see the wife and kids for the weekends.

Heigh-ho—maybe I'm taking too much for granted by expecting all of you folks to know what a grass widow is. So without wasting any more of your time, I'm going to tell you. When a man sends his wife and family out to the country the wife is referred to as a grass widow—and he is probably called a grass widower although that term isn't used much—but still 'tis true.

Now where, oh, where would that term originate? Well, after a little delving and studying, I think I have found the answer. It seems that since the days of Clive in India the British professional soldiers carried their wives along with them. When they moved from one place to another they had their wife and family tag along with them. Those of them who were stationed in India found the summers very, very hot and stifling as you might well imagine it would be and certainly any Englishman would find that heat unbearable after the balmy, cool and sometimes dampish British summers.

Well, all of the officers who could possibly afford it would send their wives and families to the hills for the hot period.

Of course when the soldier went to visit his family on his weekend leaves, the first thing that he would notice and it would be startling to him was the fact that as he came closer to the hills, that there was a lush, beautiful, green carpet of grass as compared to the burned, dried and browned terrain close to the city or the lower-lying country.

So when a man sent his wife to the country for the summer and they would ask him where she was, he would say that he "sent her to the grass" and nothing would be more natural than that statement. Seeing she had gone to the grass, the most understandable and natural expression arose and they were called "grass widows".

To me this all seems very, very simple. I hope it does to you.

Nowadays when we refer to a grass widow, we mean a woman who is separated or divorced from her husband. It also refers to a gal who enjoyed life well but unwisely and had an offspring without benefit of clergy. I hope you agree.

Orchid Tips

Here are some general tips on growing Orchids. They are simple, easy to follow and most of them of course are common sense.

They can be grown in a mixed greenhouse, in your kitchen window or even in your living room—yes, and practically any room in the house that has some light.

It is very seldom that an Orchid wants lots of sunlight. In fact I don't know of any that do. You see in their native habitat they grow in the forks of trees or on sheltered rocks or in a shady nook or ravine.

Orchids can stand it pretty cool. It's definitely sure that 40 degrees won't harm them and at 40 many other tender plants are either affected or killed. So Orchids are much hardier as you will note.

Heed . . . Orchids do not like too much heat. They can stand it but they will do much better for you if the temperature is kept somewhere around 60 or 70.

Ventilation is a must for Orchids. They want lots of it. Now, remember, no plant that I know of likes draughts and Orchids are no exception.

Every Orchid that I've ever known wanted good drainage. You see their native habitat indicates that drainage is vitally important. Use Osmunda Fibre, pieces of brick or pots or such—anything that won't let moisture cling to it very long. As Orchids grow naturally in humid areas where they get a lot of fogs, they like the humid atmosphere so you can pour water to them all you like providing it drains away quickly.

If you'll take this advice, you'll get far better results with your Orchids.

The old advice on Orchids used to be to water once every 4 or 5 days but the most recent experiments indicate that where drainage is perfect, they can be watered every day and thrive. In fact it has been conclusively proven that they will do better, give more growth and more flowers, where the water supply is given every day.

When the weather is cold they require much less water which is understandable.

Listen! This part is very important! Orchids do not like to be moved. Once they are established in a location, they stay there all their lives and they resent being moved about.

As long as we have had Orchids in our greenhouses which is about 8 years, I have never known an insect to attack them. So that speaks volumes. From my impression and experience, they are absolutely insect-free.

Any of the plants that we list or ship out are at least 3 years old and in most cases they are 6 or 7 years old. It takes at least 2 or 3 years before an Orchid is ready to bloom.

When potting or re-potting an Orchid be sure that it is set very,

very firmly and definitely only the roots should be in the growing medium . . . not the plant or the bulb—just the roots. Actually the plant should sit on the medium with the roots in the medium and the plant sitting above it.

The best time to transplant or to pot up Orchids is early in the spring—February, March or April.

Ploughshares Into Swords

I was out on the tractor Saturday morning—way back about half a mile from the office. I was preparing a field where we had decided to plant Evergreens.

I had been around thrice and still the field showed no signs of looking like I had hoped it would look—fit for planting. The sod lay here and there in strips which meant I'd have to go round at least two or three more times before it would look respectable.

I had an extra weight put on the back of the disk to dig a little deeper into the soil and cut better. But it wasn't doing much good. Yet the ground was in perfect condition for working . . . neither too dry nor too wet.

On this round when I turned and headed towards the lake, I don't know whether I heard first or saw first but there was somebody and it looked like Gerda waving to me. And I knew what it meant . . . I was needed in the office.

I sort of resented the intrusion even from a distance. Why in blazes can't they leave me alone? Why don't they let me finish this job I'm doing?

But why should I be perturbed about this? For twenty-odd years I've never hardly been allowed to finish any job at the first go at it. So why all the rage and fury now? Oh, I guess it was just one of those moments. I had hoped to get around this piece much quicker and thought it would cut up easier and better and I guess it was the disappointment that was showing through.

So I flipped the hydraulic and up went the disk and I shoved it in cruising gear and headed towards the figure that was still waving at me.

Then suddenly I felt like a warrior riding on his noble steed. Here I was . . . Cincinnatus being called from his farm in the 5th Century to defeat the Aequians and the Volscians who were threatening glorious Rome from the east and the south. I could just see myself as I marched humbly back to my farm after I had vanquished the foe. Then about 20 years later I was called again to put down the revolt of the Plebeians and when this task was done, I set out once more for my farm.

Then I saw myself on a little farm raising sheep in Israel where I had retired after serving my country for almost ten years. Then word came to my farm that I was needed and I again set out on my jeep with my grey hair flowing in the wind . . . to lead the armies of Israel against the Egyptians . . . and when victory was won, again to return to my farm.

So here was Cincinnatus Ben-gurion Tobias riding his galloping Ford steed to the administration chambers to help solve the vital national crisis. I pulled up in front of the office, turned off the key of the tractor and jumped off and there I was greeted by a guy trying to sell me some insurance!

The Forest Tree Speaks

The report is quoted from a Toronto newspaper.

"This giant Elm tree, estimated to be more than 500 years old, was cut down at Moulinette, west of Cornwall, as tree-cutting crews clear the head-pond area prior to flooding next July 1 for the St. Lawrence power project. Using I.E.L. Pioneer chain saws, these Ontario Hydro workmen levelled the old Elm tree, 10 feet across at the base and over 100 feet high".

I lay aside the newspaper, feeling the anguish of the doomed tree . . .

As the armed crew march toward her, the giant elm speaks . . .

"Ere you steer that mighty colossus at my heart, heed and take to mind . . . I will die crushed, battered, wounded, rent asunder by its herculean power. But remember, I was once your cradle . . . and the hand that rocked and lulled you to sleep in it sat on a stool made from my branches.

I was the beams that held the roof that kept the rain and snow from your head. I was the boards upon which you trod.. I was the door that kept out the wolf and the bear and the intruder.

I was the bed upon which you slept. I was the table from which you ate. I was the first utensil which you used and from which you ate your food. I was the plow with which you first broke the forest and sod. 'Twas that plow that first gave you your daily bread. I was the teeth of your first harrows and the point of your first planter. I was your first churn and pail.

I was the fuel that gave you warmth, that baked the bread, that gave you health and strength.

My supple branches made the bow that sped the arrow that enabled you to bring down for food the fleet hare, the soaring bird and the nimble deer.

Do you recall the wheel that first you made from the sinewy strips of my heartwood?

Do you recall the wagon on which you rode when first you were wed? . . . Yes, and the church where you were blessed and sought the help of the Lord? It was made of my timbers.

As a wagon I bore the burden which formerly you bore upon your back. Mine are the pillars upon which your place of God is built. My fruits have given you food and quenched your thirst. My leaves and boughs have often been your pillow.

I enabled you to chart the seven seas. I kept you afloat through wind and storm and thunder and lightning and in me you brought the spices and the raiment and the silks and foods from India, China and all other parts of the world.

I was the ship that defended your shores . . .

Hold! . . . Just one last word. Remember, 'tis in me where you will find your last repose for is it not stated in the 'Good Book' that you will return to the earth from whence you came in a simple pine box?

But some day your progeny will have cause to lament the havoc and destruction you caused. Think of the heritage that you bequeath to them. Where once stood tree-filled forests, now lie deserts and dustbowls.

Now you can strike . . . my breast is bared. I have no means to withstand the onslaught. But my progeny will carry on. They will somewhere find a resting place and somehow flourish still. . . . . But will you and your kind?"

Rose of Magnanimity

Do you recall the story you heard when you were just a wee duffer about the Ugly Duckling? . . . It turns out that the Ugly Duckling was a beautiful, glorious pure white swan. It was just that it was misplaced among a batch of ducks instead of where it belonged . . . with the swans.

Well, that's the story of the Polyantha Roses. Put them in with a bed of Hybrid Teas and they're "ugly ducklings". But plant them in groups for borders, for hedges, for screens and they'll bring you more joy than an only begotten son on pay day.

There is no class of Roses among all that glorious beautiful family that will give you more beauty per inch than the Polyanthas.

"Then why are they are not better known or more appreciated?" you ask and that, my friend, is a smart question and I deliberately reply, "It is because they have been misunderstood and misused."

I'll grant that when it comes to perfume and shapeliness that they do not rival the Hybrid Teas. But if color, profusion of bloom, hardiness and sheer beauty means anything in your lexicon, then Polyanthas are your meat or even chicken. No flower can remotely detract from the loveliness, elegance and true unmitigated beauty of the Hybrid Tea Roses.

But whereas the Hybrid Teas give of themselves sparingly—yes, some varieties even begrudgingly, Polyanthas throw their flowers at you like an over-indulgent parent.

Where, oh, where in Heaven's kingdom or on earth can you find a plant that will start to bloom in late May or June and continue relentlessly until the hard, not the light but the hard, frost ends their magnificent sway.

On my word of honor, you can on many occasions count hundreds —and I repeat—hundreds of buds on a Polyantha Rose bush—yes, on one single Polyantha Rose bush. And that's the way they continue spring, summer and fall.

Do you know why I think folks don't appreciate the Polyanthas— simply because they give of themselves too readily or too easily. If only they would learn the secret of women—to just give enough of themselves to keep Rose growers interested. Perhaps they love unwisely, but too well.

Strew, Stray, Straw

Sure, we all know that wild Strawberries can be found in practically every spot in America—excepting the bone dry desert. Even way far north—yes, even in the Yukon and probably in the Northwest Territories—wild Strawberries can be found growing.

However the Strawberry as we know it today is not an off-shoot of our native wild Strawberry. No, no such luck! The Strawberries that we know in our gardens first came from Chile early in the 1700's. They are properly known as Fragaria and this, to you uninitiated, refers to the delectable fragrance and the mouth-watering aroma that comes off the fruit.

They were originally found growing along the South American Pacific Coast from Peru to Patagonia. The common wild Strawberry of the North American Pacific Coast from California to Alaska is almost identical and is considered of the same species.

Dollar to a doughnut, you don't know where Patagonia is? Or do you say there is no such place or country? Well, there is—in South America and it comprises parts of Southern Argentina, Southeastern Chile and North Tierra del Fuego. It's quite a fabulous territory, too, with an astounding wealth of flora and fauna—yes, and minerals too.

"Skinflint Tobe"

While walking along the road here one day, I noticed in a field a huge Sunflower head. I stopped and went over and examined it and it was about the biggest single stalk and head of Sunflower I'd ever seen in my life.

"Boy, I'd like to own that fellow", thought I to myself.

So a few yards down I noticed the farmer, whom I knew. I went over to him and said, "Mornin', Fred! Would you sell me that big beautiful Sunflower head?"

"How much will you offer me for it?" he asked.

"Two bucks", says I.

"Sold", snapped the farmer.

So when it was mature (I had been watching it), I came around with an axe, chopped it off—and was it ever a beauty! Each seed was like a jewel in an enormous diadem.

I lugged the big head to the car, drove around to the house and handed friend Fred the $2.00 and drove off.

I took it into the seed office, gave it to Gerda and said, "When this is dried off, shell it for seed and we'll have some of the finest seeds that money can buy."

Well, a few days later I was walking through the potting room and the gals were having their lunch and I could hear a continuing crunch, crunch and then a sort of hissing or emitting like spitting and there on the floor I saw strewn Sunflower shells. Each one of the gals had a handful of seeds and was having a lot of fun eating them. Judging by the quantity of shells on the floor, they were eating plenty.

I could also tell by the size of those shells that they were my prize Sunflower seeds.

The plot thickens . . . I wonder do you know the Garbanzo Bean It's also called Chick Pea and its proper name is Cicer arietinum.

It's a plant that I advise my readers to sow and grow so that they can enjoy its nutty flavor.

I had quite a lot of trouble getting a bag of this seed because of some regulation or other. Besides it is not very well known in America

—but it is popular in Europe. Eventually I located some in California and got the seed here.

To the consternation of some of my employees, I have a nasty habit of wandering around at lunch time and when I came into the potting room where the girls have their lunch, there they were munching Garbanzo. As a matter of fact, the beans looked so tempting, sitting there in a dish after they had been cooked and salted, that I reached over and got a handful for myself.

As I don't know anybody in the neighboring county who sells Garbanzo seed but us, I'm quite sure it was our seed.

A short time before, I noticed an ad from a fellow down in Pennsylvania who was featuring some of the finest Sweet Chestnuts of the Manchurian type that ever grew.

So I ordered 20 lbs. because we've always grown a few of these trees and I wanted the best seed I could get . . . and in due time they arrived.

Well, one day from the greenhouse I detected a pleasant smell reaching my nostrils. I sniffed and sniffed again and, holy smokes, it reminded me of the days when I was a kid and I heard that whistling sound which bespoke one thing and one thing only—the Sweet Chestnut vendor.

I sauntered over and looked and, lo and behold, there they were roasting my good Chestnuts over the hotplate.

Heck, they looked so good and, oh, so tempting that I had one or two myself.

Well now, a mile or so down the road a friend of mine by the name of George Walker has a few good English Walnut trees and I asked him if he would get me some seed. So in October he brought me down a 6 qt. basket full and some of them were about the biggest Walnuts I ever saw grown in the northern latitudes—as big and, yes, bigger than those select Diamond Brand from old California.

So I put them in the main office where I was sure they would be safe from all harm.

I was sitting dictating one day when I heard a couple of crunches. I didn't pay any attention. It didn't seem to register. But when I took a look at the basket later, Holy Smokes, the whole top layer was gone.

And, believe me, they weren't selecting the small nuts. They were picking the largest and the best in every case . . . the ones that I prized so highly and was looking forward to planting with the hope that they in turn would produce trees that would bear nuts of similar size and quality.

Well, I didn't want to run out and rush out with that basket of nuts for fear they'd look upon their boss as a lousy old "skinflint" and a stingy old beggar.

So I casually carried them out into the seed room and when I got there, strangely enough, no one was around. I found myself a good sized card and a good thick heavy pencil and I wrote on this piece of cardboard which I stuck in front of the basket, "Gerda—For Seed— Not Feed".

Do you think it will work?

Dwarfs and Giants

What is the difference anyway between a dwarf and a giant? Do you know?

Well, I've asked myself that question and I've given myself some rather weird answers such as—size, primarily. As a matter of fact, I can't find any other difference and maybe that's the story.

But whoa! Hold up! Don't run away! There is more to this than meets the casual eye.

A dwarf plant is dwarf primarily because it hasn't got enough to eat or doesn't have room to stretch and to grow. Did you know, for example, that a Shetland Pony is only a pony when it's on the Shetland Islands? Take it off there like to America and feed him and breed him and what do you get? Three guesses—that's right—horses!

Take a pygmy from down in Africa and bring him to the West, feed him well, treat him well and in a couple of generations what have you got? . . . A normal man. . . . And later what? . . . A giant! That's right. You don't believe it—so what do I care? I still say it's true.

You take a plant—a dwarf plant. You want it to grow in your rockery. Well, if you provide rockery conditions with the soil not too rich and crowded and pressed about, you'll probably keep it dwarf. But you put it where it will get nice soil and lots of food and rain and lots of room and in a couple of generations, Buster, your dwarf plant "ain't going to be a dwarf no mo'—sure 'nuf!"

I hear you saying, "It ain't the first crazy thing Old Tobe has said and it won't be the last!"

Right as rain—you are right! You never were righter!

Now this may sound like stupidity to you but there is a garden in old Niagara wherein grows mostly my plants, roses, shrubs, trees and evergreens. There their dwarfing habit seems to have but little meaning. Dwarf Mums the second or third year become medium and the fourth or fifth year, tall. The dwarf Roses even the first year are robust and vigorous but the second or third year they are good hefty bushes.

While the evergreens are still dwarf, yet such stocky solid dwarfs, they quickly reach their maximum height that elsewhere would require many years. Petunias there grow like pigweed—robust, tall, profuse. This location seems to be the antithesis of dwarfism.

You see, he has a marvelous piece of soil with a bottom that seems to be fed from higher sources and the place is always nice and moist without being wet and the food is coming down with the water. So the normal stuff becomes giants and the dwarf stuff becomes close to normal.

You don't believe me? Well, come down some day and I'll show you.

This all leads me to believe that dwarfing is positively only caused by lack of food or difficult conditions. Why is it that so many of the dwarf plants are native to the lean, rocky, mountain areas?

Just recently I heard of experiments that were conducted with dwarf plants—in this case they were trees. They were kept cut back drastically but they didn't prune the roots and they grew rampant. What happened? In this case the leaves began to grow larger and larger and larger until they were the same size leaves as the natural large-leafed species of the same tree of which this was a dwarf.

Upon checking deeper into the topic, I found that this is the natural and usual procedure. So now do you know the difference between a dwarf and a giant? . . . Sure—Tom Thumb and Goliath—and the difference is what they eat!

Lysenko in the Toils Again

Well, it looks like over in Russia they're having their natural and chemical fertilizer battle, too. And I am glad . . . for why should they have "Paradise" and we here live in a cold competitive world?

Was just reading again about my old friend Lysenko. I say friend qualifiedly because no doubt Lysenko wouldn't have anything to do with a member of the capitalistic class. (This will make my bank manager kill himself laughing because the only thing capitalistic about me is the big fat unpaid notes that he has of mine.)

Well, now I'm going to ask—could it be that Lysenko and his Russian system is right? What a revolting thought. It's like a bad dream —or should I say nightmare?

You know sometimes I believe we ought not to let ourselves get so worked up about the Reds because when we do we get our blood pressure up and our blood rises right up into our eyes and all we can see is red . . . actually blinding us from perhaps some possible truths.

These truths may be to our advantage so we should at least look and listen.

You know we haven't been very smart in our dealings with the Reds, in my opinion. For the past 40 years they have been picking out the best of our system and using it and we've been too stubborn and blind to pick up any good thing that they've had and put it to our use. And if we keep this up long enough, they're going to get ahead of us.

So I've decided that I'm not going to be blind anyway. If the Russians come up with any good agricultural ideas or others that are applicable to my business or trade, I'm going to adopt them and I'll even say "Thank you" for them, too.

Now in truth I'm going to bare my soul here. The closest I've even been to a Red was when I leaned on the Niagara-on-the-Lake Volunteer Firemen's truck when freshly painted . . . but I'm telling you—I'm not going to throw Lysenko, or any other scientist or man from the Red country, or his theories overboard just because of the color of his convictions.

Well, Lysenko has been up and down in the Russian government's estimation for some years. It seems that Stalin thought he was a pretty smart boy but when Stalin passed away and Malenkov took charge, he wasn't so popular and it looked as though he was going to lose his head or wind up in the salt mines in Siberia. But evidently he pulled out of that and now with this guy Kruschev in power he seems to have regained his stature and position.

Of course his theories, convictions and acts are undoubtedly radical and when you say radical in Russia, brother, your red suspendered, crimson faced fireman is fighting fire with gasoline.

You know Lysenko's agricultural thinking doesn't go along the approved or academic patterns. While his name sounds very Russian, I think that guy probably is an Irishman in disguise and his name is really O'Lysenk because he doesn't agree with anybody. He thinks for himself and doesn't give two hoots in Hades if all the world disagrees with him. (I knew there was some reason why I always liked Irishmen.)

One of the greater English agriculturists, after he met Lysenko, said he was an ignorant louse or something—I forget. Well, you don't want to forget that there have been some mighty great big clever men in this world who didn't have much school or higher institutional training. A man doesn't have to have a college degree, or a high school diploma for that matter either, to be smart and capable and have a broad credit of accomplishments. Sometimes too much academic training can do harm to a man's brain. You think I'm joshin' —but no, I'm not. I mean that too much "book larnin" will codify a man's brain and make it click, clack, cluck like a comptometer and everything works so precise and fits into an approved cliche—and with such continuous regimentation the brain becomes warped and stifled . . . you know—like a robot or an automaton.

O.K.—you don't have to agree with me. Nobody's compelling you. That's just my opinion.

Some mighty smart men, when they were boys, refused to go on to higher learning because they had to master so doggone many keys, figures, formulas, equations, rules, regulations, codes, combinations and what else. And there are folks who are given to original thought who just can't be shackled by that mess of stuff and neither you nor anyone else can deny that memorizing that host of things can stifle a man's brain and when a problem arises one immediately thinks of a solution based upon those formulas and charts . . . with no originality.

A man shouldn't allow a bunch of data to block his original theories and thinking.

So where does that get me? Just where I thought it would get me— no place!

Well anyway, a recent statement or theory that Lysenko made or claimed is something like this. He maintains that his organic mineral mixture, which is comprised of the combination of peat, manure and composts with some limestone and phosphorous added, is not only more economical but also more successful from practically every angle than the regular run of chemical fertilizers.

Now don't think for a moment that he's having an easy time of it —also called cinch—because 'tain't so! Practically all of the other Russian scientists and chemical men are ridiculing him and trying to laugh him down. Me? . . . I don't think they'll succeed. I think Lysenko is right and he'll come out on top . . . not only because the fertilizer will be cheaper and more successful but also because it will be a lot more healthful for the people who eat the resulting crops.

Sphag Moss 'Lows No Loss

Insufficient attention is paid to starting mediums for seeds.

Why not view it sensibly and with an open mind? About 90% of all plants in creation are grown from seed. Therefore it should be clear to all of us that the medium in which the seed is sown is of prime importance. Of course as long as some folks continue to get fair results from the medium they have been accustomed to using, probably they're happy. But on the other hand, as a nurseryman, I know that there are a good many failures and I'm telling you truly that in most cases it's not the fault of the seed.

To be sure, when you're using the ordinary mediums like soil or sand, you've got to be a topnotch grower and one who can give painstaking care to the practice of growing seeds. However, knowing human frailties, as I learn and see fresh examples every day, I fully realize that the fault lies in our own carelessness, thoughtlessness or forgetfulness and those three factors are the cause of most seed failures.

You know a man can't spend a large part of a lifetime with something without learning a little bit about it—as long as he has an open mind instead of a hole in his head. He also learns to accept things as they are and not as he would like them to be. Sure, it's all right for green thumb artists, like you may be, to grow them in soil but why take the risk? Why place a burden on yourself when it can be avoided and, as a matter of fact, when you can use something that is better and gives many additional advantages?

Now what I'm going to tell you isn't any secret. It's common knowledge to most people. Probably the big difficulty is that most people forget or have to be reminded.

I still believe that the world's best starting medium for seeds of any kind or description is sphagnum moss. Now you've also heard me at one time or another extol the magnificent virtues of vermiculite and I honestly believe that both of them are wonderful. But if it came to a decision where I had to decide whether it would be sphagnum moss or vermiculite, I think that I'd give sphagnum moss the nod.

In the first place, sphagnum moss is nature's original method and means of seed germination and nature has ideally prepared it for its work. With it you can start the most exotic, the most difficult and even the easiest kinds of seeds. In all sincerity, if a seed has the germ viability within its coat, the sphagnum moss will encourage that little germ to sprout and grow, because it presents optimum conditions for it to do so.

Here are some of the reasons why this wonderful thing is so wonderful. To begin with, you can get complete germination. Every seed that is viable, as I said before, will grow. It is impossible to over-water. Damping off is completely eliminated. It removes the necessity of constant alertness and professional judgment. It encourages tremendous root development. Transplanting becomes a pleasure instead of a chore and, what's more, it is absolutely safe and transplanting losses can be completely eliminated.

Here I quote from a U.S. Department of Agriculture's leaflet:

"Shredded Sphagnum Moss is an ideal medium for seed germination. This has been demonstrated by long experience with several thousand species of plants at the United States Plant Introduction Garden at Glenn Dale, Maryland.

The advantages of Sphagnum deserve the attention of nurserymen, florists, vegetable growers, amateur gardeners, and other horticulturists and also of plant pathologists."

Yet there is one more very important thing I want to mention and emphasize and that is that once the seedlings become fairly well established, nutrients must be supplied or they must be transplanted. But if you are going to supply nutrients, please don't use chemical fertilizer. Get plain ordinary liquid manure if it is at all procureable and water your young seedings with it. In this way you will be giving them the ultimate in food and care.

As Dickens' Scrooge said . . . "Best and happiest of all"—Sphagnum Moss costs so very, very little. It's so very light that a pound goes a long, long way.

Change is no Rest

One of the surest signs that age is creeping up on us is our fear of making a change. Somehow we become reluctant to deviate from the patterns of the things to which we have become accustomed.

Change foods. Change drinks. Don't stick to one. Have better health. Change the path of your walks. Change your exercises. Change your mind. Change your clothes. Don't change friends . . . but do add new ones. Change political affiliations for broader vision. Substitute the plants in your garden and change their locations occasionally.

That is where youth differs from old age. Youth wants to try everything. As a matter of fact, they don't want to accept anything that has been done before. They want to try things that are different, unusual, strange and new and I guess that is the way it should be.

Well, there's no point in me trying to exhort or drive the young folks to change because you can't hold them back anyway. But there is a point if I seek to drive and encourage you oldsters not to fear a change but to be bold—dare to do things differently! Seek and try the new!

Take a leaf from the tree of life for it is eternally changing—yes, life changes momentarily everywhere on earth. Day becomes noon, noon becomes dusk and dusk turns into night. Spring becomes sum-

mer, summer changes to fall and fall turns into winter. We have warm
days, hot days, cool days and cold days. We have calm, storms, winds,
frost and rain. Don't you see that in this world change is continuous.
It is endless!

Therefore I warn you . . . Don't fear variations because when you
do you are giving ample and conclusive proof that you're really getting
old.

Why do we fear a change? I'll tell you. It is because we are going
from the known to the unknown.

Don't you realize that without change there's nothing but stark
naked death? Life is change and change is life!

Dare to be different! Dare to be young! March out boldly and
make changes—be it in your garden, in your pattern of living or in
your action and treatment of your friends and family. Be bold—
don't fear changes!

I was going to suggest changing wives but if my wife ever heard
that I'd be a gone goose, a dead duck or a slain hero. So don't ex-
change wives!

Some time ago I had two pleasant changes thrust upon me. I'd read
an article extolling the virtues of Yerba Mate—the South American
or Paraguayan Tea. You've no doubt heard of it.

I sent for some and the office crew brewed it up and served it—
same fashion as Chinese Tea. It has been a daily practice ever since.

I found it was a little different—not too much different—but because it is a different plant I felt the substitute to my body might be
beneficial. After all there would be new elements, new reactions and
I alternate it now with my regular tea and consider it very pleasant.

Then just the other day Gerda brought me in a cup and she said,
"Taste this tea."

I looked at it and it looked rather yellowish—not the deep golden
brown of regular tea. I queried, "What is it?"

She said, "Never mind what it is. Taste it."

I did and, lo and behold, it was delightful. It was really aromatic,
pleasant and even invigorating. "What is it?" I again asked.

She replied, "Don't you recognize it?"

I said, "No, can't say that I do."

"Well, it's mint tea", she told me. "I just gathered a batch of leaves
last week from the field and dried them in the greenhouse and then I
brewed them up and you've got mint tea."

Believe me, folks, if you haven't tasted mint tea you've got a pleasant,
delightful surprise in store for you. You see—change is wonderful!

In many instances folks can be coaxed into making changes. The ones that are cast upon us or forced upon us we don't like. Those are the ones that are sometimes the best for us. Our doctor insists that we must make a change. Well, we should have made it ourselves, I guess, and only when it's pointed out to us that we are endangering our health and our lives and that a change must be made, do we do it—rather reluctantly even then, with doubts and misgivings. But it must be done and 'tis done.

Sometimes a new way of life is thrust upon us. We don't want it —no part of it—yet, because of circumstances we must accept it. Then when we get into the way of it we find it pleasant—probably just as pleasant as the life we lived before. Sometimes it is even happier and better.

Remember from changes we meet contrasts and from contrasts we learn to choose that which is better and that . . . is good. There's no doubt about it, variation does in the long run create understanding.

Go forth to change with a strong heart. Never fear it. It is our finest teacher and our best friend. Remember that change is the life blood of progress. Remember the darkest day and the greatest ordeal must end. Changes must take place and they are often the best.

Changes are in most cases life restorers, strengtheners, enrichers both of our understanding and of our being. Changes invariably compensate. Yes, in change there is beauty, too—invariably . . . for it eliminates the ugliness of monotony.

Try a few changes . . . They may revitalize your life! !

Dwarf Trained Fruit Trees

I'm going to tell you something about Espalier Trees.

Probably this is not a very good idea on my part because you don't see very many of them around. But, on the other hand, where or when will the average individual get any information about Espalier trees if I don't give it to him? So turn thine ear and I'll whisper in it.

The growing of trees in Espalier fashion is an old art. How old I can't tell you. I sought and hunted for information but didn't find out very much. All I know is that the art was quite popular in the middle of the 19th Century and then its popularity was heightened by a man called Verrier who was a professor of botany and horticulture in the Sorbonne University in Paris. He is the man who was responsible for evolving the forms that we use mainly today.

Basically, the dwarf rootstock is used in growing an Espalier tree. This of course causes the tree to be sort of stunted—the reason being that you don't want much growth in Espalier trees. Then you have the advantage of heavier bearing. The fruit definitely is as good as the best from the standard trees.

The word "Espalier" evidently means "a network or lattice-work usually made of wood". It was originally built shoulder-high and on it were trained any plants or trees that were desired. The fruit trees were trained on these and they adopted or took on the name of Espalier. Throughout the world at the present time we know them as Espalier fruit trees.

It takes at least 5 years to get a decent Espalier tree. Some of our specimens at the nursery are 6, 7 and 8 years old, as a matter of fact. A lot of careful training and pruning is necessary—clever pruning, judicious pruning. Then the undesirable buds are rubbed off and those that are wanted are carefully handled and trained to grow in the proper position.

These trees are grown in various forms and I'll try to indicate them by a few sketches. Here are the names that they go by. One is a cordon. There's a single cordon, a double cordon and a triple cordon. There's also single U and double U. Then there's another type called the Palmette Verrier with either two, four or six arms. Then there's another known as the Palmette which has many arms or shoots from the base up. Some of the trees are found to have probably a dozen branches all starting at the base and angling out. Perhaps you've seen grape vines trained in this fashion.

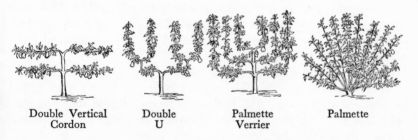

Double Vertical   Double   Palmette   Palmette
Cordon   U   Verrier

There are various and many uses for Espalier trees. Trees trained in this fashion do allow more than the usual amount of sun and air and this results in good fruit. It is advisable and suggested that Espaliers be planted below windows and between windows. Place them algonside buildings. Train them on walls, fences and trellises.

A nice effect can be gained by planting an Espalier at the corner of a building and training two branches to grow at right angles and one erect. This would give a most unusual and delightful effect to any home or abode.

Just imagine a driveway with a row of Espaliers trained on it! It would be both beautiful and useful.

Here's a very unusual way of screening out unsightly objects or places. Turn a dull spot into a thing of beauty and joy. If you're lucky enough to own a penthouse, what better or more enchanting plant can you have? They'll grow in a tub as well as anywhere else.

Try them on a terrace.

You can actually form an outdoor house of Espalier trees in your garden by making an enclosure surrounded by them. You can use this for sunbathing, your siesta or for meals. I don't know if you can visualize or dream of a more beautiful setting or a more unusual one either.

If you're bold enough to have a good rockery and are willing to bring a huge rock or if you had or made a dry wall to train an Espalier along its run . . . my, oh, my—can you visualize—can you dream of the entrancing beauty this would give to any terrain?

You could also dare to depart from the ordinary and usual and have a hedge made out of Espalier fruit trees. Everybody uses Privet and Chinese Elm and Barberry. Be different—dare to be different —and have a hedge made of Espalier trees.

I knew of a home that had an Espalier Apricot trained to grow from the lower window up to the second storey openings and the branches were trained alongside and up the window on both sides and then it had some laterals along it. When this tree was in bloom in the very, very early spring it was almost a heavenly sight. Just think, too, when the fruit is ripe you just reach out of your bedroom window and there you have your breakfast—wonderful juice and wonderful fruit. What a taste for a lovely summer morning!

The fan-shaped Espalier tree would create a focal point or point of interest in any garden. The cordon types are generally suggested for use where you want the horizontal forms because they'll stretch out—that is, they'll stretch their arms out—on either side to quite a distance if you want them that way.

Where you want them to grow in upright form, the U's—that is the single U or the double U—are adaptable and you can use them for high walls, for fences, for buildings, for screenings—yes, and for arbour plantings, too. The horizontal forms are used along walks, drives, to cover low or medium high walls, beneath windows and of course as a hedge or border line.

I haven't mentioned it yet but Espaliers are a lifelong proposition. You plant them once and they will probably last as long as you will and maybe longer. It should also be brought to your attention that a minimum amount of spraying or care is required once your Espaliers are planted and attached to their permanent locations.

Now you know the many advantages in having an Espalier tree, apart from the charm, beauty and the dignity it would lend to your home and garden.

Liming in the Limelight

I just want to sharply shout—DON'T!—when it comes to liming.

Some people and some writers for reasons known only to themselves or due to misguidance advocate the liming of the soil.

I know that my brother out here on his fruit farm for some years was liming his vineyard because some salesman or a neighbor told him that it was a good idea and would make his soil sweet. Well, if I were going to eat the soil, I'd want it sweet, too, but then I'd put some molasses or maple syrup on it—not lime.

Besides, an alert representative for the lime producing company had shown him that the government was encouraging the use of lime by subsidizing freight shipments in car load lots.

Well, I want to say—Halt! Don't lime! From my experience, from my reading and my discussions, I find that liming isn't justified in one case in a hundred. It seems that the one thing in the world that nature provided in abundance and in proper portion to soil is lime and the soil seldom, if ever, needs additional lime to benefit it in any manner or condition.

Now actually what lime does in your soil is stimulate biochemical reaction by which nutrient elements are released to the plant or to the plant roots. By adding lime indiscriminately to a soil, sure enough, you do release these nutrients. But if your plant roots aren't there to absorb it or if it is being released too fast for the plants to use, what happens? It flows out in your drainage and you lose it and your soil becomes impoverished.

Therefore in actuality our provincial government is subsidizing the destruction of our greatest heritage—our *good soil*.

Some experts will tell you that by liming your soil you are neutralizing it. Maybe they're right—but who wants a neutral soil? Looking at a plant pH requirement chart here in front of me I find that every item on the list will tolerate a soil that is below neutral in its pH reaction. Further, not one single plant on the list demands a soil with a neutral or alkaline reaction—but some will tolerate it.

With very rare or few exceptions all the major plants of the earth prefer and thrive on a soil that has definite acid reactions—to a greater or lesser degree. Therefore liming it to make it neutral or alkaline is certainly not going to help anything.

Remember, natural organic materials contain plenty of calcium which adds lime to your soil. In truth I have found that it is more necessary to get acid-producing materials for soils rather than alkalizing them or liming them—especially when you want to grow plants like Hydrangeas, Rhododendrons, Blueberries, Hollies, Azaleas, Strawberries, Gooseberries, Blackberries and such.

That doesn't mean there aren't plants that do want alkalinity or neutrality but there are, generally speaking, not very many. So remember, hold the liming. If some of these advocates suggest it, think it over very, very carefully, get some good advice and demand proof.

Better still—stick your snoot into some good advantageous reading on the subject. Ask me and I'll tell you where to get it. Most libraries can be a big help and you can do it on your own.

Sycamore, Plane, Maple

While it is difficult for even a nurseryman who has been in business all his life to tell the difference or know off hand the distinction between a Plane Tree and a Sycamore, it's high time that situation was explained to John Q. Public.

Strangely enough I had the thing all twisted up in my younger days. I thought that the Sycamore was the Plane Tree and of course the Plane Tree meant Platanus occidentalis which is the one known from coast to coast in practically all parts of the United States and sometimes in Canada. There is another form of Platanus that is better known in Europe and it is the Platanus orientalis which is the eastern Plane Tree.

There is a great deal of similarity between both trees but that's quite normal because they are of the same family and there really is no great variation.

Now back before the year 1700 someone crossed the Orientalis with the Occidentalis and brought forth Platanus acerifolia. I don't know when or who did it but the tree was definitely growing at Oxford prior to 1700.

All of these 3 varieties bear a ball of fruit instead of seed. You probably have seen them on the trees or when they fell. They are light balls—sort of fluffy and yet sort of firm. They always remind me of a huge burr and I guess that's about as apt a description as you can find handily.

But I want to stress here and now that none of these trees are the

Sycamore nor should they be called or placed in the same category with the Sycamores.

The true Sycamore is a tree called Acer pseudo platanus. Now you get that "pseudo" in there which means "false Platanus" or it resembles a Platanus. It does not have the distinguishable, attractive and unusual mottled bark as found in the Platanus group.

The leaves look very much like those of the Plane Tree and then its habit of growth is similar and also its size. Bailey refers to it as the Sycamore Maple and so does Taylor but Seymour says that the Plane Tree (Platanus occidentalis) is called Sycamore in America, whereas in Europe the Sycamore is Acer pseudo plantanus. Incidentally Acer pseudo platanus or the Sycamore Maple, as we call it, is a European tree—not American.

The easiest and safest way to distinguish these two species is by means of the seeds. The Acer pseudo platanus or Sycamore Maple, as we're calling it, has the keys of the Maple, whereas the Platanus has the balls of fruit as I mentioned above.

From my experience I would say that the Plantanus acerfolia or London Plane is by far the best of the entire group although all of them are mighty fine trees.

But for city conditions the London Plane is the best. The whole group seems to grow to a height of from 80 to 120 feet. They're clean, tall, straight and are hardy practically everywhere this side of the timberline. They're excellent for exposed windy sites. They'll grow on the tops of mountains and they'll grow near the ocean. I guess they'll grow almost everywhere and you just can't have a finer, more beautiful or more attractive tree.

So whether it be Orientalis, Occidentalis, Acerifolia, or Pseudo plantanus, my advice is to own yourself a mighty fine long lived shade tree.

Yes, 'tis confusing and bamboozling!

The Sun's Own Flower

Have you ever played the old fashioned game of "Chew and Spit"? Well, that's what you do when you masticate Sunflower seeds.

These seeds are used very extensively in many parts of Europe and Asia but in America they're not enjoying that type of popularity— probably because the spitting is looked upon here as insanitary. I guess that's the reason the old fashioned chewing tobacco is going out of style, too, and there are no more spittoons or cuspidors.

No doubt in chewing Sunflower seeds one wouldn't get that circle of black or brown around the lips that one gets from chewing tobacco

303

. . . and I'm dead sure that Sunflower seed chewing would be a lot more beneficial—healthwise.

Then let's get right down to business!

The ordinary Sunflower is cultivated rather casually in America but it is extremely highly valued and extensively grown in Russia. There they even make a good quality bread out of it and they sell the seeds on the street just as we do peanuts in this country—only they eat them raw in many cases. They don't even bother roasting them—and I can vouch for the fact that they taste good even raw. You get the most nutritional value from them when you eat them in their natural state. Yes, that is the way I prefer to enjoy them.

They have qualities that rank them as one of the finest nutritional foods in the world. And Sunflower seeds have a delicious appetizing flavor. They are commonly salted, roasted in the oven and then cracked.

Reading from an American government bulletin, here is what Sunflower seeds contain in terms of health for the body—nitrogen, calcium, phosphorous, carotene, ribo-flavin, niacin, Vitamins A, B and D and lecithin. Sunflower seeds are as high in protein content as a T-bone steak. They have more Vitamin B and D than any other field crop. And the calcium in raw Sunflower seeds is readily assimilated by the body and aids in building and maintaining sound bones and teeth.

The breakdown of the Sunflower seed is 55% protein and up to 40% fats. It contains one of the highest digestible proteins found anywhere—namely, 93.3% digestible. It is considered superior to wheat or corn germ or defatted soya bean meal as a source of Vitamin B.

Experimenters report that they are effective in benefitting throat and lung troubles, bronchitis and kidneys. It is said, too, that each seed is like a sun lamp to the body. They are beneficial to the eyesight, fingernails and complexion. They tend to lower blood pressure and curb jumpy nerves. The bracts of the flower are used to make yellow dye. The properly cured leaves make excellent food for cattle. The seeds also make exceptionally fine food for cattle—especially cows.

They are used rather extensively throughout the world as a bird or poultry feed and there's no doubt about it, birds do love them. In my day we used to call them Polly Seeds because all parrots and caged birds were fed these seeds.

It has been actually found from the point of view of oil production that the smaller seeds seem to yield better than the larger ones. The larger seeds certainly are more readily edible because there is more meat in the kernels when cracked.

The oil when cold pressed is considered equal to olive or almond oil for table use. The oil is also used for lighting, for candle and soap making.

Here are some ways and means of cracking the seeds easily. One is to use a clothespin or you can spread them out on a board and roll them with a regular, old fashioned rolling pin. Some folks use a nail file. But you can also soak them in a bowl of cold water—just barely covering them.

It is a native American plant and was used extensively by the Indians. It is properly known as Helianthus annus. The name "Helianthus" comes from the Greek and is a combination of the words "sun" and "flower", where it gets its common name as we know it.

It is the floral emblem of Peru and is revered by many in that country who are Sun Worshippers. It is also the state flower of Kansas.

I'd like to mention here, too, that the Jerusalem Artichoke is also a variety of Sunflower—properly known as Helianthus tuberosa.

But there is more to it than that. The reason it was called the Sunflower was because of the belief of the Ancients that the flower heads turned from east in the morning to the west in the evening—following the path of the sun. Well, this has definitely been proven and substantiated. So if you want to watch a Sunflower turn its big head to watch the sun, then plant some seed and pay attention.

The stems and heads of the Sunflowers make excellent paper and the stems have been used to make a very fine fibre that compares favorably with silk. When dried the fibre and the stems are used as fuel in many countries. The leaves and the tender parts of the stems are used as a fodder to feed cattle.

Bees love to work in the flower heads and therefore they aid in producing a good quality honey and an abundant supply, I might add.

Have you ever seen a huge Sunflower at its height of perfection and beauty? It does look like the sun floating in air.

I've always been fond of the daisy-like flowers as big, and sometimes much bigger, than a man's head.

If you have health problems that a balanced diet can help, I'd certainly suggest that you get yourself some Sunflower seeds and grow and eat them. They'll probably do you a lot of good.

Mountain Ballet

It is generally accepted that Switzerland is known throughout the wide world for its beautiful mountain scenery, its yodellers and its fierce love of freedom and democracy.

But there is something else evidently that Switzerland is noted for—yet not much is made of it and probably it's wise that it isn't. But often if the truth is told right out bold, the cause could be delved into and a cure or remedy found.

No, I am not playing at being mysterious or coy. I'm just trying to lead you into my topic with deliberation and an open mind.

I stood outside of one of Zurich's largest department stores waiting for my wife, who was shopping here, there or somewhere, to turn up. While I waited the "wolf" in me insisted upon being heard. So I ogled sort of surreptitiously the legs of the gals and women who went in and out of this large busy store.

For a few minutes I doubted what I was seeing. I scratched my head, I crinkled my brow, squinted my eyes and I'll wager I looked like a mighty queer nut to any of those folks who were watching these antics and expressions of my face.

But not believing or accepting what I saw, I decided to look more attentively and for a longer period of time. So I watched for at least half an hour and I'll bet you can't guess what I saw—that is, unless you've been in Switzerland and perceived the same thing that I did . . . and you wouldn't perceive them unless you were a little bit of a "wolf". But what man isnt a bit of a "wolf"? (Breathes there a man with soul so dead, who ne'er scanned a gal from toe to head?)

I've been told that here in America women have the most attractive legs in the world. But I never believed it to be true. I admit that I did see some beautiful legs in Paris but really not in too many other countries.

No, I didn't go to Europe with the specific idea of looking over women's legs. The purpose of my visit to Europe was horticultural —not pulchritudinal.

Anyway to my amazement, horror or consternation or whatever you may call it, I found that there wasn't one decent, shapely, trim pair of legs in a carload—moving in and out of this large department store. As a matter of fact, most of the legs were swollen, lumpy misshapen, with varicose veins and what-not.

Not trusting my own vision and perception, when my wife and Pearl came back a little later, I asked them to observe and see if what I had seen was true or false. So we all three stood there for another 15 minutes and they, quite perturbed, admitted that something definitely was wrong with the legs of the women of Zurich.

Well, through the rest of the tour through Switzerland I continued to observe the types of legs that the gals were walking about on and really a fine pair of legs by our standards was a rarity. Some legs were passable but by far the majority of them were in the category of poor, damaged or unhealthy.

Now you all know that Switzerland is a mountainous country that has no sea coast. I wonder if that could be the reason.

I have for many years believed and known that faulty nutrition is the cause of practically all ailments in human beings and here it was obvious . . . the fact that the people of Switzerland were denied to a great extent the fruits of the sea and this was showing up in the legs of its citizens.

There are many elements that are given to us by the sea in the form of foods or fish that are caught therein. Without these vital elements our bodies fail to develop and regenerate themselves as they should.

Another important consideration is the fact that the people of Switzerland are loath to import anything they don't have to have and they try to make their own production serve them for all food purposes. This in turn brings about diseases caused by deficiencies of the needed elements.

Shush! I'm not an alarmist nor do I pretend to be an authority. So do not assume, please, that I profess any great knowledge or wisdom. I'm just relating my observations and putting two and two together. I have given you what I believe to be the cause and effect.

Give it a little thought. Whether or not you agree with me is immaterial.

Paradise Found

Come on—follow me on an imaginary selling-bee. I'm really going out to ballyhoo, build up, beat the drums and my gums and create a big fanfare for a wonderful fertilizer.

It is the finest, the greatest, the most wonderful, the most amazing, astounding product of its kind on the market! It will make even the most sickly plant healthy and robust. It will give you the full florist-size Mums. It will create the most fragrant and most beautiful of Roses. It will make grass grow thicker than hair on a dog's back—preferably a Wire-haired Terrier or a Spaniel. It will grow vegetables that taste grand and glorious, full of flavor and vitamins and they'll be bigger and better than you ever saw them before. And if used around fruit trees, the flavor of the fruit will be such that you will never forget it and will exclaim and beam at each luscious, delicious bite. The foliage that grows from the plants that are fed with this food will be most luxuriant. The fragrance of their flowers will be exhilarating and their beauty and profusion of bloom will be unrivalled for miles around.

'Tis true—this is a prepared fertilizer but it is a natural fertilizer —an organic one! What is it? . . . Bone Meal . . . Plain ordinary bone meal—and everything I've said above comes true when you use this elixir. I know these claims are made by many chemical products but in those cases, the claims are not true. The claims I make for bone meal positively are founded on absolute facts and continued results.

Here in a hundred pound bag you get more value than you would get in at least 5 bags of commercial fertilizers—and this material is long-lasting and its effects would be felt for many months . . . yes, and often many years and it will not leave the soil worn out, impoverished and bedraggled.

I don't ask you to accept my blandishments concerning these claims. Ask any gardener, horticulturist or person who has had any experience with growing things.

I should mention here, at this time, that it is almost impossible to use too much of it but still I would use it sparingly, reasonably and with common sense.

If perchance you are a true lover of horses and animals, you may be allergic to this stuff because, in case you don't know, it comes from the glue factory and the glue factory uses horses . . . No, no—not to cart the stuff—I mean carcasses.

Ah-ha . . . Now I get it! I noticed a rather peculiar flavor in the last package of gum I chewed—something like the smell of the farm. Sure, it all fits in now . . . The name of that gum was Meadow Farm Brand.

Are Manures Better Than Compost?

A dastardly pseudo-friend of mine, with an inquisitive turn of mind and one who loves to see his friends writhe in agony, asked me this most pertinent question. . . ."Are manures better than compost?"

Had he posed this question to me when we were alone, I would have said, "Listen, my friend, I really and truly can't answer now but I'll do a little searching and researching at home in the next few weeks and then I'll let you know".

But no, that wouldn't do. He asked me that question in the presence of half a dozen or more people and therefore, I just had to have an answer or lose face (which, in truth, I can afford and as my friends say, a face like that is better lost—sooner.)

You see a man who has spent more than a quarter of a century talking and writing about composts, manure and nature just can't ignore an important question like this one . . . . and to beg off would have positively harmed the cause of organics and the natural way of doing things.

So I started by saying slowly and with much deliberation, "That is a splendid question and one that actually deserves a better reply than I am able to give. But a man can only tell what he knows, thinks or imagines and I will try to marshal the facts that I have learned through the years and give you a straightforward answer."

Inwardly I was wiggling, squirming and sweating. The truth of the matter was that this question had dogged my mind for years and I had never had the courage to face up to it and here suddenly the torch was thrust into my hands and I had to carry it. There was no turning away or time for procrastination. It was do or die!

So I started by saying, "Both are nature's best means of maintaining soil fertility and unqualifiedly if both could be used or mixed, nothing could be better. But if a choice had to be made then I would choose compost."

So, here you have my answer but that is not enough. You are entitled to either my reasons or positive proof that composts are better than manures.

Let us take the manure that you would get from one farm animal because it is a living fact that many farms throughout the world have but one farm animal. It may be a goat, a cow, an ass, a horse or a yak . . . therefore, we must consider the individual animal.

It is conceivable and understandable that the manure from one single animal could possibly be deficient in any one or many elements because a domesticated animal is almost entirely dependent upon a human being for its food—whether it is fed in a trough, a manger or is let out into pasture. So it is possible, even if remotely, that the manure from one single animal be deficient in organic or nutritive compounds.

However when you deal with compost, you are handling many materials . . . grass clippings, corn cobs, leaves of different trees, weeds, kitchen waste, sawdust, waste foods, fruits, vegetables and in general, anything of an organic nature. Therefore, it is almost inconceivable in dealing with such a wide variety of organic matter that the end result could be deficient in any of the vital elements.

Therefore I stand before you and say sincerely, after due consideration . . . that composts are better than manures! . . . In my humble unlearned opinion.

Cloven Flower Buds

Cloves are used universally and every housewife is acquainted with them. Yet very few people know what a clove really is. So let me tell you . . .

Cloves are the dried, unexpanded flower buds of a handsome, ever-green tree of the Myrtle family—properly known as Eugenia aromatica.

It is a beautiful evergreen tree in its own right—growing to a height of 40 feet, with large oval leaves and numerous groups of crimson flowers in terminal clusters.

At first the flower buds are of a pale color—gradually turning to green and later turning red, at which stage they are ready for gathering.

The clove itself is slightly more than ½ inch in length and consists of an elongated cylindrical calyx which terminates into four spreading sepals with four unopened petals that form a tiny ball in the centre.

Therefore, putting it simply, a clove is actually an unopened flower bud of the Eugenia aromatica tree.

It was originally found only in the Spice Islands or the Moluccas but now it is cultivated in many other areas, including the West Indies, Brazil, Guiana and other tropical countries.

There was great rivalry among nations, which even led to small wars, for possession of the source of this esteemed spice—involving Orientals, the Portuguese, the Dutch and the French.

The French were the first to succeed in growing it in another country —Mauritius, in the year 1770 . . . despite the great and even inhuman efforts of the Dutch to obtain a complete monopoly of this rich trade. They even attempted to kill out all the clove trees growing in their native Islands—trying to concentrate the entire world's production and subsequent control to the Amboyne Islands.

Blast O'Phaga Makes Figs

The Fig has been an important item of commerce and man's food supply for thousands and thousands of years. Only Father Time would really know how old.

It is properly known as Ficus carica. It is true that Figs can be grown with fair success in Southern Ontario without protection and farther north, with some protection.

The fruit of the Smyrna Fig, as we know it, is not a true fruit. When you've finished reading this, maybe you won't like Figs as much as you did before. Most people enjoy them. The only people that crab about Figs are those who have false teeth and the tiny seeds seem to lodge between the "falsies" and the gums and cause a lot of trouble and irritation.

Now this pear-shaped so-called fruit that we eat is in actuality a swollen hollow receptacle with a small opening in the end opposite the stem which is completely lined with tiny flowers. These develop into the true fruit or the seed of the Fig.

You see the palatability of the Smyrna Fig depends on the pollination of the flowers—and remember, these flowers line the inside wall of the fruit—by a small wasp properly known as Blastophaga psenes.

The growers of these Figs in California had to import these wasps especially for this purpose. Otherwise the Fig trees, shrubs or vines would never be able to bear fruit.

If this insect isn't around to fertilize the flowers, they will not bear seeds and the fruit will not mature properly and the all-important, vital, honey-like flavor of the Figs would be missing.

Within the hollow receptacle there are found only female flowers, incapable of pollinating themselves and that's why this wasp is so essential. The male tree is called a Capra Fig or Goat Fig where the female Blastophaga psenes lays its eggs in the cavity of the Goat Figs. The females gnaw their way out of their galls and while doing this, they become completely covered with pollen and as they emerge, they go directly to the small opening at the end of the Symrna Fig.

So actually the fine flavoured Smyrna Fig that we eat today is caused by a natural chemical process—the result of pollination which causes the receptacle to enlarge and swell because of infection or irritation. So actually the fruit is a malformation or goitre.

To think this has been going on since time immemorial . . . and all this without nature having gone to college!

I Miss Kissin' The Blarney

If there is even a wee bit, a mite, a drop, a trickle or a smidgeon of Irish blood in your veins . . . then you must dream of some day kissing the Blarney Stone.

Blarney is a small village about 5 miles northwest of the city of Cork. The village of Blarney and Blarney Castle are located in the County of Cork and the Blarney Stone is located in the castle. (Sure and begorra, I belave all Corkers have kissed the Blarney.)

It's only a small village. The population is less than 1,000.

Way back in 1446 one Cormac McCarthy built the castle. It is quite an imposing edifice and the walls in some places are 18 inches thick. While I cannot claim any green blood in my veins—tho' I once found a 4-Leaf Clover and I drink Irish Whiskey—still I went to Blarney to visit the castle with the intention of kissing the Blarney Stone.

Now this is quite a feat because you are away up high atop Blarney Castle and you have to be held by your feet, lowered, then lean and bend under and kiss the stone and that's the only way it can be done.

Well, there at the entrance to the castle was a typical Irisher. I said to him, "I've come from far off Canada to visit your most beautiful country. I have found Ireland lovely and beautiful beyond my fondest dreams . . . and oh, how I love the people. They're so fine, courageous, honest and handsome. And your colleens—they're the fairest things that ever the world has seen. Sure, and when I hear them sing, the lilt in their voices is sweeter than the strains of a harp in Heaven."

The attendant looked at me in a rather strange way but I went on, " 'Tis indeed a sublime clime that has been bestowed upon you by our Great Father. And he has given to your people—gay dispositions, souls of saints, the courage of lions, the character of Lords, the demeanor of kings and a heart full of mirth, laughter and generosity. How philosophically the Irish look at life. You have the countenance of cherubs. Nature has given of her best to the Irish!"

Then I said to him, "I have come all this way because I want to go and kiss the Blarney."

When I stopped for a moment to rest my voice, he appraised me from head to foot dreamily and then spoke up and said, shaking his shaggy, handsome head, "Mister, if you came from Canada just to kiss the Blarney, 'tis indeed a waste of time for there is nothing that you do not have that kissing the Blarney Stone will give you!"

Creator's Apprentice

This incident happens so often that it is almost getting monotonous. Yet it has a point and therefore I want to relate it to you.

It could be a man or a woman or even both. They come out and select 3, 4 or half a dozen evergreens, plants or trees and when they are about to take their leave, one of them will usually say, "We'll have to call our gardener and have him come and plant them."

Invariably, I turn around, look straight at them and say, "Well, what in Hell is the matter with you? Are you crippled? Is there something wrong with your hands, arms or elbows? Why would you be hiring a gardener to plant a few trees or shrubs? Why, I'd sooner hire someone to do my love-making for me than to get someone to do my gardening . . . or for that matter, my eating or my praying. Why would I have someone do for me the most fascinating, exhilarating task on earth?"

Then often they will say, rather shyly, "But I've never planted anything before."

"Well", I go on, "It's damned high time you got started. And let me tell you this . . . if you did your own planting once, never again as long as you live would you allow anyone else to do it for you because that is a task and a pleasure that you will always keep for yourself."

(Let me confess—this man Tobe is an awful liar. The above is what he would have liked to have said but he didn't dare. When they said, "We'll have to call our gardener", Tobe just said, "Guess that'll be O.K.—just dandy!")

Yes, folks, it's utterly unreasonable and crazy to hire and pay someone to do for you the most blessed work on the face of the earth.

Those of you who are gardeners and therefore know and love the good earth probably can understand what I'm saying. But to the uninitiated who have never felt the sublime feeling of good tilthy soil in your hands or watched the seeds swell and burst and begin the life cycle there before your eyes, then I say to you, "You have never yet had your part in creation."

It is like a medical student or a nurse who is present at the first obstetrical case. From there and then on you will relish and love the role of God's emissary in helping to create life and sustain it.

I envy those of you who are not gardeners but are about to embark on this most honored vocation or hobby.

There is another unusual factor about gardening. Once the fever takes hold of you, unlike any other fever known to medical science, it will never leave you . . . but it will be maintained and sustained to a greater or lesser degree until you are laid away . . . to once again join and become part of that good earth that you knew and loved so well.

Fitting, isn't it! Fits like the bark on a tree—eh, what?

Winsome 'Witching Womanly Wiles

Could anyone doubt that nature is a woman? Who or what else is so full of caprice? And what man with breath in his body would want it otherwise?

You know—I know—we all know that a man would be content his drab garb to wear endlessly . . . anon . . . for ever and a day, until it fell in tatters from his aging frame.

Ah, but thank heaven, nature is a woman. And she must change her raiment with every breeze that blows. With a zephyr 'twould be green . . . for a gust, mauve . . . in a ripple 'twould be blue . . . for a gush she'd wear bronze . . . for a blow she'd wear scarlet . . . for the blast she'd wear somber brown . . . and when the wind was playful, she'd wear pink . . . and in a gale she would shed them all. She knows the world is well endowed and she digs deeply into nature's rich plentiful store.

From her palette, dabbed with countless mounds of pigments and ochres, she selects with infinite care the exact hue or shade needed for each individual leaf.

Yes, and even then in a burst of effervescence, she would cast them all aside and suffer the pangs of cold so that the coming spring might have compassion upon her and deck her gaily once more.

Too, I would say that with each change of raiment, there is also a change of temperament.

A man would quake at the thought of being unsuitably clad as the winter approached. But being a woman, nature would feign be bereft of every stitch and stand chattering—yes, even freezing—as long as when spring came, she would be adorned like the rising sun in raiment new and gay, and be young and fresh again.

You know that each and every tree in the forest is an individual—more so than you and I. Sure, the trees are alike, but yet each is different and apart from every other one in stature, girth and curves. Each tree has its character more clearly defined than any human being.

How fortunate is a tree . . . In it birds find sanctuary and they appreciate and respect that haven and pay for it in song and warble. Then in return for the kindness shown to them, they stand guard against the onslaught of bugs, slugs, worms and things that would cause umbrage to the tree—their benefactor.

Even in the closely tangled wildwood, shrubs are found—seeds, fruit and berries . . . and oh, how the birds love to race, hop, cavort and play among them—dashing in and out, under and over—filling the air with trilling, singing, in keys both high and low.

Ah, then when autumn comes and the arms of winter reach to snatch the foliage from the tree, the leaves are loathe to leave their birthplace. Only under duress do they take flight . . . but before that, they rock to and fro like a hammock. And when they at last reluctantly break away, they float softly—gliding, wavering, billowing, cradling—then, gracefully sinking to the soft welcoming earth to rest. Soon Mother Nature will tuck them to sleep with a feathery blanket of white.

Wow—Yipe—Whee . . .

We're going to talk about a more or less unusual plant. I think most of you know it or have heard about it. It's known as Mandrake but properly as Mandragora. This was the name that was used by Hippocrates way back in "them thar days". Theophrastus also recorded specific instructions for the gathering of the root. It is also known as Devil's Apple, Insane Root and Devil's Candle.

The name Mandragora, or its meaning, is obscure but whatever its origin it is said that it was so named because "it was hurtful to cattle".

It is actually not considered of any great horticultural importance. But it does belong to the Potato family and it has a thick, tuberous, forked root divided into two leg-like branches and there is where it gets its common name. It's also related to the Belladonna and suspected of containing poisonous qualities.

Now don't confuse Mandrake with the plant we know here in America as the May Apple or Podophyllum.

The Arabians called it the Devil's Candle because the leaves did shine at night. This is a natural phenomena caused by glow-worms which seek shelter and thrive in the rosettes of its foliage.

If ever there was a plant that was tied up with mystery, superstition, legend, folklore and old wives' tales, this is it.

It is generally accepted to be the Hebrew "dodaim" that is referred to in the 30th Chapter of Genesis. The Hebrew word "do" means love. In the bible you will read that Reuben, son of Leah and Jacob, gathered Mandrake and gave it to his mother. Rachel, beloved but barren, begged Leah for some of the fruit . . . which Leah refused her, but later traded Mandrake for a night in Jacob's bed. Rachel, after partaking of the Mandrake, conceived and bore Joseph.

Roots were grown and dug and those that mostly resembled the form of a human being were used in medicine or drugs and were believed to have strong aphrodaisical qualities.

It is said to be a fact that even today in some Moslem countries Arab women carry a piece of Mandrake on their person in accordance with their ancient belief that the plant is a remedy for barrenness.

If you looked through the old herbals, you would see many illustrations of the Mandrake root and invariably they seem to have the definite bodily characteristics of a human being, either male or female—with leaves like hair growing out of the head. In fact so realistic is this root to the human shape that English folklore distinguishes between male and female roots—noting sex differences. In fact, they referred to them separately as "Mandrake" and "Womandrake".

Some weird tales are connected with the Mandrake and in one of these annals they told of digging up a Mandrake root that screamed and hollered and shouted like a mad man and even sweated blood. Eventually when the root was lifted out of the ground, it did resemble a man very closely.

Yarns of this nature are very common about this plant. The Biblical account in no way mentions the "hoot and holler" phase.

While it is only a small stemless plant, it still is conspicuous with thick spindleshaped roots and large stalked, wavy, marginated leaves. Early in the spring a broad disc of leaves appear—dark green, long, sharp, pointed and hairy. The leaves grow a foot long and four inches wide. Flowers, large, cup-shaped and of rich purple hue, are borne in clusters. Later a fruit is formed of oblong shape—juicy and berry-like.

I'm not suggesting you grow them but should you desire to have one for its folklore, novelty or mystery purposes, we can supply the seeds. But I won't guarantee it will scream and howl when you pull the plant out of the ground!

Roses 7 Weeks From Seed

Tobe tells 'em bigger and better all the time . . . .

If ever a statement sounded like a lie and an exaggeration, this is it. Yet it is neither a lie nor an exaggeration. It is absolutely the simple honest truth.

You don't have to believe me. I don't even expect you will. But here is where you can catch Tobe in a trap—because when I say that something will bear fruit or do this or that in 3, 4, 5 or 6 years, well, you chuckle to yourself, "He's a pretty smart guy. Maybe I won't be alive in that many years so he's pretty safe or maybe I'll forget or something will happen.

But 7 weeks—that's a very short space of time. No one's memory is that poor that he can't remember 7 weeks.

So in this case I'm sticking my neck out but good—a yard and a half long!

A man by the name of Curtis who is a respected and renowned writer of horticultural topics for one of the largest and best gardening magazines in the world, called Amateur Gardening and published in England, heard or read about this boast of mine of Roses in 7 weeks from seed and he more or less contemptuously derided the statement and chided me for the boast.

My sensitive skin was slightly pricked by the insinuation but by dint of grim determination and grit I managed to survive it. So I sent my good friend, Curtis, over there in old England, a package of Rose seed for him to try.

I felt quite certain that he wouldn't bother to do it and therefore my boast would be safe from contradictory proof—but Friend Curtis crossed me up. He called up the head gardener at Wisley which is the seat of the Royal Horticultural Society's gardens and told them that he was sending the seeds down and he wanted them to try them and to report to him when he saw anything that looked like flowers.

Now why should I go on to write a yarn when the thing is all done for me. So from now on I quote exactly as taken from Amateur Gardening, November, 1957 . . .

"Early in May I suggested that Mr. J. H. Tobe, of St. Catharines, Ontario, was 'pulling a rather fast one' by advertising dwarf roses that would flower in seven weeks from seed sowing. Mr. Tobe accepted the challenge and sent me a packet of seeds. So that everything should be fair and above board, I sent the seeds to my good friend Mr. Frank Knight, Director of the Royal Horticultural Society's Gardens at Wisley, asking him to test them and pointing out the test might interest and amuse the student gardeners.

The seeds reached Wisley at the end of July and on October 9 Mr. Knight told me, by phone, that the resulting plants were flowering. Next day he brought a specimen to the R.H.S. Hall, and gave it to me. As I write it is standing on my table; its height, including the 3 in. pot, is 8 in. Two growths rise from the base and one of these is branched. There are four slightly semi-double flowers, each about 1 in. in diameter and of a pleasing purplish-mauve colour, with a small pale yellow base to most petals. Seven unopened buds promise to prolong the little display.

It occurs to me that invalids and dwellers who live in flats and have a love for plants, might find interest in raising and flowering miniature roses. How long the plants will last I do not know, but if they are short-lived it would be possible to raise several small batches each year. My guess is that these roses belong to Rosa Chinensis minima, or the strain more or less well known as Lawranceana."

We planted 150 seeds on November 24 and 10 days later we transplanted 116 seedlings into 2 in. plant cubes. Out of 116, 109 survived. This is February 6 and the first one shows a nice sized bud—that is, nice sized for the tiny plant. Most of the plants look healthy and thriving.

From our experience with Rosa polyantha nana semperflorens, I'd say 7 weeks from germination might bring the first flower under optimum conditions and in the springtime of its normal native heath. Better allow 8 to 10 weeks under all other conditions and seasons.

Sex Determination

Females are such dowdy things!

Swish! Whop! That, ladies and gentlemen, was a wet towel that was lashed across my face undoubtedly by some member of the female sorority within earshot of my big mouth and I hurry to add while still alive that 'tis about the Feline domestica family that I am talking—and not homo sapiens feminina!

Why is it that all the nice light colored flashy fellows with soft shiny fluffy fur are invariably males? The piebald, scruffy alley-cat-like sleeksters are usually the more deadly of the species.

I am neither a cat fancier nor someone who is endowed with any special knowledge on this business of living "mouse traps". But one of the first things I can remember back to my childhood was the time I tried to save a batch of kittens that my father was drowning. As soon as my dad's back was turned, I pulled the kittens out of the water and placed them beneath folded layers of burlap which I fashioned from ordinary potato sacks. I did my very best with them—wept copious tears, brought them milk which I forced into their mouths with the aid of a pop straw—but to no avail. All failed to respond to my able, dexterous, therapeutic treatment.

In Schmoozy's recent batch of kittens—three all told—one was a neat bright looking gray and white, one was what you might call beige . . . it was the most unusual kitten and I don't recall seeing many like this. It was very light colored—almost a very light sand, it might be said. Then the third one was a sort of red or rust color. When they were about 4 weeks old some folks came in and seeing the kittens, asked if they could have one and I told them that I'd be glad to let them take their pick. So they selected one and it was this red headed fellow as I am wont to call him. He really was a cute "meower" and probably the most attractive of the litter.

"I really wanted a male cat," spoke up one of the female members of the party. "My dad says this is a female but I like its color so I think I'll take it", she said.

She had the kitten sitting in an envelope box that she found around the potting room. I reached into the box gingerly, picked up the little kitten and whirled its rear about into the air, took a quick but penetrating peak and said, "That, from my point of view, is a male kitten. But I may be wrong. I've been known to be wrong before . . . truth is, I'm seldom right!"

Then the father hurriedly explained that he only had a rear view and didn't pretend to be any expert on diagnosing the sex of kittens.

"Well", I said, "I wouldn't have even put my two cents worth in except for the fact that I have never seen a cat of that color anything but a male."

Now I don't know if that holds true here, there and everywhere but most certainly in my experience that has held true. So I therefore investigated when she said it was a female kitten.

Believe me, I can assure you that I am no expert when it comes to deciphering the sex of animals when they are very young but when I was but a wee duffer someone taught me the difference between a pistil and a stamen and two parts of a snap fastener. Then I learned the male and female parts of pipe fittings and at last the birds and the bees.

Well, when you examine even a kitten, it's not hard to apply the pistil and stamen or the snap fastener principle. But I still think the male cats are the prettiest . . . and that the red headed ones are all males. Do you know better?

Tall Tulip Tale

You know all those beautiful flowers that appear in the spring? Well, it's not by mere chance or accident that this miracle takes place it's because folks like you and I think of Tulips in the fall and plant them so that they will be there to bring beauty and loveliness when the long winter is done.

It is fitting that you should know a little about Tulips. I'm not going to go into a great long tale about all of the Tulips because most folks are to a greater or lesser degree acquainted with this wonderful branch of flower growing.

We all know the Darwin Tulips. They are sure to please, a blend of fine colors, have tall erect stems and they seem to be hardy in every part of the arable world. I don't know of any part of America where it is too cold for them to grow . . . unless you want to trip me up and say that they don't grow in Aklavik. Well, I couldn't say for sure but I have an idea that they would grow there if they were planted.

First, let's talk about the Candystick Tulip—also known as the Lady

Tulip. It is worthy of the name. It's dainty in coloring and habit. Its slightly scented flowers open widely to a flat star from April to May on 15 inch stems. The backs of the outer segments are crimson with a white margin. Inside the segments are white but tinged with crimson at the tips and with a dark blotch at the base. It was originally found in North India, Iraq and the mountainous regions of Persia. It's ideal for rockeries.

Now the largest and one of the most brilliant of all Tulip species is the Tulip fosteriana Mad. Lefeber—but known to us as Red Emperor. The flower stalks will grow 12 to 15 inches tall and these are crowned by an immense flower which opens flat in the sun—up to 8 inches across. The shape of the flowers as they begin to open is a miracle to behold . . . a study of symmetry, grace and elegance. The color is a brilliant, glossy scarlet—rather lighter on the backs of the segments. Inside a black starry blotch is boldly margined with yellow. What robust habit and how easy it grows anywhere! You will search far and wide before you will find another flower to surpass it in brightness and beauty. Makes a focal point in a rockery. It blooms very early— earlier than most varieties of Tulips found with us.

There is another fine Tulip that is famed for its large flowers and its unusual form. It is known as the Water Lily Tulip—properly Tulip kaufmaniana. It is a most hardy variety, having a very tough constitution and it produces flowers in a very prolific manner. Describing the coloring of this Tulip is rather a stickler. It's really hard to define. But that doesn't mean that it lacks interest and beauty because it has these qualities in abundance. The base color is primrose and the outer segments have a patch of light carmine on the outside with a cream colored edge. I strongly recommend this variety to you for many reasons but one of the most important is that its nymphaea-like flowers bloom in late March and early April—before any other Tulip or other flower is even dreaming of showing its face.

If you want the Tulip that is absolutely the earliest of all Tulips known to cultivation, then you want Tulip Turkestanica . . . obviously a variety that was found in Turkestan. It is neither brilliant nor showy but because of its earliness, it is worthy of a place in any garden— especially a rock garden. The flowers are not very large and open to a pointed star. As many as eight flowers can be found on a common stalk. The outer petals are heavily pigmented on the back. The inner has a single green line within the colors ivory-white with an orange blotch. It has purple or chocolate brown anthers. It is rare and scarce and it is hard to find anyone who lists it.

Having told you of the earliest flowering of all the Tulips, I'm going to tell you about the one that flowers later than all other Tulips. It is Tulip sprengeri which is a native of Asia Minor. Flowers are uniform, dull scarlet. The petals are narrow and it holds no blotch. It is very easy to grow and hardy as all get out. It will increase readily even from seed if planted in semi-shade under shrubs. While it does not have the loud desired beauty of other attractive species, it is without doubt well worth having in your garden.

Tulip biflora is a multiflowering type and you will find up to 5 flowers on short pedicles. It has yellow anthers with purple tips. It is a native of the Altai Mountains.

For the most amazing scene—that is, to anyone who sees it for the first time in a garden—you should have a few Praestans fusilier . . . a true candleabrum of glowing scarlet flowers that look like burning candles. You will have from 4 to 6 flowers on each stem. This appears to be a descendant of the "biflora".

A Dream Come True

Is it a blessing or a curse to be afflicted with the wanderlust?

Let's not go into that now, please. I want to tell you something about my journey into Sequoia National Park.

We went up there via Bakersfield and it was dark when we stopped in Bakersfield for a cup of coffee . . . and then on we went. It was a good highway but a desolate one. While that section is considered one of the most famous fruit growing sections of the world, there was little or no traffic on the highway that night.

I would very much have liked to have spent the night in Bakersfield because I had already had a hard day's driving. We left Palm Springs with the temperature at 126 degrees that afternoon . . . after I had climbed around the San Jacinto Mountains hunting for Coulteri Pine cones which are the largest cones grown by any tree in the world. Some will weigh over 10 pounds. Boy, was it scratchy and awkward carrying those claw-protruding cones in a knapsack on my back! Had I known it was somewhere around 125 degrees, I would have dropped dead in my tracks.

Now Sequoia National Park is a heck of a long way from Bakersfield . . . probably 150 miles. So we holed up in a neighboring town called Portersville for the night . . . but it was well past midnight. We started off early in the morning from there.

As you come to the perimeter of the Park you begin a steep, winding climb which, in my opinion, is about as tortuous a piece of terrain as can be found anywhere in the United States. To illustrate this, after you've climbed about three and a half miles, you have to stop your car because invariably all of them are boiling—fit to explode.

Strategically placed along a little plateau were water taps and hoses and Cadillacs, Packards, Fords, Chevs, Dodges and Studebakers were availing themselves of that God-given water. This mountain route is no respector of brand names or insignia.

A few miles up you had to stop again for the same treatment.

When you got to the top it levelled right out and you came smack into those beautiful Sequoias. I do fairly well when I have to describe beautiful, exquisite, lovely, unusual flowers but when it comes to describing these Big Trees, well, frankly my intellect just isn't up to the task.

The Founders Tree, for example, that you see there is over 375 feet tall. You have to almost break your neck to see the top. But I found a better way of getting a good look at this tree. I walked about 50 feet away from it and then lay down on the needle-littered ground and looked up at it. In this way I surveyed the tree with deliberation and care.

Now I don't know whether or not any of these trees are listed among the modern wonders of the world but to me they represented a sight more inspiring, more thrilling, more hallowed than all of the Wonders of the World combined. This was truly God's greatest handiwork.

Yes, it was more impressive than the Colossus at Rhodes, than the Leaning Tower of Pisa, than the Hanging Gardens of Babylon or the Crypt at Parnassus. These are all man-made baubles, trinkets, objects of art or bric-a-brac.

I claim that I am not a hero worshipper nor do I revere or idolize any graven image—or ungraven, for that matter. But to see standing before me something that God created perhaps 4,000 years ago, still growing, alive, vibrant and pulsating, made me feel ever so humble and grateful too.

Not very far from that noble tree was a sign in the form of an arrow that pointed and said "Crescent Meadow". I wondered what that could be because surely one wouldn't expect to find a meadow 7000 feet high in the mountains.

But within a couple of hundred yards I came upon a meadow so green that it could have been back home in Niagara about the 15th of May. Yes, there it was —a bright green, sun-splashed meadow with babbling brook, singing birds, gambolling wildlife, fish jumping in the creek, wild flowers all about us, green leaved trees—Birches, Cottonwoods, Laurels, Willows and more, surrounded by tall Pines, Firs and Sequoias. There were Big-leaved Plantain and the plants that reminded me of Skunk Cabbage, rosy, mauve and pink wild flowers that reminded me of and looked like Orchids and there were others that looked like Dandelions—the leaves were similar but not quite so toothed.

Then there was a bit of swamp or bog which was interspanned with low bridges and a causeway. We walked across. The water was clear and minnows could be seen swimming in all directions. To the left could be seen the sun as it crept over the tall trees and shone its beams on a section of the meadow. It made it look so bright—like a golden spot in a green swath. That part was on a slight incline which made it stand out even more—like a gorgeous jewel in a perfect setting.

It was just the kind of a meadow that we all dream about. I think we all shall see it because that's what it must be like in paradise. Well, if paradise is like that, then it's worthwhile waiting for!

Muses and Crap Cans

We were visiting a professional friend of ours shortly after our return from Europe . . . he asked many questions . . . I told him many tales.

Towards the close of the evening, when I had recounted what I believed to be the things of interest to him, he said, "You know, Tobe, most of my friends when they go to Europe come back and tell me about the wonderful universities they visited, the art galleries they saw, the art treasures they viewed. They talk of the Louvre, the architecture, of visiting Westminster Abbey, of watching the historic Changing of the Guard, old Heidelburg, 'unter der Linden' in Berlin, the Tivoli in Copenhagen, the lakes and ski runs in Switzerland, the dikes in Holland, The Square in Brussels, the castles of the Dogies and the canals in Venice and the lofty castles in Sweden.

"Then Tobe comes back and all he talks about is the latrines he has seen, the prostitutes parading up and down the Rue de la Paix, the flea market on the left bank of the Seine, the incommodious, unusual, outhouses in the provincial parts of Italy and France and the Bohemian bums in the Latin quarter. Is that what you went to Europe to see?"

Quite abashed and somewhat embarrassed—which is strange to me —for a moment I could not think of an answer because what my learned friend had said was absolutely true . . . shockingly correct and I was unable to deny it.

But after a moment's thought I replied speaking coldly but with emphasis, "When your friends went over to Europe, they either went on a supervised tour, were taken along or followed a well beaten path or were a part of a convention or sight-seeing party.

"I went to Europe strictly on my own. I rented an automobile and travelled in a circle around Ireland, completely around Great Britain, then made a wide circle around the continent, encompassing about 14 countries.

"Nowhere was anyone waiting to greet and welcome me. In no place were things cut and dried, expecting my arrival. At no time did I know when nightfall came where I would be sleeping. On two occasions, unfortunately both of them in England, we slept in flea bags. I didn't mind it so much but my companions were worried and frightened to death and didn't sleep a wink all night.

"Then sometimes we didn't know until one o'clock in the morning whether or not we'd find a hostelry that would let us in or had room for us. On one occasion we were lost on the moors in England and I never believed that any place on earth could be so desolate. I know what they mean when they talk about the eerie moors now. And if it weren't for a kind lady who took us into her large home and made makeshift beds for us, we would have had to spend the night in our car—or who knows what.

"I came and went as the roads lead and what I perceived was there bold, clear, unhidden—a part and parcel of the common everyday things in those countries.

"Swept thro' the French and Italian Rivieras but found it dull, tiring, monotonous—like Coney Island. The only other choice in order to get off that road was to strike for the provincial hinterland thro' tough, steep, dangerous mountains by ways that were uninviting to tourists . . . but to me it was paradise. Wound right thro' the Alps in Italy and crossed into France on the most difficult and hazardous possible terrain in both countries. Followed a river in France that had just recently gone on the worst rampage in modern history—wrecking power plants, bridges, sweeping before it innumerable homes and buildings, inundating countless farms and farmlands . . . rendering I don't know how many people homeless. I never read a word about it in the newspapers but that is what I saw with my own eyes.

"The detours we were forced to take were unbelievable in their antiquity. A motor car was never meant to travel such roads. The ancient Roman highways were much better, I assure you, for I travelled some of them. The parts of the cities and towns we saw were probably beyond the bounds or reaches of most travellers. Only Wild Man Tobe would attempt it!"

Then I continued to Friend Doc. "We saw the picture of Europe, not as anyone wanted us to see it, but just as it was in its stark reality and a heck of a lot or most of it wasn't lovely. No, it wasn't all arts, science, museums, galleries, cathedrals, castles, luxurious homes and gardens. In fact, not too much of it was that way. If I talk about latrines, prostitutes, beer halls, hovels, filth, poverty, thieving and such, it is because that is what we saw most frequently and that is what comprises much of Europe.

"Probably when you go to Europe, you'll also follow along the usual pattern and you'll come back and say that Tobe was as balmy as a bearing. And furthermore, I'll tell you what else. You won't have the spunk to go out and foot it yourself. You'll probably have a reservation in the finest, plushiest hotel in every city or town that you're going to stop at and you'll pull in about 4 o'clock in the afternoon for fear you might be out when it got dark. And if you do any sightseeing, it'll be with a limousine, liveried chauffeur, guide and bodyguard.

"If that's the way you want to see Europe, you go ahead and see it that way. But you might just as well go about wearing rose-colored glasses. What you see that way will not be the way the world really is.

"But I saw it the way I wanted to see it—natural, authentic, unvarnished, its true self—and that's the way I want to see any other country I visit!"

Yes, friends, and that was the end of a beautiful friendship!

Old MacDonald's Farm

What manner or means of men was it that made Canada the country it is today?

Now if I be so audacious as to suggest it was a Scotsman, I know I'll raise a hoot and a howl about my head and shoulders that will probably bust my bones.

"What about the French?" . . . I can hear nasally hacked at me, . . . "And the Irish and the English and the Italians and the Greeks and the Russians and the Poles—yes, and what about the Jews, the Dutchmen, the Swedes, the Danes, the Norwegians and the Germans?"

O.K.—O.K.—they all had their part in building this vast country of ours. But still must you quarrel with me if I suggest that the Scotsman showed maybe a little more willingness to tackle the wilderness. And why not?—it was somewhat like his native heath. I just wanted to pin a thistle on someone's lapel.

I often day-dream back to the early days of the settlers, when they came to Canada and found things just as God had made them and the Indians had left them . . . great noble forests with trees of enduring beauty reaching thro' the clouds—right to the high skies.

I can just see them—thousands, tens of thousands, hundreds of thousands—yes, and millions—of green suppliants waving themselves to and fro in the breeze like the Mohammedans and Jews vibrating themselves at prayer toward the East and their living God.

The rivers then flowed all year long—summer, autumn, winter and spring . . .like a panther in the spring, like a bird in the summer, like a ribbon in the winter and a silver streak in the fall. In the woods game was playfully abundant. Fish teemed in the water—pure, unsoiled, unspoiled pools . . . with color so blue they looked like the sky was inverted. Lakes—some snug against the mountainsides, others in crevices with the rugged, imposing, soaring, towering mountains of rock, snow and ice as the sides of their cradle and there were those on the plateaus and then the greater lakes of the plains. Where'er these lakes were found tall trees, sentinel-like trees lined their shores and stood like sentinels hard upon each other, guarding the boundaries.

That's the way it was when old man MacDonald came to Canada back over 150 years ago. He clove and hacked a farm out of the wilderness and a house and barn to house himself and his cattle.

Ah, them were the good old days . . . when a man was as free as the sky and the clouds let him be. That was when men were men and their women were mild, meek and mellow and did the chores and housework and gave birth and raised the children.

You, among others, remember the song that goes, "Old MacDonald had a farm" . . . Well, this was the Old MacDonald himself!

One of the vital things about a farm, in fact the most vital thing as we all know it, is not the house or the barn or the land but, strange to relate, the outhouse where the thick department store catalog hangs in a convenient place, ready to serve and do duty at the flick of a moistened finger-tip.

Would you believe it . . . it was old man MacDonald who built the first outhouse in Canada.

"Well", you ask incredulously, "What the devil did they do before that?"

And I reply with surprise and raised eye-brows, "Why, they did just what came naturally . . . same as the animals. And the barn or barnyard was the scene of this regular movement."

Well, Old Mac had seen in his youth in Scotland where some of the more advanced or intellectual farmers had erected these little mousiehouses, cannisters, booths, recreation centres, sunken boxes or, as you know them, plain old privies.

Now with all these fancy names that we're calling this place, I should of course mention the one that it was most often called and appropriately, too, I should affirm. The kind of house it was called rhymes with "wit" but for my purposes, I'll call it the outhouse. You can call it backhouse if you will. Of course nowadays they're in—not out of the house.

Well, 'tis true—Mac was mighty proud of his creation. It was the only one for miles around. In fact nobody knew of anyone else who had one. It had a gable roof with a half-moon cut on the windward side. 'Twas a single-holer but, believe me, it was plenty good enough, considering that every log had to be hand-hewn before it was made into boards fit for nailing together.

Well, as I said before, he was justly proud of his creation. It really was a monument to a great man's audacity and courage and after all, what can any man give to his fellow-man more than comfort, solace and the stimulation to think and ponder.

Well, muddy York was just becoming a good sized town then and his son forsook the farm and took up residence in the then distant town at the mouth of the Humber.

A year or two went by and the lad decided to go back for a visit to Glengarry where his father still farmed and of course it was like the return of the Prodigal Son. He was fed until his stomach resembled that of a poisoned pup and after he had reclined on an old couch for a few hours, he had the urge and decided to go out and see the old privy.

He returned about two minutes afterwards and addressed his father and said, "Dad, what happened to the outhouse? I couldn't find it. Where did you move it to? Have you hidden it somewhere out of the way?"

"No", his father replied, in a very sullen manner, which was quite unusual for old Mac, "I tore it down."

"But, Dad", remonstrated his son, "It was such a convenience—so comfortable, so elegant, so uplifting."

"Yes, son", said the old man, "I realize that, too, and felt just the way you do about it. You know we MacDonalds are a prolific clan. There's Big MacDonald, Little MacDonald, Red MacDonald, Black MacDonald, Lean MacDonald and such . . . but when all the folks around here began to call me Outhouse MacDonald, that finished it. I tore the dang thing down!"

Indians, Squaws, Summer, Autumn

Ever since I was a youngster Indian Summer to me meant the late fall days, usually in November, when the bright sun shone on a brisk, semi-frosty morning . . . when there was a sort of blue haze in the sky and the day in every way resembled the finest that the summer could offer except for the haze, the briskness, the lack of humidity and stifling heat.

However, in talking to different people, I find that Indian Summer means many things to various individuals. It seems each and every one of us has a conception of Indian Summer unlike that held by anyone else.

Some think Indian Summer days come in September—others, in October—to others it means any warm day or two that strikes in the fall. Now an occasional warm day in the fall may mean Indian Summer to you but it is not the true Indian Summer, according to what the Indians call Indian Summer. And after all is said and done, they are the ones who should know because they obviously originated the term or should I say—the term originated with them.

You know at times one can learn much from an encyclopedia or a dictionary. Yet at other times you can learn next to nothing. In fact, you can wind up being more confused after getting through than you were before you started.

Webster's Dictionary claims that Indian Summer is a period of mild weather late in autumn characterized by a cloudless sky and a pleasant haze in the atmosphere. The term is commonly assigned to the last days of October. Now remember he says the Indian Summer days come in the latter part of October.

The Encyclopedia Brittanica says that it is a season of several weeks duration in late autumn—characterized by a calm clear atmosphere and mellow sunshine in sharp contrast to the climatic conditions that precede and follow it . . . especially in eastern Canada, northeastern United States and the Mississippi valley. The haziness in the atmosphere is attributed to the smoke and the dust floating in the air which absence of rain and wind has made possible. It goes on to say further that Indian Summer is preceded by squaw winter—a cold spell when the thermometer first gets below freezing point.

Now I know that the Encyclopedia Brittanica is supposed to be the supreme authority and no one dare doubt it or argue against it. But, shucks, I believe that the bigger they are, the harder they fall. As a matter of fact, the Brittanica usually goes out and gets an expert to write on a certain topic and then quotes it and that's it. Well, I never did have any respect for experts anyway and when this expert says that the haze in the atmosphere is attributed to smoke and dust floating in the air, I think he's "off the beam".

It may be some form of dust left when the winds blew the soils in a swirl and some of the particles remain in the atmosphere. Maybe they're referring to the smoke that came out of the hole in the Indian's teepee or wigwam. Maybe they're referring to the smoke that came from the pipe of peace that old Chief Picklepuss was smoking.

Anyway, don't let anyone, including the Encyclopedia Brittanica, tell you that the haze in the atmosphere of the Indian Summer days is caused by smoke or dust.

In the first place there is usually ample moisture to prevent dust storms in the autumn. There are seldom if ever forest fires at that time of the year so therefore little or no smoke. I contend that the haze is caused by refraction—a combination of the sun's rays, the dew and the temperature and atmospheric conditions hovering at or slightly above freezing.

There is little or no smoke or dust in the north—the true north —and yet they have the Indian Summer haze. The Indians knew Indian Summer and the hazy days and certainly the smoke from their teepees could not cause the entire countryside to become smoke or dust filled.

The name, Indian Summer, seems to have been derived from the custom of the Indians to use this time in preparation for winter by laying in stores of food . . . or from their belief that these favorable winds were blowing directly from the court of their God to give them a chance to prepare for the winter. The Indians called their God, who brought these benevolent days and beautiful weather, Cautan-towwit or the Southwestern God.

In the northwestern part of the United States and Canada a frost can be expected in the latter part of September. Then during October, especially after those few early frosts, come some of the finest days of the entire year. The skies are clear and the sun is warm. There is a briskness in the air that can hardly be called a chill . . . yet it is invigorating and stimulating. This spell of glorious weather doesn't last just a day or two but usually for two or three weeks.

It is during this time of the year that the air becomes actually transparent and the skies are an azure blue that they never seem to be at any other time of the year.

It is also at this season that the evening sunsets are the most colorful . . . unmatched by any other period of the year. One sees at eventide the distant horizon aglow, gleaming, scintillating . . . the setting sun surrounded by hues of gold and scarlet, like a halo crowning the orb in all its majestic glory.

Actually it can be truthfully said that Indian Summer is a short season of the year all of its own—different in one way or another to any other period of the year. To this theory I eagerly subscribe!

Most of the folklore and data going back many years indicates that it takes place in either October or November. Now this should not be confusing because it is quite understandable. Naturally in the northern latitudes we would expect to get our Indian Summer in October. Farther south you would expect it in November. Then deeper north they would celebrate it in September. So therefore it makes sense.

Indian Summer is a carefree and happy time—not only for man but for birds and beasts as well. It is the time to rejoice with the harvest and to be grateful for the kindnesses that were bestowed upon them by heaven.

Probably the smorgasbord of the Scandinavians is another way of saying Indian Summer because at this time the sky is filled with gay colors of orange and gold. It is the haze that causes these oranges and gold to be diffused across the heavens.

For 'tis a time of harvest, when the crops from the field, the bush, the meadow and stream are brought from different sections—each bringing what his location produces best as a contribution to the festive celebration.

But with all this show of beauty, color, brightness and gaiety, we are brought to the realization by the chilly, frosty and unusually clear nights that winter is close at hand and we'd best be ready.

Of Birds and Other Things

How many folks seek a way and a means to meditate, ponder, think or cogitate? I am bold to suggest that quiet and peace are not the only requisites for meditation.

I have found the most conducive medium to sound thinking is . . . sitting on the tractor ploughing. Now you can think and ponder when disking or cultivating, also on the privy seat, but not to the same degree as you can when you're ploughing. As the plough breaches the earth's crust and lays it open and over, so it seems does it render your ears, eyes and mind permeable to intellectual stimuli. This gives leaven to your brain.

I'd actually given up the plough on the nursery except for opening furrows in which to plant larger trees and plants. For the past two years all the fields have been prepared for planting by the sole means of disc-harrowing. Disc-harrowing seems to be the ideal medium for following the practice of natural or organic gardening. After all, what's the sense of ploughing an 8 or 10 in. furrow and turning that good top soil down below where it can do little or no good? For remember, most of the plants that we grow feed off the first 4 to 6 inches of soil. So with logic and good reason, in my humble opinion, ploughing has been pretty well abandoned.

But this piece of sod had been grass for probably 6 or 7 years and it would not yield to the disk. I ran over it three times and it didn't make a big enough dent to make it worthwhile continuing. The neighbor's boy, watching me struggle with the disk, walked over and said, "I think you'll have to use the plough on that one, Mr. Tobe."

And I said, "Willy, you never were so right!"

So, much as I dislike ploughing (And here I should not say "dislike" because I enjoy ploughing. The better word would be "disfavor".) I felt in this instance that it was a necessity. Then I was glad that I hadn't disposed of my plough because a year or two ago it seemed as though I'd never use it again.

So I spaced off the distance with my eye and then ran down the centre, turning the first furrow. I hadn't gone 50 feet before the Blackbirds and Cowbirds were there to keep me company. I'm not as good a ploughman as I could be because I have to always look back to see how the plough lays open the earth, moulding it over ever so gently and orderly.

There were the Blackbirds already gobbling up the Junebug grubs as fast as they could chop them up and devour them.

So round I went—making one turn after another—swinging to the left down the long row and then again swinging to the left in a wide semi-circle and cutting another swath on the other side. Of course all this will eventually balance up and leave the entire area neatly turned over and waiting for a day or two to be disked.

And as my eyes roamed to the right, to the left, ahead of me and behind me, I thought of a political slogan of many years ago. You may remember it, too. It was something about a political farmer ploughing a straight furrow and calling for you, I and everyone else in Ontario to re-elect him because he ploughed that straight furrow.

Then I mused . . . the only man who can plough a straight furrow is one who looks straight ahead—neither to the right, to the left nor behind. Well, how can a man sitting on a tractor just look straight ahead and nowhere else? He could if he were a robot and he might if he wore blinkers like a horse. But any normal, intelligent man ploughing could not help but look to the right and to the left and behind as well as forward.

No wonder the intelligent electors of the Province of Ontario rejected that man who ploughed that straight furrow. I don't think any politician will use that slogan again.

I watched a limber, chunky Blackbird as he snapped up a big Junebug grub. Then he spied another and snatched it up, too, but he dropped the first one. He went at it again and then when he had the two in his mouth, he tried for a third . . . with the result that he lost them all and had none in his mouth for a moment. But he still kept doggedly going at it and eventually he got them all stuffed in his beak and flew away where he could nibble at them without fear of challengers before going back for a refill.

Now at the time I didn't know what kind of birds these were. I am sorely lacking in audubon lore. I wish I had studied ornithology and learned a little bit about birds earlier in life.

Ever since I've been able to get on the ground back in early April, every time I've disked a piece of ground or opened a furrow immediately the birds were upon me. In practically every case they consisted of these Cowbirds and Blackbirds. I always think that Blackbird is a poor name for it because its head and neck seem to be covered with a beautiful purplish or bluish sheen—almost like a gun barrel shining in the sun.

I've been checking up on a bird book that I have here and I'm not sure whether the bird that I saw was the Boat-tailed Grackle or the Brewers Blackbird but by the look of the female I'm quite sure it was a Brewers Blackbird. They both appear to have a sort of boat-like tail.

In and along with my ignorance of birds I thought that this Blackbird was an exceedingly lovely creature. The males are very good looking but the females are dowdily draped specimens.

Then of course there were the Cowbirds around, too, and an occasional Starling. But where were all these other birds that are found so abundantly throughout this part of the country? Evidently, I would surmise, they don't abound in the open fields because these seem to be the same birds that I've been noticing all spring. I'm going to keep a keener eye on the feathered friends that I see from now on.

You'd wonder how I could find peace and meditation on the seat of a roaring tractor but strange, you don't even notice the racing of the motor as you move along the ground. The seat has lots of spring to it and you're not jarred very often unless you hit a hole!

And oh, how small the worries of the day seem to be whilst sitting on the tractor ploughing. I can see now why farmers can carry the enormous burden that fate inflicts upon them. They shed their burdens from their backs, like a surfboard sloughs water, the moment they are out in the field ploughing and the world seems to be such a glorious, grand, enchanted place in which to live.

One feels privileged to be alive and enjoy the grand spring after the long, long winter and to be a part of this wonderful universe . . . buds bursting, green showing all around, birds singing, flying about and circling overhead and around you . . . yes, I want to be a friend to man and beast alike. I want to work with and live by the land and never forsake it.

Tall, Dark and Handsome

Do you need the answer to a maiden's prayer? Well, I haven't got it but if you want a good coverall vine that will do a wonderful job of bedecking unsightly rubbish heaps, outhouses, tree stumps, garages, fences and everything you want to conceal —like if you shot your mother-in-law or your son-in-law for that matter, you could very easily hide her or him under this vine.

Now this ipsy dipsy coverall vine is properly known as Humulus japonicus but more generally it is called the Hop Vine. Brother, this vine really grows fast. It's annual and seeds itself every year and it grows almost anywhere under any conditions and at almost any time.

Now don't get the idea that this is a poor specimen of a plant because it isn't. It's a good plant.

It also is useful for shading arbours and growing against walls and, generally speaking, it will cool an area because of its lush, green luxuriant foliage. So if you want the answer to a maiden's prayer, as I said before we haven't got it, but we've got a doggone good climbing vine.

Blue Hydrangea Lore, A La Tobe

About 20 years ago I began to offer outdoor Blue Hydrangeas to my customers across Canada.

Some of the older nurseries let it be known that Tobe was taking the people for a ride because the Blue Hydrangeas wouldn't bloom and were not hardy enough for this latitude. Well, today practically all of the leading nurseries list them. Evidently they've undergone a change of heart or mind.

You see I discovered some years ago that the Hydrangea was absolutely hardy in this latitude. But I also discovered a very important thing and that was that the terminal buds of the Hortensis variety, which is the one I'm talking about, were tender and would freeze in the severe winter.

Do you know the Hydrangea to which I refer? 'Tis the one that has these huge broad blue or violet pink flowers, floating like billows on a plant of glorious foliage. If you've ever driven through Pennsylvania or Upstate New York or further south in July or August you've seen them in front of many fine homes.

Now how do you go about seeing that your Blue Hydrangeas are sure to bloom? Well, I'll suggest one of the following treatments:

(1) About the first week in May get out there with the old pruners and cut the Hydrangea back drastically. This will promote vigorous growth during May and June and by the time the terminal buds have formed there will be no danger of them freezing. Then they should start to flower in late July or early August.

(2) For winter you can try covering your plant with straw, leaves, burlap or anything so that your terminal shoots won't be frozen.

(3) Now it might be another idea to trim your plant drastically, say late in July. Then by all reason your terminal shoots shouldn't be very tall by fall, and therefore they'll be easier to protect. So no frozen terminal buds—thus, plentiful blue blooms.

Just don't forget it and I've told you this before—I'm not an expert on Blue Hydrangeas or anything else. I just try various things and the answers maybe teach me something and this is the story as I give it to you.

So, So, Wild Oats

It seems that every man must do his share of sowing seeds of this plant . . . and according to some, until this is done, he is unfit to take his place in society.

I tried to track down the source of this expression but so far my efforts have come up against a blank, high brick wall. But I'm still trying—and my efforts may yet be crowned with success.

334

"He's sowing his wild oats" is said of someone who is passing through a period of wild and thoughtless dissipation—as in youth.

It is a known fact that wild oats do lie dormant in the earth for many, many years while still retaining full vitality and strength—ready to perk up and start to grow as soon as an opportunity presents itself.

Where once Wild Oats have become established, they are not readily eradicated and the only way known to old timers to get rid of them was by continued and repeated fallowing.

In days gone by, the awns of the Wild Oats were often used as hygrometers and fishermen used them for making artificial flies for trout. They claim they were very successful.

Where they originated, no one seems to know but some suspect that probably from the northern coast of Africa or Spain. The wild oat sometimes is actually somewhat taller than the cultivated oat, often being found as much as four feet tall. It is considered one of the most destructive of annual weeds and will choke out very easily many other important crops—especially barley.

The seed of the wild oat ripens and falls before the harvest of other crops, thus they populate the ground with their seed and are ready to go ahead and plague the farmer.

No one seems to know from whence the name came, but I have reason to believe that it is a hand-me-down from the Celtic "aten" which is from etan "to eat". This seems to be more or less a logical conclusion—especially as we know Scotsmen are very fond of oats and no Scotsman is said to have "eaten" until he has had his fill of oatmeal in the morning.

There seems to be some confusion concerning the genuine true wild oat, but by and large, I think that they accept Avena fatua as the true variety. Yet some authorities seem to confuse it with "sterilis" which is the animated oat. They are similar in many respects.

Evidently the name "animated" has been given to it because the long strong awn will twirl, twist and turn, depending upon the amount of moisture in the air which causes movements of the dry seeds. Bailey says that it is the flowerets that do this moving, but I think he is mistaken. It is the seed.

Evidently it was given its name "wild oat" because it is very, very difficult to control and readily gets out of hand.

When a horse is exceptionally high spirited and hard to handle, they usually say it is "feeling its oats" . . . and the same is often said of the young man—especially when he is strutting "like a cock" when there are gals about.

I would gather that the twisting and turning of the awns under the sun's heat is a means of getting the seed to another location more suitable for its germination and growth . . . Nature's means of auto-motion or propulsion.

An awn, incidentally, is a beard or bristle-like appendage of the outer glume of wheat, barley and many other grasses.

An 'Artful of Art

It had to go! There was no other way out. It saddened me. I was heartbroken . . . but what could I do? It had at last outlived its usefulness.

In truth, I was reluctant to part with it even yet but there comes a time when emotions, past consideration, mood and sentimentality must be put aside and one must act ruthlessly—with boldness and purpose. So this was it—the day had at last come. In this case, it was actually Gerda who was the "destroying angel". She ordered its destruction. I was just the instrument to carry out the edict—the executioner.

I hated to do it. It pained and grieved me greatly. There was sorrow in my heart. But in truth I knew, too, that the judgment was correct—it had to be done. Still, that didn't make my task any easier.

You see it had served us well . . . withstanding the buffeting of the elements for many long arduous years. How can one part forever with something that has given of itself so freely—for so long?

So I sadly steeled myself for the ordeal to be endured and said to Bill, "Will you get the old stoneboat ready?" I told him exactly where to put it so that it would be in the proper position to receive the load it was to carry.

A few minutes later Bill came to me and said, "Boss, the stoneboat is in position—all set and ready. Will you come out with me and help ease it on?"

I got the tractor and drove it down to where the stoneboat was, backed into position and hitched it up to the drawbar. Then I carefully surveyed the position of the building and the stoneboat. Then Bill and I shoved and juggled the stoneboat a little more, to be at the exact angle to receive the load in the best possible way.

I got behind the little red building with the moon cut in one side of it and I told Bill to remain in front and sort of guide it down. Then I braced my legs and began to push.

Now it wasn't too hard to heave because the little outfit had been sitting more or less precariously on a couple of logs that had always been put in this position to allow for moving from place to place as the mounting situation demanded. I pushed firmly yet slowly and the building angled forward more and more. Then Bill caught it and eased it gently on top of the stoneboat.

Eventually when the building was completely lying on the stoneboat on its side the "gaping" hole was left uncovered. No, it wasn't smelly or sickening as you "city-slickers" might say or think. Why, I bet 999 of you "city-slickers" out of 1,000 don't know what one of these things looks like—let alone smells like. Contrary to what you believe, they don't have a vile odor.

I admit it didn't smell like Coty 14 but it smelled a lot better than stale beer or the second-hand smell of whiskey or tobacco smoke off a man's breath or the general odor that emanates from a "pub" . . . even your favorite one. If you think I'm talking through my hat, make the comparison and see for yourself whether or not I'm right.

Yes, and there are people in this great big country of ours who would rather use one of these out-house outfits than modern plumbing. You could never understand that—any more than you could understand that a few grains of fresh wheat pulled off the stalk . . . rubbed in your hands to remove the husks . . .the chaff blown away . . . tastes better and is better than gum.

So I hollered, "O.K., Bill, fill her up!" And he started shovelling the good earth into the opening that didn't need much filling to begin with.

Well, there was another shovel handy so I, too, fell to the job and helped Bill fill her up. When it was finished, I climbed aboard the tractor and told Bill to follow behind because the rear of the building was dragging. The stoneboat wasn't long enough.

Turning round on the seat of the tractor, I said, "I'm taking that down to the back, Bill. We're going to burn it."

So I drove along and when I hit a rough spot or two, the load bounced and shook and trembled as though it were going to fall apart and about the fourth or fifth time that happened the poor old building rolled off the stoneboat and with a crash parts of its "innards" fell out.

I stopped the tractor, jumped off and ran behind and there Bill was dragging a board about 5 feet long and 1 foot wide that had two holes in it. While most of the old building was made of rough lumber, this piece was obviously our native Silver maple—a rather whitish wood, rubbery, smooth, tough yet soft. And the two openings had been hand-carved and bevelled just at the right places.

Now I can't take any credit for this because this building was erected long before I had bought the farm . . . although we had moved it from place to place on many occasions.

Of course the board had been worn much smoother than it was originally because of the movements that took place on it over the period of time and I would judge that would be 50 years.

Well, before I get away from the main thought here, I'd better tell you we were not entirely abandoning this mode of living. In the nursery we have a more or less modern and up-to-date bathroom and the necessary facilities. We also have one upstairs on the second floor of the shipping building. But the packing, shipping and nursery crews would rather be found dead than go into the office when the need arises. So they always use the "mousie-housie" or as I call it, "Peter Pan's Can".

A few weeks before Gerda had told me her plan. I was to get the lumber, which I did, and Dan slapped it together with loving care and understanding. It was also a two-holer but with a wall between. No more of that comeraderie and comfy coziness—and two doors to boot!

I recall that when Dan was ready to cut the apertures, he came into the office and asked me if I had a large sheet of white foolscap. I showed him the largest we had which was 8½ inches wide by 11 inches long.

He said, "No, that isn't big enough for what I want."

Then I recalled that we had newspaper dummy sheets which were the size of a newspaper but blank. And I showed them to him and he told me, "That's just what I need. That'll be fine and dandy!"

I hadn't the foggiest notion at the time what he wanted them for. So a day or two later Dan called me aside when I was out at the back and whispered, "I want to show you something."

Then he unfolded and held up in front of me one of these large blank sheets of newspaper . . . only this time there were two pictures drawn on it. One was a head of Dan and the other was a head of Bill—life size. But the heads were just about both the same size—perfect ovals.

"Well, that's pretty good drawing", I said to Dan. "Who did it?"

"I don't know", he said, "One of the gals in the packing shed, I think."

"Why", I said, "I'll have to have them do mine, too."

"You'll have to do what we did," replied Dan.

"Then tell me, what did you do to get your portraits drawn?"

Dan confessed, "As a sort of joke, I sent a couple of sheets of this large paper in with one of the kids and told her to tell the gals to give me a couple of patterns for the seats of the outhouse and this is what came back!"

"So sorry", I told Dan, "I'm afraid you'll have to cut from memory.

338

But better still, those two egg-heads are about the right size anyway. I'd just cut around them."

"Yes", mused Dan, measuring the oval drawing with his carpenter's rule. "They are just about the exact shape and size."

So as I stood meditatingly by, watching the flames licking up the old outhouse and the smoke curling upwards towards the sky, I could see my likeness à la Goya painted by the billowing smoke . . . bushy eyebrows, bald head, moustache and bow-tie. Ah, parting is such sweet sorrow. . . .

Boomerang

Bill Brent and Bob Taylor were good friends. In fact, they'd been fast chums since childhood. Now that they were men their friendship was stronger than ever . . . even after Bob got married.

They'd go hunting, fishing and on all other types of outings together . . . Bob's wife never seemed to mind a bit because, in truth, Bill was a really fine sort of guy. She recognized it and felt that Bob was in mighty good company.

Brent was born on the land and loved it but when he was just a boy his father had lost the 100 acres during the bad spell in the early 1930's. Always while performing his daily work at the rubber factory, packing and sending shipments all over the country, he kept happy by day-dreaming of his life on the farm and of some day having a farm of his own.

Yet in his heart he knew that with his meagre wage that dream could never come true—but dreams are sometimes made of heavenly fibre.

Bob had a much better position. His father had provided him with a higher education. He worked for a bank and had risen to the position of accountant. He was a handsome chap, a good talker and he had a terrific way with the ladies, whereas Bill was sort of quiet and restrained—never pushing himself forward anywhere.

They were up on Georgian Bay fishing this particular weekend— with the usual wet goods for companionship. By early Saturday evening they saw by the look of the sky that a squall was brewing . . . so they began to reel in and head for shore. They had a long way to go because they had been in a spot where the fishing was good and it was quite a distance from their base.

"Bob," Bill said, "We'd better start moving real fast if we want to get to land before that storm hits."

"Yes, I think you're right," agreed Bob, as he gazed up and appraised the darkening clouds.

So they headed the long way back to camp. They had only gone a short distance when the sky blackened, night set in prematurely and they couldn't see very clearly where they were going. One thing they did know was the general direction in which the land lay and they headed directly towards it.

The storm started, but before it had picked up its fury, they were beached. They pulled their boat well up on shore to avoid it being carried out by the mounting surf. They knew they were nowhere near camp. However, they weren't worried—they were mighty grateful that they were on dry land.

They began to walk inland to see what they could find. In a little while they came to a farm house and even in the semi-darkness, with the rain falling, Bill recognized the farm as being a good one and the home, a durable brick building of strength and character, as being selectively placed in a beautiful wooded area.

"The man who built that farm house knew what he was doing," Bill said . . . as he looked at the rolling land and the lush grain swaying in the wind, his heart longing for something just like it.

They walked up the wide, screened-in verandah, knocked at the door and a female voice called from the other side, "Who is there?"

Then quickly, through the closed door, they explained that they'd been caught on the lake in the storm, were lost and were seeking shelter for the night and they told her where they came from. At that the bolt was slid and the door opened.

The head of a lady peered through the partly opened door. She glanced at both of them, then opened the door wide and beckoned them in. As she shut the door behind them, she said, "I live here by myself and I'm rather careful as to whom I let in once it begins to get dark. But you look like two well brought up boys. I'm glad I didn't allow my scruples to prevent me from letting you in."

She was a comely lady, of good matronly build, radiant and vibrant looking, with greying hair, in her 60's . . . but yet of attractive and fresh appearance.

"I'll brew up a pot of tea and a snack while you remove your wet jackets and try to make yourselves comfortable.

"Later I'd best see that your beds are made ready for the night because you couldn't possibly find your way back tonight. I presume you are camped in the public grounds about six miles from here. You'd never be able to find your way in the dark!

"My good husband died two years ago and the children wanted me to give up the farm and come to the city. None of them wanted to stay on the land. Said they liked the life but they can make more money, faster and easier in the city than on the farm. But I chose to remain. After 40 years out here, I couldn't leave it . . . besides hereabouts are my friends."

The boys listened with keen interest and then said, "Well, thank you very much. This is a kindness we didn't expect . . . but we are indeed very grateful!"

So she deftly prepared them a little lunch, a cup of tea and they sat in the very attractive, old fashioned living room and chatted.

When about 10 o'clock rolled around, Bill said, "I'm getting a little tired. Would you mind if I went to bed? I'm not a nighthawk like Bob . . . I like to go to bed with the chickens. He can stay up till the wee hours but I can't."

So the good lady showed Bill to his room, bade him good-night and went back downstairs. As he lay in bed before he fell asleep, Bill could hear her and Bob laughing and chatting, which they continued way on into the night.

Bill was always an early riser and he was out on the land before the cock crowed—wandering about, his heart singing and crying with every step he took. He was immensely taken with the farm—its spring-fed creek, the undulating green carpeted hills, the sturdy trees on the pasture fence line, the excellent well. Then he heard the bell ringing which he knew was a summons that "soup was on".

It was a sumptuous breakfast, as often farm breakfasts are, and the boys lapped it up like bears in a beehive. The kind lady was at her best and they couldn't have been treated better if they were her "ain" folk. She took a shine to Bob and they seemed to get on famously. She looked after him like an indulgent mother.

After breakfast they bade their kind friend adieu and went on about their business—to the boat and then back to camp.

Almost a year had flown by and the pleasant interlude was well nigh forgotten, when Bill received an unusual notice in the mail from a firm of lawyers. It perturbed him no end. It puzzled him. He just couldn't figure it out. He racked his brain, he pondered, he worried . . . but he couldn't come up with a logical answer.

That evening he went over to see his friend, Bob. After the usual commonplace formalities, he said, "Let's go out for a walk, boy. I want to show you something!"

So out they went together.

"What's this you want to show me?" asked Bob.

"Well, I really want to ask you a question or two first. Remember that night we spent up north there on the farm when we got lost on the lake in the blow and sought shelter in that widow's house?"

"Why sure," Bob said, "Of course I remember. We had a very pleasant time there."

"That's coming right to the point!" said Bill. "Perhaps you can help explain about this very important letter I received today from an impressive firm of lawyers up Owen Sound way."

At this Bob paled, became agitated and nervous. "Holy Smokes!" he sighed, "Who'd have believed it? I thought it was as safe as a fort. Who would ever imagine any danger? . . . And at her age!"

Before his friend could go into the matter further, Bob blurted out excitedly, "Look, Bill, we've been good friends for many years. The truth is that I was a little indiscreet that evening. But she was such a pleasant old lady, she doesn't have much fun in life and I thought I'd be sort of repaying her for her kindness to us."

"Yeh," said Bill, "I understand all about that. After all, I haven't been so close to you all these years without knowing a little about you. But how did she get my name?"

"Well," replied Bob apologetically, holding his head, "You know how it is! I'm married and in the event of something slipping, I'd be in awful trouble with the wife and family. It's just one of those spontaneous precautions. You know how it is! You're single and it wouldn't make a bit of difference to you. So I assumed your name that evening."

"Please, please, Bill," Bob pleaded, "Don't get angry! We've been pals for over 25 years and I wouldn't want anything to break up our friendship. Don't let this interfere. Don't allow this to come between us. I beg of you, don't be mad at me. I'll do everything necessary to help you straighten it out. I'll bear the full cost—whatever it may be!"

"Look," said Bill, "I'm not mad at anybody . . . certainly not at you. I was just puzzled. And I don't know what you're talking about —sharing expenses—bearing the cost. All I wanted to tell you was that the lawyers notified me that that dear, beloved, wonderful old lady had died and left me that big beautiful farm in her will!"

"Leave Well Enough Alone!"

Well, doggone it . . . an' tan my hide . . . right here I can hear you say, "There is sound advice—the soundest ever offered. None better can anyone give."

Is that so? Tsk, Tsk, Tsk! Well, well, well . . . and what makes you think that you are able to judge what should be left alone and what should be disturbed? Just because you've got a cushy job . . .

probably working for the government, a few bucks in the bank and the mortgage interest and principal paid up to date . . . does that entitle you to think that you are the judge of what's good for mankind?

So the world's all right. You don't want any changes—you don't want anything to interfere with the way things are going now. You've got a car, a T.V. set, a washing machine and this and that and that and that . . . and you resent anyone who is trying to initiate a few reforms—to change the so-called "status quo".

Listen here, you poor simp! If it weren't for those imaginative, restless, wanderlusting, courageous souls, you wouldn't have a pot to pour in and you wouldn't have those fancy shoes and Scotch plaid socks or sheer nylon hose. In fact you'd be blamed lucky if you had a few rags to wrap around your feet—if you could steal them. And that's all you'd have to keep out the winter's cold.

A car . . . Shucks, man, you wouldn't even have a wheel—not even a spoke that begins to form it or the hub. No sir, you wouldn't even have the button to press that makes the horn blow.

Everything we've got in this grand, modern, wonderful wide world of ours we owe to those few enterprising souls who couldn't rest but had to go out into the world alone—that cold world—that hard world—that burdening one—to brave broad crushing rivers, ice, steep mountains, burning deserts, wild beasts, deadly snakes, disease-laden swamps, crags and crevices, savages, thousands of miles of open sea, hurricanes—yes, and fate a thousand times worse than death . . . all for you—to find that better land, a freer land, a more fertile country where there was greener grass, a redder and more fragrant rose, finer silks and furs to adorn your women and keep them warm and make them lovelier—to find you jewels and spices and better foods and pure water.

Yes, tis their visions that we are living in and enjoying today.

They only saw the rainbow and followed it where'er it led them. Some say 'twas lunacy. They never enjoyed any of its gold. Theirs are the bones you will find under that mound with the cross on it, a million miles from nowhere. Few of these wanderlusters ever enjoyed the fruits of their planting. But sow and plant they did and we are the ones who reap the harvest—we who never planted or sowed. Practically all we do is despoil.

Speak up . . . Do you still feel so smug and cock-sure of yourself and everything else around you? Or do you feel, as you should, like the boy who was caught with his hand in the jam jar? You know, if I were you I'd get down on my knees and thank the Boss upstairs that He made a few . . . who were not satisfied to let well enough alone, for in all truth, the progress that the world has made we owe only to such men.

Need I tell you who they were? Every child knows. You don't have to go to much trouble to find out. But don't ever say, "Leave well enough alone" . . . unless you want to label yourself a poor, unimaginative simpleton.

The Best Things in Life Are Free

I feel sort of depressed and despondent today . . . .

You know, it's one of these days that most of us come across every now and then. I wish they could be avoided but I've never found any way that I could lift them out of my life. I've just got to put up with them, I guess.

"What brought this mood on, or about", perhaps you are wondering . . . . Most likely you've begun to believe that I am one of these rare fellows who is always happy, laughing and smiling—full of appreciation of the bounties and beauties of effervescing life and such.

Well, it's like this . . . I've got a postcard in front of me. It's from the Bahamas. It's the fourth one I've received from friends of mine in the last few weeks.

In February one came from Mexico where Bob Stair had flown with his wife and entire family to enjoy the heavenly, luxurious weather that they get down around Acapulco. It read, "Swimming is grand— Service at the hotel is out of this world—and the sumptuous Mexican food would make a gourmet drool."

Then one came from Florida . . . "Well, the weather's been a little chilly down here but still the fishing is good, the company's even better, the liquor is tops (and plentiful), and I've been feeling so good that if the sun was shining, I wouldn't notice it, anyway."

Now this card from the Bahamas says, "I've chartered a yacht and have been making visits to the various islands—fishing, eating, drinking, lolling and having the time of my life."

Poor me . . . . stuck up here in the north . . . . suffering the hardships of the rigorous Canadian winter. I feel so sorry for myself that I could crawl into a hole and then drag the whole in after me.

Boy, they're all lucky to be in such wonderful businesses that allow them the privilege of long distance vacations at the finest hostelries in the world.

No, my business isn't like that . . . . and I am grateful. What am I saying? Yes, the truth of the matter is that I'm not a bit envious or jealous. You see, I know full well that these boys have got to get away from it all. Otherwise, they'd crack up. In fact, I know for sure most of them have cracked up on one or two occasions during their careers.

Sure, they make a lot more money than I do and I used to be a bit jealous at that. But then . . . do they understand or know what it's like to stand on an old wooden bridge and look down at the peaceful, placid flowing water of the creek—counting the ripples?

I watched that crooked white willow tree growing right out of its left bank with its roots and footing under mud whenever the creek overflows its banks with the melting snow in the spring and I crane my neck and arch it with the contour of the willow . . . . as the sun comes through its dense branches, it seems like shimmering gold floating down from the heavens.

Did they ever taste the sweetness and smell the aroma of a wild strawberry? Do they know the juicy succulence of the dead-ripe May apple? I don't think so! I believe they don't know such things exist.

Even when they go down to these tropical paradises you can bet that most of them never even see the plants, flowers and trees.

Often I have walked along a winding, undulating creek bank. How still, how serene, how glorious is this simple bit of nature. Every step speaks of the wondrous living world about us . . . lichens, mosses, grasses, herbs in flower, saplings and shrubs. These are the living quarters of our fauna—toads, turtles, groundhogs, rabbits, squirrels, skunks, raccoons . . . yes, and even a few deer, too.

I've reached the highest part of the bank as the sun is setting and the colors in the sky, the reflections in the water at the widening mouth of the creek where the gold of the day comes upon the blue of the night, are such as to make you feel that here and now you would like time to stop.

I'm not a "birder", as they say, but any human being whose heart and soul are in tune with nature revels in the song of a bird as the cadences and trills ring like chimes from the very alcoves of paradise.

I stop for a moment to rest under a stately Elm and nibble a sandwich that I have packed and which I carry in a knapsack on my back. I believe the Elm is the stateliest and most regal of all trees. Its branches are long and sinewy, yet so soft and pliable, but you never can break them. Tear them, yes, but break them in two—seldom ever. Both Oaks and Maples form better heads, or should I say, denser heads, and they have their own virtues but they do not possess the elegance and grace of the Elm.

Birds seem to love the Elms more than other trees. One of the reasons, I believe, is the fact that the Elms are usually so tall and even their lowest branches are so far from the ground that our feathered friends feel more secure nestled among them. No young dare-devil of a boy could scale its trunk and get up there and steal the bird's eggs . . . but they might in a Maple or Oak.

Well, I have mused enough. I am now, thanks to you for listenin', out of the mental doldrums. I'll take the natural beauties of my "ain" country and be happy as a lark . . . . Tra-la-la. Tweet-tweet-tweet.

Lust For Land

Scurried all over Europe—hopping about like a kangaroo—from country to country—over hill and dale, mount and vale . . . Ireland, England, Scotland, Wales, Belgium, Holland, Denmark, Sweden, Germany, Switzerland, Lichtenstein, Austria, Italy and France.

When I left the farm I felt the monster within me. He'd gained possession of my soul because of my discontent and dissatisfaction with everybody and everything.

The farm boy sitting in the shade of the hay stack for a little rest between loads had become a Frankenstein. He had to find glamour, art and beauty—though he had to search the wide world over.

'Twas true! For weeks now my fields and the farms that surrounded them were colorless and lacking in interest. Their charm had fled.

I had to be off to soar and to see the wonders of the world. A man was nothing until he had travelled and lain his head in many climes.

Like the great Caesar—I came, I saw . . . I conquered!

What did I conquer? Ah, it was a great conquest—a magnificent victory . . . though I came back weary, bedraggled, forlorn, with a sinking feeling in my heart that dripped down into my soul . . . Yes, truly I had conquered . . . my blindness and my stupidity.

I came back filled with the love of my country, its soil, its flora and its fauna . . . and, aye, most of all—its people!

Perchance you too are one of those disgruntled crabbers and gripers —and there are too many of them. Go off and visit the Continent. See life . . . old and new . . . for yourself. Feel its heart throbs, its vivaciousness, its upsurge, its decay. See what people are—everywhere.

Bub, when you get back, your squawking days will have ended . . . but for good!

If I loved the land before I left, then it must have been a little wee bit of a pilot light because today the love for my land and for my country glows like a beacon on a mountain top . . . an all consuming fire that will burn fiercely . . . all the days of my life.

Where'er we soared, tho' 'twas the farms atop the mountains in

Switzerland—could be through the rich fields where the men, women and children were working side by side, doing heavy manual labor in Germany—perhaps 'twas the well husbanded fields in Denmark—maybe the soft green, fairy-like fields of Ireland—or the rambling, rolling downs of England—yes, even the rugged, rollicking hills in Scotland . . . always beside what I saw was a vision—my little farm at Niagara. That was where my thoughts roamed. That is the spot I sighed for and where I wanted to be forever.

I enjoyed my travels. If I did not learn what to do, at least I found out what not to do.

When I returned, never did my fields look so green. Never did a piece of land look so wholesome. All the farms around me glowed with the luscious richness of the foliage of the trees and the colored fruits that shone from out them. All were heavenly balm to my tired, aching eyes.

I am back . . . a sadder, poorer but . . . I hope, a wiser man!

Lassies Love the Land???

'Twasn't yesterday but yet is wasn't too long ago either. A chap walked up to me and asked me if I knew "so and so" and I said, "Yep, he's a good friend of mine."

"Well," the chap said, "He told me to come and see you. He's a cousin of mine. I'm visiting from New York and wanted to come up and see what Canada looked like and I'm having a wonderful time."

We chatted a while and I soon found out that he really was a splendid sort of individual . . . frank, clean-cut, intelligent and filled with the love of life.

As the conversation continued I found out that he was born on a farm and raised on one. But he'd married a city girl and that ended his farming career.

He was a big strapping fellow, probably 6 ft. 2 in. with a big frame and shoulders like a wrestler. He told me his work consisted of hauling beef carcasses for an abattoir and, believe me, be could haul a carcass no matter how large.

Well, he was a nice lad and he spent a couple of days with me and, God, how he loved the land! Never saw a man so completely lost to its possibilities and beauty. Each step he took on the good earth was like a dream. To see him breathing the country air with affection was something worthwhile.

I can't describe his exuberance or his enthusiasm for the land. They are above mere words. Taking note of this, I then said to him, "Why don't you have a farm?"

He replied, "There's nothing more in life that I'd love to do."

"Well, why don't you?" I said, "Nobody is stopping you. There are lots of farms available cheap, and good farms too."

He was silent and his face was troubled and he shook his head negatively. I looked at him. His face was sad. So I pressed him, "Why?"

"Just this", he said, "The wife wouldn't hear of it".

So he left and went back to New York—but not without making me promise that I would at least call him on the telephone if and when I came to New York.

Each and every year I make a pilgrimage to the big city and this year when I went down and after I was comfortably ensconced in my hotel I thought I'd phone him and I did.

Well, in about 15 minutes he was at the hotel and he brought along his young son . . . a youngster of about 9—built like his father. We chatted for a few minutes and then he asked me if the wife and I would come to his place for dinner at 7 o'clock that night. We gladly accepted. So at 6.45 promptly he called for us and drove us down to his abode.

He lived on the east side. I'm pretty sure it was First Avenue. You could see the United Nations' building being erected at the time. The section in which he lived, which you would know if you knew New York, was a decrepit old section with old, old shops, warehouses and what have you. In our jargon we'd call it an out and out slum area.

We walked up three flights of rickety stairs to get to his apartment which was on the top of a three storey building. When we got to the upper landing his wife was there to greet us. She was a beautiful looking woman . . . gracious, intelligent, tidy, neat and pleasant.

When she ushered us into her home we were amazed to find it sparkling with cleanliness and hominess, too. As is the custom we gossiped for a while, had a drink and then sat down to dinner. It was a sumptuous repast. One wouldn't wish for or desire anything finer nor could a better served or prepared meal be had anywhere.

We chatted as we ate and bantered pleasantries back and forth. He was a wonderful host and she was a charming hostess. The children were well behaved too. There were two of them—a boy, whom we met before, and a girl.

Then we relayed to and relaxed in the living room and from these comfy quarters could be seen the waterfront and the United Nations' building—so close you could almost touch it. I talked of my farm, the nursery, the land and, as I did, I watched her and him very closely. The sound of the land made lights glance and dance in his eyes and

348

to her it brought shadows and her brow darkened and her eyes narrowed. I found that as much as he loved the country and the farm she hated it twice as much.

She was born in a slum area on the east side and she loved it. The stenches, the characters, the beggars, the dope pedlars and the dope fiends, the drunks, the prostitutes, the thieves and the gamblers . . . to her these spelled life. Yet she was strong enough in character and upbringing to remain unsullied by the abominables that brushed by her daily.

To him only the farm meant life. There it was—the never ending turmoil. Obviously, she was the stronger character of the two and her will prevailed. It was either that or he loved her so much that he just couldn't live without her but he could exist without the farm. As it was he had to dwell in the city where he dreaded the dawn of every new day and his daily trek to the abattoir. So he told me definitely but sadly.

She would rather exist in this speck of Hell than live on the best farm on the continent. She didn't want the land or any part of it— ever!

Well, there it was. That's the picture as I saw it . . . I am foiled. I can't understand it. I never did find out the reasons nor the why's nor the wherefore's and I probably never will. But there is the situation and I present it to you for what it is worth.

I wrote to them thanking them for their hospitality. They never replied from that day to this and I think I know why.

Tobe's Folly

To begin with, let me exphasize that I'm not talking about "follies". I was trying to explain to some of my girls of foreign birth what folly meant and, believe me, I had quite a time of it.

I cited the episode of Seward's Folly and then of Fulton's Folly— although both of these boomeranged and the years have shown them to be wise. But those were due to fortunate turns of events—which I can't count upon.

But now out here at the nursery the girls call a certain group of plants Tobe's Folly and I will admit there are grounds and justification for this name calling.

I go to great ends, a lot of trouble and through many difficulties to procure seeds, plants and trees of various special, new or sensational items but all of which wind up leaving me in the red.

But I say to my crew, "Look, these are sterling, splendid, unusual, wonderful and rare horticultural items and I must try to make them known and offer them to my customers."

So this year when I go to list them, I get into a hassel with my left and right bowers. "What's the sense of growing and listing these items?" they said, "They don't pay their way."

"But think", purrs I, "of the beauty, the grandeur and the loveliness of the Dawn Tree, the Metasequoia glyptostroboides . . . Just fathom —this tree was first discovered only a few short years ago and it's considered to be the oldest living tree on the face of the globe. Why it's like having a museum piece in your garden! Shouldn't I be able to offer this to my friends and customers?"

"Yes", pipes up Gerda, "You should—but last year we sold two of them."

"Now think", says I, "of the Acer ginnala—that beautiful low growing Maple that has the finest color of all Maples with graceful habit and unusually handsome foliage that turns bright red in the autumn—a really much better tree than the Japanese Dwarf Maple and much hardier, although its leaves are not red during the summer."

Then Pearl tells, "I didn't see one order come through for that item last season."

"Well", I continued, "Think of those beautiful Deodara Cedars. That's the genuine Cedar. It was undoubtedly the handsomest, gayest and most interesting item that we had in our evergreen fields this year and everybody who saw them admired them and asked its name and its history and origin."

"But how many did we sell?" asks Pearl.

"Two of them," says Gerda, "And four hundred asked questions about them and kept me from my work."

But stoicly I went on, "Think of those beautiful Cedar of Lebanon that I had. They are the first that I've known to be grown in this area. They do make a beautiful specimen and think—it's a tree that was described in the Bible and is still growing throughout that hallowed land."

Gerda jumped in, "Yes, and all of the specimens that you started with are still out in the fields."

I had to ignore this uncouth type of interruption so I smilingly pursued my course. "Just think—we have these lovely Hollies growing in our fields . . . the real, genuine English Holly with the sharp prickles and those luxuriant, thick leaves."

"Yes", said Pearl, "And you haven't sold one in two years."

"Come, follow me," I held forth, brushing aside that hurdle. "Let me show you these beautiful Pieris japonica. You remember how striking they were in the early spring with those grand blossoms hanging down by the million from each plant. It was like a little tree covered with Lily-of-the-Valley flowers and they were nicely perfumed too. Look at them now. They are changing color. They really have a different tone or shade for every month of the year and they retain their leaves through the winter too. What a wonderful shrub it is!"

"I haven't been asked for nor have I sold one during the entire summer or fall", chirped Gerda.

Disregarding the interlopation, I walked over to the Koster Dwarf Globe Spruce. "There", I said, "Is something that the horticultural world has been looking for for many, many years—a dwarf specimen of a genuine Blue Spruce and here it is and I am one of the few people in the North American continent who has it."

"We sold the first two the other day for a cemetery planting", says Pearl, "It seems clearly obvious that people are just dying for it."

"Look at those Cotoneasters", I went on, blithely undisturbed by the hindrance. "They are one of the finest of all shrubs that I know and I'm trying to educate people to appreciate them."

"I think we've sold three of them in four years", admitted Gerda, "I don't remember which variety it was. But most people who come to the nursery don't know how to pronounce the name—and I can't even help them."

Hanging on like a bull-dog, I pointed and said, "Now aren't these Espaliers a grand sight and we've been eating delicious pears and apples from these trees since early August."

"Yes", Gerda effused, "And think of the work, the effort and the years it takes to grow one of them. You sell them as cheap as borscht and even then nobody buys them. When somebody does send in an order once in a blue moon, two girls have to spend a day to pack up one tree because they're so difficult to handle."

"HMMmm", it was not possible to ignore the outburst any longer and clearing my throat, I orated, "A man has to have a little latitude. Grant me a sliver or two of foolishness, won't you?"

"But you've listed innumerable unusual, new, rare types of bulbs, seeds, plants and trees for the past 25 years and most of them haven't paid off. Why continue to list these crazy items? Why not let the other fellow do the experimenting and you stay with the sound, popular and in-demand items where there is an element of profit?" the girls chorused.

"But", wails I, "A man can't live on bread alone."

"Nor can we women", they sang out again, "We'd like some raisin bread, cake or pie, too. But if we keep up at the rate we've been

351

going, we won't even have bread. Why not face it? You like handling these unusual items. So why not call it your hobby and let it go at that? Some men drink, others play the horses or gamble and there are some who hunt and others who fish or go boating or collect stamps. You like searching or locating strange and unusual plants and convincing other folk that they have genuine merit."

Says I, "That's a little different angle . . . one well worth thinking over."

So that's it, folks. It's my hobby. I think they're the finest and most unusual items in the world. They're yours at a very reasonable rate— far less than they would cost if you tried to buy one individually from somewhere else.

I can't plant the seed of the love of the rare, the meritorious or unusual in your soul but I can try to tell you about it anyway.

The Weaker Sex

If we are to accept the Gospel of the Bible, woman was the Lord's second choice. And it is also clear as crystal that she actually was an afterthought . . . when the Lord, upon seeing his handiwork in Adam, realized that man was incomplete. Therefore he created woman.

But let me tell you that while woman may be second choice and an afterthought, she is not to be trifled with—and don't get the idea she is inferior.

I've learned to respect women very, very highly. The average woman makes the average man look like a monkey. Yes, I mean in deed, in action, in thought and such. Women, according to my thinking, are undoubtedly the superior sex and it is as natural a conclusion as breathing air.

After all is said and done, she performs the most important function of life and therefore the power that the good Lord had to give in most every way, he gave to women.

Of course I see it every day of my life. I have in the main female help and if I thought that male help would do the job better and faster, I'd have them quick—no fooling.

Well, the superiority of women was made so starkly obvious to me on my trip to the Yukon and Alaska a couple of years ago. I'm sure you realize that while men hack and bulldoze their way through the bush, it is the women back in the tents, huts and cabins who keep those men fed, comforted and happy . . . and to do that with the little that is usually available is a tribute to their capabilities.

352

At the early stages of the Alaskan tour I didn't make any special effort to study women but after a few stops, I was pulled up with a jolt when I heard myself and companions stating and repeating phrases like . . .

"Wasn't that a remarkable woman?"

"There was a superior feminine creation!"

"Didn't that woman handle that entire outfit like a general?"

"That woman amazes me with her masterly way of directing and handling that household and business."

"That was a pleasant stopover. Everything was just in apple-pie order. She certainly made us feel right at home. What a delightful person!"

"She certainly made the best of a situation. It is surprising how many things a person can improvise—if no money is available."

"My that was a remarkable woman that we met there at the last stop. Sure as fate, there was a dandy one the time before. Then, by Jove, weren't they all capable, alert, intelligent, polite, strong, observant and most of all, understanding?"

So from there on out I began to take a little keener note of the women that we met and they were a remarkable lot. Now there are lots of good women in other places besides Alaska and the Yukon but the ones up here were by far a superior breed.

So skimming along the road I began to think the thing out. A man won't go or stay long anywhere without a woman. If the woman won't go, it spells the end to his dreams of adventure . . . for seldom will a man stay long anywhere without a mate. Of course to a man, going off into the unknown means adventure. To a woman, it means hard work, drudgery, self-denial, privation . . . yes, but it also means freedom and moreover it also proves what a woman will do for a man —because, remember, about 75% of all the dirty work has to be done by the woman. The man will go out and hunt and fish but in all probabilities, the woman has to turn a smelly, scaley old fish into a delectable repast. She has to skin and disentrail the animals before a man can get his belly full.

Yes, the women of the north are real women . . . and don't you ever underestimate them!

Scots Wa Hae

As we moved along the English countryside, past Westmoreland County and then into Cumberland, in a little while I began to notice a change in the topography. It didn't seem the same. It had a familiar note about it. Definitely we were in a terrain that seemed homey.

I began to see the same kind of weeds that we had at home. Furthermore the fields and the hills seemed to have lost their lustre. As to what had happened I pondered and scratched my head and suddenly it dawned on me. We had crossed from England into Scotland.

Really the roadsides did very much resemble the kind of country we have just north of Toronto. Had I not known where I was, I would have guessed that we were somewhere near Barrie or Orillia.

But then we began to climb a hill and right before me unfolded a scene, a panorama, a vision or a sight or any other name you might call it, that just couldn't be duplicated around home.

Now again these hills are entirely different from the hills of Ireland. Whereas those in Ireland were green, lush, fertile and luxuriant, the Scottish hills had a more sombre, hard look. They didn't have anything about them like the Irish hills that lilted, "Come loll and relax. Life is slow and easy."

The Scottish hills said hoarsely, "I am here if you want me but I present a challenge. You've got to dig for anything that I'll give you."

Yes, there is no doubt about it . . . the challenge of the Scottish soil made those Scotsmen what they are in the world today. It isn't hard to understand how Scotsmen have paved the way through the universe to its most difficult accesses and recesses so that other strong men may follow.

Until you have actually seen the soils upon which men live, you cannot understand from where men derive their character and strength.

My friends in Canada, before I left, had been careful to warn me that when I reached Scotland never to call a Scotch man a Scotchman and that they wanted to be called Scotsmen and would resent being called Scotchmen because Scotch referred to whiskey, whereas the men were Scots. So the first few men I met in Scotland I queried about this and in every case they said either, "It makes no difference" or I wouldn't know the difference" and some of the others said, "Either one is as good as the other."

While motoring through England at different times we felt like something to eat or a "cup of taye" and we passed many and more tea shops, or whatever you might call them, than you could shake a stick at but wherever there happened to be one, there was no place to park. We did notice cars, the small English cars, parked everywhere and at every angle right in the crowded sections of the narrow streets and, believe me, they were narrow. But I didn't dare park there. I'm accustomed to getting a ticket hung on my windshield whenever I do something that I shouldn't do and therefore I didn't take the chance in

England. I didn't want to have any "bobby" chasing me down the English country lanes and taking me in tow—handcuffed, to the bloody tower.

So we kept on, hoping that we'd find one somewhere. Well, we were quite a few miles into Scotland before we found a little inn. I said little but it really wasn't so little. It was quite spacious but compared to our big establishments, I guess it was small.

There seemed to be two, three or four large rooms in which one could drink beer and then we came upon the dining quarters and they were really delightful. They were prim, neat, proper, cute and cozy. You just do not see any such establishments in Canada or the United States nor, as a matter of fact, in the rest of Europe either—as we found out.

Well, we drank tea and had sandwiches and cakes until our bellies began to look like pin cushions. We were all hungry and we would have preferred something more substantial but this establishment didn't supply anything but tea and sandwiches or do they call it high tea, low tea or mid-tea—or whatever it is?

Then when I got the check, it was 4 shillings, 6 pence—in other words, slighty less than 60c in good Canadian money . . . for all three of us, mind you. Now I can see how Andrew Carnegie made his money.

The next stop was Glasgow. It's a seaport and a ship-building city and you just wouldn't expect it to sparkle like a jewel on the firmament. Well, it's not going to surpass your expectations—it didn't ours.

The railroad station is right in the centre of the town and a large tunnel brings all the trains into the centre of the city . . . a sort of subway. Then with the smoke belching high into the sky, it just wouldn't be the place for the prim and proper lady to hang her fresh, bleached, snow white washing.

There were millions of pigeons atop the buildings right down town, too. After having a few drops of "guano" drop on my balding dome, I heaved a groan of thanks that cows have yet not learned to fly and the citizens of Glasgow should pray every night that they never do.

But then when the day wound up and it was finished, I thought to myself, "At 6.30 that morning we were in Wynn's hotel in Dublin —down to breakfast—then around the corner to get the bus—and At 8.30 Aer Lingus took us across the Irish sea to Liverpool. There our "drive-yourself" car was waiting for us and we streaked our way northward towards Glasgow. So we had breakfast in Ireland, a cup of tea in Liverpool, lunch in a little town called Kirkland where we had to

355

climb two flights of stairs to get to the dining room and had a most delightful homey lunch. There wasn't too much to eat but the price wasn't very steep either so I guess it was even. Then we had tea at that cute little place at 5.30 in the Gingham Room and our dinner in dear old Glasgow at about 7.30."

We spent the night in one of the better down town hotels but we didn't sleep a wink. There was a street car and a bus stop just in front of the hotel where, unfortunately, we were trying to sleep. Evidently oil must be quite scarce in Glasgow because the squeaking of the brakes of the buses never stopped a second and they squeak and, brother, I mean squeak! It's the only place in the world where street cars are equipped with square wheels instead of round ones and you can imagine the slap, slap, slap of the steel against these every time the square object turned about to propel the car forward. I didn't examine the wheels—I'm just judging by the sound and the fury.

We were so glad when morning came and we could get out into the Trossacks where peace and quiet once more reigned supreme. 'Twas heavenly!

When an Indian dies, he wants to go to the "Happy Hunting Ground"—a Scandinavian, to his Valhalla—a Mohammedan to Mecca—a Jew to Jerusalem—a Scotsman . . . no, not to Glasgow but to the Trossacks, near "bonnie Loch Lomond".

Boy, I sympathize with the Scotsmen and I'll tell you more about our trip through the Trossacks and dear old Loch Lomond another time.

You know I'm very fond of plaid ties. In fact, I have practically every tartan I can get hold of. I like them because I think they're pretty. Besides that, they wear forever and they're not expensive. Well, every time I stopped at a shop in Scotland I went in and inquired about tartan ties and do you think I found any? . . . Nary a one did I find in Scotland! Know why? . . . They ship them all over to Canada and the United States. So if you want to buy a good tartan tie, the place to get it is in dear old Toronto. I think they sell more tartan ties in Toronto than they do in all of Scotland. But those folks in Toronto are canny, too.

Weeds and the Desert

Probably you, like many other people who come to the nursery to visit, will be disappointed. No, you won't be disappointed in the variety or the vigor of the plants we grow but you probably will be shocked when you see a lot of weeds around the place.

I'm a good cook, I write pleasant things for you to read, I go all over creation hunting up new plants for you, I am pleasant and civil to my friends and associates, I don't beat my wife and I have never yet been in the penitentiary. So what if I'm not neat!

Neatness and tidiness are ingrained in a person's soul. Usually a person is born with that trait. While I'm not particularly sloppy or careless, I'm just not meticulous and weeds grow here and there at the nursery.

Now look at it from my angle for a moment. I've just come back from California and in my travels to get there and back I had to cross parts of Oregon, Idaho, Nevada, Utah and Colorado. Each and every one of these states has within its borders many thousands of miles or acres of desert. Maybe they're not as big as the Sahara but they're just as dry and as forlorn, desolate and heartbreaking.

On this last trek, because I insisted upon seeing some unusual horticultural specimens, I had to make my way into some inaccesible places. To do this I had to cross a lot of desert—a total actually of over 3500 miles of it up and back, north and south, east and west. The thermometer registered 131 at a place called Baker in Nevada when I was there. It was 126 in Palm Springs and just above in the San Gorgonian range. And 'twas in that heat I was clambering up and down mountainsides hunting Coulteri Pine cones. Besides it was always 114-120 during the day wherever we were in the desert.

And did I have troubles! The only green things that we saw here and there and now and then were some Mesquite bushes, Joshua trees, some Sage and occasionally a Cactus. 90% of this terrain wouldn't even grow a respectable Cactus.

So when I returned home the first thing that greeted me at the entrance to the nursery was a nice big batch of weeds . . . Lambsquarters, Goldenrod, Queen Anne's Lace, Ragweed, Plantain and a host of others. Brother, did they look good! I could have pressed them to my bosom and inhaled their hayfever-inducing grand fragrance.

You think I'm nuts, don't you? Well, you get out there on the desert and drive thousands of miles without seeing the faintest sign of anything that looks green and fresh and healthy and then come back and look at our native weeds. You'll love them as much or maybe more than I do.

So help me Hannah, unless a weed is actually standing in my road or doing me some harm, I hate to pull it out . . . I hear you whisper in an aside, "That guy Tobe is getting crazier every minute!"

The fact remains that we have to mow down the weeds with our cultivator in the fields and occasionally I get so ashamed of the weeds around the nursery buildings that I send Bill out with the scythe. But I've got to turn my back or go away because I can't bear to see him cut those weeds down in their prime. And I wouldn't even cut them if it weren't for the fact that I'm scared you'll come down and say, "Heck, the only thing that guy Tobe can grow is weeds!"

Wonderful—but you Keep it

The tiller of the soil, the farmer, the gardener, the horticulturist or whatever you might call him is thrice blessed. I say thrice but it could be many more times—certainly not less.

In all this great country of ours . . . and the same pattern is probably repeated in every other country on the face of the earth . . . everyone seems to be running away from the land. And if this continues, God will have to learn to till the land himself and I'm afraid that day's a-coming.

Perhaps herein lies an analogy. When I was but a wee lad, my mother taught me that when the Lord had prepared his word, the Good Book, and his Ten Commandments, he was pondering the best way to handle this situation. So he started at the beginning of the alphabet, A for Alpha, and approached the various nations. Each in turn refused it. You know how easy it is to refuse something you don't want. You can term it neatly by saying, "Oh, I am unworthy of such a noble undertaking" or "There are other people much more capable of handling that task than I". On the other hand, some might say bluntly, "What do you want to give it to me for? I've got enough trouble."

Or some of the other nations might have said, "We're always apprehensive of gifts from above. No thanks, we'd rather not have it."

Then some of them, having the Trojan horse in mind, might have declined saying. "No thank you, we must beware of Greeks bearing gifts."

So on goes the tale . . . nobody wanted it. At last he came to Zion and having run the gamut, the good Lord was in no mood for further horse-play, dilly-dally, polite refusals, evasions or whatever might be the case. So he said, "Here you sons of Zion. Here is the good book. It's yours and you've got to carry it as long as you live." And the sons of Zion have carried it along with the thousand and one burdens, persecutions, hatreds and spites ever since.

It's going to take a lot of kindness up in the heavens to repay those people for the suffering they've endured because they carry that cross

358

of David. I doubt if there are enough gifts in heaven to repay them for the millions that have been murdered because of God's gift. It seems to me that they were the victims of the greatest hoax in the annals of time.

But wait . . . could be I'm wrong. At least they have existed for four or five thousand years, whereas many other nations who turned the deal down have long since been forgotten except when we read about them in the ancient history books.

But back to my tale. Farming is the forsaken profession. Every succeeding year there are fewer tillers of the soil. Lucky for us, due to improved methods of soil tilling, mechanization, machinery and such, these small numbers of farmers can still produce sufficient to feed at least the western world.

Years ago I used to believe that teaching and farming had a great deal in common, chiefly because a man went into both of these professions with but one thought uppermost in his mind . . . devotion to an ideal, service to mankind, doing what one likes to do without thought of remuneration. Of course the farmers haven't improved their lot and still remain in this category. The teachers have fared more fortunately because their salaries have been increased and their pill has been greatly sweetened so they are no longer the suffering profession.

From what I can see and gather, the farmer's lot has not improved any. He still worries from crop to crop, he never dies rich (at least, not from what he made on the land unless he struck oil or uranium) and he has to work hard seven days a week, 52 weeks of the year. But still I do believe that the good Lord should start rewarding the farmers a little more generously . . . because if he doesn't, they're going to leave the land and He's going to have to till it himself.

Best Time to Plant

We're back again once more to the why's and wherefore's of fall planting.

At least on a few hundred occasions during the year I'm asked, "Which is the best time to plant—spring or fall?"

And my answer never varies. When we're approaching spring or into spring, I always say to plant in the spring. And when we're approaching fall or into the fall, I always say to plant in the fall.

Now do you know of a more logical answer? If you do, I would be delighted to hear it.

You may say that's a sort of an ambiguous answer like the kind that the oracle of Delphi used to give in the old days when Greece was the centre of the universe. I'll reply that the old oracle gave some mighty good advice in those days and what's more . . . the advice I'm giving you above is mighty good advice, too.

After all, why put off till fall what you can plant in the spring and by the same token, why put off till spring what you can plant in the fall?

It is an absolute, honest statement and a proven fact that fall planted trees and shrubs will positively make root growth during the fall, winter and early spring days and months and if it makes root growth, it means that the plant is developing in your favor, fall, winter and spring. When the temperature is above 40 degrees at the ground level, and there are many days during the fall, winter and spring when the temperature is above that at soil level, therefore the plants make root growth for many days and long periods during the time that elapses from fall till the growing season.

For years and years and years I made the erroneous statement that nature does her planting in the fall and what I should have said was that nature does most of her planting in the fall. After all, there is no use trying to hoodwink you. I've walked ankle-deep through fallen seed pods and wings and other forms of seeds of Maples, Elms, Birches and who knows what other kind of trees along the streets of Niagara and on my walks on the Lakeshore Road and into the bush . . . and these pods or seeds fell in the spring. So it cannot be truthfully said by me or anyone else that nature does her planting only in the fall.

But you and I will agree that most of nature's planting is done at the end of the summer's growth and the year's harvest takes place in the fall.

One of the finest things about fall planting is that it is usually unhurried and conditions are at their best—that is, there are usually ample rains, the weather is cool, it is pleasant to work and above all, the soil is in optimum friable condition.

If there are some items that you want to plant and you are ready for them in September or October or November, it would be foolish of you to wait until spring to plant them because there are enough other things you'll want to do then anyway. So what you can get done in the fall is a step in the right direction.

There really and truly is no comparison between a plant set out in the fall and one set out in the spring because during the period from the fall till the spring, the plant has ample opportunity to get well established and with the rains seeping through the soil, the roots get neatly placed in the angles and directions in which they want to grow.

You know you can get some mighty hot days in the spring and it doesn't do newly planted stock any too much benefit.

A good many varieties of perennials and things can be planted in September. So can bulbs and such. But deciduous stocks—that is, stock that has leaves—can't be planted then. You must wait until October or November when the leaves have fallen naturally. Then is the right time for planting.

It is very important when planting in the fall to make sure that the plants are kept watered. Usually we have ample rain but in case anything happens and you don't have enough rain, give them a couple of good soakings so that the trees or plants will go into the winter well supplied with moisture. By that I don't mean that you've got to have puddles around them or have them swimming. I just mean that the soil should be in a good moist condition.

Some folks worry about heaving during the winter. This need cause you no concern because earth provided with ample tilth and good drainage does not heave. Therefore if your soil needs humus, add peat moss or compost. If your soil does not drain properly, provide that drainage and your plants once set will stay in the ground.

Mulching around the plants after the first good frost is a very, very wise precaution. It will keep the frost in—and that is what the plants want—not keep the plants warm as some people imagine. It is the thawing and freezing that causes most troubles and winter-killing.

Fall is also an excellent time to ship plants. Whereas in the spring one might run into difficulties if we hit a warm spell and plants might suffer somewhat, in the fall this seldom ever happens. Besides, the plants are dormant with no intent or desire to get started quickly and therefore the plants do not suffer at all in transit when planted in the fall.

Nectar of the Gods

I'm a firm believer in drinking pure wholesome water from a spring or a well or even rainwater from a cistern.

City water that has been fluorinated or chlorinated is actually an abomination. Oh, I drink it, too, at times—when I'm in the city and can't get anything else. But I usually keep my thirst quenched at the nursery with the water from our own deep well. And the water is always cool and refreshing. Yes, it tastes sweet really because no chemicals have been added nor has anything been removed or released.

When I make this statement within earshot of city folks with a sanitation complex, they usually are horrified and say, "I wouldn't dare drink any water that hasn't been tested, approved and chlorinated. Why it isn't safe . . . typhoid, diphtheria and such."

Says I, "You're right. For example, here in Niagara our water supply comes out of the river and 32 miles up at Buffalo the refuse of three-quarters of a million people, and factories as well as chemical plants is dumped into it. Even the world's largest cataract at the falls isn't potent enough to purify that cesspool. But why drink it at all when you can pull up all the water you need from below and it would require no treatment whatsoever and be sweet and beneficial?"

The water in a well has in most cases seeped down through the soil, taking along with it on its sojourn all of the water soluble minerals and elements that were available. This nourishes plant roots as well as the microorganisms found in the soil. If a human being is lucky enough to get this kind of water for drinking purposes, his entire system benefits from this nectar.

The working of bacteria in the soil combines humus and the minerals. This in turn releases or yields vital acids which add to the solvent power of the water as it finds its way through top soil to sub soil.

I believe that the further the water penetrated, the more minerals it would pick up.

So friends, take a drive out to the country onto a farm and get yourself a drink of life-giving water.

Azaleamum

Cradled in the East in darkness
'Mid glacial chill and snows
Snuggled against the mountains
This robust flower grows.

Striving thro' the springtime
First glowing midst summer's heat
Their all they give in the autumn
Till harsh winter stills their beat.

Death and Taxes

You must admit that a great deal of publicity has been given to this business of cancer and the smoking of cigarettes.

Now I'm not trying to take sides on the matter because I have enough troubles looking after the nursery business without getting involved with such broad, deeprooted problems.

But just the other day I was listening to a couple of fellows having a discussion on the subject and I heard one of them say, "Well, if it's really serious why doesn't the government step in and take some action and prevent people from being killed by cigarettes?"

At this outburst I began to laugh and probably I laughed a little too loudly and volubly and both my friends turned to me and said, "What the heck is so funny? What are you laughing about? What's more, this is a very serious business. People are dying of lung cancer by the thousands and you think it's so funny you're laughing."

"Well", I replied, "It's just like the fighter and his manager. The manager tells the fighter to get in there and take everything that the other fighter can give him and come back and knock him out. Sure, that's all right for the fighter's manager to say that . . . he doesn't meet one of the punches, whereas the poor boxer is just getting himself half killed."

As yet I haven't got lung cancer and because I smoke very little, I don't ever intend to have it. But that wasn't what I was laughing at. I do consider cancer of the lung, or any other part of the anatomy, a very serious business and I wouldn't laugh at that.

What I was laughing at was when they said that government should step in and take action.

So just listen a minute. . . . It is an actual fact that in Great Britain the government collects over 2 billion dollars annually from tobacco alone. Now I assume that the self-same government collects three or four times that amount in taxes from alcoholic beverages or alcohol in any form . . . whether it be beer, whiskey or wine.

Well, both of these items pooled are without doubt the largest source of revenue for the British government and I guess that pretty well holds true in all countries of the world—perhaps with the exception of Canada and the United States where income taxes take a big toll.

However, the point that I want to make here is . . . can you just imagine the father—a family man with a wife and a batch of children to provide for and winter coming on—taking the roof off his house and leaving it exposed to the elements? Well, that would make as much sense as the government notifying or spending good money to tell its citizens that smoking is no good for them or that alcohol may kill them. Besides, I guess the government knows full well that the people wouldn't pay any attention to them anyway.

Since the articles have appeared about the cancer danger in cigarettes, cigarette sales have gone up. That's right. They sort of dipped for a few days after the announcement was made but since then they've gone up above the figures that prevailed before the announcement was made.

Of course I think that by taking the short view the government eventually defeats itself. You see a man paying tribute until he's 63 or 70 years old is of much greater value to them than a man paying taxes until he is 45 or 50 and then dropping dead.

Let the thought permeate through your cranium and see if it doesn't make sense!

INDEX

365

366

367